Avignon and Its Papacy, 1309–1417

Avignon and Its Papacy, 1309–1417

Popes, Institutions, and Society

Joëlle Rollo-Koster

ROWMAN & LITTLEFIELD
Lanham • Boulder • New York • London

Published by Rowman & Littlefield
A wholly owned subsidiary of
The Rowman & Littlefield Publishing Group, Inc.
4501 Forbes Boulevard, Suite 200, Lanham, Maryland 20706
www.rowman.com

Unit A, Whitacre Mews, 26-34 Stannary Street, London SE11 4AB,
United Kingdom

British Library Cataloguing in Publication Information Available

Library of Congress Cataloging-in-Publication Data

Rollo-Koster, Joëlle.
Avignon and its papacy, 1309–1417 : popes, institutions, and society / Joëlle Rollo-Koster.
pages cm
Includes bibliographical references and index.
Summary: "Through a blend of political and social history, the author tells the tale of the transplanted
papacy in Avignon, bringing to life the fourteenth-century capital of Christianity"— Provided by
publisher.
ISBN 978-1-4422-1532-0 (cloth : alkaline paper) — ISBN 978-1-4422-1534-4 (e-book) 1. Avignon
(France)—History—14th century. 2. Avignon (Papal city)—History—14th century. 3. Avignon
(France)—Population—History. 4. Avignon (Papal city)—Population—History. 5. Catholic
Church—France—Avignon—History. 6. Catholic Church. Curia Romana—History. 7. Catholic
Church—Europe—Bishops—Appointment, call, and election—History. 8. Schism, The Great West-
ern, 1378–1417. 9. Papacy—History. I. Title.
DC801.A96R59 2015
262'.1309023—dc23
2015014639

Printed in the United States of America

I would like to thank URI Center for the Humanities
and the University of Rhode Island Division of Research and
Economic Development for their support at the various stages
of this book.

My thanks also to Anna Bennett and Joe Pearson for their patient reviews
and editorial comments.

This book is dedicated to my girls, Zézé, Auriane, Laudine,
and my beautiful chocolate Lab, Léa, gone too soon.

Contents

Author's Note

Throughout the manuscript, French names have been standardized to "de" if followed by patronymics and "of" if followed by toponymics; thus Charles of Blois, Robert of Anjou, but Jacques de Molay. I have respected the Italian form of spelling.

Maps

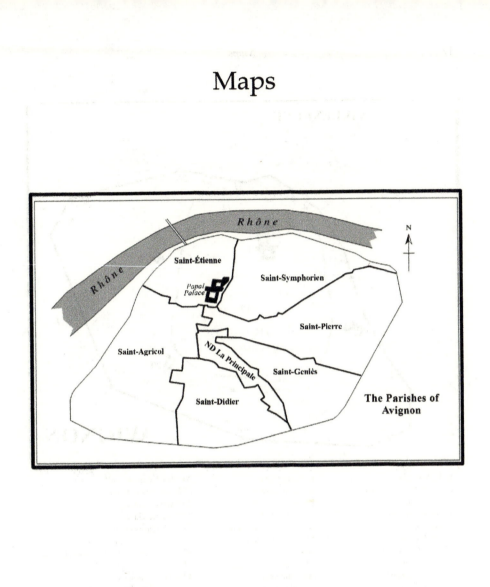

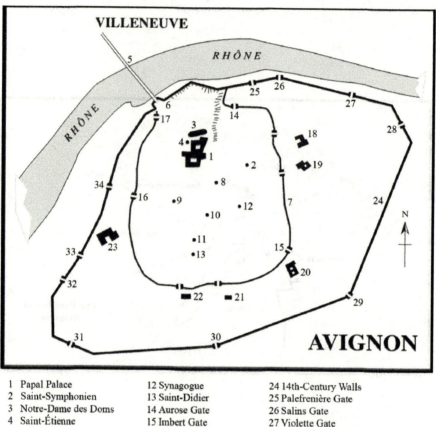

1 Papal Palace
2 Saint-Symphonien
3 Notre-Dame des Doms
4 Saint-Étienne
5 Bridge
6 Bridge Gate
7 13th-Century Walls
8 Saint-Pierre
9 Saint-Agricol
10 Saint-Geniès
11 Notre-Dame la Principale

12 Synagogue
13 Saint-Didier
14 Aurose Gate
15 Imbert Gate
16 St. Agricola's Gate
17 Eyguière Gate
18 Carmelites
19 Augustinians
20 Franciscans
21 Celestines
22 Saint-Martial
23 Dominicans

24 14th-Century Walls
25 Palefrenière Gate
26 Salins Gate
27 Violette Gate
28 St. Lazarus Gate
29 New Imbert Gate
30 St. Anthony's or St. Michael's Gate
31 Gate of Miracles
32 Stone Cutter's Gate
33 Gate of the Dominicans
34 St. James' Gate

Introduction

"When the Good Lord comes to doubt about the world, he remembers that he created Provence," the great French poet Frédéric Mistral (1830–1914) is said to have offered in praise of his beloved homeland. Few other words better celebrate the region that hosted the papacy for the one hundred years that closed the Middle Ages. The French Southeast, open to the rest of the world via its Mediterranean shores, the broad highway of its Rhône River, and the byways of its Alpine passes, became the papal residence first by historical accident in 1309 but later by choice. The following pages tell the tale of this transplanted papacy at Avignon, the city the popes transformed into their capital. It is the tale of an institution growing and defending its prerogatives, of men both high and low who produced and served its needs, and of the city they built up together. As I reconsider the Avignon papacy and the Great Western Schism (1309–1417) within the social setting of late-medieval Avignon, I hope to recover some of its urban texture, the fabric of its streets, the noise of its crowds and celebrations, and a bit of its people's joys and pains.

The story of Avignon and its inhabitants is crucial to our understanding of the institutional history of the papacy in the later Middle Ages. Between 1309 and 1378, seven popes ruled the Western Church from Avignon (French today but Provençal territory until 1348, when Pope Clement VI bought the city from the Countess of Provence). Pope Gregory XI returned the papacy to Rome in 1377, but his subsequent death in March 1378 and the tumultuous Roman election of his successor in April shattered the unity of the Church in the Great Western Schism (1378–1417). The increasing dissatisfaction of the cardinals after the election of Urban VI led the majority to withdraw their support from him and to elect a challenger, Clement VII. Both popes considered themselves legitimate. The two contenders established rival courts, and Christendom split into a divided obedience. Clement VII and his court resettled in Avignon while Urban VI remained, sometimes tenuously, in Rome.

The Avignon papacy and the Schism encouraged fundamental institutional changes in the history of early modern Europe—effective central-

1

ization linked to fiscal policy, efficient bureaucratic governance, court society (*société de cour*), and conciliarism—but the dubious legitimacy of a divided and non-Roman papacy has cast a shadow over the entire period. The Schism only fueled the scathing criticism of Petrarch, who himself grew up near Avignon in the early years of the fourteenth century. His judgment that "the worst of all things are there in Babylon on the fierce banks of the Rhône where the infamous prostitute fornicates with the kings of the earth" has echoed throughout history. [1] His fame stigmatized Avignon and its popes. With his flair for invective, the negative effect of Petrarch's acid-tongued propaganda against the papal capital city has taken centuries to undo. Indeed, the scholarly consensus today concerning papal Avignon differs little from Petrarch's. How could someone possibly show interest in a topic dismissed by the father of humanism in these kinds of disparaging terms?

> Now I am living in France, in the Babylon of the West. The sun in its travels sees nothing more hideous than this place on the shores of the wild Rhône, which suggests the hellish streams of Cocytus and Acheron. Here reign the successors of the poor fishermen of Galilee; they have strangely forgotten their origin. I am astounded, as I recall their predecessors, to see these men loaded with gold and clad in purple, boasting of the spoils of princes and nations; to see luxurious palaces and heights crowned with fortifications, instead of a boat turned downward for shelter. We no longer find the simple nets which were once used to gain a frugal sustenance from the lake of Galilee, and with which, having labored all night and caught nothing, they took, at daybreak, a multitude of fishes, in the name of Jesus. One is stupefied nowadays to hear the lying tongues, and to see worthless parchments turned by a leaden seal into nets which are used, in Christ's name, but by the arts of Belial, to catch hordes of unwary Christians. [2]

Several centuries passed before, in 1866, a single author, Alphonse Daudet, took up the challenge of rehabilitating the city and its popes; but again, as it had been with Petrarch, Avignon was fictionalized. In one of his short stories, *The Mule of the Pope*, Daudet offers a caricature of papal Avignon joyous to the point of insouciance, peaceful and industrious—in fact, a city that never was. [3] At both ends of the spectrum, from the fourteenth to the nineteenth centuries, Petrarch and Daudet constructed the city as though inhabited by dramatis personae, both authors inserting a large dose of fiction into their contrived representations.

For more than six hundred years, historical scholarship concerning the fourteenth century has either neglected the Avignon papacy or vilified it as a French puppet—immoral, worldly, and materialistic in outlook. As Daniel Waley astutely remarks, the Avignon papacy has been treated until recently as an inconvenience, detrimental to Rome and the papacy in general. Surveys of papal Avignon have been close to nonexistent. And it seems that very few ever questioned the sources fabricated by Petrarch, Giovanni Villani, and their like, chroniclers whose basic interest was to defend a Roman papacy regardless of the location of the papacy, either in Rome or elsewhere in Italy.[4]

With such historical polarization, the work of a single author, Étienne Baluze (1630–1718), needs to be highlighted for his contribution to Avignon's reevaluation. This seventeenth-century scholar, an antiquarian and director of the rich and impressive private library of Jean-Baptiste Colbert, was the first to attempt a somewhat historical approach to the Avignon papacy, by focusing on source work. For many decades long after his death, he remained the sole scholar to edit documents related to the Avignon papacy. Born in Limousin in the French Southwest (like many of the Avignon popes), Baluze used his in-depth knowledge of archives to collect fourteenth-century documents that recounted the lives of the popes; these became the two volumes of his *Vitae paparum avenionensium* published in 1693.[5] Baluze was not intrinsically interested in the Avignon papacy per se; rather, this specific work evolved from his general interest in manuscripts related to Christian institutions of the Middle Ages. He produced a great many editions of Christian documents, texts, and treatises, and his edition of the lives of the Avignon popes seemed a natural continuation of his monumental endeavors. Yet with one caveat: the Avignon papacy was still an unwelcome bête noire, and in 1698 the volumes were put on the Index (the Catholic Church's list of prohibited books). Despite censorship by the Catholic Church, Baluze's edition of the popes' lives stood (and still stands) as the foundation of modern studies of the Avignon papacy before the opening of the Vatican Archives in 1881.

In 1917, Guillaume Mollat masterfully edited Baluze's *Vitae paparum*. Mollat extended Baluze's two-volume edition with an additional two that enlarged and analyzed the sources Baluze had utilized.[6] As Mollat notes, Baluze never worried about a rigorously scientific approach to his edition, never identifying, for example, the provenance of his material. Baluze's critical apparatus was close to nonexistent. Quite uncritically, he simply collected together various "lives" for each pope, which he organized sequentially. Thus, each pope had a first, second, or third life, each authored by various medieval chroniclers. Mollat's task was to identify and check Baluze's sources (original material from the royal collections and from Colbert's library, the Sorbonne, the Abbey of Saint-Denis, transcriptions of Vatican material done by Cardinal Casanata, and other material from elsewhere) and to analyze the sources' reliability, utility, and content. To complete the edition, Mollat clarified ambiguities, filled voids, and added documents that he found during his research.[7] Thus was born the four-volume edition of the popes' lives, the foundation of all subsequent work dealing with the Avignon papacy.

The opening of the Vatican Archives in 1881 and the knowledge derived from that rich collection initiated a marked change of perception: literary and somewhat amateur interest was slowly replaced by a historical narrative reliably grounded in true archival research. The German School of Rome, led by Heinrich Denifle and Franz Ehrle, produced seven volumes of documentary editions concerned largely with texts dealing with the Avignon papacy (*Archiv für Literatur und Kirchengeschichte des Mittelalters*).[8] Their focus fell on ecclesiastical, intellectual, institutional, and theological sources. During roughly the same period, the first volumes of the *Analecta Vaticano-Belgica* appeared, a series published by the *Institut historique belge de Rome*, from 1906 to 1987. These editions concerned the institutional history of dioceses in the medieval and early modern periods that today form Belgium. In the Middle Ages, they included Brussels, Cambrai, Liège, Thérouanne, and Tournai.[9]

This early interest in the institutional history of the Avignon papacy led logically to a study of its financial history. In 1911, Karl H. Schäfer began his transcription of the most important apostolic financial records regarding the Avignon papacy in his *Vatikanische Quellen zur Geschichte der päpstlichen Hof- und Finanzverwaltung (1316–1378)* for the *Historischen Institut* of the *Görres-Gesellschaft*.[10] The records of the Apostolic Chamber opened a window into the day-to-day life of the papal court. Expenses were itemized around several categories that evolved with each pope but generally dealt with the sustenance and functioning of the court. The kitchen, bread, and wine office itemized purchases of food, drink, and medicine; the stables' registers recorded expenses related to transportation and horses. All in all, within these categories scribes noted additional expenses relating to the purchase of wax, paper, clothing, fabrics, arts, jewelry, and the papal library, for example. Apostolic scribes also recorded the salaries of curial servants, alms, and finally all expenses related to construction and war. Historians discover invaluable information in these records—from the payments going to cobblers for making the pontiffs' red slippers, to physicians' salaries and the medication they ordered for certain popes, to the very names of the papal laundresses, messengers, and purveyors of wheat, wine, and fishes. Over the years, historians have refined the edition of these expense registers, but the early German editions remain the first points of reference for any basic research. The exploitation of these financial records was complemented in 1899 with the initiation of the project of the French School of Rome. If the Germans focused on finances, the French opted to decipher the papal correspondence and began publication of the papal letters; to date, their research has produced some fifty-four volumes of the *Registres et lettres des papes du XIVme siècle.*[11] As we will see later, the papal correspondence evolved somewhat with each pope but remained organized around two poles, internal politics and external diplomacy. There always remained the larger division between secret and curial letters for diplomacy and sensitive correspondence and communal letters for internal nominations and responses to petitions.

Ironically, the wealth of archive material is itself the result of the effective administration of the Avignon papacy. Because popes knew that they would not remain forever in exile from the Eternal City, they requested that administrative documents be archived twice, creating the so-called Avignon paper registers, the *Registra Avenionensia*, and the Vatican parchment registers, or *Registra Vaticana*. The chancery systematically recopied in the Vatican registers what was contained in the less durable paper registers. After Innocent VI's reign (1352–1362), recopying became less systematic, only privileging items deemed more important, such as papal bulls. Still, this double record keeping allowed for better conservation of the material. If registers were lost in transport between Avignon and Rome, the odds were good that other copies existed. The registers provided raw material to a small number of scholars (primarily French) who, between the two world wars, produced scores of "local" studies that remain invaluable even today.

Interest in major archives like the one at the Vatican sparked systematic and thorough research in local repositories, such as the communal and departmental archives of the Vaucluse (to which Avignon belonged). Gustave Bayle, Robert André-Michel, Robert Brun, Léopold Duhamel, Joseph Girard, Léon-Honoré Labande, and Pierre Pansier pored over local material, and their names still today find an honored place in the bibliography of any work concerning papal Avignon. Gustave Bayle was an early antiquarian (and something of an ethnologist, too), one of the first to draw from the communal archives. Relying on a methodology akin to folklore studies (he was, for example, interested in women's history, medicine, and prostitution), he integrated this approach to his reading of the medieval past and paved the way for a future social and cultural history of the city. [12]

During a brief career cut short by the outbreak of World War I, Robert André-Michel (1884–1914) turned the keen eye of a trained social historian to studying the papal capital. [13] He published a series of articles on Avignon's first clock, the building of its surrounding walls, and its defense against the companies of mercenaries (the infamous *routiers*). [14] A few years later, Robert Brun (1896–1978) became one of the first economic historians of the Middle Ages. Brun focused on commercial exchanges operated mainly by the Italian merchant class of Avignon. In his research, he understood quite early the great importance of the Pratese archives, the documentary history of one of Avignon's most famous merchants, Francesco di Marco Datini. [15] These archives became over time a research focus for his understanding of the economic history of the Middle Ages. [16] On a different spectrum, one more closely aligned with archival studies, Léopold Duhamel (1842–1922) initiated a long trend that eventually bound the office of archivist closely to the city's history. A professional archivist/paleographer, he directed important French archives, including those of the *département* of Vaucluse, of which Avignon is a part. He also directed the archives of the *départements* of Vosges and Corsica, organizing and classifying documents in his charge, compiling several inventories and repertories. Besides compiling the first inventory of the communal archives of Avignon, he also edited other series detailing the modern period, for example, *Répertoire numerique détaillé de la série L: Administration révolutionnaire, 1790–1800*. [17] His impeccable knowledge of the archives allowed him to publish several books on the pope's palace, architecture, and art. But more importantly, he is the one who facilitated the move of the papal archives from the *Préfecture de Vaucluse* into the pope's palace (in fact, an old chapel of Benedict XII), where they remain today. A few years later he convinced the communal authorities to grant him control of the communal archives; little by little, the departmental archives of Vaucluse grew into a research center investigating all aspects of Avignon and the papacy.

Another scholar associated with the preservation of the city's history is Joseph Girard (1881–1962). He is identified above all with the *Musée Calvet*, which he directed for some forty years before becoming the conservator of the pope's palace. The museum was a semi-independent institution founded and supported by the eighteenth-century physician and collector Esprit Calvet (1728–1810). Still open today, the museum preserves a collection of stone architectural remains (*musée lapidaire*), paintings, and ironworks. Of interest for the history of Avignon, the museum acquired under the leadership of Girard a large collection of manuscripts emanating from Avignonese antiquarians and historians (*fonds* of the Abbé Requin, Léon-Honoré Labande, and Pierre Pansier).[18] Active with the *Académie de Vaucluse* (the quintessential academia for erudite scholars), Girard focused his scholarship on cataloguing his museum and writing a history of Avignon's monuments.[19] Léon-Honoré Labande (1867–1939) is also closely associated with the Calvet Museum. He was a *chartiste*, that is, a graduate of the prestigious *École des chartes*, which still prepares France's conservators and archivists to this day. In 1890, Labande was named conservator of the *Musée Calvet* and of the *Bibliothèque d'Avignon*, a position that allowed him to examine all of Avignon's manuscripts deposited in the communal library. His work culminated in a comprehensive catalogue of the manuscripts in France's public libraries (*Catalogue général des manuscrits des bibliothèques publiques*). He spent much of his career as conservator of the archives and library of Monaco Palace (1906–1939). While in Avignon, Labande's scholarship focused on textual documentation and urban archaeology, and it extended to the periods both before and after the papal sojourn, so he broadened the scope of research interest in the city from the thirteenth to the fifteenth centuries.[20]

The last antiquarian/historian to be considered is Pierre Pansier (1864–1934). An ophthalmologist and chief surgeon at Avignon's hospital, Pierre Pansier's initial interest in the history of his profession grew into an insatiable appetite for the city's history at large. I cannot cite here his immense bibliography, and I would be hard pressed to offer a selection of his most relevant work, signaling in my footnotes only the books that pertain closely to the present study.[21] Pansier worked on everything from medieval doctors to repentant prostitutes to the history of the city's streets. He is the first source that historians interested in Avignon turn to (even if sometimes some of his transcriptions are erroneous). We can note that early in his career he joined Joseph Girard to discuss the history of the Temporal Court of Avignon, the judicial institution that monitored the lay population of the city.[22] He produced scores of articles in the *Annales d'Avignon et du Comtat Venaissin* and the *Mémoires de l'Académie de Vaucluse.*

Avignon advanced from the realm of merely local and antiquarian studies when four French historians—Léon Mirot, Guillaume Mollat, Charles Samaran, and Yves Renouard—opted to focus their research on the Avignon papacy. Léon Mirot (1870–1946) was an archivist and paleographer trained at the *École des chartes*, a member of the French School in Rome, and a conservator at France's National Archives. Like Robert Brun, he focused on the Italians active in France and Provence. Yet unlike Brun, who researched the well-known Florentines of Avignon, Mirot studied the Lucchese families who settled abroad, such as the Spiafame.[23] Note that Mirot also published one of the first manuals of historical geography of the modern period, a topic dear to the *Annales* School.[24] Mirot's interest in the Avignon papacy led him to a study of the papal return to Rome in 1376[25] and most importantly to transcribe and edit the letters of Pope Gregory XI.[26]

Guillaume Mollat (1877–1968) left an immense body of scholarship, including seminal works about Avignon's history such as the first comprehensive survey of the Avignon papacy and (as seen previously) the edition in four volumes of Étienne Baluze's lives of the Avignon popes *(Vitae paparum Avenionensum)*, still the standard work in the field. He edited the papal letters of four popes, John XXII (sixteen volumes), Clement VI (four volumes), Urban V (one volume), and Gregory XI (one volume).[27] His intimate knowledge of the archival material survives in countless articles in the *Revue d'histoire ecclésiastique, Provence Historique,* and the *Mémoires de l'Académie de Vaucluse.*[28] Although his interest remained institutional, he never shied away from addressing the men who worked within the system and, to a lesser extent, Avignon curial society. Although Mollat was a member of the clergy, he trained at the *École française* of Rome under the direction of another ecclesiastic, the famous Church historian Louis Duchesne (1843–1922). Mollat pursued his research even while fulfilling his priestly functions, traveling back and forth between Rome and France, where he served as chaplain in Mont-martre and vicar of Notre-Dame de Passy.[29] Guillaume Mollat's interest in the men who administered the curia, papal justice, and finances paved the way for the next generation of scholars.[30] One of Guillaume Mollat's closest friends was Charles Samaran (1879–1982); together in 1905 they published the first study of the Avignon popes' finances.[31] The extraordinary longevity of Charles Samaran (he died at 104) made him the dean of Avignon historiography, whose work influenced the next wave of economic historians like Yves Renouard (1908–1965) and Jean Favier (1932–2014). Samaran was a humanist in the old sense, a true erudite scholar, a Renaissance man with a deep literary culture and the perfect mastery of Latin so dear to the *École des chartes*.[32]

The study of papal finances pointed to a few truisms. When the papacy moved to southern France in 1309, it was still a Roman curia. Even if accused of being manipulated by the French crown, the curia comprised individuals still labeled "followers of the Roman court," despite where it was located. The highest echelons of papal government were French, but a large segment of the bureaucratic and financial institution was in the hands of Italian nationals. It was a fact that the French papacy kept close ties with Italy if only because of the large tracts of land it needed to reconquer in order to consolidate its papal states in the area. Conquest and war meant funds, and Italian bankers ran papal finances on a daily basis.

The last historian of the mid-twentieth-century group of economic historians, Yves Renouard, understood this and clearly linked papal Avignon to Italy. Yves Renouard may be considered the first modern economic historian. In a 1971 review, Brown University's Italianist David Herlihy underscores Renouard's originality, his mode of thought that privileged administrative sources: "The novelty of Renouard's work in administrative history was his shift of emphasis from the theoretical functions of the various papal offices to the practical operations of the papal government. He sought to explore, as he says in the *Études*, 'the reality, the life, which is usually covered or masked in the official texts.'"[33] In 1968, the sixth section of the *École pratique des hautes études* compiled two volumes containing the majority of Yves Renouard's articles (approximately seventy of them) completed between 1934 and 1965.[34] These articles serve as an introduction to his scholarship. Renouard navigated between three poles of interest—the Avignon papacy,

Italian cities, and the French Southwest—all of which he linked with the Italian merchants who traveled from one to the other. As David Herlihy explains, "To judge from his first publication he [Renouard] had been concerned initially with the political and institutional history of the papacy in the Avignon period, but with characteristic alertness he soon recognized the value of these archives for economic history. These documents were the basis of his thesis, published in 1942, on the relations of the Avignon papacy with the banking companies of Italy."[35] Renouard's thesis, *Les relations des papes d'Avignon et des compagnies commerciales et bancaires de 1316 à 1378*, and its continuation, *Recherches sur les compagnies commerciales et bancaires utilisées par les papes d'Avignon avant le Grand Schisme*, made him the foremost specialist on the Avignon merchant class.[36] His work led him to conduct a survey of medieval businessmen and to write another history of the Avignon papacy.[37] Renouard thus became the second historian, after Guillaume Mollat, to synthesize the era. Studies of the Avignon papacy became important enough to be translated into English—in 1963 for Guillaume Mollat[38] and 1970 for Yves Renouard.[39] To date, the best survey in English of the Avignon papacy remains Patrick Zutshi's chapter in the sixth volume of *The New Cambridge Medieval History*, which deals with the years 1300 to 1415.[40]

Fourteenth-century Avignonese records lend themselves to historical demographic analysis and quantitative studies, a growing methodological trend in the 1960s. Once the papal administration settled in Avignon in the early fourteenth century, it organized its services based on local resources. For example, curial officers in charge of finding shelter for curialists compiled lists of available housing. Throughout the period, these assignation and taxation records tracked lodging locations as well as rent charged and paid to property owners. These registers, now housed at the Vatican, were completed with lists of all expenses encountered by the curia. Such accounts offer a glimpse into the day-to-day administration of the curia, from data relating to tax collection by the Apostolic Chamber, to food and clothing purchases, to the making of knives, medicine, laundry lists, and names of mercenaries defending the palace and city walls. Record keeping was rigorous and surprisingly well developed for the time.[41] Any person who had a transaction with the curia could expect to have his or her name recorded by papal scribes. Using scores of these documents, Bernard Guillemain, in his 1962 book *La cour pontificale d'Avignon: Étude d'une société (1309–1376)*, wrote the first social history of the fourteenth-century curia.[42] His contemporary, Jean Favier, published in 1966 a study of the papal finances during the Great Western Schism (1378–1409).[43] Both works (each close to one thousand pages long) remain impossible to ignore for any study of papal Avignon.

Bernard Guillemain describes in minute detail the members of the papal government and bureaucracy as well as the numerous immigrants (*cortisiani* or *curiam romanam sequentes,* "the followers of the Roman court") attracted to the city by the presence of the popes. He identifies the geographical origins and occupational activities of these curialists and other immigrants, who had hoped to better their lives within the walls of the Provençal city by offering their services to the curia. Because of its scope, Guillemain's study of the city during the first seventy-five years of the fourteenth century became a landmark in the social history of medieval Avignon even though it contains some errors.[44] For his part, Jean Favier pursued the analysis of the trademark of the Avignon papacy, its growing financial and administrative centralization, a trait already noted by Guillaume Mollat, Yves Renouard, and Bernard Guillemain. *Les finances pontificales à l'époque du Grand Schisme* made Favier's career, which culminated with his nomination as keeper of the French National Archives.[45] *Les finances* remains notable today because it is the sole monograph focused on Avignon during the Great Western Schism. Favier used his study as a means to direct attention to the financial structures of the papacy, essential for its survival during this period of trouble, but also to the men who ran the institution. Like Guillemain's, his social approach linked religion, politics, and economy to society. He framed his methodology around preoccupations of human interest, focusing on the tax collectors, money changers, and merchants without whom church government would not have functioned, as well as on the means by which it functioned. All in all, Guillemain's and Favier's socioeconomic studies presented the papal city as one of the great medieval metropolises, worthy of being placed on the historical map alongside Paris, Florence, and London.

In 1979, there appeared under the leadership of Sylvain Gagnière the first and only synthesis of the history of the city throughout the ages, the *Histoire d'Avignon.*[46] Each chronological chapter was authored by a specialist of the period. Sylvain Gagnière came to history by way of archaeology. The son of a wealthy family, he abandoned a promising career in industry after World War II to pursue his interest in archaeology. A researcher at the *Centre national de la recherche scientifique* and specialist in Provence's prehistory, he eventually became conservator of the *Palais du Roure* (a fifteenth-century palace built by a Florentine exile, Piero Baroncelli) and of the pope's palace. In that capacity, he initiated several digging campaigns subsequently documented in published reports and eventually leading to the first in-depth study of the papal palace.[47] Quintessential historian of the palace, he founded the *Société des amis du Palais des Papes* that is still active today with meetings and a journal, the *Annuaire de la Société des amis du Palais des Papes*. He may be the sole modern historian who gave his name to a street in Avignon. There is a *Rue Pierre Pansier*, but it is in Carpentras!

Since Bernard Guillemain, Jean Favier, and Sylvain Gagnière, the glitter of Avignon's archival wealth has attracted more French historians, mainly disciples of the *École des chartes* and the Annales School. Anne-Marie Hayez for the former, and Jacques Chiffoleau for the latter, continue to be their best representatives. Anne-Marie Hayez's immense knowledge of the archives and their content makes her the ideal interlocutor for anyone interested in the Avignon papacy. This study is deeply indebted to her many publications on taxes and *gabelles*, the construction of the palace, papal life, and fourteenth-century Avignonese citizens. She has edited countless numbers of papal letters and is responsible for several volumes of papal correspondence published by the *École française* of Rome, especially regarding Urban V and Gregory XI.[48]

Anne-Marie Hayez also edited an important volume indispensable for the knowledge of medieval Avignon, the *Terrier Avignonnais de l'évêque Anglic Grimoard*.[49] Administrative documents (usually labeled *terrier* or *censier*) offer an abundance of information on property ownership with detailed descriptions of people and geography. Medieval ownership is a complicated concept somewhat incomprehensible to the modern mind. People owned vacant and arable lands, houses, courtyards, vineyards, and gardens that they or their forefathers had bought from a "lord." The "owners" could dispose of their property at will with a caveat; they needed to recognize a right of ownership to that same "lord" or his successors. That right of "direct" ownership to another entity was materialized through the payment of a yearly tax, a *cens* (hence the word *censier* or *terrier* for the listings) to the person (a descendant or his representative, often called procurator). Usually that legal persona, or "lord," was an institution, a diocese, a cathedral chapter, an abbey, a convent, or a monastery. Well-organized lordships compiled registers that listed and counted the parcels, whether lands, houses, or vineyards, and listed their payment due dates in currency and in kind. Hayez edited one of the most important *terriers*, compiled under the directives of the bishop of Avignon, Anglic Grimoard, by a certain Sicard du Fraisse between 1366 and 1368. Further, she appends an important biographical apparatus to the individuals listed in the *terrier*, allowing thus a clear identification of who was where in 1360s Avignon. The work is an invaluable tool.

Anne-Marie Hayez's husband, Michel Hayez, is also a historian of Avignon. While director of the Archives of the Vaucluse, he edited a guide to the archives, essential when navigating the massive documentation contained there. He also produced other repertories of archival material unrelated to the Avignon papacy.[50] He was a coeditor, with his wife and other collaborators, of the *École française* edition of Urban V's letters, and he also coauthored several articles with his wife.[51] As sole author, he produced two articles on the departure of the popes from and their return to Avignon.[52] Their son, Jérôme, is continuing the familial involvement with the papal city. *Chargé de recherche* at the *Institut d'histoire moderne et contemporaine*, he has focused his research on the epistolary exchanges between Avignon and Italy, producing an anthropological study of medieval migration.[53]

Among contemporary historians, Jacques Chiffoleau has become the French specialist on the city's religious history and justice. He produced two groundbreaking studies in the 1980s: *La comptabilité de l'au-delà: Les hommes, la mort et la religion dans la region d'Avignon à la fin du moyen âge*, and *Les justices du pape*.[54] *La comptabilité* is a study based largely on notarial archives and testaments from which Chiffoleau measures the impact that crises of the time—plague, war, and immigration—had on religious mentalities. He evokes a world of familial isolation where deep ties of kinship gave way before interclass marriage, the alliances of friends and neighbors, and the abruptly truncated nuclear family—in sum, the birth of modern kinship structures. *Les justices du pape* uses Vatican and communal material (for the most part) to survey the many justices—or, rather, judicial systems—that ruled Avignon. Two additional French historians have focused on Avignon as well. Jacques Rossiaud has published a study of medieval prostitution and of occupations related to the Rhône River (boatmen and longshoremen), while Daniel Le Blévec has studied charity and the assistance given to the poor in the Avignonese region.[55]

In spite of the dominance of French scholars in the field, a few English-speaking modern historians have been attracted to the Avignon papacy and its capital city. Richard C. Trexler started his career with a study of the *Liber divisionis,* a census of Avignonese immigrants in 1371, researching a thesis that examined the strained relations between Florence and Avignon that led to the 1376 papal interdict over the city.[56] Daniel Williman has researched papal chamberlains and the Apostolic Chamber.[57] And a few papal biographies have appeared in English: Sophia Menache authored a life of Clement V, Diane Wood concentrated on Clement VI, and Paul Thibault wrote about Gregory XI.[58] I will return to them while addressing specific popes. Most recently, the Avignon papacy has resurfaced to prominence somewhat. Other scholars have intensively studied the sources, and their research has led to new studies, often fresh perspectives considered through a social and cultural lens. I will engage them in the discussion that follows.

In this work, I attempt to rehabilitate the effectiveness of papal governance and to recover the creativity and civic dynamism of the period. The significant contribution of this study resides in its retrieval of the complex interrelationship of court and city, enlarging what might otherwise be a narrowly institutional approach within the wider perspective of a newer urban history. This is not the rhetorical Avignon of Dante, Petrarch, St. Catherine of Siena, or Bridget of Sweden, but the day-to-day Avignon of popes, bureaucrats, and merchants. The first three chapters survey the history of the seven popes of Avignon. These chapters canvass the many issues they dealt with, whether internal or external, and how each pontiff responded. Contrary to older assumptions, there is little doubt that the popes of Avignon defended papal authority rather than acquiescing to the French crown. Many of them were experienced diplomats whose skill at temporizing with somewhat arrogant rulers could mistakenly be perceived as complacency. The fourth chapter elucidates the many innovations of Avignon's papal administration, the veritable founder of what we would call today "red tape." Since papal government implanted itself in the city, the chapter also scrutinizes the relationship between administration and Avignon's space and topography. The fifth chapter addresses directly how city and pope related and the effect of the court's arrival on Avignon's physical and social topographies. The last chapter addresses the birth and history of the Great Western Schism as it connected to Avignon's policies and society.

The Avignon papacy was notable for its economic efficiency—for example, it organized and centralized tax collection, money changing, and banking. Yet institutions are nothing without the people who create and run them. The story of the city and its inhabitants is knitted into the institutional history of the papacy. So this volume examines not only the popes and the people of their courts (cardinals, chamberlains, tax collectors, Italian merchants, scribes, papal messengers, and the myriad bureaucrats necessary for the curia's functioning) but also the laboring classes drawn to the city to provide the many ancillary services necessary for the court's comfort, from butchers and fruit sellers to cooks, from shoemakers to laundresses. Late-medieval Avignon experienced tremendous demographic and spatial growth within a short time, forcing the city to face early some of the issues that typically affect modern capitals: unchecked immigration, urban sprawl, social tensions and geographic segregation, health and hygiene issues, poverty, and widespread prostitution, to name a few. The aim of this volume is to give readers a vivid sense of what it was like to live in the crowded fourteenth-century capital of Christianity even as we survey the history of the popes and their court.

NOTES

1. Robert Coogan, *Babylon on the Rhone: A Translation of Letters by Dante, Petrarch, and Catherine of Siena on the Avignon Papacy* (Madrid: José Porrúa Turanzas, 1983), 13.

2. "Petrarch's Letter to a friend, 1340–1353," in *Readings in European History*, ed. James Harvey Robinson (Boston: Ginn, 1904), 1:502.

3. "He who never saw Avignon in the time of the Popes has seen nothing. Never was there such a city for gayety, life, animation, and a succession of fetes. There were, from morning till night, processions, pilgrimages, streets strewn with flowers and carpeted with magnificent tapestries, cardinals arriving by the Rhone, with banners flying; gayly bedecked galleys, the soldiers of the Pope singing in Latin on the squares, and the bowls of mendicant friars: and then, from roof to cellar of the houses that crowded humming about the great Papal palace, like bees about their hive, there was the tick-tack of the lace-makers' looms, the rapid movement of the shuttles weaving gold thread for the vestments, the little hammers of the carvers of burettes, the keyboards being tuned at the lute-makers, the songs of the sempstresses; and, overhead, the clang of the bells, and always a tambourine or two jingling down by the bridge. For with us, when the common people are pleased, they must dance and dance; and as the streets in the city in those days were too narrow for the farandole, the fifes and the tambourines stationed themselves on Avignon Bridge, in the cool breezes from the Rhone; and there the people danced and danced, day and night. Ah! the happy days! the happy city! Halberds that did not wound, state prisons where they put wine to cool. No famine; no wars. That is how the Popes of the Comtat governed the people; that is why the people regretted them so bitterly." Alphonse Daudet, *Alphonse Daudet's*

Short Stories, trans. George Burnham Ives (New York: G. P. Putnam's Sons, 1909), 47–48.

4. Daniel Waley, "Opinions of the Avignon Papacy: A Historiographical Sketch," in *Storiografia e Storia: Studi in onore Eugenio Duprè Theseider* (Rome: Bulzoni, 1974), 1:175–188.

5. Étienne Baluze, *Vitae paparum avenionensium, hoc est, Historia pontificum romanorum qui in Gallia sederunt ab anno Christi MCCCV usque ad annum MCCCXCIV*, ed. Guillaume Mollat (Paris: Letouzey et Ané, 1914), 4 vols. The text has been recently digitalized following the edition of Guillaume Mollat, making it easily accessible. See http://baluze.univAvignon.fr/v1/read_index.html.

6. A first volume focused on the lives of the popes collected from various medieval manuscripts ranging between 1305 and 1394 (appended with Baluze's notes), and a second volume contained the various documents that Baluze used for his notes.

7. Mollat explains his rationale and edition in Guillaume Mollat, *Etude critique sur les Vitæ Paparum Avenionensium d'Etienne Baluze* (Paris: Letouzey et Ané, 1917).

8. Heinrich Denifle, O.P., and Franz Erhle, S.J. (eds.), *Archiv für Literatur und Kirchengeschichte des Mittelalters* (Berlin: Weidmannsche Buchhandlung, 1885–1890), 7 vols.

9. Ursmer Berlière, *Suppliques de Clément VI (1342–1352): Textes et analyses* (Rome: Institut historique belge, 1906); Arnold R. Fayen, *Lettres de Jean XXII (1316–1334): Textes et analyses* (Rome: M. Bretschneider, 1908), 2 vols.; Alphonse Fierens, *Lettres de Benoit XII (1334–1342): Textes et analyses* (Rome: M. Bretschneider, 1910); Ursmer Berlière, *Suppliques d'Innocent VI (1352–1362): Textes et analyses* (Rome: M. Bretschneider, 1911); Alphonse Fierens, *Suppliques d'Urbain V (1362–1370): Textes et analyses* (Rome: M. Bretschneider, 1914); Karl Hanquet, Ursmer Berlière, Hubert Nelis, Marie Jeanne Tits-Dieuaide, Pervenche Briegleb, and Arlette Laret-Kayser, *Documents relatifs au grand schisme: Textes et analyses* (Brussels: Institut historique belge de Rome, 1924), 7 vols.; Philippe Van Isacker and Ursmer Berlière, *Lettres de Clément VI (1342–1352): Textes et analyses* (Rome: Institut historique belge, 1924); Alphonse Fierens and Camille Tihon, *Lettres d'Urbain V (1362–1370): Textes et analyses* (Rome: Institut historique belge, 1928); Ursmer Berlière, *Les collectories pontificales dans les anciens diocèses de Cambrai, Thérouanne et Tournai au XIVe siècle* (Rome: Institut historique belge, 1929); Georges Despy, *Lettres d'Innocent VI (1352–1362): Textes et analyses* (Brussels: Institut historique belge de Rome, 1953); Camille Tihon, *Lettres de Grégoire XI (1371–1378): Textes et analyses: Documents relatifs aux anciens diocèses de Cambrai, Liège, Thérouanne et Tournai* (Brussels: Institut historique belge de Rome, 1958), 4 vols.; Micheline Soenen, *Lettres de Grégoire XII, 1406–1415: Textes et analyses* (Brussels: Institut historique belge de Rome, 1976); Marguerite Gastout, *Suppliques et lettres d'Urbain VI (1378–1389) et de Boniface IX (cinq premières années, 1389–1394): Textes et analyses* (Brussels: Institut historique belge de Rome, 1976); Jeannine Paye-Bourgeois, *Lettres de Benoît XIII (1394–1422)* (Brussels: Institut historique belge de Rome, 1983); Monique Maillard-Luypaert, *Lettres d'Innocent VII (1404–1406): Textes et analyses* (Brussels: Institut historique belge de Rome, 1987).

10. Karl-Heinrich Schäfer, *Die Ausgaben der apostolischen Kammer unter Johann XXII nebst den Jahresbilanzen von 1316–1375* (Paderborn: Ferdinand Schöningh, 1911); *Die Ausgaben der apostolischen Kammer unter Benedikt XII, Klemens VI und Innocenz VI* (Paderborn: Ferdinand Schöningh, 1914); and *Die Ausgaben der apostolischen Kammer unter den Päpsten Urban V und Gregor XI (1362–1378)* (Paderborn: Ferdinand Schöningh, 1937). These editions concern the Vatican Archives *introitus et exitus* series.

11. The full edition of the letters is as follows: Jean XXII (1316–1334), *Lettres communes* (Paris: BEFAR, 1904–1947), 16 vols.; Jean XXII (1316–1334), *Lettres secrètes et curiales relatives à la France* (Paris: BEFAR, 1900–1972), 4 vols.; Benoît XII (1334–1342), *Lettres communes* (Paris: BEFAR, 1902–1911), 3 vols.; Benoît XII (1334–1342), *Lettres closes, patentes et curiales se rapportant à la France* (Paris: BEFAR, 1899–1920); Benoît XII (1334–1342), *Lettres closes et patentes intéressant les pays autres que la France* (Paris: BEFAR, 1913–1950), 2 vols.; Clément VI (1342–1352), *Lettres closes, patentes et curiales se rapportant à la France* (Paris: BEFAR, 1925–1961), 3 vols.; Clément VI (1342–1352), *Lettres closes, patentes et curiales intéressant les pays autres que la France* (Paris: BEFAR, 1960–1961); Innocent VI (1352–1362), *Lettres closes, patentes et curiales se rapportant à la France* (Paris: BEFAR, 1909); Innocent VI (1352–1362), *Lettres secrètes et curiales* (Paris: BEFAR, 1959–forthcoming), 5 vols.; Urbain V (1362–1370), *Lettres secrètes et curiales se rapportant à la France* (Paris: BEFAR, 1902–1955); Urbain V (1362–1370), *Lettres communes* (Paris: BEFAR, 1954–1989), 12 vols.; Grégoire XI (1370–1378), *Lettres communes* (Rome: BEFAR, 1992–1993), 3 vols.; Grégoire XI (1370–1378), *Lettres secrètes et curiales relatives à la France* (Paris: BEFAR, 1935–1957); and Grégoire XI (1370–1378), *Lettres secrètes et curiales intéressant les pays autres que la France* (Paris: BEFAR, 1962–1965). The letters are now available in an online database; see *Ut per litteras apostolicas/Lettres Pontificales/Papal Letters online* (Turnhout: Brepols, 2005).

12. See, for example, Gustave Bayle, "Une bourgeoise Avignonnaise au moyen-âge," *Mémoires de l'academie de Vaucluse* (henceforth *MAV*) 6 (1886): 295–306; "Habitudes somptuaires des Avignonnais au moyen-âge," *Bulletin historique et archéologique de Vaucluse* 5 (1883): 311–335, 431–452; and 6 (1884): 455–474; "Les médecins d'Avignon au moyen-âge," *Annuaire de Vaucluse* (1882): 1–102; "Notes pour l'histoire de la prostitution au moyen-âge dans les provinces méridionales de la France," *MAV* 6 (1886): 233–245; "Un trésorier général de la ville d'Avignon au XIVe siècle: La messe de la concorde," *MAV* 9 (1889): 137–163.

13. American readers may be familiar with him through his young wife, Rose-Marie Ormond André-Michel, favorite model of her uncle John Singer Sargent. Like her husband, she died young, a tragic death following German bombardments of Paris.

14. Robert André-Michel, "Les premières horloges du palais pontifical d'Avignon," *Mélanges d'archéologie et d'histoire* (henceforth *MAH*) 29 (1909): 212–224; "La construction des remparts d'Avignon au XIVe siècle," in *Congrés archéologique de France (Avignon, 1909)*: 341–360; "La défense d'Avignon sous Urbain V et Grégoire XI," *MAH* 30 (1910): 129–154; "Anglais, bretons et routiers à Carpentras sous Jean le Bon et Charles V," in *Mélanges d'histoire Louis Halphen* (Paris, 1913), 341–352; "Avignon au temps des premiers papes," *Revue historique* 118 (1915): 289–304; "Le palais des papes d'Avignon: Documents inédits," *Annales d'Avignon et du Comtat Venaissin* 1–2 (1917–1918): 3–42.

15. Robert Brun, "Quelques italiens d'Avignon au XIVe siècle: Naddino di Prato médecin de la cour pontificale," *MAH* 49 (1923): 219–236; *Avignon aux temps des papes: Les monuments, les artistes, la société* (Paris, 1928); "A Fourteenth-Century Merchant of Italy: Francesco Datini of Prato," *Journal of Economic and Business History* 2 (1930): 451–466; "Notes sur le commerce des objets d'art en France et principalement à Avignon à la fin du XIVe siècle," *Bibliothèque de l'École des chartes* (henceforth *BEC*) 95 (1934): 327–346; "Annales Avignonnaises de 1382 à 1410 extraites des archives Datini," *Mémoires de l'institut historique de Provence* 12 (1935):17–142; 13 (1936): 58–105; 14 (1937): 5–57; 15 (1938): 21–52 and 154–192; "Notes sur le commerce florentin à Paris à la fin du

XIVe siècle," *Cooperazione intellettuale* 6 (1936): 87–96; "Notes sur le commerce des armes à Avignon au XIVe siècle," *BEC* 109 (1951): 209–232.

16. See, for example, Jérôme Hayez and Diana Toccafondi, eds., *Palazzo Datini a Prato: Una casa fatta per durare mille anni* (Florence: Edizioni Polistampa, 2012), 2 vols.; and http://www.istitutodatini.it/schede/archivio/eng/arc-dat1.htm.

17. His inventories are as follows: Léopold Duhamel, *Inventaire-sommaire des archives communales antérieures à 1790 de la ville d'Avignon* (Avignon: Impr. P. Bernard, 1906); *Inventaire-sommaire des archives communales antérieures à 1790 de la ville d'Avignon: série AA* (Avignon: impr. de P. Bernard, 1906); with Paul Achard, Félix Achard, and Claude Pintat, *Inventaire sommaire des archives communales antérieures à 1790 de la ville d'Avignon: Grandes archives* (Avignon: Archives départementales, 1863); with Félix Achard, *Inventaire-sommaire des archives départementales antérieures à 1790: Vaucluse: Archives civiles: Série B* (Paris: P. Dupont, 1878); *Inventaire sommaire des archives départementales de Vaucluse séries C et D* (Avignon: F. Seguin, 1913); *Inventaire sommaire des archives communales antérieures à 1790 supplément à la série E* (Epinal: Veuve Gley, 1867); with Léo Imbert and Jacques de Font-Réaulx, *Inventaire sommaire des archives départementales du département de Vaucluse: Série G: Archevêché, chapitre, cathédrale, séminaire et Inquisition d'Avignon* (Avignon: Archives de Vaucluse, 1954); with Aimé Autrand and Jacques de Font-Réaulx, *Répertoire numérique des archives municipales d'Avignon: Documents de l'époque révolutionnaire* (Avignon: Archives de Vaucluse, 1955). He then produced a registry for the notarial archives, with *Les archives notariales d'Avignon et du Comtat Venaissin* (Paris: A. Picard, 1895). The rest of his production concerning Avignon related more specifically to art and architecture; see *Les origines du palais des papes* (Tours: P. Bousrez, 1883); *Les oeuvres d'art du monastère des Célestins d'Avignon* (Caen: H. Delesques, 1888); *Inventaire du trésor de l'église métropolitaine d'Avigon au XVIe siècle (1511–1546)* (Paris: Impr. Nat, 1880); *Les architectes du palais des papes* (Avignon: Seguin frères, 1882); and *Les origines de l'imprimerie à Avignon: Note sur les documents découverts* (Avignon: Seguin frères, 1890).

18. In archival practice, a *fonds* represents "the entire body of records of an organization, family, or individual that have been created and accumulated as the result of an organic process reflecting the functions of the creator"; see http://www2.archivists. org/glossary/terms/f/fonds.

19. Joseph Girard, *Musée Calvet de la ville d'Avignon: Catalogue illustré* (Avignon: Musée Calvet, 1921); *Catalogue des tableaux exposés dans les galeries du Musée-Calvet d'Avignon* (Avignon: François Seguin, 1909); *Histoire du Musée Calvet* (Avignon: Impr. Rullière, 1955); *Avignon: Histoire sommaire, guide des monuments* (Avignon: Dominique Seguin, 1923); with F. Detaille and Adolphe Detaille, *Avignon: Ses monuments, ses hôtels, ses trésors d'art* (Marseille: F. Detaille, 1931); *Les Baroncelli d'Avignon: Publications de l'institut méditerranéen du Palais du Roure: Avignon, Fondation Flandreysy-Espérandieu* (Avignon: Palais du Roure, 1957); *Évocation du vieil Avignon* (Paris: Les éditions de Minuit, 1958).

20. Léon-Honoré Labande, *Catalogue général des manuscrits des bibliothèques publiques de France* (Paris: Plon, 1894); *Les Doria de France, Provence, Avignon et Comté Venaissin, Bretagne, Ile-de-France et Picardie: Études historiques et généalogiques* (Paris: A. Picard, 1899); Le palais des papes et les monuments d'Avignon au XIVe siècle (Marseille: Detaille, 1925), 2 vols.; *Avignon au XVe siècle* (Marseille: Laffitte Reprints, 1973); *Avignon au XVe siècle: Légation de Charles de Bourbon et du Cardinal Julien de La Rovère* (Marseille: Laffitte Reprints, 1975); *Avignon au XIIIe siècle: L'évêque Zoen Tencarari et les Avignonais* (Marseille: Laffitte, 1975).

21. Pierre Pansier, *L'oeuvre des repenties en Avignon du XIIIe au XVIIIe siècles* (Paris: H. Champion, 1910); *Les palais cardinalices d'Avignon aux XIVe et XVe siècles* (Avignon: J. Roumanille, 1926–1931); *Dictionnaire des anciennes rues d'Avignon* (Avignon: J. Roumanille, 1930); *Les Boucicaut à Avignon (1371–1490)* (Avignon: J. Roumanille, 1933).

22. Joseph Girard and Pierre Pansier, *La cour temporelle d'Avignon aux XIVe et XVe siècles: Contribution à l'étude des institutions judiciaires, administratives et économiques d'Avignon au moyen-âge* (Paris: H. Champion, 1909).

23. Léon Mirot, *Études lucquoises* (Paris: Imprimerie Daupeley-Gouverneur, 1930).

24. Léon Mirot, *Manuel de géographie historique de la France: Quarante-trois cartes hors texte* (Paris: A. Picard, 1929).

25. Léon Mirot, *La politique pontificale et le retour du Saint-Siège à Rome en 1376* (Paris: É. Bouillon, 1899).

26. Léon Mirot, Guillaume Mollat, Henri Jassemin, and Edmond René Labande, *Lettres secrètes et curiales du pape Grégoire XI (1370–1378) relatives à la France, extraites des registres du Vatican* (Paris: De Boccard, 1935).

27. Guillaume Mollat, *Les papes d'Avignon (1305–1378)* (Paris: V. Lecoffre, 1912); Jean XXII, *Lettres communes analysées d'après les registres dits d'Avignon et du Vatican*, ed. Guillaume Mollat (Paris: De Boccard, 1904–1946), 16 vols.; Clément VI, *Lettres closes, patentes et curiales se rapportant à la France publiées ou analysées d'après les registres du Vatican*, ed. Eugène Déprez and Guillaume Mollat (Paris: De Boccard, 1910–1961), 3 vols.; Clément VI, *Lettres closes, patentes et curiales, intéressant les pays autres que la France, publiées ou analysées d'après les registres du Vatican*, ed. Eugène Déprez and Guillaume Mollat (Paris: De Boccard, 1960–1961); Grégoire XI, *Lettres secrètes et curiales intéressant les pays autres que la France*, ed. Guillaume Mollat (Paris: De Boccard, 1962–1965); Urbain V, *Lettres secrètes et curiales du pape Urbain V (1362–1370) se rapportant à la France*, ed. Paul Lecacheux and Guillaume Mollat (Paris: A. Fontemoing, 1902).

28. For example, Guillaume Mollat, "Les changeurs d'Avignon sous Jean XXII," *MAV*, series 2, 5 (1905): 271–279; "Les conflits de juridiction entre le maréchal de la cour pontificale et le viguier d'Avignon au XIVe siècle," *Provence historique* 4 (1954): 11–18; "Contribution à l'histoire de l'administration judiciaire de l'église romaine au XIVe siècle," *Revue d'histoire ecclésiastique* 32 (1936): 877–928; "Contribution à l'histoire de la chambre apostolique au XIVe siècle," *Revue d'histoire ecclésiastique* 45 (1950): 82–94; "Deux frères mineurs Marc de Viterbe et Guillaume de Guasconi au service de la papauté (1363–1375)," *Revue d'histoire ecclésiastique* 50 (1955): 1092–1096; "La diplomatie pontificale au XIVe siècle," In *Mélanges Louis Halphen d'histoire du moyen-âge* (Paris, 1951), 507–512; "Fin de la carrière du cardinal Pierre d'Estaing (1376–1377)," in *Académie des inscriptions des belles-lettres* (Paris, 1956), 422–425; "Grégoire XI et sa légende," *Revue d'histoire ecclésiastique* 44 (1954): 873–877; "Miscellanea avenionensia," *MAH* 44 (1927): 1–11; "Réglements d'Urbain V sur les insignes des sergents d'armes, des portiers et des courriers de la cour pontificale," In *Mélanges Eugenes Tisserant* (Paris, 1964), 165–169; "Les relations politiques de Grégoire XI avec les siennois et les florentins," *MAH* 68 (1956): 335–376; "Les vacances à la cour pontificale au XIVe siècle," *MAH* 65 (1953): 215–217.

29. For his eulogy see, Henri-Charles Puech, "Éloge funèbre de Mgr Guillaume Mollat, membre libre de l'Académie," *Comptes-rendus des séances de l'Académie des inscriptions et belles-lettres* 112.2 (1968): 160–161, and another eulogy by his dear friend, the centenarian scholar Charles Samaran, in *Comptes-rendus des séances de l'Académie des inscriptions et belles-lettres* 112.2 (1968): 245–249.

30. See Guillaume Mollat and Jean Glénisson, *L'administration des états de l'église au XIVe siècle: Correspondance des légats et vicaires généraux Albornoz et de la Roche, 1353–1357* (Paris: De Boccard, 1964).

31. Guillaume Mollat and Charles Samaran, *La fiscalité pontificale en France au XIVe siècle* (Paris: A. Fontemoing, 1905).

32. Robert-Henri Bautier, "Notice sur la vie et les travaux de Charles Samaran, membre de l'Académie," *Comptes-rendus des séances de l'Académie des inscriptions et belles-lettres* 127.4 (1983): 581–604.

33. David Herlihy, "Yves Renouard and the Economic History of the Middle Ages," *American Historical Review* 76.1 (1971): 129.

34. See the review of this publication by Philippe Braunstein, "Yves Renouard, Études d'histoire médiévale," *Annales: Économies, Sociétés, Civilisations* 24.5 (1969): 1183–1186.

35. Herlihy, "Yves Renouard and the Economic History of the Middle Ages," 129.

36. See Yves Renouard, *Les relations des papes d'Avignon et des compagnies commerciales et bancaires de 1316 à 1378* (Paris: De Boccard, 1941); *Recherches sur les compagnies commerciales et bancaires utilisées par les papes d'Avignon avant le Grand Schisme* (Paris: Presses universitaires de France, 1942).

37. Yves Renouard, *Les hommes d'affaires italiens au moyen-âge* (Paris: Colin, 1949); *La papauté à Avignon* (Paris: Presses universitaires de France, 1954).

38. Guillaume Mollat, *The Popes at Avignon, 1305–1378*, trans. Janet Love (London: T. Nelson, 1963).

39. Yves Renouard, *The Avignon Papacy*, trans. Denis Bethell (Hamden: Archon, 1970).

40. Patrick N. R. Zutschi, "The Avignon Papacy," in *The New Cambridge Medieval History*, ed. Michael Jones (Cambridge: Cambridge University Press, 2000), vol. 6, 653–673.

41. For a detailed discussion of this administration, see *Aux origines de l'état moderne, le fonctionnement administratif de la papauté d'Avignon, actes de la table ronde organisée par l'École française de Rome, Avignon, 23–24 janvier 1988* (Rome: École française de Rome, 1990).

42. Bernard Guillemain, *La cour pontificale d'Avignon: Étude d'une société* (Paris: De Boccard, 1962).

43. Jean Favier, *Les finances pontificales à l'époque du Grand Schisme (1378–1409)* (Paris: De Boccard, 1966).

44. See Joëlle Rollo-Koster, *The People of Curial Avignon: A Critical Edition of the Liber Divisionis and the Matriculae of Notre Dame la Majour* (Lampeter, GB, and Lewiston, NY: Edwin Mellen, 2009), 39–72 for a discussion and criticism of Guillemain's analysis of the *Liber Divisionis*.

45. In 2006, after a brilliant career and multiple interests within the medieval period, Favier returned to the Avignon papacy with the publication of a new synthesis, *Les papes d'Avignon* (Paris: Fayard, 2006). He died in August 2014.

46. *Histoire d'Avignon*, ed. Sylvain Gagnière (Aix-en-Provence: Édisud, 1979).

47. See Sylvain Gagnière, *Le palais des papes d'Avignon* (Paris: Caisse nationale des monuments historiques, 1965); *Les pierres utilisées dans la construction du palais des papes* (Avignon: Maison Aubanel Père, 1966); with Jacky Granier, *Contribution à l'étude du palais des papes* (Avignon: Imprimerie Rullière, 1966). More recently, Dominique Vingtain has offered a new history of the building with *Avignon: Le palais des papes* (La Pierre-qui-Vire: Éd. Zodiaque, 1998).

48. Urbain V, *Lettres communes analysées d'après les registres dits d'Avignon et du Vatican*, ed. Marie-Hyacinthe Laurent, Michel Hayez, Anne-Marie Hayez, Janine Mathieu, and Marie-France Yvan (Paris: De Boccard, 1954–1989), 12 vols.; and Gregory XI, *Lettres communes analysées d'après les registres dits d'Avignon et du Vatican*, ed. Anne-Marie Hayez, Janine Mathieu, and Marie-France Yvan (Rome: École française de Rome, 1992–1993), 3 vols.

49. Anne-Marie Hayez, *Le terrier Avignonnais de l'évêque Anglic Grimoard: 1366–1368* (Paris: CTHS, 1993).

50. Michel Hayez and Claude-France Rochat-Hollard, *Guide des archives de Vaucluse* (Avignon: Archives départementales, 1985); Claude-France Rochat-Hollard, Françoise Chauzat, and Michel Hayez, *Répertoire numérique des archives communales d'Avignon antérieures à 1790 déposées aux Archives départementales* (Avignon: Conseil général de Vaucluse, 1995).

51. See, for example, Anne-Marie Hayez and Michel Hayez, "L'hôtellerie Avignonnaise au XIVe siècle à propos de la succession de Siffrede de Trolhon (1387)," *Provence historique* 25 (1975): 275–284; "Juifs d'Avignon au tribunal de la cour temporelle sous Urbain V," *Provence historique* 23 (1973): 165–173; and "Les saints honorés à Avignon au XIVe siècle," *Mémoires de l'academie de Vaucluse*, series 7, 6 (1985): 199–223.

52. Michel Hayez, "Avignon sans les Papes (1367–1370, 1376–1379)," in *Genèse et début du grand schisme d'occident*, ed. Jean Favier (Paris: Éditions du CNRS, 1980), 143–157; "Le retour à Rome du pape Grégoire XI," *Bulletin mensuel de l'académie de Vaucluse*, 93 (Avignon, 1976).

53. Jérôme Hayez, "La maison des fantômes: Un récit onirique de ser Bartolomeo Levaldini, notaire de Prato et correspondant de Francesco Datini," *Italia medioevale e umanistica* 47 (2006): 75–192; "Tucte sono patrie, ma la buona è quela dove l'uomo fa bene: Famille et migration dans la correspondance de deux marchands toscans vers 1400," in *Éloignement géographique et cohésion familiale (XVe–XXe siècles)*, éd. Jean-François Chauvard et Christine Lebeau (Strasbourg: Presses universitaires de Strasbourg, 2006), 69–95; "Le rire du marchand: Francesco Datini, sa femme Margherita et les gran maestri florentins," in *La famille, les femmes et le quotidien, XIVe–XVIIIe siècles : Textes offerts à Christiane Klapisch-Zuber*, ed. Isabelle Chabot, Didier Lett, and Jérôme Hayez (Paris: Publications de la Sorbonne, 2006), 407–458; "Un facteur siennois de Francesco di Marco Datini: Andrea di Bartolomeo di Ghino et sa correspondance (1383–1389)," *Opera del Vocabolario italiano: Bollettino* 10 (2005): 203–397; "Le carteggio Datini et les correspondances pratiques des XIVe–XVIe siècles;" and "L'archivio Datini, de l'invention de 1870 à l'exploration d'un système d'écrits privés," *Mélanges de l'École française de Rome, moyen âge-temps modernes* 117 (2005): 115–222; "La voix des morts ou la mine de données: Deux siècles et demi d'édition des correspondances privées des XIIIe–XVIe siècles"; and "Les lettres parisiennes du carteggio Datini: Première approche du dossier," *Mélanges de l'École française de Rome, moyen âge-temps modernes* 117 (2005): 257–304; "Avviso, informazione, novella, nuova: La notion de l'information dans les correspondances marchandes toscanes vers 1400," in *Information et société en Occident à la fin du Moyen Age: Actes du colloque international tenu à l'Université du Québec à Montréal et à l'Université d'Ottawa (9–11 mai 2002)*, ed. Claire Boudreau, Kouky Fianu, Claude Gauvard, and Michel Hébert (Paris, 2004), 113–134; "'Veramente io spero farci bene . . .': Expérience de migrant et pratique de l'amitié dans la correspondance de maestro Naddino d'Aldobrandino Bovattieri, médecin toscan d'Avignon (1385–1407)," *Bibliothèque de l'École des chartes* 159.2 (2001): 413–539.

54. Jacques Chiffoleau, *La comptabilité de l'au-delà: Les hommes, la mort et la religion dans la region d'Avignon à la fin du moyen âge* (Paris: De Boccard, 1980); *Les justices du pape* (Paris: Publications de la Sorbonne, 1984).

55. Jacques Rossiaud, *Le Rhône au Moyen Âge: Histoire et représentations d'un fleuve européen* (Paris: Aubier, 2007); *Medieval Prostitution: Family, Sexuality, and Social Relations in Past Times* (New York: Blackwell, 1988); Daniel Le Blévec, *La part du pauvre: L'assistance dans les pays du Bas-Rhône du XIIe siècles au milieu du XVe siècle* (Rome: École française de Rome, 2000), 2 vols.

56. Richard C. Trexler, "A Medieval Census, the *Liber Divisionis,*" *Mediaevalia et Humanistica* 17 (1966): 82–85; *Spiritual Power: Republican Florence under Interdict* (Leiden: Brill, 1974).

57. Daniel Williman, *Records of the Papal Right Spoil, 1316–1412* (Paris: Éditions du centre national de la recherche scientifique, 1974); *Bibliothèques ecclésiastiques au temps de la papauté d'Avignon* (Paris: Éditions du centre national de la recherche scientifique, 1980); *The Right of Spoil of the Popes of Avignon, 1316–1415* (Philadelphia: American Philosophical Society, 1988); *Calendar of the Letters of Arnaud Aubert: Camerarius Apostolicus 1361–1371* (Toronto: Pontifical Institute of Mediaeval Studies, 1992); *The Letters of Pierre De Cros, Chamberlain to Pope Gregory XI, 1371–1378* (Tempe: Arizona Center for Medieval and Renaissance Studies, 2008).

58. Sophia Menache, *Clement V* (Cambridge: Cambridge University Press, 1998); Diana Wood, *Clement VI: The Pontificate and Ideas of an Avignon Pope* (Cambridge: Cambridge University Press, 1989); Paul R. Thibault, *Pope Gregory XI: The Failure of Tradition* (Lanham, MD: University Press of America, 1986).

ONE

Early Popes

If any common thread links the popes who resided at Avignon in the fourteenth century, it is their attempt to preserve their institutional legitimacy as successors of St. Peter even while they resided away from the traditional Christian capital, Rome. Legitimacy was constructed both administratively and politically. In our first three chapters, we survey each pope's career in view of his effort to promote and centralize papal authority, while chapter 4 is dedicated to the Avignon papacy's success at centralizing its administration and tax collection. Erroneously labeled the first Avignon pope, Clement V perhaps has suffered more abuse than any other pope of the period. To begin with, he was accused of having brought the papal court to Avignon to please Philip IV the Fair, the king of France (r. 1286–1314), henceforth initiating the so-called Babylonian Captivity. In fact, Clement did not settle his court in Avignon, nor is there any evidence that he ever had intended to do so. A transient pope waiting for the right moment to reclaim his Roman residence, Clement had no intention of remaining either in France or in Avignon (which, incidentally, was not French at the time). Stigmatized as a puppet of the king of France, Clement deserves better than his egregious reputation.[1] At a precarious moment for the Church's liberty, Clement perceived that a pretended passivity might counterbalance the impatience and arrogance of Philip the Fair. The pope tempered as much as he could the grandiosity of the king of France, who, in the words of an Aragonese ambassador, claimed to be at once "king, pope, and emperor" and who conceived of his office in terms of absolute independence.[2] The chronically sick Clem-

23

ent may have been frail, but his timidity, evasiveness, and restraint were signs of the diplomatic talent that made him a match for the ambitious Philip. Rather than allowing Philip to grossly manipulate him, Clement responded with the weapons available to him. He temporized. He defended the interests of the Church throughout two great crises: the French demonization of his predecessor, Pope Boniface VIII, and the downfall of the Knights Templar. But most of all, Clement used his position to advance his own priority, the reconquest of the Holy Land. Some historians have argued that his crusading agenda dictated most of his policies.[3] Seen in that light, Clement did not break with tradition; rather, his policies were largely in line with those of most medieval popes.

BEFORE CLEMENT: BONIFACE VIII, PHILIP THE FAIR, AND ROME

In large part, the history that preceded him directed Clement's actions. Since Pope Urban II and the call of the First Crusade in 1095, the quest for Christian Levantine territories gave medieval popes moral leadership throughout Europe. The initial success and subsequent failure of the crusades kept the papacy in a position to intervene more or less at all levels of Christian society. In the words of the late Yves Renouard, a foremost historian of the Avignon papacy: "Christian Europe had been feudally united to the papacy when western kings had sworn oaths of vassalage to the popes."[4] The Roman pontiff regulated the newly formed universities that taught dogma to the Dominican friars, who maintained orthodoxy in Christendom, as Franciscans served the new urban population of western Europe as spiritual guides. In addition to the Church's control over religious and moral matters, the crusading effort led popes to promote taxation for the ongoing conquest, levying tithes in most European countries. Eventually kings appropriated these levies, but they still needed to negotiate their release by the pope. This advantageous position led the papacy to arbitrate international politics and assert and centralize its authority.

It is traditional when describing the thirteenth-century papacy to emphasize the pope who revolutionized it, Innocent III (r. 1198–1216). He is often considered the most powerful and most successful of medieval popes. Innocent positioned himself as Vicar of Christ (more than a mere successor of St. Peter), and with his theory of the two swords, one religious and one temporal, he allowed ecclesiastics to discipline sinning laymen (because the religious sword always overpowers the temporal one).

In this way, he defended his intervention in all secular affairs. Innocent kept track of all great secular rulers of his times, kept them in check, and inserted himself in their undertakings. He was able to moderate France's and England's encroachment on ecclesiastical taxes, he managed to control the nomination of the Holy Roman emperor, and he let papal dominion over central Italy generally dictate his external policies. The pope never hesitated in calling crusades against his opponents, as he did against Emperor Frederick II, and enmeshed religious with secular concerns—as in the case of the Albigensian Crusade or the intrigues surrounding the Sack of Constantinople during the Fourth Crusade. It is true that no other medieval pope succeeded like Innocent.

To minimize secular intervention in religious affairs, he and his successors commissioned legal treatises implying that canon law affirmed the far-reaching claims of papal power. The early thirteenth century established the protocol of canonical papal elections (again to minimize secular interference) as the papacy regained control over ecclesiastics, taxing clergymen for their nominations. A tax of one third of yearly revenues was enacted whenever a bishop or abbot acceded to their benefice (*servitium commune*). Popes staffed or "provisioned" benefices when they (and no one else) named their holders; they offered dispensations, that is, waivers to candidates for ecclesiastical positions who did not meet requirements of legitimacy, and they reorganized and expanded the curia. Later popes of the thirteenth and fourteenth centuries did not alter this policy. But the greatest success of fourteenth-century popes was to centralize and control their government and develop efficient tax collection like no popes had before them.

Not all thirteenth-century popes were as successful as Innocent. In Rome, arguments over the appropriate limits of communal versus papal sovereignty sometimes led to short papal exiles in Viterbo or Anagni, Orvieto or Rieti. As the popes became physically estranged from their city, so papal rituals of accession became detached from their Roman setting. Ceremonies closely linked to Rome, like the pope's enthronement in St. Peter's or his episcopal possession of the Lateran, lost symbolic ground to a papal coronation that could take place anywhere. Like their fourteenth-century successors, thirteenth-century popes relied on close kin and on their households to rule papal territories. They also centralized their ecclesiastical administration to strengthen their grip over their own government. We see, then, that fourteenth-century popes brought to conclusion innovations that had their origins a century earlier.

The culmination of papal influence came with Clement's predecessor, Boniface VIII (Benedetto Caetani), who ruled between 1294 and 1303.[5] Boniface VIII thought that he could establish an absolute "papal monarchy," a kind of super imperium over kings, as Innocent III had aimed to do at the start of his century. Boniface's public and spectacular failure eventually taught his successors the pitfalls to avoid. Drawing on the advances made by his predecessors, Boniface VIII attempted to impose his conception of an absolute papacy on the monarchies of his time. With the canonization of St. Louis in 1297 and the foundation of the first Roman Jubilee in 1300, Boniface's successes testify to his political intelligence.[6] As demonstrated by Agostino Paravicini Bagliani, the pope's heightened sense of his role was reflected in the greater reliance on the symbolic representation of the pope's persona and the care taken of the body of the pope. The pope surrounded himself with medical doctors to sustain his good health. Likewise, he banned the long-standing practice that allowed the evisceration and dismemberment of corpses for multilocational burials. The goal of his now famous bull, *Detestande feritatis*, aimed at preserving the unity and integrity of the pope's body, a fitting metaphor for the ecclesiastical body. Boniface also multiplied his symbolic presence in the many statues that portrayed him, often wearing his newly designed triple tiara.[7] On the other hand, Boniface had the misfortune to follow Celestine V (r. 1294), the only medieval pope to resign voluntarily, making his successor an easy target for blame in that dubious affair. As they circulated rumors of Boniface's role in Celestine's decision (defamatory words reinforced by Boniface's imprisonment of Celestine after he stepped down), the pope's enemies pressed for Celestine's canonization.

Philip the Fair's own heightened conception of his kingship halted Boniface from establishing a firmer hold on the European monarchies. The long-lasting skirmishes and war between France and England necessitated an increase in governmental revenues. Philip opted to tax his French clergy directly, without the pope's permission. Boniface responded in 1296 with his bull *Clericis laicos*, which forbade clerical taxation without papal consent under the threat of excommunication. Philip responded by preventing taxes raised in France from reaching Italy.

By 1297, Philip found support for his antipapal campaign among the traditional enemies of the Caetani pope, the members of the Colonna family. They attacked the papal treasury on its way to Rome from the pope's favorite summer residence in Anagni. As a result, Boniface backtracked, allowing Philip's taxation of the clergy in exceptional circumstances. In 1301, Philip the Fair intervened again in ecclesiastical affairs, this time imprisoning Bernard Saisset, the bishop of Pamiers, who had been sent to protest the king's anticlerical measures—Philip invested bishops and relentlessly taxed the clergy. Boniface responded with his 1301 bull *Ausculta Fili*, demanding the king change his ways. In 1302 Boniface took his quarrel with Philip a step further, publishing in *Unam Sanctam* the strongest statement a pope had ever made on the primacy of a pontiff over secular rulers:

> Urged by faith, we are obliged to believe and to maintain that the Church is one, holy, catholic, and also apostolic. We believe in her firmly and we confess with simplicity that outside of her there is neither salvation nor the remission of sins . . . of the one and only Church there is one body and one head, not two heads like a monster; that is, Christ and the Vicar of Christ, Peter and the successor of Peter. . . . We are informed by the texts of the gospels that in this Church and in its power are two swords; namely, the spiritual and the temporal. . . . Certainly the one who denies that the temporal sword is in the power of Peter has not listened well to the word of the Lord commanding: "Put up thy sword into thy scabbard" [Mt 26:52]. Both, therefore, are in the power of the Church, that is to say, the spiritual and the material sword, but the former is to be administered *for* the Church but the latter *by* the Church; the former in the hands of the priest; the latter by the hands of kings and soldiers, but at the will and sufferance of the priest.[8]

In startling terms, Boniface here defined the primacy of spiritual over temporal power and the deference of temporal power to the spiritual. Philip responded swiftly. The pope was declared a heretic (in return, he excommunicated Philip), after which Philip sent his counselor Guillaume de Nogaret to Anagni to capture Boniface and seize his treasury (September 1303). Nogaret raised enough commotion for the inhabitants of Anagni to allow his entry and sack of the papal treasury. He seized the pope, intending to bring him back to France on charges of heresy, simony, sodomy, and illegitimacy. Since his predecessor, Celestine, had resigned in 1294 and not died in office, charges of electoral manipulation were brought against his own election. Boniface was held by his French captors for some three days before Anagni's citizens had a change of heart. Much has been traditionally made of the violence the pope suffered during his captivity; it would seem that the pope might have been hit once (perhaps during his initial capture) by one of his Roman opponents. Saved by the townspeople, Boniface died of shock a month later, in October 1303. A letter of William of Hundleby describes the affront:

> At dawn of the vigil of the Nativity of the Blessed Mary just past, suddenly and unexpectedly there came upon Anagni a great force of armed men of the party of the King of France and of the two deposed Colonna cardinals. Arriving at the gates of Anagni and finding them open, they entered the town and at once made an assault upon the palace of the Pope. . . . Many of them heaped insults upon his head and threatened him violently, but to them all the Pope answered not so much as a word. And when they pressed him as to whether he would resign the Papacy, firmly did he refuse—indeed he preferred to lose his head—as he said in his vernacular: "E le col, e le cape!" which means: "Here is my neck and here my head." . . . The soldiers, on first breaking in, had pillaged the Pope, his chamber and his treasury of utensils and clothing, fixtures, gold and silver and everything found therein so that the Pope had been made as poor as Job upon receiving word of his misfortune. Moreover, the Pope witnessed all and saw how the wretches divided his garments and carted away his furniture, both large items and small, deciding who would take this and who that, and yet he said no more than: "The Lord gave and the Lord taketh away, etc."[9]

The violence of the events in "the Outrage at Anagni" in September 1303 is, of course, representative of the rancor produced by the growing pains of nation-states attempting to break free from centuries-long traditions. It is also prime evidence of Philip the Fair's callousness. But these events also need to be contextualized within a purely Roman setting. One cannot comprehend the actions against Boniface, and his successors' motivations in staying away from Italy, and the eventual move of the papacy to Avignon, without first discussing Rome.

Since the mid-twelfth century, in an attempt to mitigate the growing powers of the patrician aristocracy and papacy, a republic (that is, a commune with an elected senate housed at the capitol) had won the right to rule Rome nominally. The city was divided into fourteen *rioni* (regions); these had originally elected senators to represent their interests, but in fact aristocratic clans controlled these regions. One of the major aims of the commune was to wrest temporal governance of the city from the papacy. In order to do so, the commune aligned itself with the Holy Roman emperor for support, turning itself to Ghibelline allegiance, the name given to the supporters of imperial rule in Italy. Partisans of papal control of the city and other Italian states were labeled Guelphs.

The Roman political situation was so precarious that popes sometimes had to fight the republic to gain entrance into their city. Rome was essential for papal liturgical functions, including the pope's consecration and coronation. Thus, occasionally popes aligned themselves with the Holy Roman emperor in order to regain the city. By the end of the twelfth century, all powers were more or less reconciled in a treaty that allowed Romans to elect their own magistrates, the emperor to name the prefect of the city, and the pope to hold rights over his territories. This situation did not last long. In 1197 Pope Celestine III replaced the Senate with two senators and a council that he named. From then on, the pope's control of the commune, and hence of the middle class, was perceived as a threat to the aristocracy, who in 1255, for example, attacked the capitol. But as a rule, horizontal social alliances were not as disruptive as vertical ones. Clans, regrouping aristocratic magnates, and their clienteles directed Roman political life. And since the Church employed many of the magnates' descendants, it is difficult to disentangle the politics of the aristocrats from that of the Church.

Throughout the Middle Ages, the city of Rome had a long tradition of insurrection tied to its political situation. The medieval *popolo minuto* (commoners) fought the aristocratic barons and the papacy. Both latter groups were politically intertwined with popes, usually chosen from the ranks of the aristocracy. These families, of which the Annibaldi, Colonna, Conti, Orsini, Frangipani, Pierleoni, and Savelli were the oldest, controlled land in the city and the Roman countryside (known as the Latium). Each clan's leader solidly defended his lineage's interest, guiding a system of clients that served his "house" when needed. These barons controlled a mass of "hands" available to serve at their whim, fighting other clans when needed. Clans were used to staff the city and church government; they rivaled each other in power but also rotated among the highest offices as bishops, cardinals, and popes. While the rotation of power among them maintained a status quo that allowed their differences to explode in the frequent quarrels that marred the peace of the city, they resented the establishment of new "houses," such as Boniface's Caetani, for example.

Barons controlled various quarters of the city and constantly wrestled for space, making the city a precarious place to govern. These networks of allegiances and territorial rivalries endangered the seat of the papacy and the popes themselves. Clients fought territorial wars for their patrons, a situation that greatly imperiled Roman and papal stability as ecclesiastics from the Roman baronage embroiled the Church in these neighborhood quarrels. The Savelli were established on the Aventine; the Colonna on Monte Citorio and the Quirinal; the Frangipani on the Palatine; the Orsini on Monte Giordano; and Pierleoni on Tiber Island. Clans also occupied the ancient monuments: the Conti controlled the Market of Trajan; the Frangipani and Annibaldi fought for the Colosseum; the Savelli, Pierleoni, and Orsini took turns occupying the Theater of Marcellus; and the Frangipani controlled the Arches of Titus and Constantine and the Via Sacra and also fortified monuments of the Septizonium toward the Great Circus. The Colonna occupied the Baths of Constantine and the Mausoleum of Augustus (that previously had been held by the Orsini). The Orsini possessed the Mausoleum of Hadrian (Castel Sant'Angelo) and controlled the Tiber. Although Roman clans thrived in their quarrels and accepted the traditional rotation of power among themselves, they balked at the interference of new blood or foreigners within their rivalries.

By the end of the thirteenth century, three families overshadowed the others: the Orsini, positioned north of the city; the Colonna, east; and the new players in this drama, the Caetani, who held Anagni and eastern portions of Rome on the road to Naples but did not control strong alliances within the city. Originally rooted in Pisa, the Caetani's only success had been the short-lived but tumultuous election of Pope Gelasius II in 1118. Gelasius had been seized by the Frangipani (of Ghibelline allegiance); eventually freed by the Romans, he escaped to his homeland of Gaeta and reclaimed Rome with the support of the Normans, but was forced into exile once again by the Frangipani.

Boniface VIII's turbulent years resembled his forefathers' and demonstrate how the lack of a local supporting power base endangered papal rule in Rome. The Caetani owed their success in establishing Boniface on the papal throne to an alliance with the Orsini. That partnership aggravated the Colonna, who in turn instigated a war of propaganda against

Boniface and eventually joined the French in their antipapal attacks.[10] By the late 1290s, the rivalry between the Caetani and Colonna was intensified by the fact that the new pope used the papal treasury to buy lands in the Pontine Marshes for the Caetani. Stephano Colonna paid his family back on May 3, 1297, when he robbed the papal treasury upon its return to Rome from Anagni.[11] Boniface's response was to hold hostage the two Colonna cardinals (Giacomo and Pietro) until their cousin returned the funds, which he eventually did. After this episode, Colonna wrath against the pope turned virulent. They accused Boniface of heresy, simony, and illegitimacy. Feeling unsafe in Rome, the pope left for Orvieto, called for a crusade against the clan, demoted the two Colonna cardinals, confiscated their goods, and excommunicated them. After their escape from prison, the Colonna cardinals traveled to France, where they rejoined Pietro's brother, Giacomo, alias the infamous Sciarra Colonna. The French king was happy to support the Colonna in their quest as long as it served his own purpose. Colonna troops joined the French in Anagni when they attacked the pope.[12] According to Teofilo F. Ruiz, it would be wrong to assume that Europeans constructed this assault as an attack on the Church. Most medieval contemporaries viewed it purely in political terms.[13] This episode demonstrates how Rome's internal clan rivalries affected international politics. Any pope had to maneuver between local Roman allegiances that might easily take on an international character; they themselves brought their divisions to the papal court, and to a large extent, cardinals brought their tribal quarrels with them as well.

The conclave that opened at the death of Boniface elected Benedict XI in October 1303. A Dominican, Benedict distanced himself as much as possible from the quarrel between the Caetani and their French and Colonna adversaries. He temporized with Philip the Fair, absolving most participants of the Anagni coup with the exception of the main protagonists, Sciarra Colonna, Nogaret, and the Italian robbers of the treasury, whom he excommunicated. But the cardinals Giacomo and Pietro Colonna were not pardoned, and Benedict did not bow to Philip's demand for a council that would judge Boniface. When Benedict died in Perugia under suspicion of poisoning, the conclave opened in the city of his death, as prescribed by the rules of the conclave.[14] As expected, the conclave was racked by dissension caused by the Boniface/Colonna parties. Led by Cardinal Matteo Rosso Orsini, the majority of the Italian cardinals were still upset by the Outrage at Anagni and took a stance against French interests. Napoleone Orsini steered the "French party": he lobbied for the reinstatement of the Colonnas and a papal alliance with France. The deposed cardinals were actually in Perugia, ready to defend French interests in this election, buttressed by Nogaret himself, who darkly intimated, "If some Antichrist invade the Holy See, we must resist him."[15] As expected, tensions among the cardinals lengthened deliberations considerably. The conclave lasted close to a year, opening in July 1304 and finally reaching an agreement on the election of Bertrand de Got on June 5, 1305. Bertrand was in Lusignan, Poitou, when he learned of his election as pontiff in June 1305 and traveled south via Bordeaux (where he took the name of Clement V), Agen, Montpellier, Bezier, Nîmes, and Viviers, before reaching Lyons for his coronation, an occasion attended by the French king and his royal household.

CLEMENT V: FRENCH PUPPET OR ABLE DIPLOMAT?

The fifteen cardinals who elected the Gascon chose someone outside their own ranks, a non-Italian perceived as immune or at least untouched by the Italian cardinals' divisions. But the famous Italian chronicler of that time, Giovanni Villani, accused the pope of having bowed down to the French king, promising papal submission to the crown if he were elected.[16] Historians have been quick to point out the many inaccuracies of the tale; but Villani's propaganda soon took hold and continues to this day to mar the Avignon papacy as a French "puppet."[17]

Bernard Guillemain, in his *La cour pontificale*, suggests that Clement received the tiara in these difficult times because of his talent for keeping everyone content. A great diplomat and an open and friendly man, Clement was called a "pleaser" by Guillemain to the point of indulgence.[18] For Jean Favier, Clement was chosen because of his talents as a canonist and administrator; he was at the time archbishop of Bordeaux. That both the kings of France and England liked him was an added advantage working in Clement's favor.[19]

Born in Guyenne, Bertrand de Got apprenticed diplomacy early as a vassal of the king of England. Guyenne belonged to the cluster of French territories possessed by the Crown, and subsequently, de Got understood intimately the meaning of dual allegiance. He was at his core a man of compromise. He studied civil and canon law and followed an ecclesiastic career patronized by his namesake, his uncle Bertrand de Got (the elder), bishop of Agen, and most importantly by his brother Béraud, archbishop of Lyons. Bertrand de Got was promoted to cardinal by Celestine V. Pope Celestine also made him his chaplain; his successor, Boniface VIII, maintained Bertrand's position until his nomination to the see of Comminges in 1295 and the archiepiscopal see of Bordeaux in 1297.

The disruption of his pontifical coronation easily demonstrates the popularity of such ceremonies but also their volatility and unforeseen dangers. Of the five versions of Clement's life recorded by Étienne Baluze, two mention a dramatic accident that dampened the inaugural celebrations on November 14, 1305. According to Clement's second recorded life, authored by the Dominican Ptolemeus Lucensi, when the pope's cavalcade left the Cathedral of St. Just in Lyons for its parade, the sustaining wall of a narrow street collapsed under the weight of onlookers, tumbling onto members of the procession. Many nobles buried in the rubble were injured, including Charles, brother of the king of France, who eventually recovered from his wounds. Many died from their injuries, however, including the Duke of Brittany. Even the pope was put in danger when he fell from his horse and lost his crown, which tumbled to the ground. He got up, unscathed, with minor scratches, but his tiara, topped with precious gems, lost a ruby worth some six thousand florins. While the stone was eventually recovered, the chronicler could not stop himself from adding that such events were a warning, a bad omen, a *signum notabile* (without really clarifying of what).[20] The next author who discusses the event, Bernard Guidonis, bishop of Lodève, describes the press of a crowd that rushed after the passing of the cavalcade as if they were seeing "King Solomon with his diadem" and adds that twelve people died of their injuries.[21] He also comments that many considered the event a presage, negatively marking the beginning of this new papacy. Still, it is interesting to note that several authors avoided discussing the incident, choosing to either disregard popular "superstition" or to pass over in silence a possible "curse" on the papacy.

THE PAST CATCHING UP: BONIFACE AND THE TEMPLARS

Clement inherited a papacy that rested on shaky ground after the Anagni affair. It is worth remembering that his tenure and many of his decisions cannot be separated from the constant demands pressed by France that a posthumous trial condemn Boniface and that all involved in the attack be completely absolved. It is this convoluted past that directed many of Clement's policies. Clement first gave in to Philip the Fair, abrogating in 1306 *Clericis laicos* and *Unam sanctam*. In doing so, the pope backed down from the high-ground theological stance previously taken by Boniface. But more issues surfaced. Clement, as a Gascon, was also preoccupied by the situation in his native Guyenne (Gascony belonged to Guyenne). The king of England, unsatisfied by the marital policies that united both crowns, could not be happy with the loss of Guyenne's sovereignty. He was but a vassal of the king of France for these lands. [22] Skirmishes between both armies spoiled this province's daily life, and in his long-term plans, the pope understood that the recapture of the Christian Holy Land started with peace in Europe. He needed concord between Philip the Fair and Edward I in order for them to shift their interest toward the Levant. Taking in mind Helen Nicholson's summary of Clement's early years, it is easy to understand why the pope faced a hard path ahead. She states: "He inherited a papacy that had lost both prestige and power over the past decades through its involvement in factional infighting, its involvement in Sicily and its inability to assist the Latin Christendom in the East. The political situation in Rome was so heated that Clement decided not to set up his court there." [23]

In order to discuss so many pressing affairs, the pope decided to remain in Lyons longer, forgoing a quick return to Italy. Clement understood full well that the Italian situation was untenable for the pope and was well aware of Rome's peculiarly turbulent history. After long and strenuous negotiations, he reached a deal with France in spring 1307 that allowed him to avoid Boniface's posthumous trials: Clement absolved Nogaret and the assailants at Anagni and reintegrated the Colonna cardinals into the college. Ever a shrewd politician, Clement staffed his government with a new promotion to the rank of cardinal of the king of England's confessor, two French ecclesiastics, and seven Gascons—five of whom were the pope's relatives! With this promotion, Clement pleased both rival kings and thwarted any accusation of favoritism by doing so; at the same time, he also surrounded himself with people he could trust and rely upon, his family. For modern readers, his actions smack of nepotism, and quite a few historians have severely judged Clement's partiality for his own people.

Jean Favier does not shy away from describing the many advantages that the de Gots received from this "stroke of good luck." [24] Still, he does not mark out this nepotism as exceptional. It was commonly practiced in all courts of the Middle Ages. Feudal princes were obligated to keep relatives at court to maintain their rank; especially in cases of poorer relatives, they needed to support those who bore their last names. Princes relied on familial counselors, who had (or were supposed to have) the prince's best interests at heart. Brothers, nephews, cousins, and in-laws were part of the political entourage of princes, whether lay or ecclesiastic.[25] In this way, Clement only continued a centuries-long practice well entrenched in the European nobility. Accusing the pope of nepotism is an anachronistic objection that no one would have understood during Clement's lifetime.

Nevertheless, his transformation of the composition of the college of cardinals shocked his contemporaries, especially the Italians. His second and third promotions to the cardinalate (in 1310 and 1312) changed the majority for years to come. The college of cardinals became largely French, and it remained so for close to a century. The great Italian families' response to their loss of influence at the curia was one of bewilderment, certainly because of their loss of power but also at the success of the de Got lesser nobility. The Italian elites implicitly assumed it natural to reward one's "house" with multiple positions and offices; this followed political mores. It shocked them, though, that a representative of the lesser nobility and gentry like de Got was able to do the same.

If modern readers are not well versed in the internal politics of the medieval Church and unfamiliar with Clement's revolutionary alteration of the college, they still may know Clement for his infamous participation in the well-known "Affair of the Templars." On October 13, 1307, Clement learned of the arrest of the French Templars. This important historical event marked the quick downfall of the great military order and requires scrutiny in and of itself. But it also precipitated Clement's decision to leave French territories for more neutral ground—up to then he had been traveling between Bordeaux and Poitou, where he felt his presence needed. His itinerant papacy was a handicap for the court, which had a hard time finding decent quarters in the varied cities where they sojourned. The long stay in France also suggested the influence of French policies on ecclesiastical affairs. On August 8, 1308, the pope called a council to deal with the matter of the Templars and other pressing issues. Weighing his options, Clement preferred the city of Vienne on the Rhône river (south of Lyons) over the Lateran Palace in Rome, feeling relatively more comfortable there under the pressure of the nearby French than being at the mercy of the Italian clans. Vienne belonged to the county of Provence, was controlled by the Angevin kings of Naples, and was thus (in theory) liege of the Holy Roman Empire. Vienne was close to France but outside its control, an easy destination for clergymen who needed to reach the city for the council's opening on October 1, 1310 (an event in fact delayed until October 1, 1311, in order to finish various investigations). In the meantime, Clement chose Avignon for his own quarters; the city was near Vienne and centrally located, easy to reach by land or sea. In August 1308 the pope set out, arriving ill in Avignon on March 9, 1309.[26] Like Vienne, Avignon did not belong to France but to Provence, and the city neighbored the Comtat Venaissin, papal territory since Philip III of France granted it to the pope in 1274. France was also on the other side of the Rhône, across the Pont Saint-Bénézet, on its western side. Clement found lodging in the large Dominican convent at Avignon and traveled back and forth from there to Carpentras, where he prepared for the council. Cardinals and the curia struggled to find accommodations in Avignon, however, causing half of the prelates to miss the council because they could not find appropriate lodging nearby.

Once the council and location were established, Clement was able to focus on the Templars. The affair can be viewed as the cornerstone of Clement's reign. The Templars had been created shortly after the success of the First Crusade in the early twelfth century. The order's mission, as indicated in their founding documents, was to protect pilgrims visiting the Holy Land, "defending the land from the unbelieving pagans who are the enemies of the son of the Virgin Mary."[27] Eventually their knowledge of the terrain made them the "special forces" of the Levant, superb in warfare but also outstanding in their knowledge of Islamic society. Because their existence rested on the defense of the Christian Levant, their demise is linked to the end of the "crusading spirit" and the fall of Acre in 1291. With the loss of Acre, the Templars were dealt a huge blow, and they became an easy target for rulers in need of cash and scapegoats. As Helen Nicholson explains, they lost a great number of men in their last battles and all bases of operation in the East. Subsequently, they retreated to the island of Cyprus. After his election as grand master in 1292, Jacques de Molay traveled to Europe to discuss his options with Pope Boniface VIII, requesting funding for a new crusade.[28] Boniface offered him some financial advantages and asked Europe's kings to help supply Cyprus. But the kings of France and England were too distracted by their own wars to go crusading, while Pope Boniface was busy in Sicily supporting the Angevin attempts at regaining the island from the Aragonese.[29]

By the beginning of the fourteenth century, the papacy understood that a Christian Levant required permanent forces on the ground. The Templars and the Knights of St. John of Jerusalem were the best fitted for the task. But they had a long tradition of squabbles and conflict. The religious military orders bore the brunt of criticism for the failure of Christian armies and politics in the East. A proposal to combine both orders had been circulating for several decades, but it was systematically refused. Clement had planned on bringing it up again when Philip arrested the Templars.[30]

In addition to losing Acre, the Templars' wealth and perceived greediness disturbed many. According to Jean Favier, Philip the Fair's strong dislike of the order may have originated in their treatment of his grandfather St. Louis (Louis IX), after whom he modeled his own reign.[31] During the Seventh Crusade in 1250, Mamluks had captured Louis at the Battle of Fariskur and then ransomed him. According to Joinville (Louis's knight and bio-/hagiographer), the seneschal of the order refused to lend funds to complete the ransom. Renaud de Vichiers, a marshal, solved the issue. When Joinville asked for the loan (the money rested in a coffer on a galley off the cost of Damietta), Vichiers indicated to Joinville that if he took it by force, he would not interfere; Joinville did.[32] The story may be apocryphal, but it indicates the general frame of mind that regarded the Templars as greedy bankers.

As an international force, the Templars were in contact with European leaders. At some point, Philip the Fair had used Templars in his administration of the realm, which suggests that he had recently deemed them trustworthy enough to support his rule.[33] But the changing circumstances of the dawning fourteenth century altered this relationship when France's pressing financial needs, born of the exigencies of the battlefield, loomed large. The Templars' most obvious miscalculation was to have been, like Lombards and Jews, with the king's creditors. In traditional medieval fashion, when a king fell short of cash for reimbursement, he could always exert his right of reprisal on his creditors, expel them, and confiscate their goods. For the order, the loss of the Levant coalesced with France's pressing monetary issues. One solution tabled for a possible meeting between Clement V and de Molay was to join together both crusading orders, Templars and Hospitallers, into a single community. Yet the Templars were incarcerated before discussions could take place.[34]

After their surprise arrest on October 13, 1307, the French Templars were imprisoned and interrogated. The charges leveled against them had more to do with their accusers than with their actual crimes. They were charged with a bizarre assortment of incredible crimes: denying Christ, defiling the cross, exchanging obscene kisses during induction ceremonies, practicing sodomy, keeping secrets, adoring a cat, venerating a bearded head as an idol, not believing in the sacraments, not being charitable and hospitable enough, receiving absolution from their lay superior, lying for the order, and, finally, robbery.[35] If we turn to the charges leveled during the same period against Boniface VIII by the same French legal team led by Guillaume de Nogaret, many parallels arise. The late pope was accused of illegitimacy, heresy, simony, sodomy, and general malignancy. Boniface supposedly criticized the power of the sacraments, including the Eucharist, penance, and marriage, and did not believe in the immortality of the soul. He was said to have called believers idiots. He was accused of statements insinuating that "he had everything he wanted in this world and did what he wished"; and it was said that he often quoted the proverb "No dead, no grass in the meadow"—a statement that seemingly questioned his belief in an afterlife. He was also charged with having sex with men and women.[36]

The French court orchestrated propagandistic accusations against both Boniface and the Templars that aimed to shape public opinion favorably toward France's role in the events at Anagni. They played on late medieval fears of heresy and pollution. Helen Nicholson shares the virtually unanimous verdict of historians that the Templars were attacked because Philip the Fair needed funds for his wars and "to demonstrate that he was the most Christian king of Europe."[37] Pushing this argument further, Julien Théry proposes that the Templars were instrumentalized to achieve Philip's desire to construct France as a mystical body. In this scheme of things, Philip the Fair guaranteed a higher faith above the pope, attacked the pope's prerogatives, and provoked the pope by parodying papal rhetoric. For Théry, the eschatological leaning of Philip and Nogaret "pontificalized" the French monarchy.[38] They attacked Boniface VIII and then his memory after his death, persecuted Jews, moneylenders, and holy women such as Marguerite Porete—in sum, anyone whose fall would propel their own mysticism and benefit the king's coffers.

Regardless of the veracity of the charges, French Templars were tortured and as a result confessed. Tried in 1308, they largely recanted their earlier assertions made under duress. According to a rather controversial article by Barbara Frale, Philip tried to stop the pope from meeting with the imprisoned Templars but eventually, using all his acumen, the pope did hear and absolve scores of them at Poitiers in June 1308.[39] Frale, insisting on the power play that took place between king and pope, suggests that later (in August 1308) a special papal commission exonerated the leaders, de Molay included. Clement thus played on Philip's infatuation with his grandfather, Louis IX. In his bull *Ad preclaras sapientie*, the pope chastised the king for being less saintly than Louis, offering him a chance to redeem himself by handing the Templars and their property back to the pope.[40] When he met the prisoners, Clement's astuteness surfaced:

> Clement V asked a number of questions that the French Inquisitor had neglected to address in his own proceedings: did the Templars hear mass, go to Holy Communion, go to confession and comply with their liturgical duties? Naturally, the pope mostly wished to analyse the faith and the religious habits of Templars; on the contrary, the royal party had placed in evidence just those things which would be useful to gain a condemnation.[41]

In his bull *Faciens misericordiam*, dated August 12, 1308, Clement called for the Council of Vienne. Scheduled to meet in 1310, it instead opened in 1311 because of lengthy preinquests. Clement's diplomatic persuasion had won the king over; a council, and not the king, was charged with investigating both Boniface's memory and the allegations against the Templars. In 1311, the case against Boniface was quickly closed when three cardinals defended him, buttressed by a knightly call for a trial by combat against challengers. None stepped forward. The council, working in committees, moved ahead with several items touching on ecclesiastical reforms reminiscent of previous conciliar efforts.[42] These resolutions were later labeled *Clementinae*, and eventually they were incorporated into canon law as *Liber Septimus*, or the seventh book of the *Decretals*. In 1312, the pope announced to the council the dissolution of the Templars. On March 22 of that year, the bull *Vox in excelso* suppressed the order without condemning it.[43] Another bull, *Ad providam*, issued May 2, 1312, provided for the devolution of the Templars' goods and property to the Hospital of St. John of Jerusalem.[44] Note that Clement had obtained from France the right to distinguish between trials of persons and a trial of the order. If the order was suppressed without being charged, individual French Templars given to the Inquisition were punished severely: some, like de Molay, were burned at the stake in 1314. Satisfied by the turn of events, the French king and his family took an empty vow of crusade.

WHY NOT RETURN TO ROME?

Clement's preoccupations with rehabilitating the memory of his predecessor and the affair of the Templars were encapsulated in his relation with France. But he still had to address additional pressing concerns. He knew that he could not return to Rome as long as aristocratic rivalries made the city unsafe. This issue may not have been the most pressing, however. A papacy away from Rome was not specifically new. Thirteenth-century popes had frequently resided in Anagni and Viterbo, and few had died in Rome. In 1260, the great canonist Henry of Segusio (Hostiensis) declared, "It is not the place that sanctifies the man, it is the man who sanctifies the place."[45] This justification for a papacy away from Rome worked to the advantage of Avignon, a reminder that "Rome is where the pope is" (*ubi est papa, ibi est Roma*).[46] The situation in the Papal States compounded the difficulty of quickly resettling the papacy in Rome (or Viterbo, or Anagni, for that matter) and also worked in favor of an Avignon that could be Rome. Reaching the city was in itself a difficult task.

The pontifical territories, or Papal States, existed long before the fourteenth century; they were more or less founded when the Carolingians gifted the papacy with lands conquered from the Lombards. These grants allowed the papacy temporal sovereignty over territories that varied in size with time but ranged from central to northern Italy. Hierarchical rapport between popes and Holy Roman emperors was never regulated, leaving open the question of dominance. The ebb and flow of their relationship is an abiding theme of the history of the Middle Ages. The Papal States did not form territorial unity and counted several provinces that were united under papal authority. During the late medieval period, popes appointed rectors who embodied the pontifical administration locally. The local population historically viewed these officials negatively.

Often they itched for autonomy, playing a game of shifting allegiances between the papacy, the Holy Roman Empire, and the French Angevins, who attempted to control southern Italy. These allegiances were additionally splintered within the large communes of the city-states, communes riven by the turmoil of popular and aristocratic parties, the *popolo minuto* and *grasso*, creating complex webs of Ghibellines and Guelphs.

At the time of Clement V's rule, Guelphs were still fractured in their allegiance to either the Colonna or the Caetani families, with open hostilities between cities such as Florence and Bologna. It is evident that the unity of the Guelph party was of primary interest to the Church. In 1306, Clement sent Napoleone Orsini as legate to Italy to pacify its northern states. Orsini had the experience of name and age. A scion of the great Roman family, he had been a member of the college since 1288 and sat for fifty-four years until his death in 1342; he was a leader of the curia, he was extremely well connected as a nephew of popes and cardinals, and (along with his family) he held large tracts of land in the Papal States. Napoleone Orsini had participated in all the conclaves since 1292, and Bernard Guillemain attributes the election of Clement to Orsini's skills. [47] Orsini had held a previous legate position in Italy in 1301 in Spoleto and Ancona and had been successful in seizing the town of Gubbio for Boniface VIII. What had seemed like a good choice unfortunately backfired, however; Orsini was a staunch defender of the French party (he later reneged on the Colonna) and failed at pacifying Arezzo, Florence, and Bologna. He returned to meet Clement in Avignon in June 1309. As we will see later, Orsini was to play an important role during the Franciscan poverty debate.

Clement's November 1308 confirmation of the election of the new Holy Roman emperor, Henry VII of Luxembourg, exemplifies the complex network of papal politics. In a move that showed some independence, Clement sanctioned the election quickly, derailing Philip the Fair's hope of seeing his brother Charles de Valois receive the title. By tradition the emperor received his title along with his crown in Rome and was thus compelled to journey to the old capital. The pope proposed February 1312 as the date of Henry VII's coronation, a date the emperor considered tardy. The presence of the Ghibelline leader in Italy was an additional source of instability for the Italian peninsula and the French, leading Clement to temporize, even if he viewed the emperor as a safeguard against French pretensions in southern Italy (the Angevin held Naples

but had lost Sicily to the Aragonese). To complicate matters, in May 1309
the king of Naples, Charles II of the house of Anjou, died, succeeded
shortly thereafter by his son Robert. Clement quickly crowned Robert of
Anjou king of Naples in Avignon in August 1309 to assure Naples of his
support.

Henry's so-called journey southward allowed the pope to parlay
France into favorable terms. France did not want to see the emperor's
army marching down the Italian peninsula and thus destabilize its own
interests in the south. In addition, Henry was overlord of Provence and,
as such, of the king of Naples, who held both kingdoms, of Naples and
Provence (of whom the pope was a guest in Avignon until its purchase in
1348). Robert of Anjou still owed the emperor homage in person as a
vassal. Robert of Anjou complained to the pope, who proposed to mediate the situation if Philip the Fair abandoned his vendetta against Boniface and promised to lead a crusade. Simply put, Clement yielded in
order to gain support for his own priorities. To further please Philip, he
agreed to excommunicate Flanders if the county were unable to pay its
indemnity at the end of the Franco-Flemish War and forced it to hand
over Lille, Douai, and Béthune to France. The bull *Rex gloriae virtutum* in
August 1311 exonerated Philip of any wrongdoing against Boniface and
sealed the case. The pope then invited the king to the Council of Vienne,
where, as we saw previously, he agreed to drop his revenge against
Boniface and discuss crusading plans. The pope had procrastinated to
reach his aim, but in 1311 he still contemplated the danger presented by
the Angevin alliance with the house of Hungary in southern Italy
(Charles II of Anjou had married Mary of Hungary, making Robert's son
de facto king of Hungary).

As Clement negotiated with Philip, Henry of Luxembourg started his
march down to Rome.[48] Milan, Verona, Pisa, Lucca, and Sicily supported
the emperor and Ghibelline aspirations. In cities like Florence and Pistoia,
Guelphs were divided between Black and White parties based on their
willingness to see external influences (Black) or not (White) intervene in
their city. The political situation was so fluid that with the success of the
Black Guelphs in Florence, Pistoia, and Bologna, the White Guelphs ironically ended up pushed toward the emperor's Ghibelline party, and the
papacy was criticized by both Black and White Guelphs (with the White
leaning toward Ghibelline affiliation!). During his march, Henry faced
insurrection from Guelph cities such as Cremona, Lodi, and Brescia. The

pope intervened to calm the situation, negotiating the payment of indemnities to save the lives of the rebels. The emperor's strategy was to besiege rebel cities (such as Genoa and Padua) in order to raise the funds necessary for the continuation of his quest toward Rome. Still faced with strong resistance from the Guelphs, who were supported by the Angevins, Henry retreated to Pisa and negotiated his coronation with the pope's envoys from there. In Rome, John of Anjou (Robert's brother) took control of the city while the Colonna defended the emperor's position; the Eternal City was again in turmoil. Henry eventually made his way to Rome but was unable to reach the Vatican for his coronation; he capitulated for a ceremony at the Lateran. Papal legates crowned him on June 29, 1312. His ambition did not stop there. After spending three weeks in Rome, the emperor began his exit and opted to besiege Guelph Florence on the return trip. The Florentines agreed to receive Angevin help and surrendered to Robert for five years. This complicated even more the situation for the pope by giving control north of Rome to Robert of Anjou. Anjou's support of the Florentines infuriated the emperor, who declared Robert a traitor (he was Henry's vassal, after all) and confiscated his lands. In response, the pope threatened to excommunicate the emperor (who was *his* vassal) if he decided to march toward Naples. The emperor died, perhaps conveniently for Clement, on his way to Rome on August 24, 1314, while still planning an attack on Naples. The contest between his possible successors, Frederick of Austria and Louis of Bavaria, lasted close to ten years and became a major sore point for the next pope, John XXII.

The importance of these Italian campaigns cannot be minimized. In *The Italian Crusades: The Papal-Angevin Alliance and the Crusades against Christian Lay Powers, 1254–1343*, Norman Housley argues from his reading of contemporary texts that even though perceived as a political struggle, the fight between insubordinate Italian states and the Holy Roman Empire was a full-fledged crusade. Taxes were levied; fighters received indulgences and stitched a cross on their garments; and Guelphs commuted their pilgrimage to the Levant in order to fight in Italy. Defense of the Papal States equaled defense of papal authority, and no general opposition hindered the popes. It was understood that any attacks on the sovereignty of the Papal States hindered the papacy in its spiritual mission. As we will see (in chapter 4, regarding papal administration), the legacy of these Italian crusades resides in the development of banking.

Short in their levy of subsidies to cover all their costs, the early Avignon popes relied on merchant bankers for advances and the subsequent collection of the funds necessary to their victory.

Criticized by many historians for his various weaknesses, one can agree with Sophia Menache that Clement did his best to temporize and save the Church from powerful enemies: France, the Holy Roman Empire, and a dire situation in Italy. Following the great historians of Avignon Yves Renouard and Guillaume Mollat, Menache calls Clement modern because he defended the interest of the Church against the rising monarchies of western Europe. To the complex situation described in the previous pages, one can add the beginning of the Hundred Years' War that kept Clement close to France and England and the theological threats of Beghards and Beguines, who rebelled against traditional Church authority. In his dealing with the Templars, Clement managed to prevent Philip the Fair from seizing their property; in return, he received what he wanted: a promise of a crusade and the abandonment of all charges against Boniface. In her afterword, Sophia Menache locates Clement within his time, adding:

> The pope's image, as designed by fourteenth-century authors and often echoed in historical research, was isolated from the historical background and the many limitations imposed on the curia. This is not to say that Clement V was an exemplary pope; it is to assert that he was a true reflection of his age, with political and legal skills above the average. Neither an exemplary pope nor a weak subject of Philip the Fair, Clement V, or more accurately his image, was often sacrificed on the altar of unhistorical judgments, of longings for a more militant papacy that could no longer exist. [49]

Unaware of the historical legacy of the "Avignon papacy" and "Babylonian Captivity" with which he would be burdened, Clement remained in the city until he felt his end near. He died in Roquemaure on April 20, 1314, on his way to his beloved Gascony, where he was buried at Uzeste.

CENTRALIZATION: JOHN XXII

It took some two and a half years to elect a successor to Clement V, evidence enough that the college was still not strongly unified, regardless of the mounting significance of the French party. Ever a fine diplomat, Clement V had anticipated the fissures that would emerge during the election of his successor. In his bull *Ne romani* (1311), he ordained the opening of the conclave within ten days of the pope's death in the diocese where the curia resided (Carpentras in this case). The division of the college between a Gascon group of ten, a fractured Italian group of seven, and eight undecided voters hindered a swift resolution. No agreement was reached after a three-month-long deliberation that ended in chaos when Gascons and Italian courtiers started fighting. Things got even worse when the pope's nephew, Bertrand de Got, Viscount of Lomagne, entered the city with mercenary troops in order to claim the pope's body; the troops chanted, "Death to the Italian cardinals, we want a pope!" De Got's army ransacked Carpentras and the conclave and plundered the papal treasury.[50] These actions led to the dissolution of the conclave on July 24, 1314. The cardinals escaped the city, and it took much convincing from French authorities to rally the college into meeting again, this time in the safety of the Dominican convent in the French city of Lyons. Jacques Duèse, who took the name of John XXII, was then elected on August 7, 1316, and was crowned in the same city.

The experienced Napoleone Orsini had nominated the aged Jacques Duèse for several reasons. His advanced age made him a transitional pope, and his origins (he was from Cahors in Quercy) pacified those who refused another Gascon like his predecessor. But Orsini's intentions rather backfired. The seventy-two-year-old pope the college elected was not a fragile, uninvolved administrator. To the contrary, he was engaged, a brilliant and efficient organizer, a relentless workaholic, and what we would label in modern parlance a micromanager. John XXII involved himself in all the facets of his papal responsibilities, from architecture and construction to taxation and theology. His conception of a supreme and absolute papacy delineated to a certain extent the characteristics of the Avignon papacy.

Jacques came from the bourgeoisie of Cahors. He was a southerner who spoke and read Latin before *langue d'oil*, the French of the north. His legal mind was framed while studying law at Montpellier and Orléans, where he received his doctorate. Enrolled in theology in Paris, he never finished his degree and probably taught law in Toulouse, supported by the Neapolitan house of Anjou. He was in the entourage of both Charles II of Provence and his son Louis. There is no doubt that his education and experience made him an efficient administrator. Jacques collected several benefices (archpriest and archdeacon) before being named archbishop of

Toulouse in 1297. He was elected bishop of Fréjus in 1300, and in 1308 Charles II asked him to take the helm of the Kingdom of Sicily as its chancellor. Clement V transferred him from Sicily to the diocese of Avignon when the pope moved there in 1310 (Jacques returned to his episcopal palace when elected pope). He played a large part in the discussions related to Boniface's trial and the Council of Vienne. Clement promoted him to cardinal of San Vital in 1312, adding the bishopric of Porto in 1313.

SATANIC BEGINNINGS

Shortly after his election, rumors flew at the curia of a possible plot to assassinate the pope. The first report of a Gascon conspiracy to eliminate the pope and his *Quercynois* compatriots in the middle of a consistory was rapidly quelled. Why kill an old man? But a real plot involving several bizarre elements indeed unraveled soon afterward.[51] Hugues Géraud, bishop of Cahors (thus head of a diocese close to the pope's heart) decided to poison the pope and his confidants when Géraud was threatened with deposition for several offenses (involving mostly his simony). Notably, in the wake of the accusations against Boniface and the Templars, times were propitious to accusations of enchantment and sorcery. As treason became the benchmark accusation of the later fourteenth century, sorcery was the accusation of choice in the earlier years. Still, in this case the threat was real. Géraud resided in Avignon, and with his two accomplices he quickly acquired the necessary accoutrements, arsenic and wax dolls. The first doll needed to be baptized to become efficacious so that the devil would recognize it and was named after Jacques de Via, the cardinal-nephew of the pope. Since de Via died on June 13, 1317, his death ensured Géraud of the effectiveness of his method. The bishop then decided to kill the pope and two other cardinals. He found accomplices working in the pope's household to bring the dolls to court and another bishop to baptize them. The dolls, which contained inscriptions stating "May pope John die and no other," "May Bertrand du Poujet die," and "May Gaucelme de Jean die," traveled back to Géraud, after their baptism, inside hollowed breads. On their way, the poisoners' suspicious behavior alarmed guards, who stopped them at the gate of the city. They found overwhelming evidence fairly quickly. Géraud, who had not yet been publicly denounced, nonetheless became alarmed and started talking. Arrested in March 1317, he was condemned and burned in September. Afraid of opening a Pandora's box of wrongdoing, John pardoned most of the accomplices. As Jean Favier states, this affair plunged the papacy back into its traditional Roman milieu. The Orsini and Colonna may have been far away, but the French, Gascon, and Italian rivalries easily replaced them.[52]

It is highly possible that the Géraud affair impressed John enough to leave him suspicious of the crimes of poisoning and black magic and of antipapal conspiracies in general. He seemed to have genuinely feared a Jewish-Christian "magical" scheme, which led him to expel Jews from the Comtat Venaissin in 1321–1323. But the pope also accused the Visconti of Milan of practicing magic against him, and he was not afraid to fend off poison with poison. In March 1317, the pope thanked a certain Marguerite de Foiz for a poison antidote she had sent him; in February 1318, the pope asked the bishop of Fréjus to search for necromancers.[53] But most of all, John established the link as a kind of rationale that bound demons and the devil to heresy. In short, John instigated the mode of thinking that produced the witch crazes of the early modern period. In his *Satan the Heretic: The Birth of Demonology in the Medieval West*, Alain Boureau traces this evolution. Throughout the 1320s John created a commission of theologians to investigate black magic and heresy; it concluded the assimilation of the one into the other.[54] Enrico del Carretto, a member of the commission, searched for causes behind the successful use of images and hosts in sorcery, arguing that Satan was "the signified in the sign."[55] According to his logic, a baptized image became the site of the pact with Satan and proof of devil worship, thus a heretical object.

Earlier views had minimized demonic power over humans as a mere superstition. Authorities usually regarded magic as a practice for the weak of mind. But the pope broke the tradition that regarded heresies as intellectual (a matter of faith) and dissociated magic from doctrinal/dogmatic issues. John upgraded magic to a powerful reality as dangerous and unorthodox dogma. In 1326, John promulgated his bull *Super illius specula,* handing black magic to the Inquisition as "perverse dogma" that "infected" the Church.[56] It is highly possible that John's broadening of the concept of heresy to magic demonstrated his concern for protecting the Church and its sovereignty at a time when the Spiritual Franciscans' discussion of absolute poverty led the pope toward a redefinition of what was acceptable debate and what was not.

THE FRANCISCAN POVERTY DEBATE AND ITS
EUROPEAN IMPLICATION

The dispute over Franciscan poverty polarized much of John's early rule, and the debate was not new. Shortly after St. Francis's death in 1226, his followers split into two distinct groups: the Spirituals, who endorsed strict adherence to the rule, and the Conventuals, willing to accept change. Christianity has an ancient tradition of detachment from the world and the embrace of radical voluntary poverty dating even to its earliest origins, and St. Francis, by following in Jesus's footsteps to the permissible extent, marked himself as radically different from other contemporary religious leaders by the absoluteness of his commitment to poverty. In 1279, Pope Nicholas III's *Exiit qui seminat* had facilitated that same commitment to poverty on the part of individual Franciscans and the order as an institution when it stated that the papacy owned the goods used by Franciscans.[57] The bull established that Christ and the apostles had lived without individual or communal possession; they had used property but rejected its possession. Most discussions over poverty insisted on the separation between ownership/possession and use. In short, Franciscans had *usus facti* of the goods they used, but they did not possess them, the Church did. Hence individuals in the Franciscan order could avoid the "burden" of ownership and claim total poverty since they owned nothing and simply benefited from the pope's assistance. Franciscans could thus practice poverty without the inconvenience of ownership.

The majority of Franciscans were satisfied with this arrangement, but Angelo da Clareno and Ubertino da Casale headed a minority, the Spirituals, that championed a strict adherence to St. Francis's lifestyle: utter destitution. Tensions rose steadily between followers of the two observances and reached the breaking point under the rule of John XXII. But this did not prevent the general Franciscan practice to put them at odds with all the other orders that possessed and used goods. Clement V had called Franciscans to discuss the issue at the Council of Vienne. He admonished moderation without reaching a conclusion on the place of the Spirituals.

Upon his nomination, John returned to the poverty issue, asking the Inquisition to examine the friars. The leaders of the Spirituals were called to Avignon in 1316, where Angelo da Clareno, Ubertino da Casale, and

Bernard Délicieux (a strong opponent of the Inquisition) tried to compel the pope to join their ranks. The pope did not appreciate their initiative. Bernard was imprisoned and Angelo and Ubertino demoted. In 1317, a papal bull condemned the Spirituals (labeling them *Fraticelli* for the first time), and in his next bull the pope advanced obedience as the greatest of all vows. He stated, "Poverty is great, but unity is greater, obedience is the greatest good if it is preserved intact."[58] The argument reached a new level in 1321, when a heretic was burned by the Inquisition in Narbonne for advocating a total poverty that was quite similar to the Spirituals' model. A local Franciscan appealed to the pope against this injustice, and John acted as any good manager would. He consulted experts, collected their opinions, read all discussions, convened specialists, and listened to arguments, finally making a decision in 1322. He abrogated *Exiit qui seminat*. When Louis of Bavaria, the emperor-elect, appealed his decision, John answered, "Scripture can contradict the poverty of Christ."[59] He added that he could in fact change an earlier pontifical act when it endangered the present. His *Ad conditorem canonum* granted property ownership back to the Franciscans.[60] The bull scandalized all Franciscans who in a council in Perugia reasserted their strict adherence to the ideal of apostolic poverty, following the lead of their general, Michael of Cesena. The pope answered in 1323 with another bull, *Cum inter nonnullos*, that condemned the Perugian defense and rendered moot any further discussions of Christ's poverty.[61] The Franciscans split, with a majority obeying the pope and a minority sticking with Michael of Cesena to the strict ideal of poverty. This alliance between Michael and the emperor-elect Louis of Bavaria lent a further political dimension to the religious crisis that will be addressed later.

In his book *Pope John XXII and His Franciscan Cardinal: Bertrand de la Tour and the Apostolic Poverty Controversy*, Patrick Nold revisits the historiography of the Franciscan poverty debate of the early fourteenth century, noting how it usually reflects negatively on the pope, making him the villain of the affair. He reevaluates the pope's position (roughly 1322–1325) and studies how John managed the crisis, looking for the counsel of specialists and relying on Franciscan supporters at the curia, such as Cardinal Bertrand de la Tour, to counterbalance opinions. Nold contends essentially that if John listened to a Franciscan, then the chasm that separated him from Cesena was not as wide as traditionally thought. In essence, Nold argues that John actually followed the recommendation of the Franciscan de la Tour and cannot thus be condemned alone for the split. He portrays a pope more prone to compromise than previously perceived, willing to review all the arguments of the controversy. Most of all, he describes John XXII as a centralizer who brought important theological matters to the curia instead of leaving them in the hands of councils or universities. [62]

The question remains, however: Why did John cast off absolute poverty so adamantly? In her recent dissertation, Melanie Brunner focuses on the reason behind John XXII's rejection. She questions the pope's dislike of the Franciscans and his support of the Dominicans and probes the pope's vision of Franciscan ideology as a threat to ecclesiastical authority. She restores John to the context of his earlier training in natural law and offers a legal rationale for John's objection. John hinted that absolute poverty hinged on heresy and that Jesus was bound to have held property. The papal dominion (*dominium* equaled lordship and property) over Franciscan goods set the papacy sharply at odds with the secular clergy (which controlled its own property). Further, the pope conceived dominion as part of human nature, a divine institution that could not be refused or rejected. For the pope, obedience was more important than poverty, and a refusal to own property seemed like contempt for the material world, a dangerous and familiar heretical position. As Brunner aptly states,

> Evangelical poverty was not characterised by lack of *dominium*. The crucial point about Christ's poverty from the papal point of view was not that he did not have any dominium, but that he had dominium yet chose not to use it. The fact that Christ refrained from using his rights was the distinguishing factor of his poverty and humility. [63]

The pope made the case in his bull *Quia vir reprobus* (1329) that reproved the theories of the former Franciscan general Michael of Cesena and ended further discussion. [64]

Of course, this debate may sound abstract and quite remote to the concerns of a modern reader. Its importance, however, may be suggested by its relevance to the perennially important issue of legacies and inheritance claims. The debate over apostolic poverty is a perfect example of the ties that bound law to religion. Like many other religious orders, the Franciscans' charisma attracted the support of many individuals, most notably in towns, where they spiritually counseled a population that felt torn, like Francis of Assisi himself, between an ideal of absolute poverty and the birth pangs of early capitalism. A sense of pollution remained attached to money and to the wealth amassed by the new merchant class. One way to mitigate it was to transform this ungainly wealth into charity. Bequests to the Franciscans alleviated the guilty conscience of the wealthy and in turn supported the urban poor through Franciscan activities. The testamentary practice of the time shows that in Avignon Franciscans were tremendously popular with the merchant and laboring classes, widely accepted as they were within European urban settings. In Avignon, some 60 percent of cultivators, 44.5 percent of merchants, and 27 percent of artisans chose to be buried within Franciscan churches and cemeteries.[65] The amount of property they received as bequests held in trust also testified to their immense popularity. But, of course, the Franciscans' extreme position muddled many inheritance cases, especially when disinherited friends, kin, and relatives used the legal system to their advantage and challenged how bequests could be made to the Franciscans because of their attachment to absolute poverty. A pragmatic man like John XXII was bound to comprehend the deep ramifications of Franciscan "intransigence" over poverty. It put at risk the survival of the trust holder, the Church.

John's conflict with the Franciscans occasioned some of the most provocative Christian soul searching of the time. Authors such as Marsilius of Padua, William of Ockham, Peter John Olivi, Ubertino of Casale, and Bonagratia da Bergamo questioned papal authority in view of their reading of the scriptures, addressing topics such as the apparent conflict of papal and imperial authority and the theory of papal infallibility as they attempted to reframe the dominant discourse. They discussed political theory and ecclesiology, pushing boundaries like no one else had done before them. The lengthy continuation of the Spirituals affair aptly demonstrates how medieval political discourse was embedded in theology. Since the publication of *Ad conditionem canonum*, the Franciscan general Michael of Cesena had changed sides and joined the Spirituals; he could not tolerate the papal defense of Christ's and Apostolical possessions. In a show of authority, John summoned Michael to Avignon, where he imprisoned him. In 1328, the latter escaped, accompanied by William of Ockham; they both found refuge at the court of Louis of Bavaria, Holy Roman emperor-elect, who supported their cause.

After the death of Emperor Henry VII in 1313, polarized German electors supported two rival emperors: Louis of Bavaria, crowned in Aachen, and Frederick of Austria, crowned in Bonn. The issue was resolved militarily when Louis defeated and captured Frederick in September 1322.

John chose this moment of imperial "weakness" to assert his sovereignty over Italian territory. He announced the Italian (imperial) vicariate vacant and offered it to Robert of Anjou, King of Naples. Supporting his Ghibelline cause, Louis backed the activities of the Milanese Visconti against Anjou. In retaliation, the pope questioned Louis's legitimacy, which led the emperor to support the Spirituals.

The pope's special envoys, known as papal legates, could not pacify the land and were overextended trying to rule southern Italy and the rebellious north. John trusted first Bertrand du Poujet to contain the Visconti of Milan and the Ghibellines' northern cities of Lombardy and Romagna; but ultimately he failed. John then divided the Italian legacy in two, keeping du Poujet to the north and granting southern Italy to Cardinal Giovanni Orsini. The pope expected that Orsini's Roman experience with local politics would buttress papal support. He also failed, bringing to his legation the fractured politics of Rome. Sebastian Zanke, working with some 67,000 or so letters preserved in John XXII's papal registers, has been able to gauge the interest that the pope paid to foreign policy, and unsurprisingly, the affairs of the Italian States monopolized most of his attention. The pope sent up to twelve nuncios, who supplemented the local administration, and his two legates. All other aspects of European politics came second. Zanke cites the quite astonishing lack of interest on the pope's part at the deposition of King Edward II of England, for example. He describes papal policies as "responsive" or "reactive" to specific requests and not the results of an overarching planned and calculated foreign policy. Only the petitioners and foreign representatives who were able to reach the pope's attention (through the curia) received attention.[66]

By 1324, the pope had excommunicated the emperor, who had first accused John of heresy. Louis's stance was strengthened by one of the most controversial pamphlets of its time, Marsilius of Padua's *Defensor pacis*. In his treatise, the Italian scholar weakened papal authority, promoted imperial secular sovereignty (and councils of ecclesiastics and laymen) over the pope, denied ecclesiastical rights over temporal justice, taxation, and property, and repudiated ecclesiastical prerogatives such as excommunication. In short, according to Marsilius of Padua, the emperor granted the pope his power. Marsilius's formulations (a reversal of Boniface VIII's utterances) were radical for the time, and he deserves a place among the greatest political thinkers of his time. Marsilius breached the "modern" world of politics with the following declaration:

> Now we declare according to the truth and on the authority of Aristotle that the law-making power or the first and real effective source of law is the people. . . . For temporal power and greed, and lust of authority and rule is not the spouse of Christ, nor has He wedded such a spirit, but has expressly repudiated it, as has been shown from the divine Scriptures. . . . The recent Roman popes do not defend her who is the spouse of Christ, that is, the Catholic faith and the multitude of the believers, but offend her; they do not preserve her beauty, that is, the unity of the faith, but defile it. Since by sowing tares and schisms they are tearing her limb from limb, and since they do not receive the true companions of Christ, poverty and humility, but shut them out entirely, they show themselves not servants but enemies of the husband. [67]

As Cary J. Nederman states, Marsilius "set the individual into a communal setting while maintaining a meaningful role for personal volition and achieved this precisely by turning diversity of function—divergence in 'ways of life'—into a virtue, indeed a necessity." [68] Louis could not have found a better intellectual support than Marsilius's *Defensor pacis*. With this defense of his authority in mind, the emperor marched into Italy in 1327, crowned himself king of Italy in Milan, and continued toward Rome, where he was again elected and crowned emperor by the Romans and a few rebellious bishops. The new regime, led by Sciarra Colonna, benefited Roman aristocratic Ghibellines. In January 1328, John XXII predictably deposed the emperor, who retorted by deposing the pope and supporting the election of a counterpope, the Franciscan Pietro of Corvara, as Nicholas V. Louis's *iter italicum* eventually became unsustainable, however, and he returned north, leaving his pope (also excommunicated) in Pisa. John eventually pardoned Nicholas, who abdicated in 1330 and died in an Avignonese jail three years later. [69] Still, between 1330 and 1346, Louis attempted to have the pope annul the sentences levied against him. But in order to do so, he had to swear absolute obedience to the mandates of the Church, a step he was not willing to take, especially when the pope refused to accept his stance on equal negotiation between them.

BEATIFIC VISION

A review of John XXII's rich pontificate cannot end without discussing his controversial "beatific vision" theory. His theological stance created enough buzz to garner the criticism of all his enemies, Ghibellines and Fraticelli included; some called him a heretic while others questioned the pope's infallibility. On All Saints' Day 1331, John, while discussing verses from the book of Revelation (especially the term "under the altar" found in Rv 6:9), argued that the "blessed souls" could only contemplate Christ's humanity. Their visions of God's essence and Christ's divinity had to wait for their bodily resurrection and Last Judgment. For John (and to the contrary of what most medieval Christians believed), beatific vision was achieved only after resurrection. John's revisionist view followed his logical mind. What was the point of a Last Judgment if all received punishments and salvation *before* judgment? He continued his defense in several sermons, up to his death, when he retracted his views *in articulo mortis*. His successor, Benedict XII, ended the controversy, proclaiming in his conciliating *Benedictus Deus* (1336) that

> By this Constitution which is to remain in force for ever, we, with apostolic authority, define the following: According to the general disposition of God, the souls of all the saints who departed from this world before the passion of our Lord Jesus Christ and also of the holy apostles, martyrs, confessors, virgins and other faithful who died after receiving the holy baptism of Christ—provided they were not in need of any purification when they died . . . —and again the souls of children who have been reborn by the same baptism of Christ . . . all these souls, immediately after death and, in the case of those in need of purification, after the purification mentioned above, since the ascension of our Lord and Saviour Jesus Christ into heaven, already before they take up their bodies again and before the general judgment, have been, are and will be with Christ in heaven, in the heavenly kingdom and paradise, joined to the company of the holy angels. Since the passion and death of the Lord Jesus Christ, these souls have seen and see the divine essence with an intuitive vision and even face to face, without the mediation of any creature by way of object of vision; rather the divine essence immediately manifests itself to them, plainly, clearly and openly, and in this vision they enjoy the divine essence.[70]

It seems preposterous nowadays to consider that such a theological statement could create an international crisis. But it did, entangling all of

Europe's secular and religious authorities into a defense or criticism of the pope. While historians have argued that the debate remained a scholastic squabble among savants, irrelevant to "simple Christians," Jérémie Rabiot demonstrates in a recent article that an educated merchant like Giovanni Villani was interested enough to send missives asking questions to clarify the debate and became a cultural mediator, analyzing in his chronicle the dogmatic, political, and ecclesiological stakes of the issue.[71] For this merchant, the debate highlighted two distinct conceptions of ecclesiastical authority: one, authoritarian and uncompromising, defended by the position of John XXII, and one, collegial and more open, defended by the college and universities. For Villani, the controversy affected the cult of saints and their intercessory relevance, indulgences, and the Church's power in remitting sins—in summary, a large part of the medieval Christian belief system. This example, limited in time and topic, demonstrates that the boundary separating popular from scholastic culture was not as marked as one might expect.

In any case, on December 3, 1334, a day before his death, the pope (pressured by cardinals and family members) confessed "that souls separated from bodies and fully justified . . . see God and the divine essence face to face and clearly, as much as the state and condition of the separated soul can bear."[72] Understanding the damage his words had done, John died with the assurance that his last confession eased the turmoil he had created. It is worth noting that in his chronicle, Giovanni Villani discussed the pope's death and his last words, taking time to translate the pope's renunciation words that he had received from his brother who resided at court, evidence enough of the impact of the pope's utterance. Villani adds further that the pope left his treasury in excellent shape with some eighteen million gold florins in currency and liturgical objects worth an additional seven million.[73] We can take the chronicler's words as evidence of the pope's administrative and fiscal successes. John E. Weakland, who has studied the pope's administrative achievements, describes him as an efficient and talented administrator, energetic, eloquent, frugal, unwavering, confident, a tough opponent, a "burning genius" according to his contemporary, and a pope who was engaged with a high conception of his office and a deep sense of preserving Church unity.[74] We could go a step further: John XXII defined the Avignon papacy. Its centralization, tight administration, and self-awareness marked the institution for years to come. John symbolized the Avignon papacy.

Travelers to Avignon can still see today what is left of John's magnificent Gothic mausoleum in the treasury of Notre-Dame des Doms.

MONASTICIZATION: BENEDICT XII

According to the well-informed Giovanni Villani, the conclave that elected John's successor was splintered into two parties. In spite of the division, it ended up electing "a man of good life," the Cistercian monk Jacques Fournier. He chose the name of Benedict in honor of the founder of his order. The humble new pope supposedly responded to his nomination by commenting wryly: "You have elected an ass."[75] To English-speaking readers, Jacques Fournier is better known as the inquisitor who provided Emmanuel Leroy Ladurie with the material for his fabulous ethnohistory, *Montaillou: Occitan Village*, than as a pope of Avignon.[76] Benedict XII's short rule was certainly a respite after the frenetic pace with which his predecessors had responded to relentless issues. Benedict XII died early in his tenure, on April 25, 1342, making his reign the shortest of the Avignon papacy. Because of its brevity, fewer international crises plagued his reign.

The conclave that elected John's successor was also notable for the fact that none of the cardinals but Cardinal Jacopo Stefaneschi had ever before participated in one, and thus the proceedings relied heavily on the institutional knowledge of the old man.[77] This serves as a key reminder that sometimes institutions, too, need to rely on "memory." It seems quite logical to assume, as Jean Favier did, that the election of the "orthodox" Jacques Fournier by the twenty-four cardinals present in conclave was a direct response to the dogmatic vagaries of his predecessor.[78] According to Giovanni Villani, the tiara was first proposed to the archbishop of Toulouse, Jean-Raymond of Comminges; he refused after French cardinals set an electoral precondition that the new pope not return the papacy to Rome. Out of spite, the French cardinals chose the "lesser" candidate: the cardinal who was associated with the "small nation" of Toulouse (a recently created province). But Villani does add that he was "a man of good life."[79] Regardless of the historical truth, the Italian chronicler's biases are quite apparent here!

Jacques Fournier's rectitude and dogmatism certainly affected the cardinals' vote. Fournier was a Cistercian monk of humble origins (his father was rumored to have been a miller), who had followed his maternal uncle Arnaud Nouvel to the monastery of Boulbonne, today in the Midi-Pyrenées. He studied theology at the Cistercian College of St. Bernard in Paris and headed the Abbey of Fontfroide in 1311. Fournier was reputedly a brilliant theologian. In 1317 he became bishop of Pamiers, where he pursued heretics relentlessly. His "Fournier Register" recorded the interrogations of some 578 Cathars; the register became a mine of information for daily life in the medieval French Southwest.[80] His unique interrogation skills allowed him to minimize physical torture, and his record keeping was meticulous. There is no doubt that his zeal and organizational skills pleased John XXII. In 1326, Fournier was transferred to the diocese of Mirepoix, and in 1327 John XXII elevated him to cardinal with the title of Santa Prisca, a post held previously by his uncle Arnaud Nouvel. Once at court, he became one of John's advisors, the court's theologian, and one of those who urged the pope to recant his "wayward" understanding of beatific vision.

Benedict was an austere man. His interest focused largely on theology and philosophy, and he showed little patience for politics or the law. As cardinal and pope he kept his white Cistercian habit (hence his name, "The White Cardinal"), and he embraced orthodox dogma and behavior. Of him, Paul Amargier writes, "With more depth and constancy than his two predecessors, Clement V and John XXII, he grasped the essentially religious aspect of his position. He remained a monk."[81] He announced shortly after his election that his nearest kin should expect nothing from him (it is worth remembering that his maternal uncle had been a cardinal, so he indeed benefited from traditional nepotism). In 1336, his *Benedictus deus* ended the beatific vision controversy. After his election, he rejected all the requests from petitioners attracted to Avignon by the election of a new pope, and he ordered those charged with benefices to reside where they served a purpose; that is, they had to leave the court and reside where they had been nominated. The new pope deplored the accumulation of benefices and residence exemptions for ecclesiastics.[82]

The pope's interest in reducing abuses led to his personal involvement in the nomination of thousands of benefices of all ranks—from bishops and abbots to lower offices—in which he demonstrated his fairness by granting positions even to the illegitimate sons of ecclesiastics, at the same time centralizing the decision-making process in his own hands.

It was the reform of religious orders that first merited Benedict's care and attention, initiating these efforts with his bull *Pastor bonus* in June

1335, which compelled abbots to search out and recall to religious life wayward monks who had abandoned their calling.[83] With *Fulgens sicut stella*, promulgated on July 12, 1335, Benedict focused on his own Cistercian order. Rigorous changes were initiated, including rules that stipulated: "In certain monasteries the monks have the right to a certain part of the corn, the bread, the wine and the income. That must no longer happen; everything will be common to all. It will no longer be possible for anyone to have any revenue or pension for his sustenance, his clothing or for anything else"; and "Likewise to be abolished is the sharing of the revenues among the Abbot, the officers and the community. The Abbots opposing this decision are to be deposed, the monks to be imprisoned for life."[84] The pope was obviously attempting to restore fairness and equity in practice and lifestyle. In June 1336, he turned to the Benedictines, whose organization he attempted to centralize with the bull *Summi magistri*. Again, in May 1339, he summoned the Augustinian Canons Regular to reform with the bull *Ad decorum ecclesie*. Papal enthusiasm for reform did not sit well with many orders, and his relations with the Franciscans soured to the point of irreconciliation. J. B. Mahn, discussing the pope's *Redemptor noster* of 1336, states, "[This text] today still earns him the stubborn hostility of all the sons of St. Francis, no matter which branch they belong to."[85] In some thirty articles the pope totally reformed the order in ways that may have shocked purists. The most radical points were the opening of conventual schools that would allow gifted students to be educated and the elections by communal chapters of conventual custodians and guardians.[86] Last, the pope attempted to reform the Dominicans, but they resisted so strongly that he first considered dissolving the order before abandoning his plan.

A fervent opponent of heresies, Benedict was also active in expanding the frontiers of Christendom. He sent an embassy of four missionaries to Kublai Khan, grandson of Genghis, headed by the renowned Parisian theologian Nicholas Bonet. Leaving Avignon in 1338, the embassy reached Peking in 1342. They were well received and permitted to found several missions throughout the Mongol Empire. The embassy returned from the east in 1346, arriving back in Avignon in 1354; Bonet had died in 1343. The chronicle of Arnald de Sarrant recounts the event quite inaccurately, emphasizing the great love Kublai showed for the Franciscans, especially a certain Brother Francis of Alessandria, who had cured the emperor of cancer and a fistula and converted him! In any case, Kublai Khan's successor eradicated Christian influence in the Mongol Empire.[87]

STAYING IN AVIGNON

Benedict was not solely interested in proselytizing faraway lands. He was deeply uncomfortable with the location of the papacy and chose to return to Rome as early as 1335; in his first consistory, he dedicated fifty thousand florins for the reconstruction of the basilicas of St. Peter and the Lateran.[88] He sent the archbishop of Embrun to revamp the ultramontane papal administration, but the Italian barons still dominated the peninsula. Benedict negotiated with local rulers in exchange for their support. He recognized the vicariate of the della Scala in Verona and Vicenza, the Gonzaga in Mantua, the Este in Modena, and the Visconti in Milan, thus reinforcing their authority. Bologna, which had entered the Guelph party in 1327, had rebelled against John XXII in 1334, and it took several years to quell the uprising. In 1337, Benedict was forced to excommunicate the revolt's instigator, Taddeo Pepoli, and put the city under interdict. The situation was remedied three years later in 1340, when Bologna surrendered and offered its allegiance to the pope, agreeing to the payment of a feudal tax. Thenceforth, Taddeo became the ecclesiastical administrator of Guelph-dominated Bologna.

Realizing that the political situation in Italy remained unresolved and facing strong opposition at the court, Benedict decided to remain in Avignon. The city had been without a bishop since 1334. After a two-year-long vacancy, in 1336 the pope finally named Jean de Cojordan to that see. After purchasing the Petit Palais (a group of houses owned by the late cardinal Arnaud de Via), Benedict personally kept what had been episcopal property up to that point and offered the newly acquired Petit Palais to the bishop of Avignon. He then charged architect Pierre Poisson to rehabilitate and transform the episcopal residence into what became the first austere papal fortress, the Palace (now labeled the Old Palace to distinguish it from Clement VI's upgrading).[89] The fate of the papacy in Avignon was definitively sealed in 1339, when the pope recalled the papal archives from Assisi to Avignon.[90] There is no doubt that foreign policy also dictated the building of a new impregnable fortress as the threat of invasion by Louis of Bavaria still loomed.

Benedict's alliance with the Visconti had deprived Louis of a traditional Ghibelline ally. The emperor also constantly feared the association between the papacy and the French house of Anjou in Naples and the Valois who ruled France. Louis sent embassies to the new pope and readied himself to comply with Benedict's imperatives for reconciliation. The pope was eager; the houses of Anjou and Valois were not. Their ambassadors criticized the German emperor for his notorious heresies and the utter disregard with which he treated the Church. Discussions went back and forth with no solution; the French pressured the pope to refuse or defer negotiations. Long delays created new resolutions, and (in traditional fashion) the enemies of France became the friends of Germany. Louis and Edward III of England allied and ceased negotiating with Avignon. According to Henry Knighton, both Louis and Edward met in the city of Coblenz among great ceremonies. "There in the presence of all the assembled people the Emperor declared and made known to all the unnaturalness, disobedience, and wickedness with which the King of France had acted towards him; defied the King of France; and declared him and all his adherents to be under forfeiture. Then the Emperor made King Edward his Vicar, and gave him all the power he himself had, over Cologne and from there to the sea." [91] In response, the pope laid an interdict on Germany. In 1338, German bishops begged the pope to resume discussions. He refused. They then decided on a radical course of action. In July 1338, Louis received from the six imperial electors (with the support of the German episcopate) the recognition that an emperor elected by the majority had the right to rule, regardless of the pope's confirmation. With this Treaty of Rhens, imperial legitimacy officially circumvented papal approval. Three years later, a new agreement reconciled the emperor to the pope and France with Germany. It was left to the next pope, Clement VI, to end this convoluted imperial affair.

Modern historians of the period largely followed Guillaume Mollat's assessment of the relationship between France and the papacy. The relations were not "tainted with servility." [92] The popes supported France because it advanced their own interests, and the popes' interests lay in a crusade. It would be successful only if England and France solved their difficulties and worked together on the (re)conquest of the Levant. [93] Once the Valois dynasty was recognized after the demise of the last Capetian, it needed to affirm its authority over the six great fiefs of the French monarchy: Flanders, Burgundy, Brittany, Armagnac, Foix, and

Aquitaine. This authority legitimated its position. All were relatively quiet except Aquitaine, English since 1152 and stuck between the hegemonic tendencies of both France and England. Benedict stalled Philip when he proposed to intervene in British-Scottish affairs, and he tried to dissuade Philip from invading Guyenne.[94] Between 1337 and 1340 the pope further restrained Philip from attacking Edward when the latter was isolated. Pierre Roger, the future Clement VI, became the legate deployed to maintain the peace necessary to the papacy's long-term crusading plans. Ironically, Edward seized the moment to join with the emperor and plan his conquest of France. Conversely, Benedict put much energy in preventing Flanders from supporting British politics. In the end, the pope's efforts on both sides were all for naught. In 1337 Philip invaded Gascony, initiating the Hundred Years' War, and a year later Edward landed in Flanders as Philip attacked Guyenne. In January 1340, Edward declared himself king of France. In the midst of this turmoil, Benedict did manage to negotiate the short-lived Truce of Esplechin in 1340. Karsten Plöger's examination of diplomacy at the papal court details the back-and-forth discussions and travels that put the papacy at the center of European negotiations. He qualifies the rapport between Avignon and Edward III's representatives thus:

> The rarity of letters of procuration for English envoys dispatched to Avignon in the mid-fourteenth century is a reflection of the nature of Anglo-papal relations in this particular period. The use of *plena potestas* had long since become a characteristic feature of negotiations both between equals and between rulers and their subjects in which the representatives of either side would try to reach some form of mutually binding agreement. Bilateral talks between English envoys and the pope, however, did not normally involve the kind of give-and-take typical of such discussions. Unlike their compatriots sent abroad to negotiate with secular rulers, Edward III's diplomats travelling to the curia in those years did not go there with the aim of "striking deals" and entering into contractual agreements (this also distinguished them from the plenipotentiaries of Louis of Bavaria who came to Avignon between 1335 and 1344 to negotiate the terms of the emperor's absolution; their procurations were closely scrutinized in consistory and played a central role in the subsequent discussion). Instead, as has been suggested above, they would usually try to influence papal decisions regarding such problems as provisions, peace and marriage dispensations by force of legal argument and persuasion.[95]

In summary, the papacy's efforts on behalf of England may have been half-hearted.

In 1340, Benedict became afflicted with several ulcers on his legs. Gangrene eventually killed him on April 25, 1342. His tomb can still be seen in Notre-Dame des Doms. As Bernard Guillemain stated, while the pope's enemies described him as a vulgar fool, instead "he appears to us simple, unpretentious, hardworking, devoted to the habits of monastic life."[96] He took counsel before making difficult decisions, and his brilliant theological mind granted him self-assurance and reliability. His distribution of benefices was fair, calculated, and impeccable. Benedict defined his office first and foremost in religious terms and after becoming pope remained a monk in practice and mind. He had pressed heretics to confess; once they recognized their errors, they needed to be treated with indulgence.[97] The castle that he ordered to be built protected the papal administration and the pope as well. But it was devoid of grandeur and elegance, neither ostentatious nor luxurious. The humblest of all the Avignon popes, Benedict remained the only one who did not succumb to the temptation to shower his family and friends with favors.[98] The conclave that elected his successor chose a man dramatically different.

NOTES

1. Alain Demurger, "Clement V," in *The Papacy: An Encyclopedia*, ed. Philippe Levillain (New York: Routledge, 2002), 333–335, defends him to a certain extent, arguing that he was not under the control of France. Still, he agrees that his nepotism was flagrant, as was his financial centralization, two items that gave him bad press.

2. Jean Favier, *Les papes d'Avignon* (Paris: Fayard, 2006), 62.

3. Sophia Menache, *Clement V* (Cambridge: Cambridge University Press, 1998); see also Norman Housley, "Pope Clement V and the Crusades of 1309–10," *Journal of Medieval History* 8.1 (1982): 29–43.

4. Yves Renouard, *The Avignon Papacy: The Popes in Exile 1305–1403*, trans. Denis Bethell (New York: Barnes and Noble, 1994), 14.

5. His direct predecessor was the short-lived Benedict XI, elected in March 1304, who died of food poisoning in Perugia on July 7, 1304, after having eaten, according to Giovanni Villani, a basket of fresh figs brought to him by a young man disguised as a nun. See *Key Figures in Medieval Europe: An Encyclopedia*, ed. Richard Kenneth Emmerson and Sandra Clayton-Emmerson (London: Routledge, 2005), 143–144.

6. In a recent article, "Boniface VIII, Philip the Fair, and the Sanctity of Louis IX," *Journal of Medieval History* 29.1 (2003): 1–26, M. C. Gaposchkin argues that Boniface canonized Louis to show his grandson what good leadership meant.

7. See Agostino Paravicini Bagliani, *Boniface VIII: Un pape hérétique* (Paris: Payot & Rivages, 2003), 231–253, 279–299.

8. Henry Scowcroft Bettenson and Chris Maunder, *Documents of the Christian Church* (Oxford: Oxford University Press, 1999), 121–122.

9. For a copy of the letter, see Henry G. J. Beck, "William Hundleby's Account of the Anagni Outrage," *Catholic Historical Review* 32.2 (1946): 190–220, also available at http://www.fordham.edu/Halsall/source/1303anagni.asp.

10. Favier, *Les papes d'Avignon*, 18–22, clearly navigates the labyrinth of Roman alliances.

11. Regarding the specifics of this robbery, see Joëlle Rollo-Koster, *Raiding Saint Peter: Empty Sees, Violence, and the Initiation of the Great Western Schism (1378)* (Leiden: Brill, 2008), 136–138.

12. Jean Coste, "Les deux missions de Guillaume de Nogaret en 1303," *Mélanges de l'École française de Rome, moyen-âge-temps modernes* 105.1 (1993): 299–326 discusses the succession of events.

13. Teofilo F. Ruiz, "Reaction to Anagni," *Catholic Historical Review* 65.3 (1979): 385–401, argues that medieval society viewed growing secularization essentially as a political affair.

14. With his 1274 bull *Ubi periculum*, Pope Gregory X regulated the conclave. The three-year-long vacancy that preceded his election made him well aware of all the shortcomings associated with unregulated political transitions. Mandatory enclosure ("conclave," the technical term for papal elections, is from the Latin *cum clave*, a phrase meaning "with a key") isolated cardinals (who were the sole papal electors) from external influences and gave them (at least in principle) freedom of choice—the idea being that they were not supposed to choose under duress. The bull stated that the conclave would open wherever the late pope died and asked the cardinals to wait ten days before entering the conclave, allowing the absent cardinals to join them. It regulated who enforced the integrity of the meeting and who guarded it, and it detailed what cardinals did, said, ate, and slept. See Rollo-Koster, *Raiding Saint Peter*, 94–100, for more details.

15. Guillaume Mollat, *The Popes at Avignon: The "Babylonian Captivity" of the Medieval Church*, trans. Janet Love (New York: Harper & Row, 1965), 3.

16. See *Villani's Chronicle Being Selections from the First Nine Books of the Croniche Fiorentine of Giovanni Villani*, trans. Rose E. Selfe and ed. Philip H. Wicksteed, M.A. (London: Archibald Constable, 1906), book VIII, chap. 80, "How Pope Benedict Died; and of the New Election of Pope Clement V," at http://www.gutenberg.org/files/33022/33022-h/33022-h.htm#VIII_80.

17. See, for example, Mollat, *The Popes at Avignon*, 4–5, who counters Villani's statement point by point.

18. Bernard Guillemain, *La cour pontificale d'Avignon: Étude d'une société* (Paris: De Boccard, 1962), 129–130.

19. Favier, *Les papes d'Avignon*, 38.

20. Étienne Baluze, *Vitae paparum avenionensium, hoc est, Historia pontificum romanorum qui in Gallia sederunt ab anno Christi MCCCV usque ad annum MCCCXCIV*, ed. Guillaume Mollat (Paris: Letouzey et Ané, 1914), vol. 1, 24–25.

21. Baluze, *Vitae*, vol. 1, 60–61.

22. See Favier, *Les papes d'Avignon*, 48–49.

23. Helen Nicholson, *The Knights Templar: A New History* (Thrupp, Stroud: Sutton, 2001), 225.

24. Favier, *Les papes d'Avignon*, 50–51.

25. Favier, *Les papes d'Avignon*, 166–167.

26. The pope suffered from stomach or intestine cancer. His illness made him frail and affected somewhat his character and behavior, making him reclusive for weeks at a time during bouts of his illness. Aggravating his misery, one of the common remedies his doctors prescribed consisted of mixing gold with his meals. See Agostini Paravicini Bagliani, *The Pope's Body*, trans. David S. Peterson (Chicago: University of Chicago Press, 2000), 228; Menache, *Clement V*, 32.

27. From the text of the rule translated by Judith Upton-Ward, *The Rule of the Templars* (Woodbridge: Boydell, 1992), http://www.the-orb.net/encyclop/religion/monastic/t_rule.html.

28. Nicholson finds no evidence that they were unpopular by the early fourteenth century, even though their frequent fund-raising in Europe had negatively affected public perception. In the West, people had little appreciation of the politics and difficulties of waging and winning a war in the Levant and perceived them as money-hungry. What made them a target was that they had a job to do and they were failing. See Nicholson, *The Knights Templar*, 11–12.

29. Nicholson, *The Knights Templar*, 220–221.

30. Malcolm Barber, *The New Knighthood: A History of the Order of the Temple* (Cambridge: Cambridge University Press, 1994), 115.

31. Favier, *Les papes d'Avignon*, 54.

32. Jean de Joinville, *The Memoirs of the Lord of Joinville: A New English Version*, trans. Ethel Wedgwood (London: J. Murray, 1906), 192.

33. Barber, *The New Knighthood*, 296.

34. Barber, *The New Knighthood*, 115.

35. Nicholson, *The Knights Templar*, 230.

36. Jean Coste, *Boniface VIII en procès: Articles d'accusation et dépositions des témoins, 1303–1311* (Rome: L'Erma di Bretschneider, 1995), 413–415.

37. Nicholson, *The Knights Templar*, 13.

38. Julien Théry, "A Heresy of State: Philip the Fair, the Trial of the 'Perfidious Templars,' and the Pontificalization of the French Monarchy," *Journal of Medieval Religious Cultures* 39.2 (2013): 117–148.

39. Barbara Frale, "The Chinon Chart," *Journal of Medieval History* 30.2 (2004): 109–134. The article is controversial because Frale accepts the charges against the Templars, arguing that they represented a misunderstood rite of passage that exemplified what would happen to a Templar if caught by Muslims (denying and spitting on the cross). Aware of the questionable initiation rites, Clement wanted to reform them but was cut short by Philip's imprisonment of the Templars.

40. Frale, "The Chinon Chart," 122.

41. Frale, "The Chinon chart," 126.

42. *Council of Vienne, 1311–1312*, http://www.ewtn.com/library/councils/vienne.htm, has most of the council's decrees.

43. The bull has erroneously been called *Vox clamantis*; see Anne Gilmour-Bryson, "Vox in Excelso Deconstructed: Exactly What Did Clement V Say?" in *On the Margins of Crusading: The Military Orders, the Papacy and the Christian World*, ed. Helen Nicholson (Farnham: Ashgate, 2011), 75–88.

44. Helen Nicholson insists that Clement did not declare them guilty, and charges against them were "not proven"; see Nicholson, *The Knights Templar*, 11.

45. As cited by Favier, *Les papes d'Avignon*, 26.

46. See also Bagliani, *The Pope's Body*, 60–63.

47. Guillemain, *La cour pontificale*, 241.

48. See William M. Bowsky, *Henry VII in Italy: The Conflict of Empire and City-State, 1310–1313* (Lincoln: University of Nebraska Press, 1960), who considers Henry ill prepared and foolish in his decision to make this "journey."

49. Menache, *Clement V*, 307.

50. The papal treasury counted precious objects and rich vestments necessary to the pontifical ritual (liturgical clothing, reliquaries, crosses, chalices, candlesticks, and ornaments), all offerings in kind and currency, and, most important of all, the papal archives in the form of registers and books. At a time when appropriate documentation was crucial to establishing legal claims, the loss of archives could be devastating.

51. See Favier, *Les papes d'Avignon*, 114–118.

52. Favier, *Les papes d'Avignon*, 118.

53. Robert André-Michel, *Avignon, les fresques du Palais des Papes; le procès des Visconti* (Paris: A. Colin, 1926), 168.

54. Alain Boureau, *Satan the Heretic: The Birth of Demonology in the Medieval West*, trans. Teresa Lavender Fagan (Chicago: University of Chicago Press, 2006).

55. Boureau, *Satan the Heretic*, 60.

56. Isabel Iribarren, "From Black Magic to Heresy: A Doctrinal Leap in the Pontificate of John XXII," *Church History: Studies in Christianity and Culture* 76 (2007): 59.

57. The bull is available at the *Franciscan Archive*, http://www.franciscan-archive.org/bullarium/exiit-e.html.

58. Gabrielle Gonzales, "The King of the Locusts Who Destroyed the Poverty of Christ: Pope John XXII, Marsilius of Padua, and the Franciscan Question," in *The World of Marsilius de Padua*, ed. Gerson Moreno-Riaño (Turnhout: Brepols, 2006), 73.

59. Gonzales, "The King of the Locusts," 84.

60. The bull is available from Macquarie University, http://www.mq.edu.au/about_us/faculties_and_departments/faculty_of_arts/mhpir/politics_and_international_relations/staff/john_kilcullen/john_xxii_ad_conditorem_canonum/.

61. The bull is available online at the *Franciscan Archive*, http://www.franciscan-archive.org/bullarium/qinn-e.html. It is titled: *The opinion, which asserts, that Christ and His disciples had nothing, and in regard to those things, which they did have, they had no right, is erroneous and heretical. This extravagant [opinion] is indeed striking, and has profound implications, which have been drawn from the founts of sacred scripture. If one diligently inspects the preceding extravagant [opinion] and the one [which] follows [it], he would say, in my opinion, that it has been assigned this apt designation [i.e., heretical].*

62. See Patrick Nold, *Pope John XXII and His Franciscan Cardinal: Bertrand de la Tour and the Apostolic Poverty Controversy* (Oxford: Oxford University Press, 2003).

63. Melanie Brunner, "Pope John XXII and the Franciscan Ideal of Absolute Poverty" (PhD diss., University of Leeds, 2006); available online at http://etheses.whiterose.ac.uk/1095/, 237.

64. The bull is available from Macquarie University, http://www.mq.edu.au/about_us/faculties_and_departments/faculty_of_arts/mhpir/politics_and_international_relations/staff/john_kilcullen/john_xxii_quia_vir_reprobus/.

65. Jacques Chiffoleau, *La comptabilité de l'au-delà: Les hommes, la mort et la religion dans la région d'Avignon à la fin du Moyen-Âge* (Paris: De Boccard, 1980), 261.

66. Sebastian Zanke, *Johannes XXII, Avignon und Europa: Das politische Papsttum im Spiegel der kurialen Register (1316–1334)* (Leiden: Brill, 2013).

67. "Medieval Sourcebook: Marsilius of Padua, from *Defensor Pacis*, 1324," available at http://www.fordham.edu/halsall/source/marsiglio4.asp.

68. Cary J. Nederman, *Community and Consent: The Secular Political Theory of Marsiglio of Padua's "Defensor pacis"* (Lanham, MD: Rowman & Littlefield, 1995), 145.

69. Losing their motivations, Romans then submitted petitions to the pope asking his forgiveness.

70. The full translation is available at EWTN, http://www.ewtn.com/library/papaldoc/b12bdeus.htm.

71. Jérémie Rabiot, "La culture théologique d'un grand marchand florentin: Échos de la controverse sur la vision béatifique dans la *Nuova cronica* de Giovanni Villani (XIVe siècle)," *Mélanges de l'École française de Rome, moyen âge–temps modernes* (2013): 125-1, available at http://mefrm.revues.org/1143.

72. Louis Duval-Arnould, "John XXII," in *The Papacy: An Encyclopedia*, ed. Philippe LeVillain (London: Routeldge, 2001), vol. 2, 850–851.

73. Giovanni Villani, *Cronica di Giovanni Villani*, ed. and trans. Ignazio Moutier and Pietro Massai (Florence, 1823), vol. 6, 53–57.

74. John E. Weakland, "Administrative and Fiscal Centralization under Pope John XXII, 1316–1334," *Catholic Historical Review* 54.1 (1968): 39–43.

75. Villani, *Cronica di Giovanni Villani*, 59.

76. Emmanuel Le Roy Ladurie, *Montaillou: Village occitan* (Paris: Gallimard, 1975), trans. Barbara Bray as *Montaillou: The Promised Land of Error* (New York: George Braziller, 1978).

77. Marc Dykmans, *Le cérémonial papal de la fin du moyen âge à la renaissance: Les textes Avignonnais jusqu'à la fin du grand schisme d'occident* (Brussels: Institut historique belge de Rome, 1983), vol. 2, 168–169.

78. Favier, *Les papes d'Avignon*, 126.

79. Villani, *Cronica di Giovanni Villani*, book XI, chap. 21, 58–59.

80. Currently it is being translated into English by Nancy Stork at San José State University; see "Inquisition Records of Jacques Fournier," available at http://www.sjsu.edu/people/nancy.stork/jacquesfournier/.

81. Paul Amargier, "Benedict XII," in *The Papacy: An Encyclopedia*, ed. Philippe Levillain (New York: Routledge, 2002), 161.

82. Favier, *Les papes d'Avignon*, 127–128.

83. Philip Hughes, *History of the Church: The Revolt against the Church, Aquinas to Luther* (Westminster: Sheed and Ward, 1947), vol. 3, 178.

84. A partial text of the bull is available on the website of the Order of Cistercians of the Strict Observance at http://www.ocso.org/index.php?option=com_docman&Itemid=120&lang=en.

85. Cited in Amargier, "Benedict XII," 161.

86. See Bernard Guillemain, "Benedetto XII," at Treccani, *Enciclopedia dei Papi*, http://www.treccani.it/enciclopedia/benedetto-xii_(Enciclopedia_dei_Papi)/.

87. Arnald of Sarrant, *Chronicle of the Twenty-Four Generals of the Order of Friars Minor*, trans. Noël Muscat, O.F.M. (Malta: TAU Franciscan Communications, 2010), 79–80, 530.

88. Favier, *Les papes d'Avignon*, 130.

89. A detailed account of the construction of the palace is addressed in a later chapter.

90. Franz Ehrle, "Zur Geschichte des Schatzes, der Bibliothek und des Archivs der Päpste im vierzehnten Jahrhundert," *Archiv für Literatur- und Kirchengeschichte des Mittelalters* 1 (1885): 296–299.

91. *The Wars of Edward III: Sources and Interpretations,* ed. Clifford J. Rogers (Woodbridge: Boydell, 1999), 70.

92. Mollat, *The Popes at Avignon,* 252.

93. Mollat, *The Popes at Avignon,* 252; Favier, *Les papes d'Avignon,* 402.

94. Edward III had a claim to the throne of France as grandson of Philip the Fair. France was at the time trying to recover lands controlled by the British in France, remnants of Eleanor of Aquitaine's inheritance.

95. Karsten Plöger, *England and the Avignon Popes: The Practice of Diplomacy in Late Medieval Europe* (London: Legenda, 2005), 181.

96. Guillemain, "Benedetto XII."

97. Guillemain, *La cour pontificale,* 134–136.

98. Guillemain, *La cour pontificale,* 156.

TWO
Papal Monarchy

There is no doubt that the seventeen cardinals who quickly decided on the election of Pierre Roger as Benedict XII's successor chose the "star" of the college. Étienne Baluze's *Lives of the Avignon Popes* accentuates the rapidity with which Clement VI was elected in order to underscore the unanimous decision of the college. "He was *immediately* [my emphasis] elected pope in Avignon" on May 7, 1342, and was crowned in the large Dominican convent on May 19; the apostolic see had remained vacant for only thirteen days.[1] Clement's close rapport with the French crown in combination with the attendance of the Duke of Normandy (the future king of France, John the Good) led detractors to insist on his French partiality. On the other hand, expectations for Clement's pontificate ran so high that the second chronicler of his life reports that since he was crowned on the day of Pentecost, a tongue of fire illuminated his crown's jewels, as if he himself received the blessing of the Holy Spirit.[2]

In his history of the Avignon popes, Jean Favier clarifies, "He [Pierre Roger] had acquired the reputation of a skillful and intelligent diplomat, an impartial mediator, and an expert in political life."[3] For Favier, the cardinals unanimously elected an exceptional man. Pierre Roger chose Clement as his papal name to emphasize what he considered the emblematic qualities of a pope: mercifulness and leniency. Like his predecessors, Clement staunchly defended the sovereignty and infallibility of the papacy and acted to protect the Church from secular infringement. Ironically, Clement's accomplishments have disappeared behind the dark veneer laid down by his detractors. He has become the emblematic repre-

sentative of the Avignon popes, their ostentatiousness, venality, and pro-
clivity for worldly court life. While the latter description partially exag-
gerates the truth, Clement was indeed remembered to have said, *"Prede-
cessores nostri nesciverunt esse papa"* (Our predecessors did not know how
to be pope), stressing his own elevated conception of his office. [4]

Still, it is important to remember that Clement dealt with many pressing issues during his papacy, including the traditional foreign policy
quagmire in Italy, the Hundred Years' War between England and France,
and the condemnation of Louis of Bavaria in the empire. He is the pope
who defined the Christian jubilee and the theology of indulgences and,
above all, faced the greatest existential crisis of the Middle Ages with the
arrival of the Black Death in 1348. As his biographer Diana Wood states:

> Clement VI was a fascinating and controversial figure. He has often
> been regarded as the most typical of the Avignon popes, and has there-
> fore tended to be the most vilified of them. He has been seen as the
> symbol of the period of 'Babylonish captivity', a period said to be deca-
> dent and devoid of ideas, and sullied with nepotism and vice, a period
> when the popes were entirely in thrall to the French monarchy. This
> apart, his pontificate, 1342–52, was an exceptionally eventful one. [5]

HOW TO BE POPE: THE PAPAL MONARCHY OF CLEMENT VI

Pierre Roger was a native of southern France, from Limousin, born into
the minor nobility (his father was Lord of Rosières) at the Castle of Mau-
mont, in the diocese of Tulle. Pierre Roger's career accelerated at lightning speed. After studying with the Black Monks at a local priory, in 1301
he joined the Benedictine abbey of La Chaise-Dieu; Pierre was ten years
old at the time. In 1307 he left for Paris in order to pursue his studies in
theology and canon law. There "the young monk's reputation as a theologian, canonist, orator, and teacher began to increase by leaps and
bounds." [6] In one famous discourse, he compared Aquinas to Augustine;
in another, he debated against the *Defensor pacis*. An anecdote attached to
his time at La Chaise-Dieu insists that Pierre continued to travel often
between Paris and his alma mater, even though he was once attacked by
robbers in the forest of Randan in Auvergne and suffered a head wound.
The prestigious abbey gained further fame through the accomplishments
of its brilliant monk.

Pierre was promoted to master in theology, *laudabiliter*, in 1323, and after receiving a few smaller benefices was nominated abbot of Fécamp in Normandy in 1326. This new office made him at once vassal to the kings of both England and France, as he continued to "serve" the French king as councillor and preacher. It is at the French court that he met the future Holy Roman emperor Charles IV, who explains his friendship with the future pope:

> One of his [Philip's] councilors was a very sagacious man, the abbot of Fécamp originally from Limoges, a persuasive person of cultured and upright character. He preached on Ash Wednesday, the first year of Philip's rule as king, and then he celebrated Mass so quickly that he won everyone's gratitude. After King Charles' death, with whom I had lived for five years, I lived with Philip whose sister became my wife. The command of language and beauty of expression in that sermon of the abbot, while I looked at him and listened to his words, pleased me so much that I was suddenly moved to question why so much grace flowed down upon me from him. I came to know him intimately, and he lovingly helped me like a father even teaching me the Holy Scriptures privately.[7]

With the recommendation of Pope John XXII, Pierre was made bishop of Arras in 1328, an appointment that received the strong support of the new king of France, Philip VI of Valois. With this additional charge, the young monk became versed in temporal and ecclesiastical affairs, gaining experience and doing favors that worked to his advantage. He entered the French parliament in 1329 and was elevated to archbishop, first of Sens and then Rouen in 1330. Pierre quickly became the confidant of Philip VI, entering the royal council, the Chambre des enquêtes of parliament, and finally heading the Chambre des comptes, that is, the treasury, all in the same year. The culmination of Pierre's rapid rise at the French court came with his promotion to chancellor of France, which he also achieved in 1330. It is of note that these promotions initiated by the king occurred as he argued against French royal taxation of the clergy and vehemently defended the Church's jurisdiction against the crown. Clement showed his rectitude in that he did not yield to what could be perceived as his employer's pressure—he considered himself a man of the Church before he was a servant of the king. His diplomatic skills were put to the test during the beatific vision controversy, when John XXII turned to Pierre and his skills to regain the confidence of the house of France.[8]

It is during his tenure at Rouen that, according to John Wrigley, Pierre Roger supported several of his kinsmen who had joined the ranks of the clergy. Wrigley lists a long series of collaborators and friends who profited from Pierre's new position to demonstrate that Pierre's nepotism mainly touched his ecclesiastical collaborators instead of his kin. This favoritism continued when Benedict XII promoted him to cardinal of Santi Nereo e Achilleo in 1338.[9] Still, Pierre Roger's behavior was not unusual for his time and station. Most medieval historians argue that nepotism as practiced in Avignon offered the popes a trustworthy elite on whom they could rely. As Pierre Jugie emphasizes, once Pierre became pope,

> Although he [Clement] allowed his lay relations to profit from his fortune, to which they owed, in large part, their riches, it is particularly to ecclesiastics of his family that he ensured brilliant careers. Of the 25 cardinals he created, 19 came from the South of France among them 11 Limousins (the others were 2 French from the North, one Castilian, and 3 Italians). Among them were his own brother Hugues and five cousins, including Pierre Roger de Beaufort, the future Gregory XI. He peopled the Curia with Limousins, especially in key posts.[10]

When the college chose Pierre Roger as the next pope in 1342, "Cardinals did not choose to elect a paragon of piety. They knew that Pierre Roger had nothing in him of a humble man. The conclave chose deliberately a great lord and a statesman."[11] Perhaps what distinguished Clement from other Avignon popes was his willingness to bring the grandeur of "Rome" to its new city. As his predecessors had only assuaged "exile," Clement constructed an Avignonese papal identity that paralleled that of Rome. In Avignon he legitimated Italian leaders such as Cola di Rienzo and Joanna of Naples, and he was the first pope to use the palace for ritual functions that paralleled those that had been performed in Rome. Clement's new palace actually replicated Rome's sacred space; thus, he brought the sacred city within his palace's walls.

It is difficult to assess whether the population at large lauded Clement's election in the late spring of 1342. In Baluze's *Lives of the Avignon Popes*, the election is first discussed with reference to the floods that plagued Germany, France, and the "entire world" the first summer of his rule. It rained so much that in many cities, people desperately clung to life on city walls as bridges and towers collapsed; in Avignon, people had to navigate the streets in little boats.[12] One of Clement's earliest acts was to attend to the thousands of poor clerics who crowded the city in hopes of receiving his "grace," that is, a benefice. Peter of Herenthals put their number at one hundred thousand, and (even though he certainly exaggerated) this provides a sense of the population surge that followed a papal election. [13] Next, Clement met with Roman representatives begging for his return to the banks of the Tiber. Although the Romans urged him to reconsider his position, Clement insisted on remaining in Avignon, but he offered them an important gift, both spiritually and materially rewarding: he declared 1350 a jubilee year. It was Boniface VIII who had first begun the practice of the "jubilee year," first declaring 1300 a year of special grace for pilgrims visiting Rome and its basilicas. An occasion of great spiritual benefit to Christian believers, in the jubilee year pilgrims received special indulgences and remission of the penalties for their sins to be suffered in the afterlife. But of equally important benefit materially, a jubilee was an economic boon for the city and became a distinctive highlight in the reign of the pope who mandated it. Clement, of course, did not know at the time that the arrival of the Black Death in 1348 would give special meaning to his jubilee. Clement explained his decision to halve the span of time separating holy years, from a century to only fifty years, as a means of accommodating infinite spiritual graces to limited human proportions. Few humans lived one hundred years, thus a shorter span afforded greater numbers the opportunity to partake in the benefits of the jubilee.

Although he could not have known it at the time of its publication, Clement's bull *Unigentius Dei filius*, dated January 27, 1343, came to define the Catholic Church's theory on indulgences and ultimately helped to lay the foundations for the revolt of Martin Luther and the Reformation. The bull recognized the existence of a "treasury of merits of the Church in Heaven" that was solely available to the pope who, as Vicar of Christ on earth, could dispense these merits at will (as he did with the Church's temporal goods). The pope thus began to define the theology of indulgences; he could distribute the "treasury of merits" as he distributed benefices in the temporal world. [14] An additional text specified which churches pilgrims needed to visit and how long they had to remain in the city (fifteen to thirty days) to receive their full indulgence. [15] The promulgation of the Jubilee Year of 1350 underscored the solicitous care that the pope showed for Rome's spiritual and economic survival. [16]

CLEMENT VI AND ROME: COLA DI RIENZO

Amid the group of Roman citizens who petitioned Clement for his return to Rome stood a young notary, the humble son of an innkeeper with a most unusual future, Cola di Rienzo. In Avignon Rienzo met and struck up a friendship with the great Petrarch, and their correspondence details their relationship. It was under Petrarch's direction that Rienzo read avidly about the rich history of the Eternal City. According to Rienzo's anonymous biographer (the *Anonimo romano*), his travel to Avignon in 1342 marked the culmination of a series of events that had started with the presumed unavenged murder of Rienzo's younger brother. He blamed this personal loss on Rome's endemic violence, exacerbated by poor municipal governance. Cola's thirst for revenge drove his personal ambition, political education, and rise, and finally secured his nomination to the Roman embassy to the papal court at Avignon. [17] According to Ronald Musto's recent biography, Rienzo "was regarded even then as the best orator in Rome and would soon be known as the best of his age. Cola knew well the art and technique of public speaking." [18] It is quite easy to understand how the brilliant orator at once intrigued and captivated a pope who was fascinated with words and rhetoric. Clement made him a papal notary. [19] In 1344, Rienzo returned to a Rome still in the clutches of the inevitable bad governance of the Orsini and Colonna families and their political networks. [20]

In May 1347, Rienzo took action. Backed by the anti-Colonna barons and their respective networks, he staged a coup to restore imperial Rome, making himself a tribune. His "revolution" harked back to the city's mythical past and yearned for the return of the so-called good governance (*buono stato*) of the virtuous Romans. Petrarch, who could not participate, supported the movement from afar and enjoined his friend to exemplify the merits of those ancient worthies he had encountered in his studies. Rienzo organized an army that defeated the baronial resistance (November 20, 1347) but then quickly dismissed them, owing perhaps to his unstable and volatile temperament or his own hubris. Unfortunately for Rienzo, in December the Colonna took the city back and he was expelled. In the meantime, he had managed at once to threaten mutual enemies (such as the Avignon pope and the Roman barons) and to alienate the Roman commune, who soon grew tired of his taxes and tyranny.

As recent historiography has shown, Rienzo—who may be viewed variously as a tyrant, patriot, or martyr—became enthralled with Rome's imperial history and was most skillful at manipulating myth, symbols, and ritual. He knew how to exploit both the collective memory that Romans had of their own past and their common frustration with baronial violence, intimidation, and exactions. After his expulsion, Rienzo continued his endeavors, prophesying the fall of the current pope and the rise of a new saint, Francis of Assisi. He found refuge in the Abruzzi during the Black Death and eventually made his way to Prague, where he presented his case to the Holy Roman emperor Charles IV. He was arrested there in 1350, brought to Avignon, tried by the Inquisition, and eventually released by Clement's successor, Innocent VI, in 1352.[21] Supported by the new pope, Rienzo was sent to Cardinal Albornoz, papal legate in Italy for the reconquest of the Papal States, who planned to use him as leverage against the Roman barons. Rienzo reentered Rome in 1354. By that time, he had been appointed senator. But Rienzo quickly fell into some form of madness or delusion that rendered him violent and somewhat incoherent, costing him the support of the Roman people. The barons, especially the Colonna, exacted long-sought revenge, motivating an angry mob to hack Rienzo to death two months later.

The pope's role in Rienzo's story exemplifies how the Avignon papacy never lost oversight of the old capital. Involvement with Rome, city and myth, was the linchpin of papal authority and policy. Melding Avignon into Rome legitimated Avignon and allowed the papacy to project its authority in temporal and spiritual matters. As Diana Wood states, "It was vital that the identity between Rome and the universal Church should be accepted by all Christians, and it needed to be spelt out especially to Eastern Christians, those who had no Roman conditioning on which to draw."[22] Clement remained intransigent with the Eastern Christians, making little effort to reunite Catholic and Orthodox churches but instead sending mendicant missionaries to Armenia and the Caucasus, for example, to convert them to Latin Christianity.

CLEMENT VI AND JOANNA OF NAPLES

Southern Italy also remained on Clement's mind. The life and rule of Queen Joanna of Naples (1326–1382) is closely associated with the Avignon papacy since she led the powerful Kingdom of Naples, a vassal and staunch supporter of the papacy. Her long and tumultuous rule involved many popes, from Clement VI to Clement VII, and she played a significant role in the diplomacy of many pontiffs. Joanna was the daughter of Robert of Anjou's eldest son, the Duke of Calabria. More to the point, she was the great-granddaughter of the founder of the Angevin dynasty in Italy, Charles I of Anjou, brother of Saint Louis. Charles I had received Naples and Sicily from the papacy in the 1260s as a reward for his conquest of what was then Hohenstauffen territory. From that point on, the King of Naples became a vassal of the pope. This Angevin southern kingdom buffered the papal territories from southerly attacks; preserving them from unfriendly Ghibelline hands was an absolute necessity. The Angevins eventually lost Sicily to Aragon (during the Sicilian Vespers in 1282), but the dream of Italian conquests remained a cornerstone of French foreign policy for many years. Joanna of Naples was also Countess of Provence and Forcalquier, a role drawing her closely to the Avignon papacy as she was overlord of the territory on which it resided. This is why she was easily convinced to sell Avignon to the pope in 1348. Last, as titular queen of Jerusalem (a somewhat empty title since the Christian Levant had vanished in the fourteenth century), Joanna's rule represented hope for future crusades.

Born in 1326, Joanna was betrothed as a child to Andrew of Hungary; they wed in 1342. Andrew was a somewhat distant relative, the son of Carobert (himself a son of Robert of Anjou's brother and, as such, her cousin thrice removed). He represented the eastern branch of the Angevins, who considered Naples their own. In any event, dynastic politics backfired. Once married, Joanna insisted that her husband remain strictly a prince consort. This caveat greatly peeved her Hungarian in-laws, especially her brother-in-law King Louis of Hungary, who resented the fact that Andrew could not rule.[23] As a result, Naples divided into several factions, variously defending or reviling Joanna for fully assuming her role as queen. Her detractors, uncomfortable with Joanna's enthusiastic embrace of her royal duties, sent envoys to the pope in order to convince him to allow Andrew to rule with and for her—and be crowned. Joanna's behavior was construed as a reversal of the natural order, one that must be corrected. Petrarch was unsparing in his disparagement of the city and its queen, accusing her of all sorts of things, but deploring especially her tolerance for gladiator games within the city. He fumed, "But is it any wonder that they act brazenly under the cover of darkness without witnesses, when in this Italian city in broad daylight with royalty and the populace as spectators infamous gladiatorial games are permitted of a wildness that is greater than we associate with barbarians?"[24]

But Joanna stood firm, defending her administration and refusing to allow the coronation of her spouse. She argued that as his wife she was the person most likely to advance his best interests. At first the pope agreed with her and was not inclined to see Naples allied with Hungary, but the kingdom grew so fractious that in 1345 he decided to send his legate, Aimery de Châlus, to oversee her administration and coronation (alongside her husband). The issue became moot, however, when, on September 18, 1345, on the eve of his coronation, Andrew was brutally murdered, strangled, stabbed, sexually mutilated, hanged, and defenestrated.[25]

Joanna was immediately considered the instigator of the murder, labeled a she-wolf and unfit to rule. Andrew's brother, King Louis of Hungary, and his mother, Elizabeth, requested her deposition and her crown, but Clement (as overlord of Naples) temporized. He sided with Joanna's cousins, Charles of Durazzo and Robert of Taranto, allowing a purge of her court as a compromise. Infuriated, Louis of Hungary invaded Naples in 1347–1348 while Joanna fled to Avignon with her new husband, her cousin, Louis of Taranto (Louis and Robert were sons of Philip of Taranto, Robert of Anjou's brother). It was while in Avignon that Joanna "mortgaged" the city to the pope for the sum of eighty thousand florins. At the same time, Emperor Charles IV, as suzerain of Provence, surrendered to the pope his feudal rights to the city (a testament to Clement's negotiating skills).[26] With her coffers refilled, Joanna was able to regain Naples and her throne in July 1348. She was eventually crowned alongside her husband in 1352.[27] As for Louis of Hungary, after a second failed attempt to take Naples in 1350, he abandoned that effort in order to pressure Venice and to further crusades in Lithuania and Bulgaria. The inept rule of Louis of Taranto, who basically seized control of Naples from Joanna, and the failed attempt at regaining Sicily kept Joanna at least in the thoughts (if not in the favor) of the pope. In December 1352, Clement died (Louis lived on until 1363), but there is no doubt that the queen's adventures weighed heavily on Clement's mind.[28]

CLEMENT VI AND ITALY: MILAN AND LOUIS OF BAVARIA

Rome and Naples were not the pope's only Italian preoccupations. Clement wavered for many years in his relations with traditionally Ghibelline Milan. The archbishop of this powerful city in north-central Italy had been an early supporter of Louis of Bavaria and his antipope, Nicholas V. After Louis's excommunication, Giovanni Visconti returned to Avignonese obedience and received his archbishopric. This did not stop him from invading Bologna, an act that incurred papal excommunication. Clement then recanted, choosing to appease rather than antagonize, and he offered Visconti the vicariate of Bologna for twelve years.[29] His hesitations may be indicative of Clement's diplomatic savvy; offering a high position to a Visconti may have been a way of ingratiating the Ghibellines to the pope. Still, the Ghibelline party was buttressed by Louis of Bavaria's positions (even if erratic). Louis's alliance with Edward III against France lasted until 1341; the emperor then returned his support to France. The emperor's use of dynastic policies (rewarding his wife, son, cousins, and nephews with lands) allowed him to concentrate more territory into his hands and alienate German princes. In July 1346 Clement opted to support the election of his former student, Charles IV of Luxembourg, as rival emperor. In doing so, the pope received assurances that the new emperor would defend the Church and steer away from Italian affairs, abandoning large chunks of land in Provence to the pope. Meanwhile, Louis maintained the allegiance of the Teutonic Knights, whom he supported in their northern and Eastern "crusades," and of the Hanseatic and imperial cities. The struggle between both emperors could have festered a long time and divided German allegiances, but Louis died in October 1347, putting an end to some twenty years of papal and imperial contention.[30] It is quite remarkable that even before Louis's death in 1347, Cola di Rienzo, taking his office as tribune of Rome extremely seriously, called on both rival emperors, the imperial electoral college, and representatives of the free cities of Italy to conduct a new election![31] But no one listened. With the disappearance of Louis of Bavaria, the pope became free to focus on his main preoccupation: negotiating a long-lasting peace between England and France.

CLEMENT VI: ARBITER OF THE HUNDRED YEARS' WAR

Clement's rise to prominence paralleled the end of the French Capetian dynasty and the advancement of the House of Valois. When Charles IV of France died in 1328, the circumstances of his succession brought to light a painful reality. As the last of Philip the Fair's sons, Charles died without any living male descendants. The lack of male heirs allowed Philip's daughter Isabelle and her male descendants a possible claim to the throne of France. Capetian lawyers made sure that this would not happen, reenacting the early medieval Salic law that prohibited a woman (and her children) from ascending the French throne. One is forced to wonder whether the law would have been revived were Isabelle of France and Edward II of England not married. British hopes were doused when the throne passed to Philip VI of Valois, a cadet branch of the Capetian (he was the son of Charles, a brother of Philip the Fair). This election left Edward III of England, son of Isabelle and Edward II, bitter and crestfallen. Herein lies a central cause of the Hundred Years' War.

Regardless of French dynastic policy, Philip VI favored Pierre Roger (as had his cousin, the late French king Charles). There is no doubt that the French crown favored an influential rising star of its own in the Church. Philip named Pierre Roger bishop of Arras shortly after his coronation. The king further advanced Pierre Roger with promotions to the archbishopric of Sens and later Rouen, even though Roger opposed some of Philip's policies (especially his taxation of the French clergy).[32] Pierre participated in the king's assembly at Vincennes in December 1329, which attempted to settle ecclesiastical and royal prerogatives; the archbishop valiantly protected the French church. Philip also requested in 1328 that Pierre accompany the failed embassy requiring Edward of England to present his homage to the king of France for his territory in Guyenne (Bordeaux and the Gascony coast). Edward at first refused, and the territory was confiscated until he finally relented in June 1329. In turn, Pierre met Edward for the confirmation and fealty that the English king owed the king of France for the archbishopric of Rouen and, as such, established the personal rapport that he used later as pope. On numerous occasions, the archbishop attempted without success to mediate a peace between Philip and Edward that would allow their eventual departure together for a crusade.[33]

When the idea of a crusade failed, French and British antagonism revived even further, and Pierre Roger's role as mediator also increased. Still, in 1338, the pope's ally, France, condemned the alliance between Edward and Louis of Bavaria (a staunch enemy of the papacy), justifying posthumously France's confiscation of Guyenne. Edward argued that he went to Louis in retaliation for this seizure of English-claimed territory. Named cardinal in 1339, Pierre assumed greater diplomatic responsibility for this issue, filling a position that John Wrigley defines as "special secretary of state for English and French affairs."[34] There is no doubt that when Pierre ascended to the papal throne he was the best-informed person on the situation. But his partiality and financial support of France made successful negotiations close to impossible. Most authors of the time accused Clement of favoring France; but William of Ockham summarized their views most bluntly when he said, "The said lord Clement is schismatic because he creates schism between the kings of England and France, and favours one side, and provokes wars and strife between them."[35] Clement cannot be accused of not having tried a peaceful solution, however.

Soon after his election in 1342, the pope sent Cardinals Pierre des Prés and Annibaldo Caetani of Ceccano to Brittany in order to negotiate the ineffective Truce of Malestroit (January 19, 1343), which aimed to end the civil war that had originated with the death of the duke of Brittany in 1341. Jean de Montfort, one of the claimants to the duchy of Brittany, was moved by fears of his rival claimant, Jeanne of Penthièvre, wife of Philip VI's nephew, Charles of Blois, and thus had offered his allegiance to England. Montfort's alliance with Edward allowed the English control of several of Brittany's ports, giving them easy access to Normandy and the rest of France. From 1343 to 1344 the pope attempted to organize a conference among all parties to bring them to a peaceful settlement; Clement again acted as mediator.[36] Yet the talks only deadlocked. France viewed the conflict through the lens of its suzerainty over Guyenne, while the English claimed the French crown for themselves, creating an obvious barrier to compromise.

By 1346 the English controlled Brittany and had regained lost territories in Guyenne.[37] Edward prepared to land his forces in Normandy and make his way to Paris to defeat its king, which he accomplished at the Battle of Crécy (August 26, 1346). Before the battle, Edward received cardinals who offered France's terms. According to these terms, Edward could have Guyenne if he were willing to offer his homage to the king of France. He flatly refused and was encouraged in the legitimacy of his claim with his resounding victory in the famous Battle of Crécy. The pope was again embroiled in the talks that led to the Truce of Calais in September 1347, sending Cardinal Annibaldo a second time, accompanied, however, this time by Étienne Aubert, the future Innocent VI. While the Black Death decimated Europe's populace, the truce was extended until 1355.[38] This truce followed the long siege of Calais, where the frustrated Edward III, eager to return to English soil, demanded the lives of the six most prominent bourgeois of the city to spare the rest of the population. Rodin's sculpture has immortalized the moment when the defeated captives presented themselves to the king, nooses around their necks, ready to die for their city. Their lives were spared only when Edward's pregnant wife Philippa interceded with the king on their behalf. Still, Calais's population was expelled and replaced by English inhabitants. The truce maintained something of a status quo between both exhausted camps; England kept its control over Calais, Brittany, Gascony, and Scotland, while France kept its king. In his study of the diplomacy between England and the popes, Karsten Plöger argues that Clement's efforts were never more than the exertions of a "mutual friend" rather than an "arbitrator."[39] Both sides attempted to revive the conflict, but scarce resources and the scourge of the Black Death prevented any large-scale operations.[40]

Clement may have also considered his own papal finances among the many reasons that pushed him to mitigate a costly war. In English eyes, the payment of ecclesiastical taxes to the pope benefited French war coffers; Edward III issued writs preventing papal collectors from levying taxes and calling for their arrest.[41] Edward's earlier statements bloomed into the Statutes of Provisors of 1351 that prevented the pope's handling of the collation (that is, the making of appointments) of English benefices. Considering Clement's considerable investment in making peace between England and France, a peace he pursued for the common good of all parties, there must be no doubt that his failure in this endeavor weighed heavily on his conscience. But the Truce of Calais provided only short relief for the pope and Western Europe.

THE ARRIVAL OF THE BLACK DEATH

The Black Death reached Avignon around Candlemas 1348.[42] The chronicler of Clement's first biography insists on the uniqueness of the event, the appearance of plague on a scale unknown previously in human history. This plague caused ulcers and bumps (buboes, or *bossa*) in the groin area and armpits; its survivors were too few in number to bury the dead. In its throes, parents abandoned children, children abandoned parents; it was a disease that even killed cats, dogs, chickens, and other animals.[43] The impact of the disease will be discussed later, in chapter 5, dedicated to papal Avignon, but here we must pause to examine Clement's actions at the start of the epidemic.

Louis Heyligen of Beeringen accurately described the two early forms of the disease, both pneumonic and bubonic (also mentioning the buboes in the groin and armpits areas); and he attests that on the pope's orders, anatomical examinations were carried out in Italian cities and in Avignon.[44] These efforts to establish the biology of the plague according to the medical standards of his day suggest that Clement possessed a remarkably scientific mind for the time. Heyligen reported that half the population of Avignon died of the plague, requiring the pope to purchase additional burial ground. Clement offered extraordinary spiritual comfort to the immense numbers of dying, granting a plenary indulgence to all those who were both "confessed and contrite."[45] John Aberth reports from contemporary sources that the shortage of priests necessitated a radical solution, and he finds evidence that bishops permitted, in an extraordinary concession, that the dying might confess to anyone (even to a woman) if they could not find a priest.[46] Clement reluctantly allowed penitential processions of flagellants in Avignon on certain days of the week.[47] The pope had condemned flagellants in his bull of October 29, 1349, *Inter solicitudines*.[48] But in time Clement came to withdraw his opposition at the urging of the French crown and the University of Paris.[49] According to contemporary chroniclers, a popular flagellation movement had started in Germany and descended on France, gathering all classes "noble and ignoble" who publically professed for thirty-two days. In one of the most volatile and radically apocalyptic of the popular religious movements of the Middle Ages, the flagellants practiced their peculiar form of penance night and day, half naked, threatening violence if the pope forbade clergy to participate. Tearful and loudly lamenting their sins, the flagellants sang a special song as they fell to the ground in prostration.[50] A chronicler describes the flagellants as *penitentes cruciferos* (penitent crusaders) who counted priests and mendicants among their ranks and in some instances were even led by women. No wonder the pope had anathematized them, for the unconventional organization and radical spirit of the flagellants goes far in helping to explain their condemnation![51]

As often is the case in periods of radicalization, scapegoating occurred. The flagellants' behavior, their songs and religious devotion incited participants and onlookers to anti-Jewish violence in the towns through which they passed. Although in his research John Aberth has refuted any link between the movement and Jewish pogroms, it remains a fact that attacks against Jews multiplied during the plague years. In particular, Jews were accused of poisoning wells, a claim that ran counter to the contemporary logic that surmised the disease was airborne.[52] Clement reacted courageously, protecting the Jewish population by the best means he could. In July 1348 he reissued the 1120 bull *Sicut Judeis*, which originally aimed to protect the Jewish population in the aftermath of the First Crusade. Again in September 1348 Clement instructed his clergy to protect the Jews; he spoke out against the pogroms one more time in October when he pointed to the financial motivations behind the attacks.[53] In this last bull, Clement stated:

> We are nevertheless mindful that Our Saviour chose to be born of Jewish stock when he put on mortal flesh for the salvation of the human race . . . following in the footsteps of our predecessors . . . we have taken the Jews under the shield of our protection, ordering among the rest that no Christian presume in any way to wound or kill Jews, or take their money or expel them from his service before their term of employment has expired . . . it has been brought to our attention by public fame—or, more accurately, infamy—that numerous Christians are blaming the plague with which God, provoked by their sins, has afflicted the Christian people, on poisonings carried out by the Jews . . . yet we should be prepared to accept the force of the argument that it cannot be . . . because throughout many parts of the world the same plague, by the hidden judgment of God, has afflicted and afflicts Jews themselves and many other races who have never lived alongside them.[54]

Clement's bull shows a certain moral courage and logical mind, but he was still a man of his age. Clement spent the entire epidemic, according to Mathias of Neuenburg, "shut up in his chamber where he had large fires continually burning."[55] In addition, Clement composed the text of a special votive Mass to be said in times of plague, a work that remained in use in the Roman Catholic Church until the twentieth century and that earned whoever heard or said it 260 days' worth of indulgence. Popular belief held that people who heard Clement's Mass for five days while carrying a burning candle would not die suddenly.[56]

CLEMENT VI: THE HUMANIST

In her biography of the pope, Diana Wood sees the fledgling signs of early humanism in Clement's official and private behavior. On the one hand, Clement was a man of his time, and his actions were consistent with his era and his preeminent position: he preached, granted indulgences, wrote a Mass, reluctantly allowed the flagellant movement, and credited the belief that the plague was retribution for the grievous sins of his time, perhaps most notably Queen Joanna's murder of her husband, Andrew. Yet on the other hand, the pope perhaps anticipated the interests of later humanist princes: he demonstrated a keen scientific interest, as we have seen, in the anatomical studies he permitted. A collector and student of ancient texts, he patronized scholars and artists at his court, described as Europe's most brilliant.[57] Ronald Musto concludes that Clement must be regarded as an important figure of transition:

> Often called an early humanist pope, he was more a medieval polymath. His interests ranged from crusading history to astronomy; and in the papal library he supplemented the liturgical, legal, and theological collections of John XXII and Benedict XII with the classics, especially Cicero, but also Pliny, Valerius Maximus, and Macrobius, and with books in Hebrew and Arabic. Yet while his many sermons also quote Seneca, Cicero, and Boethius, they reveal not a secular man but one deeply familiar with Scripture, the early church fathers, and Bernard of Clairvaux. Clement was also a great patron of learning and the arts, and his generosity to both office seekers, such as Petrarch, and diplomatic guests was unmatched, his reputation for opulence unrivaled, his ceremony, feasts, and festivals the envy of all other European princes.[58]

The special minted coat of arms that he had etched in the stones of his "new" palace (*d'argent à la bande d'azur accompagnée de six roses de gueules boutonnées d'or, trois en chef et trois en pointe*) tied the pope to that place and the man to his office. The keys of St. Peter and the triple-crowned papal tiara supported the azure band and stars of his family crest. Clement imprinted the stones of the palace with his name and redefined the Avignon papacy. In a campaign to remake Avignon as an *altera Roma,* he renamed many sites in the city so that they might mirror their Roman originals. In 1344 he renamed the Chapel of St. Michael, located above the Tower of the Wardrobe, *Roma.*[59] Clement also built his own great Chapel of St. Peter, intended for papal coronations, in Avignon. Rome's outdoor coronation ritual, which spanned the city between the great axis of the *Via papalis* from St. Peter to St. John Lateran, was now replicated inside the newly revamped palace between the chapels of St. Peter and St. John—the latter decorated by Matteo Giovanetti to honor (just as at the Lateran) both the Baptist and the Evangelist. Bernhard Schimmelpfennig was the first papal historian to identify how Avignon's popes, and especially Clement, linked papal ritual to the palace, uniting the popes and their residence.[60] An architectural history of Clement's new palace shows how his constructions (the Tower of the Wardrobe, the new Audience, the Great Chapel, the gardens, the decorations and painting of the Chambre du Cerf and of the chapels of Saints Martial, Michael, and John) all reflected the brilliant, colorful character of the pope and bound the pope to his French residence.[61] Further, Clement used the large chapel attached to the palace's kitchens to recount the life of the French Saint-Martial, sent by Peter to evangelize his native Limousin. Clement commanded Giovanetti to paint the exquisite frescoes on the chapel's arches that still charm visitors today, a masterpiece of the fourteenth century ordered by a pontiff who certainly proved true the judgment of his times about him: *he knew how to be pope.* Most importantly, Clement was the living incarnation of the saying, "Rome is where the pope is."

Clement VI suffered from gout, gallstones, and purulent abscesses that plagued him his entire life and as a consequence kept many doctors at his court. Despite their efforts, Clement died from a severe hemorrhage on December 6, 1352, after the rupture of a tumor found on his back.[62] His body lay in state in the Cathedral of Notre-Dame des Doms until March 1353; it was then transported to La Chaise-Dieu in accordance with his last wishes. His large and impressive tomb is still visible there today. The cortège that accompanied Clement to La Chaise-Dieu left on February 28, 1353; his successor, Innocent VI, offered the sum of five thousand florins for the journey. The procession included Hugues Roger, the late pope's brother, cardinal of San Lorenzo in Damaso; Guillaume de la Jugie, cardinal deacon of Santa Maria in Cosmedin; Nicolas Besse, cardinal of Santa Maria in Via Lata; Clement's nephew Pierre Roger de Beaufort, the future pope Gregory XI, cardinal deacon of Santa Maria Nova; Clement's cousin, Guillaume d'Aigrefeuille, cardinal of Santa Maria in Trastevere; and Count Guillaume Roger de Beaufort, Clement VI's older brother. Still, the cortège was not as numerous as the forty-four figures who surrounded the pope's tomb at La Chaise-Dieu, representing the kin and friends whom Clement had supported during his reign. In death, as in life, Clement showed himself magnanimous.[63]

LAWYER AND CONQUEROR: INNOCENT VI

The college of twenty-five cardinals that elected Clement VI's successor again acted swiftly. They entered the papal palace in conclave on Sunday, December 16, 1352, and chose Étienne Aubert, cardinal bishop of Ostia, just two days later. But the speediness of the process did not belie the importance of this conclave. The initial choice of the cardinals was a holy man, the Limousin Jean Birel. His lack of experience, according to Cardinal Talleyrand of Périgord, did not fit with the times or circumstances.[64] The college relented and opted instead for Étienne Aubert, who, while not as flamboyant as his predecessor, nevertheless bore the same profile. He was an experienced administrator extremely familiar with the French court. Again the seat of the Holy See was filled by a pope who had served both the courts of France and the Church.

Étienne Aubert was born into the minor nobility of Limousin sometime in the late 1280s. He studied law in Toulouse and received his doctorate in 1330. His began his legal career as a judge in Toulouse in 1321, continuing in this post in the employ of the French crown until 1334. At that date, Philip VI made him his commissioner, counselor, and clerk of the parliament. As such, the king sent Aubert to Avignon on several occasions from 1337 to 1338. Pleasing both the king and pope, he received the bishoprics of Noyon in 1338 and Clermont in 1340. Clement VI named him cardinal of Santi Giovanni e Paolo in September 1342; and in 1348 Aubert became the pope's Grand Penitentiary (dealing with cases of high-ranking confessor-penitents). In February 1352 Clement also named him cardinal-bishop of Ostia and Velletri. This title was prestigious: the cardinal-bishop of Ostia occupied an important liturgical office. He acted as the consecrator of the pope in the papal coronation liturgy. Thus the choice of the cardinals would seem logical—if Aubert had not been old, frail, and in poor health at the time of his election. His physical state betrays the cardinals' intention. They chose someone they could control. As Yves Renouard suggests, he was a pope who "would be harmless" to the cardinals.[65]

The second event that marked this conclave was of great historical significance. Before they named a pope, all the cardinals signed a "conclave capitulation"—the first of its kind in papal history. A papal conclave is a complicated business, not effected in a single stroke. It was, and is, of course, a spiritual affair to determine the leader of the Catholic Church. But leadership entails relations of power and politics, personality, and diplomacy. Christianity evolved significantly over the course of the first millennium of its history, and so did the nomination of a pope and the type of power he wielded. Similarly, the cardinals' role grew with time, from solely liturgical functions in Rome's great basilicas to papal advising and diplomacy. If their freedom of action was limited during a pope's rule, cardinals usually argued in favor of heightened responsibilities during the vacant see. In the thirteenth century, canonists such as Henry of Segusio (the Hostiensis) proposed that during a period of *sede vacante*, in which there was no reigning pontiff, cardinals should supervise the Church's spiritual and temporal matters. The Hostiensis voiced what the cardinals really yearned for, a form of oligarchy in which a council of cardinals ruled alongside the pope. Their dreams were shattered with Gregory X's 1274 bull *Ubi periculum*, which created the conclave. The bull decreed without any ambiguity whatsoever that the sole responsibility of the cardinals during the *sede vacante* was to elect a new pope.

In the conclave of 1352 at Avignon, the cardinals, perhaps motivated by the change of location and Clement's monarchic rule, attempted to regain some of their former power in a context they considered conducive to negotiations: the conclave. They returned to the old dream, putting pressure on all members of the college to accept the capitulation which stipulated that anyone elected would limit his college to twenty cardinals. This rule also stated that a pope would not demote, nominate, or expel any member of the college without that member's consent; that he would ban papal nepotism; and that he would consult cardinals before levying any new subsidies, which should in the event be borne by the treasuries of both the pope and the cardinals. Last, they requested total freedom of expression. Some cardinals accepted the capitulation, solemnly swearing to respect its conditions; others stalled. Étienne Aubert swore "that if one of them were elected, he would observe it insofar as it did not conflict with church law, and that, on election, he would investigate with care the validity of the terms of the document, and, therefore, the validity of their oaths."[66] After researching the topic, on July 6, 1353, Innocent decreed *Sollicitudo pastoralis*, which repudiated the capitulation on the legal grounds that it breached Gregory X's *Ubi periculum*. A conclave could not reform; it only elected a new pope. Innocent also made it clear that as supreme pontiff the pope could not be limited in his actions by anyone.[67] The issue was solved temporarily. But it would reappear again with the Great Western Schism (1378–1417), which brought the cardinals' oligarchic agenda to its full conclusion. It will be discussed in depth in chapter 6.

Once crowned amid great festivities, Innocent settled into the business of ruling. He was not his predecessor; Bernard Guillemain describes him as a pontiff of good intentions but indecisive and somewhat overwhelmed by the task.[68] One of the main issues at hand was the state of the papal treasury, depleted by the grand politics of his predecessor. Even if he wished to, Innocent did not have the means to continue Clement's policies. Thus he had to choose carefully where he would invest his resources. Innocent picked Italy and the reconquest of the Papal States; he was the first pope in many years who considered a return of the papacy to Rome. One could not go without the other. But the task was daunting and expensive; it necessitated almost the entire revenues of the papacy. Numbers are telling. According to Herman Hoberg, the wars in Italy cost the pope 1,549,000 florins at an annual average of 235,000 florins. The papacy income during the entire reign of Innocent reached only some 1,811,622 florins. Hence the treasury could barely survive with this scale of expenses. The pope used his system of tax collectors and raised the funds from Italian taxes at an average of 135,000 florins a year.[69] For the rest, he sold precious objects from the treasury and started borrowing from Italian bankers.

THE LANDS OF ST. PETER

In June 1353 Innocent VI promoted Cardinal Albornoz (the Castilian Gil Álvarez Carillo Albornoz) to vicar general for all the lands of St. Peter and papal legates. Peter Partner has shown that the legates yielded "quasi monarchical powers," going so far as to call them "satrap-legates" to indicate the range of control they held.[70] A member of the Spanish aristocracy (he was of the Luna and Carillo families) and a descendant of the royal lines of Léon and Aragon, Albornoz studied law in Toulouse, where he probably took classes from Étienne Aubert. He entered the court of King Alfonso XI of Castile and occupied several positions there before becoming the leader of the Spanish Church and a political force in Castile. Albornoz was at once archdeacon of Calatrava, canon regular, and chaplain. He became archbishop of Toledo in 1338 and chancellor of Castile in 1339 as he served his king in crusades against the Moors. Jean Favier describes him as energetic, generous, cultivated, a fine politician, and a great warlord (he led the victories of Tarifa in 1340 and Gilbraltar in 1349).[71] A man of the law, he also legislated and drafted the *Ordenamiento de Alcalá* that harmonized Castilian laws and participated in several Spanish synods aimed at reforming the Church. In sum, Albornoz was the most prominent Spaniard of his time. But at the death of Alfonso XI in 1350, he lost his influence at the Castilian court when he quarreled with the king, Pedro the Cruel (Peter of Castile, who sided with Edward III in the Hundred Years' War). That same year Albornoz left for the court of Clement VI in Avignon, where he was made cardinal of San Clemente. Two years later, Clement VI, finding that the man had the qualities required for the task, named him legate and papal vicar of Italy. Innocent similarly trusted in Albornoz's qualities.

The last serious attempt to reconquer the Papal States had occurred more than a generation earlier, in the reign of John XXII (r. 1316–1334), when the failed attempt of Bertrand du Pouget had been distracted by Louis of Bavaria. The Papal States had evolved into a concatenation of petty tyrants who basically ruled for themselves, recognizing papal suzerainty only when it fit their needs, if ever. Albornoz learned the lessons of the past and turned his focus initially on Rome, leaving Lombardy and Milan, along with Archbishop Giovanni Visconti (who had also controlled Bologna since 1350), aside for a while. The legate initiated a strategy that used tactics marked by heavy casualties and collateral damage, mercenary tactics originally tested by the English and French during the Hundred Years' War. The fourteenth century witnessed the result of a tactical move that had gradually replaced the feudal hosts and communal militias of the earlier Middle Ages: paid troops that were largely organized in small independent units, well trained and disciplined and efficiently commanded by their captains, known as *condottieri* (from the Italian word for "contractor" or "captain"). They remained the leitmotif of the Italian campaign; at once used, disbanded, and paid off when necessary.

Albornoz arrived in the Papal States in November 1353 and headquartered in Montefiascone. The city was only one of three that had remained out of Giovanni di Vico's hands. Vico was Rome's hereditary prefect, of Ghibelline allegiance, who controlled most of the Papal States and according to some was attempting to carve out for himself a kingdom on the Italian peninsula. Clement VI had originally excommunicated Vico when he seized the papal cities of Viterbo in 1338, Orvieto in 1352, and later Corneto in 1353. Vico also controlled Umbria (including Perugia, Spoleto, Assisi, and Nocera), a traditionally Guelph region. By late 1353, Clement had freed Cola di Rienzo from his Avignonese jail; now exonerated of heresy, the tribune of Rome joined the legate in his labors. But Cola's imprisonment in Avignon had not solved the Roman issue; the city was still racked by strife, and Vico's unrestrained claims were growing. Thus in September 1353 Innocent decided to send him to Albornoz to "curb [the barons'] criminal appetite with the bit of justice and so that, having stifled all hatred and rancor, he will, with the favor of God and with our aid, cause you and your compatriots to enjoy the prayed for quiet and peace."[72] Following through with Clement's excommunication, Innocent declared Vico contumacious and decreed the legal seizure of his territories. Helped by Rienzo and the Roman militias, Albornoz won hard victories and retook Tuscania, Orvieto, and Viterbo in 1354. He gained the support of his enemy, however, when in a tactical move he returned the seized territories to Vico in the 1354 Treaty of Montefiascone, with the hope of placating Vico's ambition with his recognition of the pope's lordship, of course. As for Cola di Rienzo, he made his fateful reentry into Rome in August 1354 and was stabbed to death in October.

Albornoz, buttressed by the armies of the infamous and expensive German "great companies" and supplemented by troops from Florence, Siena, and Perugia, then aimed his forces against the tyrants of the Romagna region. He confronted first the Malatesta of Rimini, Pesaro, Ancona, and Ascoli. The Malatesta were *condottieri* who had carved out a patrimony in central Italy. Innocent excommunicated the Malatesta in 1354, and in 1355 the pontifical army first took Rimini and quickly seized the rest of the March of Ancona. Albornoz showed a genius for understanding Italian politics when he gave the vicariate of Rimini first to Galeotto Malatesta for ten years; he then changed his mind and replaced him with Albornoz's nephew Blasco Fernandez, judicially keeping Malatesta *gonfaloniere* (standard-bearer) of the papal army.

Albornoz continued his successful strategy of defeat and alliance, sealed by an oath of allegiance to the pope from several tyrants. His approach usually meant returning the conquered territory to the defeated party as a vicariate held in the name of the pope. In return, the vicar provided the papal army with troops and paid an indemnity to the apostolic chamber (the pope's finance ministry) that paid for the next conquests. If this policy worked in the short term, in the end, as Peter Partner argues,

> the apostolic vicariate gave a legitimate title to the formerly abusive domination of certain families in the Papal State, and . . . partly as a result of this it became impossible to eradicate the dominion of these families for the rest of the Middle Ages. Albornoz is usually represented as the great innovator in the imposition of papal sovereignty in the Papal State, but viewed in this light his actions seem very different; he was in another way the man who began a policy of explicitly granting away a lot of important papal government rights.[73]

In 1357 Albornoz ended his first campaign in Italy with his *Constitutiones Sanctæ Matris Ecclesiæ* (*Constitutions of the Holy Mother Church*, usually known as the Egidian Constitutions) that regulated the states of the Church until 1816. In a meeting at Fano he redrew the states into five provinces (Campagne and Maritima, the Duchy of Spoleto, the March of Ancona, the Patrimony of St. Peter, and the Romagna), codified the internal mechanism of each Papal State, and centralized their administration. He called for a papal-appointed rector at their head, who in turn named a council of seven judges for his province. The rector also named the head of his army, with the stipulation that this position could not be granted to a member of his own family.

With his success in central Italy achieved, Albornoz was free to turn to the tyrants of Lombardy, including one of the most powerful enemies of the Church in Italy: the Milanese Visconti family. The papacy used what could be anachronistically labeled a Machiavellian policy with Milan's rulers. The pope temporized with Milan while Visconti, as vicar of Bologna, furnished Albornoz with revenues and troops while the papacy also fought against the ruler of Milan! Sharon Dale estimates that Giovanni Visconti "was the largest single contributor, besides the papal treasury, to Albornoz's military efforts."[74] The Visconti maintained close contact with the papal court, and well-placed lobbyists defended the family's interests. As Peter Partner suggests, it is highly probable that cardinals (like Talleyrand of Périgord) maintained pro-Visconti pressure and that some cardinals were possibly "bought off."[75] Still, keeping peaceful relations in the north, by whatever means necessary, was preferable to war.

In 1354 Archbishop Visconti died, opening the field for internal rivalries between his nephews. Visconti's captain in Bologna, Giovanni di Oleggio, seized the city for himself in 1355. The choice was now in the hands of the Church. It could either defend Matteo Visconti's claim to Bologna or make Oleggio an apostolic vicar, an occasion for the Church to reclaim the city (an idea defended by Albornoz). In 1356 Matteo Visconti asked for papal support against Oleggio, and (after some delay) Innocent sent Androin de la Roche, the abbot of Cluny, to Italy; he eventually replaced Albornoz as legate in May 1357. Jean Favier considers the move "a stab in the back" to Albornoz, arguing that the Milanese ambassadors who came to Avignon spread rumor and intrigue to convince the pope that Albornoz's war was costing the Church a fortune.[76] They were not wrong; yet their attempt first and foremost was to eliminate Albornoz from Italian soil, not restore funds to the Church. The anti-Albornoz cabal won a grand victory when the pope replaced him with Androin de la Roche, a man with no experience in Italian politics, government, or leadership. He presented himself to Albornoz and ordered the legate to deliver Bologna to Visconti. An incensed Albornoz passed his command to de la Roche and returned to Avignon, accompanied by Malatesta and a group of Romagnan nobles now allied with the Church, a definite show of Albornoz's success in his role. It took less than a year for Innocent to realize the gravity of his mistake and to reinstate Albornoz as legate in September 1358. Albornoz then took Forlì in 1358, satisfying its defeated *signore* Ordelaffi with the vicariate of Forlimpopoli. In October 1360 he installed his nephew Blasco Fernandez as rector of Bologna. Visconti attempted in vain to retake the city; Bernabò Visconti lost the Battle of

Rosillo in June 1361, leaving Albornoz's anti-Visconti policies in place until the death of Innocent.

Albornoz had been somewhat successful for Innocent. He had regained at least nominal control of the Papal States but left important territorial charges to vicars who could change their minds at whim. The consequences of Albornoz's legation may have been as psychological as they were military. Partner characterizes the legate called the "Angel of Peace" in these terms: "Albornoz brought a passionate temperament and the highest political and military ability to the task of pacifying central Italy—if 'pacifying' is the right word to use of a man who drenched the Italian countryside with blood from the Po to the Garigliano."[77] The success of the legate was a combination of his strategic use of governance, violence, and fear. These politics of reconquest also underscored new players in the Italian equation: the great companies of mercenaries that remained a thorn in the side of Italy, and France, for that matter, for the rest of the fourteenth century.

THE HUNDRED YEARS' WAR: POITIERS AND ITS AFTERMATH

The Avignon papacy, by virtue of its location and personal ties, followed French politics closely, and all popes remained attached to the idea of peace between France and England. Innocent VI repeatedly sent nuncios to both parties, organized "peace conferences" at the court, but systematically managed little success. The most he could achieve from both parties were prolongations of truces. Innocent chose the cardinal of Porto, Gui of Boulogne, for the task, initially as a nuncio and mediator rather than a legate. Gui of Boulogne was far from being an impartial judge since his niece, Jeanne of Boulogne, had married the king of France, John II the Good, in 1350. The cardinal was at once an uncle of the French king and a cousin of Charles of Navarre, also known as Charles the Bad, who played an important role in all French-English transactions. The English usually viewed Boulogne with suspicion because of his French ties; still, he managed to extend the truce of Calais.[78]

In 1354, Boulogne also negotiated the short-lived Treaty of Mantes between Charles the Bad and John II. Charles held extensive lands in Normandy and set himself up as arbitrator of the war between Edward III of England and John II of France, shifting his allegiance according to his whims and interests. He was John's son-in-law but dreamed of an impossible claim to the throne of France through his mother, the daughter of the late Louis X. Unfortunately for him, Salic law denied his cognatic descent to the throne. In January 1354, Charles openly conspired in the murder of John's favorite, the constable Charles de la Cerda, toward whom he felt marked jealousy. Inconsolable, John decided to arrest Charles and confiscate his Norman property. Charles responded by opening negotiations with the English, forcing John to sign the Treaty of Mantes in February 1354. From that point forward, relations soured quickly, leading John to retake his Norman territories as the pope organized a new peace conference in Avignon.

Edward III was willing to drop his claim to the French crown in exchange for enormous territorial gains in France (the old Aquitaine of Eleanor, Touraine, Ponthieu, Guînes, and Calais) and full suzerainty. The cardinal of Boulogne thus negotiated a meeting in Avignon, this time to ratify the so-called Treaty of Guînes that virtually dismembered France, with the prior approval of all parties. Ambassadors of both kings arrived in the city in November 1354, and discussion began with Charles the Bad, who had been invited for good measure. Unsurprisingly, negotiations went nowhere fast, and both sides recanted their previous approval, leaving the pope and Gui of Boulogne destitute of this long-sought-for peace. The only person who viewed this failure in a good light was Charles the Bad, who seized the occasion to negotiate the partition of France between Edward and himself. Charles did not succeed, however; even the English could not trust him, and their negotiations stalled. John eventually imprisoned Charles in 1356 after catching wind of his scheme.

At this stage, Innocent had few choices but to change course, especially when rumors surfaced blaming Boulogne of having facilitated meetings between Charles the Bad and the Duke of Lancaster, the English representative in Avignon. In general, the historical record has not treated Gui of Boulogne kindly. Still, Pierre Jugie argues that most concessions the cardinal granted the English were directed toward achieving peace at all costs. For Jugie, Boulogne was a grand lord, an aristocrat who leaned toward the pro-Navarre policies of his "house" and aimed at reconciling all parties, regardless of the means. Jugie exonerates the cardinal of any scheme to dismantle France between Navarre and Edward but accuses him of having been dragged into a diplomatic game where his pride got the best of him. [79]

Disappointed in his initial efforts to achieve peace between the French and English, Innocent doggedly pursued his goal, next charging the cardinal of Périgord, Hélie de Talleyrand, often accompanied by Cardinal Niccolo Capocci, to mediate another truce. Since 1355, Edward's son, the Black Prince of Wales, had been raiding Aquitaine from Bordeaux up to the Loire Valley, as papal nuncios ran from one camp to the other attempting to prevent the battle that all felt was inevitable.[80] The famous chronicler Jean Froissart dramatically represented the cardinal of Perigord's speech to the king in these terms:

> Most dear sire, you have here with you all the flower of knighthood of your kingdom against a handful of people, such as the English are, when compared to your army; you may have them upon other terms than by a battle; and it will be more honourable and profitable to you to gain them by this means than to risk such a fine army, and such noble persons as you have now with you. I therefore beseech you, in all humility, and by the love of God, that you will permit me to go to the prince, and remonstrate with him on the dangerous situation he is in.[81]

As the cardinal reminded Edward, "Fair son, if you have well considered the great army of the king of France, you will permit me to make up matters between you both, if I possibly can."[82] All this was to no avail. On September 19, 1356, the impressive forces of John the Good were thoroughly defeated by a lesser army commanded by the Black Prince in one of the most famous and consequential events of the Middle Ages, the Battle of Poitiers. This stands as one of the greatest victories in England's long and distinguished military history. The Black Prince not only won a resounding triumph but captured King John and his son Philip; scores of nobles and elite troops of the French army were killed. All that remained to the cardinals was the challenging task of trying to convince the prince to temper his ire and show magnanimity toward the defeated.

In the wake of this battle, Pope Innocent wrote to the Black Prince reminding him that the forthcoming crusade against the Turks would depend on his grace; terms with France needed to be favorable in order to allow reconciliation and foster a long-lasting peace. Meanwhile, Talleyrand needed to convince the king of France that he should relent and accept English terms. In Bordeaux, Talleyrand proposed to grant all of Aquitaine, in full suzerainty, to the English. Later in London, the king and cardinals discussed the liberation of John the Good, while his son the dauphin (the future Charles V) ruled in the name of his father. Papal nuncios who repeatedly insisted on keeping the French crown on John's head did not convince the English of their goodwill. Even with the pope's replacement of Talleyrand, the English always considered the nuncios little more than representatives of the Valois. According to Henry Knighton, a chronicler from Leicester, a limerick circulating at the time read, "Thus the pope is now French, and Jesus English. Let us see who can do more, the pope or Jesus?"[83]

While negotiations remained active to conclude the English victory of 1356 with a treaty, France went to war with itself; the country suffered the depredations of the free companies of mercenaries that terrorized the countryside now that a truce had been concluded. Their violent, destructive ravaging required the dauphin to raise an army from his *Dauphiné* to fight them. At the same time, the ransom payment needed to free the king antagonized the French nobility. The bourgeoisie of Paris, led by Étienne Marcel, revolted against the dauphin in 1358. The peasantry too, oppressed by taxes, mercenaries, and the nobility's failure to protect them, followed suit that same year in their own rebellion, the infamous *Jacquerie*. The dauphin managed to respond to every threat with the help of his father, who negotiated the Treaty of London with Edward III in 1358. It was a treaty that granted a third of France to England and the payment by France of a ransom of three million gold ecus, while Edward renounced his claim to the French crown.

The Treaty of London precipitated events in Paris. Étienne Marcel, outraged by the "treacherous" clauses of the treaty, attacked the dauphin in Paris and killed his three marshal-generals with the hope of controlling the young man himself. Assisted by the Estates General, Marcel instituted a constitutional regency, naming the dauphin regent. The dauphin grudgingly accepted this guardianship but balked at the liberation of Charles the Bad—who was greeted by many as the savior of France and granted an army. After escaping Paris, the dauphin could only witness the brutal repression of the *Jacquerie* by Charles the Bad and other barons such as Gaston of Foix. By then, the peasants' resentment against the nobility, their anger at the numerous French defeats and the increased burden of higher taxation, and the lack of protection against the roaming free companies had reached Paris. Étienne Marcel seized the occasion to join the movement. Marcel supported the peasants for a while only, until they stopped serving his larger purpose: an alliance with Charles the Bad to install in France a form of parliamentary monarchy.

After his victory against the peasantry, Charles the Bad entered Paris as captain of the town, hoping that an "urban league" could change the political dynamics, creating a situation in which he might be offered the crown. But many French nobles, naturally suspicious of his behavior, joined the dauphin in exile and left the Parisian defense of Charles the Bad in the hands of his English mercenaries. In June 1358, the dauphin began to besiege Paris, supplemented by troops of mercenaries anxiously waiting to loot the city. Charles the Bad's English mercenaries became his Achilles' heel. The Parisians (unsurprisingly) revolted against them after they had killed many citizens in skirmishes clearly drawn along nationalistic lines. Fearing Charles the Bad would bring reinforcements with the arrival of more English mercenaries, the Parisians returned their allegiance to the dauphin and killed Étienne Marcel. The dauphin reentered his city on August 2, 1358, while Charles the Bad and his English troops ransacked the Île-de-France until they retreated to Navarre. Still, companies of *routiers*—roaming mercenary troops—harassed the countryside for the rest of the century, pillaging and ransoming people, whole villages, sometimes entire cities, even going so far as to attack the neighborhoods of Avignon.

It was in this context that the Treaty of Brétigny, which freed John the Good from English captivity, was negotiated. Innocent VI sent Androin de la Roche to the kings, who agreed to the thirty-nine articles of the treaty on May 25, 1360. They ratified the document in Calais that October, both kings accompanied by their eldest sons. Edward III received Aquitaine more or less in free suzerainty but gave up Touraine, Anjou, and Maine and suzerainty of Brittany and Flanders, and he rescinded his claim to the throne of France. John had to pay a ransom of three million gold ecus and was to be freed, along with ten other prisoners, after a third of the ransom was paid. He left two of his sons, several nobles, and some of the French bourgeoisie as surety. The rest of the ransom was to be paid in sixths, every six months, with one fifth of the hostages freed in each instance. Shortly after his liberation, John decided to travel to Avignon to discuss with the pope the proposed marriage of his son Philip to Joanna of Naples and the possibility of leading a crusade, an act he hoped would rehabilitate his kingly image. Most of all, his visit served to thank the pope and the Apostolic Chamber, who had produced nine hundred thousand ecus for his ransom. John learned of Innocent's death in 1362 as he was making his way toward Provence.[84] Thus, after close to sixty years of mediation, the papacy had still not succeeded in pacifying France and England in order to resume its crusading effort. Brétigny offered a temporary truce that ended up lasting nine years, but it was no permanent solution.

THE FREE COMPANIES IN PROVENCE

The events in the aftermath of the Battle of Poitiers were, in an indirect way, of dire consequence for the Avignon papacy. In the last clause of the Treaty of Brétigny, Edward condemned all acts of war perpetrated by English soldiers:

> [A]nd as it may fall out or happen that some warriors from our king-
> dom, or other of our subjects, may endeavour to do or undertake things
> contrary to the said peace by taking or detaining forts, towns, cities and
> castles, or in pillaging and arresting persons, and taking from them
> their goods, merchandise or other things, acting against the said peace
> (the which will highly displease us, and we cannot nor will not suffer
> it, nor pass it over under any sort of dissembling); We, willing to reme-
> dy these aforesaid things with all our powers, wish, desire, and ordain,
> by the deliberation of our council, that none of our subjects or allies,
> whatever their state or condition may be, do, or endeavour to do, any
> thing contrary to the said peace, by pillaging, taking, or detaining forts,
> persons or goods of any sort in the kingdom of France, or belonging to
> our said brother, his subjects, allies or adherents whomsoever.[85]

Yet this grave warning had little effect on the European continent.

The free companies of mercenaries, unemployed in the north since the 1356 truce, subsequently made their way down to more promising lands. As early as May 1357 the company of the archpriest Arnaud de Cervole invaded Provence.[86] Froissart is again our guide to the events. He states:

> About this period, a knight, named sir Arnold de Cervole, but more
> commonly called the Archpriest, collected a large body of men at arms,
> who came from all parts, seeing that their pay would not be continued
> in France, and that, since the capture of the king, there was not any
> probability of their gaining more in that country. They marched first
> into Provence, where they took many strong towns and castles, and
> ruined the country by their robberies as far as Avignon. Pope Innocent
> VI., who resided in Avignon, was much alarmed, as not knowing what
> might be the intentions of the archpriest, the leader of these forces; and,
> for fear of personal insult, he and the cardinals kept their households

armed day and night. When the archpriest and his troops had pillaged all the country, the pope and clergy entered into treaty with him. Having received proper security, he and the greater part of his people entered Avignon, where he was received with as much respect as if he had been son to the king of France. He dined many times with the pope and cardinals, who gave him absolution from all his sins; and, at his departure, they presented him with forty thousand crowns, to distribute among his companions. These men, therefore, marched away to different places, following, however, the directions of the archpriest.[87]

But Froissart, as a grand admirer of these men-at-arms, obviously exaggerated. Papal sources demonstrate that indeed the curia feared Cervole's incursions, but there are no records of any dinners and entertainment! The registers of the Apostolic Chamber are filled with expenses incurred from the dispatching of couriers and troops that closely followed the mercenaries' movements and attacked them when needed.[88] In July 1357 Innocent clearly designated Cervole (alias the Archpriest) as a captain of a company.[89] The pope then dispatched one of his squires with a letter requiring Cervole to make his intentions clear, brandishing the spiritual punishments he would incur if he entered papal territory. Cervole responded that he planned to attack only Louis, King of Sicily, and not the pope. But a skeptical Innocent called for the help of the emperor and of the captive king of France. With their aid, by the end of July Innocent had committed hundreds of troops to the defense of the Comtat Venaissin and Avignon.[90]

Cervole was eventually bought off with one thousand florins and joined the ranks of Charles the Bad's troops. A couple of years later, additional bands of mercenaries, the so-called *Tard-venus* (in French, literally "the late-comers") and *Grandes compagnies* pillaged a path through Burgundy and Beaujolais, finally arriving in the neighborhood of Avignon at Pont-Saint-Esprit by the end of 1360. After taking this city, they controlled access to Avignon and Languedoc, disrupting vital supply lines to the region. In response, the pope initiated the construction of Avignon's protective new ramparts still visible today. (Their construction is discussed in chapter 5.) The pope proclaimed a crusade against Charles the Bad and Cervole after their excommunications but continued to pay them off when needed. In his letters, Innocent rationalized the crusade by the fact that the bands menaced the papacy and thus constituted an attack on Christendom itself, but in fact the crusade went nowhere.[91] In 1361 the *routiers* agreed to leave Pont-Saint-Esprit for campaigns in Languedoc, Italy, or Aragon. Some eventually made their way back to the north, and others joined the troops of Henry of Trastámara and his efforts to claim the Castilian throne, while others pursued further mercenary adventures elsewhere.

The complicated and precarious situation in France had not prevented the pontiff from contemplating the affairs of Spain and pursuing the policy of his predecessor. Clement VI had encouraged the marriage of Pedro of Castile to a French princess, the fourteen-year-old Blanche of Bourbon. Medieval diplomacy and international politics were often carried through by means of marital alliances. Such an alliance, sealed by proxy in July 1352, reinforced the diplomatic ties binding Castile to France just as the Hundred Years' War erupted. Unfortunately for Blanche, the young Pedro only had eyes for his mistress Maria de Padilla, and throughout his rule, Innocent VI sent numerous letters exhorting the young man to consummate his marriage. Pedro never consented to recognize the union, however, and attempted to extricate himself from it by an unusual strategy. He requested papal approval of a convent of Poor Clares—one that happened to be his mistress's foundation. Recognizing Maria, a known royal mistress, as a founder of a religious house would have legitimated her position (and contrition!) as it simultaneously reinforced Pedro's so-called attempts at breaking free from her charm. Pedro was thus showing his willingness to simultaneously protect the virtue of his former mistress and embrace his royal obligations. But it did not matter since Pedro abandoned both Maria (for another mistress) and Blanche. Pedro eventually sided with England and demonstrated his break with France by having Blanche imprisoned. She died of poison or natural death in 1361. But Pedro's ruthless actions eventually caught up with him. A few years later his half-brother Henry of Trastámara challenged him for the throne during a civil war that had originally been encouraged by Innocent VI, who was happy to see bands of French *routiers* joining the fray.

Henry of Trastámara was one of the many illegitimate children of King Alfonso XI of Castile, begotten from his noble mistress Eleanor of Guzmán. Henry had been raised at the Castilian court and married into the kingdom's most prominent noble family, the Manuel. But with Alfonso's passing in 1350, the situation of his illegitimate descendants became precarious, as the legitimate ruling heir, King Alfonso XI's son Pedro the Cruel, viewed them with suspicion. Pedro ordered the execution of Henry's mother, Eleanor, and Henry and Pedro fought on and off for several years until Henry found shelter at the French court. In France Henry became the equivalent of a "noble" captain of mercenaries, supporting Aragon in its wars with Castile and eventually fighting in the Castilian Wars that joined Henry's Castilians, Aragonese, and French troops under the leadership of the famous French *condottiere* Bertrand du Guesclin against Pedro the Cruel.

In 1362, Henry and his brother Sancho marched into Languedoc and from there penetrated into Provence, supposedly on their way to Castile. They ransomed the region. A letter from Pope Innocent suggests that they were bought off with a tax levied on local inhabitants and clergy.[92] But this was not enough; once paid off, the free companies became available to fight other companies. The systematic and commonplace mismanagement of such mercenary companies explains why their presence did not diminish in the latter half of the fourteenth century: they had no compelling reasons to go away but plenty of compelling reasons to stay — money being the principal one. The popes systematically bought them off as they continued to hire their services.[93] As we will see later, Urban V devised what must have seemed at the time a radical solution when he promised mercenaries absolution if they entered the Christian army against the Turks.

Meanwhile, Pedro the Cruel, who at first committed the misstep of engaging his Castilian troops across the Pyrenees into English-held southern French territory, ended up allying with the Black Prince. Queen Joanna of Naples's third husband, James of Majorca, defeated Henry and Du Guesclin at the Battle of Nájera in 1367. Escaping to France once again, Henry regrouped his men and re-formed his alliance with Du Guesclin. When the brothers next met in the field, Henry delivered Pedro a crushing defeat at the Battle of Montiel in March 1369 and killed him. Thus, Henry became the next king of Castile. Because of his title and martial activities throughout Europe, until his death in 1379 Henry more or less remained a constant presence in the Avignon papal registers, especially for the reigns of Innocent VI and Urban V.

In any case, what remained in the wake of the mercenary companies was a ravaged and destabilized Provence. The old argument made fifty years earlier against returning to Rome's "malaria-infected, crumbling, mob-infested, and baron-torn wreck" began to weaken.[94] Thus the mercenaries' depredations helped convince the popes eventually to return the curia to Rome.

HOLY ROMAN EMPIRE

Compared with policies of his predecessors, Innocent's foreign policy was less concerned with the Holy Roman Empire. The usual grand descent on Rome for the emperor's coronation did not happen. The emperor spared the Italian peninsula and the papacy the Guelph-Ghibelline instabilities that traditionally accompanied his formal coronation. Instead, the emperor came and left Rome quickly once his coronation was granted in 1354. On January 13, 1356, Charles IV emancipated the empire from the overarching authority of the papacy with the publication of the Golden Bull. According to this document, seven prince-electors would, by a majority ruling, name the King of the Romans, who would then be crowned by the pope. This effectively removed the pope from the electoral process by eliminating the papal confirmation of the elect. The Church's vicariate of Italy during imperial vacancies also disappeared with the Golden Bull.[95] Guillaume Mollat argues that Innocent's lack of resistance to it demonstrates his relief to see that "the bull weakened imperial authority, and so indirectly furthered papal claims in Italy."[96] But most of all, the pope obliged the emperor because he needed the support of Charles IV in his fight against the Visconti and the *routiers*.

While preoccupied with this complex international situation, Innocent never abandoned his agenda to reform the Church. He thinned the numbers of petitioners idling at court, warning them either to return to their benefices or be excommunicated, and he required candidates to benefices to be literate and qualified. He also reduced the expenses of the court at Avignon, an action taken more by necessity than conviction since the Italian campaigns had emptied his treasury.[97] In his relations with religious orders, Innocent was as intransigent with the Spiritual Franciscans as his predecessors had been. Evidence of this can be found in the words of St. Bridget of Sweden, who compared the pope to Judas and Pilate and condemned the Avignon cardinals to the fires of Sodom.[98] The saint, living in Rome from 1349, constantly harangued the Avignon popes to return the curia to Rome. The Avignon popes were no strangers to critics from within the religious orders. Innocent kept the prophet, alchemist, and Spiritual Franciscan Jean de Roquetaillade in prison until the end of his life for his relentless criticism of the papal court, accusing him of heresies, false prophecies, and magic. Imprisonment did not quiet the Franciscan, however, as he continued writing and circulating his apocalyptic visions with the help of his jailers.[99]

Innocent's reforming spirit also attempted to control Dominicans' zeal. Mendicant orders and their role in medieval society, especially in England, were frequently discussed at the curia, especially by the archbishop of Armagh, Richard FitzRalph, who deeply resented mendicant intrusion into the ministry of the secular clergy (clergymen not affiliated with a religious order). An older bull, decreed by Boniface VIII (*Super cathedram*) in 1300 and confirmed by the Council of Vienne (1311), had already established that mendicants who preached and heard confessions needed to be preapproved by the local ordinary. They also needed to share with local clergy the income they received from bequests and legacies. FitzRalph vigorously argued that the Church had survived for centuries without the mendicants, and he questioned their methods and motivations. Innocent decreed a renewal of *Super cathedram* in England and in 1357 charged a commission of cardinals to further evaluate the question. Acrimonious debates went on between mendicants and the archbishop until Innocent's October 1358 decree, *Gravem dilectorum*, a bull that supported mendicant ministry. FitzRalph's death in 1360 abruptly ended the proceedings.

By the end of his life, Innocent VI was a dispirited and broken man who felt overwhelmed by the constant wars that surrounded him. Matters worsened when an outbreak of plague returned to Europe in 1361, terrifying the population and killing in even higher numbers than during the first onslaught. Chroniclers remarked that this plague killed more "nobles and notables," vindicating the widespread fear of the disease. Werner, author of a biography of the pope, mentions the death of eight cardinals and innumerable people during the 1361 outbreak.[100] The famous surgeon Guy de Chauliac wrote in his *Chirurgia magna* that this plague affected the rich and nobility, many children but few women. Perhaps overcome by grief and exhausted from his hard labor and responsibilities, Innocent died on September 12, 1362, asking to be buried in Villeneuve-les-Avignon, across the Pont Saint-Bénézet in the Carthusian monastery that he had founded.

The popes who had anchored the central years of the Avignon papacy faced unprecedented challenges: plague, the Hundred Years' War, and attacks of mercenary companies. They responded to the best of their abilities. For many years to come, the surviving European population learned to live with the epidemic. As they maintained a steady grip on the reins of the Church, advanced Church reform, and pacified Rome and the Papal States, Clement VI and Innocent VI broadened their diplomatic activities on the European stage. Nuncios and papal legates crisscrossed the fields of action of a war that would take years to bring to an end. There is no reason to question the genuine interest the popes showed in bringing to term both kings of France and England in an enduring peace and in pacifying Italy. War brought violence, and the pressures on Avignon compelled the popes to rethink their position. As companies of mercenaries threatened the new capital of Christendom, Innocent must have pondered whether the city was indeed so much safer than Rome. His successors decided it was not.

NOTES

1. Étienne Baluze, *Vitae paparum avenionensium, hoc est, Historia pontificum romanorum qui in Gallia sederunt ab anno Christi MCCCV usque ad annum MCCCXCIV,* ed. Guillaume Mollat (Paris: Letouzey et Ané, 1914), vol. 1, 241.

2. Baluze, *Vitae,* vol. 1, 263.

3. Jean Favier, *Les papes d'Avignon* (Paris: Fayard, 2006), 134. My translation.

4. Baluze, *Vitae,* vol. 1, 299.

5. Diana Wood, *Clement VI: The Pontificate and Ideas of an Avignon Pope* (Cambridge: Cambridge University Press, 1989), xi.

6. John E. Wrigley, "Clement VI before His Pontificate: The Early Life of Pierre Roger, 1290/91–1342," *Catholic Historical Review* 56.3 (1970): 441.

7. As quoted by Wrigley, "Clement VI before His Pontificate," 444. Of course, this relationship favored the pope's rapport with the empire.

8. Wrigley, "Clement VI before His Pontificate," 454–456.

9. Wrigley, "Clement VI before His Pontificate," 451–452, 467–469.

10. Pierre Jugie, "Clement VI," in *The Papacy: An Encyclopedia,* ed. Philippe Levillain (New York: Routledge, 2002), 336.

11. Favier, *Les papes d'Avignon,* 134. My translation.

12. Baluze, *Vitae,* vol. 1, 305.

13. Baluze, *Vitae,* vol. 1, 299.

14. See Christopher Kleinhenz, *Medieval Italy: An Encyclopedia* (New York: Routledge, 2004), 1209–1210. A Latin transcription of the text (based on Heinrich Joseph Dominicus Denzinger's *Enchiridion Symbolorum et Definitionum*) is available online at http://catho.org/9.php?d=bxy#bt). On purgatory, see Jacques LeGoff, *The Birth of Purgatory* (London: Scolar, 1990).

15. Baluze, *Vitae,* vol. 1, 299–303.

16. It should be noted, however, that robbers and pirates plagued pilgrims. Many documents attest to the high incidence of robbery and attacks committed by "thieves,

robbers and pirates," which forced pilgrims en route to Rome to conceal their identity as much as possible (see Baluze, *Vitae*, vol. 1, 253).

17. "Cola di Rienzo and Fourteenth-Century Rome," in *Medieval Italy: Texts in Translation*, ed. Katherine L. Jansen, Joanna Drell, and Frances Andrew (Philadephia: University of Pennsylvania Press, 2009), 295–300.

18. Ronald G. Musto, *Apocalypse in Rome: Cola di Rienzo and the Politics of the New Age* (Berkeley: University of California Press, 2003), 70.

19. On Cola in Avignon, see Musto, *Apocalypse in Rome*, 58–82.

20. See Wood, *Clement VI*, 74–95, for the situation of Rome at the time of Clement VI.

21. Wood, *Clement VI*, 79, explains: "Clement's accusation against Cola was that he had not scrupled to blaspheme against the 'holy, catholic, and universal Church' by asserting that the universal Church and the city of Rome were the same *(prefatam Ecclesiam civitatemque Romanam idem esse asseruit)*. What really incensed the Pope was Cola's identification of the city of Rome with the universal Church, rather than with the localised church of Rome. He had confused Clement's two brides: he had made possession of the city of Rome a sine qua non for possession of universal authority, rather than vice versa. He had turned the city of Rome into the head of the Church and thus usurped the position of the papacy."

22. Wood, *Clement VI*, 77.

23. Louis of Hungary was a grandnephew of Joanna's father, so again an Angevin relative of the queen.

24. Ronald G. Musto, *Medieval Naples: A Documentary History, 400–1400* (New York: Italica, 2012), 267–268.

25. See Musto, *Medieval Naples*, 274–275.

26. Wood, *Clement VI*, 48–50.

27. See Musto, *Medieval Naples*, 278–298.

28. After Louis's death, Joanna married the unreliable Jaime IV, titular king of Majorca, on September 26, 1363. He died in 1375. During the Schism, she rallied the Clementist side and saw herself attacked by the Urbanists. She was deposed by Urban VI and attacked by Charles III (son of Charles) of Durazzo. Childless, Joanna adopted Louis of Anjou as her heir. Her new husband, Otto of Brunswick, helped her fight Durazzo's invasion, but to no avail. Durazzo took Naples in 1381, but realizing the imminent advance of Louis of Anjou toward Naples, he removed Joanna from the city and had her strangled in 1382.

29. Wood, *Clement VI*, 38.

30. See Wood, *Clement VI*, 142–176, for the pope's relations with the empire.

31. Wood, *Clement VI*, 79.

32. Wrigley, "Clement VI before His Pontificate," 447–448.

33. Wrigley, "Clement VI before His Pontificate," 460–463. See Wood, *Clement VI*, 123–141 for a detailed history of Clement's involvement in the diplomacy between France and England.

34. Wrigley, "Clement VI before His Pontificate," 472.

35. Wood, *Clement VI*, 123.

36. Karsten Plöger, *England and the Avignon Popes: The Practice of Diplomacy in Late Medieval Europe* (London: Legenda, 2005), 30–36.

37. Robin Neillands, *The Hundred Years War* (London: Routledge, 1990), 88–91.

38. Plöger, *England and the Avignon Popes*, 36–40.

39. Plöger, *England and the Avignon Popes*, 38–41, esp. 33–34.

40. John A. Wagner, *Encyclopedia of the Hundred Years War* (Westport, CT: Greenwood, 2006), 73–75.

41. Wood, *Clement VI*, 133–134.

42. Baluze, *Vitae*, vol. 1, 305.

43. Baluze, *Vitae*, vol. 1, 251.

44. Rosemary Horrox, *The Black Death* (Manchester: Manchester University Press, 1994), 42.

45. Horrox, *The Black Death*, 44.

46. John Aberth, *From the Brink of the Apocalypse: Confronting Famine, War, Plague, and Death in the Later Middle Ages* (New York: Routledge, 2000), 121.

47. Horrox, *The Black Death*, 44–46.

48. Baluze, *Vitae*, vol. 1, 303; Aberth, *From the Brink of the Apocalypse*, 133–156.

49. Aberth, *From the Brink of the Apocalypse*, 145.

50. Baluze, *Vitae*, vol. 1, 550.

51. Baluze, *Vitae*, vol. 1, 307.

52. Aberth, *From the Brink of the Apocalypse*, 153–163.

53. Horrox, *The Black Death*, 221.

54. Horrox, *The Black Death*, 221–222.

55. Aberth, *From the Brink of the Apocalypse*, 120.

56. J. Viard, "La messe pour la peste," *Bibliothèque de l'École des chartes* 61 (1900): 344–48.

57. Wood, *Clement VI*, 66–71.

58. Musto, *Apocalypse in Rome*, 62.

59. Musto, *Apocalypse in Rome*, 66.

60. Bernhard Schimmelpfennig, "Eleven Papal Coronations in Avignon," in *Coronations: Medieval and Early Modern Monarchic Ritual*, ed. János M. Bak (Berkeley: University of California Press, 1990), 179–193.

61. Dominique Vingtain, *Avignon: Le palais des papes* (Saint-Léger-Vauban: Zodiaque, 1998), 181–394.

62. Baluze, *Vitae*, vol. 1, 303.

63. Eugène Déprez, "Les funérailles de Clément VI et d'Innocent VI d'après les comptes de la cour pontificale," *Mélanges d'archéologie et d'histoire* 20 (1900): 238–239.

64. Guillaume Mollat, *The Popes at Avignon: The "Babylonian Captivity" of the Medieval Church*, trans. Janet Love (New York: Harper & Row, 1965), 44. Norman P. Zacour, "A Note on the Papal Election of 1352: The Candidacy of Jean Birel," *Traditio* 13 (1957): 456–462, questions this assertion.

65. Yves Renouard, *The Avignon Papacy: The Popes in Exile 1305–1403*, trans. Denis Bethell (New York: Barnes and Noble, 1970), 49.

66. Zacour, "A Note on the Papal Election of 1352," 460.

67. Pierre Gasnault and Marie-Hyacinte Laurent, eds., *Innocent VI (1352–1362), Lettres secrètes et curiales* (Paris: Bibliothèque des Écoles françaises d'Athènes et de Rome, 1959–2006), vol. 5, no. 435.

68. Bernard Guillemain, *La cour pontificale d'Avignon: Étude d'une société* (Paris: de Boccard, 1962), 141.

69. Hermann Hoberg, ed., *Die Einnahmen der Apostolischen Kammer unter Innozenz VI. Zweiter Teil: Die Servitienquittungen des päpstlichen Kamerars* (Paderborn: Ferdinand Schöningh Verlag, 1972).

70. Peter Partner, *The Lands of Saint Peter: The Papal State in the Middle Ages and Early Renaissance* (Berkeley: University of California Press, 1972), 332.

71. Favier, *Les papes d'Avignon*, 474.

72. Musto, *Apocalypse in Rome*, 312.

73. Partner, *The Lands of Saint Peter*, 344.

74. Sharon Dale, "*Contra damnationis filios*: The Visconti in Fourteenth-Century Papal Diplomacy," *Journal of Medieval History* 33.1 (2007), 11.

75. Partner, *The Lands of St. Peter*, 346.

76. Favier, *Les papes d'Avignon*, 478.

77. Partner, *The Lands of St. Peter*, 340.

78. Plöger, *England and the Avignon Popes*, 38–41.

79. Pierre Jugie, "L'activité diplomatique du cardinal Gui de Boulogne en France au milieu du XIVe siècle," *Bibliothèque de l'École des chartes* 145.1 (1987): 99–127.

80. Baluze, *Vitae*, vol. 1, 317.

81. John Froissart, *Chronicles of England, France and Spain and the Surrounding Countries*, trans. Thomas Johnes, Esq. (London: William Smith, 1848), chapter 160, 215.

82. Froissart, *Chronicles of England, France and Spain*, chapter 160, 216.

83. Favier, *Les papes d'Avignon*, 410. My translation.

84. Favier, *Les papes d'Avignon*, 410.

85. Froissart, *Chronicles of England, France and Spain*, chapter 212, 289.

86. Kenneth Fowler, *Medieval Mercenaries: The Great Companies* (Oxford: Blackwell, 2001), 61–64.

87. Froissart, *Chronicles of England, France and Spain*, chapter 176, 238.

88. Karl Heinrich Schäfer, *Die ausgaben der Apostolischen kammer unter Benedikt XII., Klemens VI. und Innocenz VI. (1335–1362.)* (Paderborn: F. Schöningh, 1914), 647, 681, 726, 751, and 821.

89. Cervole's nickname came from his possession of an ecclesiastical benefice in Dordogne.

90. Heinrich Denifle, *La désolation des églises, monastères, hôpitaux en France, pendant la guerre de cent ans* (Paris: A. Picard et fils, 1897–1899), vol. 2, 196–198.

91. ASV, Reg. Vat. 25, fol. 378v. (March 8, 1361).

92. ASV, Reg. Aven. 28, fol. 505 (May 2, 1362).

93. See especially for that period Denifle, *La désolation des églises*, vol. 2, 406–410.

94. Musto, *Apocalypse in Rome*, 66.

95. The bull can be found on the website of Yale Law School at http://avalon.law.yale.edu/medieval/golden.asp.

96. Mollat, *The Popes at Avignon*, 228.

97. Baluze, *Vitae*, vol. 1, 343, 347.

98. Denis Michael Searby and Bridget Morris, *The Revelations of St. Birgitta of Sweden* (Oxford: Oxford University Press, 2006), vol. 2, 245–246; and Mollat, *The Popes at Avignon*, 46.

99. See the recent Leah DeVun, *Prophecy, Alchemy, and the End of Time: John of Rupescissa in the Late Middle Ages* (New York: Columbia University Press, 2009) for an overview of this extraordinary character.

100. Baluze, *Vitae*, vol. 1, 327, 340; vol. 2, 490.

THREE
Returning to Rome

Jean Froissart, the famed chronicler of the Hundred Years' War and insider to the politics of the high nobility, used the following words to recall the nomination of pope Urban V:

> About Christmas pope Innocent VI departed this life: and the cardinals were in great discord about the election of another, for each was desirous of that honour; more particularly the cardinals of Boulogne and Périgord, who were the greatest in the college. Their dissensions kept the conclave a long time shut up. The conclave had ordered and arranged everything according to the desires of the two beforementioned cardinals, but in such a manner that neither of them could succeed to the papacy: upon which they both agreed, that none of their brethren should wear the papal crown, and elected the abbot de St. Victor of Marseilles, who was a holy and learned man, of good morals, and who had laboured hard for the church in Lombardy and other places. The two cardinals sent to inform him of this elevation, and to desire he would come to Avignon: which he did as soon as possible, and received this gift with joy. He was called Urban V, and reigned with great prosperity: he augmented much the power of the church, and did great good to Rome and other parts.[1]

Froissart, like his patrons, was well aware of the fractures that had divided the college. When Innocent died on September 12, 1362, eighteen of the twenty-one cardinals composing the college were French. The Spaniard Albornoz was at the time in Italy, and Androin de la Roche, who had been named cardinal in September 1361, still had his cardinal's voice "closed." He had yet to be introduced into the consistory and needed a special derogation in order to participate in the conclave. A certain few of his colleagues refused him the privilege. The college eventually mandated a commission, however, which decided that he could vote.[2] When the time came to choose the next pope, the conclave divided along geographical lines between a Limousin party of six cardinals, who lobbied for the election of a compatriot, opposed by the anti-Limousins, who refused this course of action on the grounds that Limousins had been in control of the papacy for too long. In addition, the Limousin region was at the time in English hands, a state of affairs that did not sit well with nascent French nationalism.

The cardinals' vote went first to Hugues Roger, brother of Clement VI, cardinal-priest of San Lorenzo in Damaso. He refused because of his age. The second round brought only eleven votes to Cardinal Raymond of Canillac, thus under the required majority of two-thirds. The latter was also related to Clement VI and cardinal-bishop of Palestrina. As Froissart remarks, the cardinals of Périgord and Boulogne also unsuccessfully manifested their desire to wear the papal tiara. Since neither wanted to yield to the other, however, the college decided on someone outside its own membership; this sometimes happened when negotiations deadlocked. They named as papal-elect the current nuncio in Naples, Guillaume de Grimoard. The cardinals kept the election secret until Grimoard acquiesced, afraid that resentful Italians would keep him in Naples and return him to Rome to bring back the papacy to Italy. Grimoard accepted his nomination in Marseille as he was making his way back to Avignon in October 1362. He then entered the city on October 31. Following protocol, Étienne Aubert, the cardinal of Ostia, consecrated Grimoard bishop of Rome and crowned him inside the palace on November 6.

URBAN V

Guillaume de Grimoard (who took the name of Urban, perhaps in reference to the biblical "city on the hill") was a Benedictine monk like Benedict XII and Clement VI, foreign to the politics of the curia and college and devoid of diplomatic experience with France.[3] In some ways, he represented new blood. Guillaume de Grimoard was born in 1310, the oldest son and namesake of his father, Guillaume de Grimoard, a knight who held the Castle of Grizac near Mende. The Grimoards were related to the Sabrans, a family who received medieval fame when Elzéar and

Delphine de Sabran, though married, lived chastely together for the rest of their lives. Elzéar epitomized a masculine virtuous sanctity that encompassed men who could control their bodies as well as armies.[4]

According to legend, Guillaume was born deformed, but during his baptism the prayers of his godfather Elzéar worked a miracle that cured him.

Guillaume de Grimoard had six siblings. Thus, as Pope Urban V he could have followed his predecessors' example and elevated kin and friends to high positions. To some extent he did, but in decided moderation. As soon as he became pope, Urban named his younger brother Anglic de Grimoard to the vicariate of Avignon; he was later made cardinal in 1366 and vicar of Bologna. Anglic was a talented administrator whose sound management of the Avignon diocese produced a detailed listing of the episcopal revenues of the city (a *terrier*) that remains a valuable source for historians of the city. Urban could rely on his brother. He also brought to the court his elderly, widowed father, who appears to have been a medieval anomaly since he was nearly a centenarian at the time of his death in 1366, four weeks after having celebrated Anglic's promotion to cardinal. Since old Grimoard's sons all died with no descendants, Urban bequeathed his patrimony to his sister's son, Raymond de Montaut, whom he also made sergeant and squire at the court. The pope also shared limited friendship with every cardinal except for his close relationship with Guillaume d'Aigrefeuille, who had tabled his name during the election.

Guillaume de Grimoard the son followed the traditional career of a bright, literate young man. At twelve years old he left his homestead for schooling in Montpellier, where his rapid progress landed him at Toulouse University. He studied civil law and opted for a career in the regular orders. It is notable that he chose to enter monastic life outside of typical parental pressure. Grimoard joined the priory of Chirac in 1327 to become a Benedictine monk; he later moved to the ancient and famous Abbey of Saint-Victor in Marseille. He continued his education after joining the order, studying in Toulouse, Montpellier, Paris, and Avignon to become a doctor in canon law in 1342. Indeed, Grimoard was a renowned canonist of his time. He taught law at Montpellier, where he survived the first onslaught of the plague in 1348. He was promoted vicar and prior of several benefices before Clement VI made him legate to Lombardy in February 1352. There, Grimoard discovered the court of Bishop Giovanni

Visconti in Milan and honed his diplomatic skills. He negotiated with Visconti for the return of Orvieto to the pope in exchange for the vicariate of Bologna (that Visconti had previously seized) for twelve years and 12,000 yearly florins. Grimoard was then named abbot of Auxerre as a reward for his activities. Starting in 1354, Innocent VI selected him for diverse missions in Italy. He seconded Albornoz in Rome and Milan, where he convinced Bernabò Visconti (Bishop Visconti's nephew) to let Bologna go and gathered funds for the reconquest of the Papal States. But Albornoz's troops crushed the Milanese, and Grimoard's travels ended there. Innocent VI named him abbot of Saint-Victor in Marseille in August 1361 and shortly after, in May 1362, appointed him Italian nuncio at the court of Naples following the death of Joanna of Naples's second husband, Louis of Taranto. It is in Naples that Grimoard learned the news of his election to the papal throne.

Urban appears to have been a man of contradictions. He was before all else a monk, frugal and ascetic, who could do without the luxury of the court; he supposedly slept in the palace on a wooden pallet. He was interested in reforming the Church and especially in reversing the rampant secularization of the court; a patron of education, he supported hundreds of scholars. As pope, he used his position to found colleges and ameliorate schools and universities. Urban's love of intellectual pursuits was unrestricted, and on the subject of education, he stated: "I know that all the ones [students] I support will not enter ecclesiastic life. . . . Some will become either regular or secular clergymen; some will remain in the world and become fathers. Regardless of their choice, even if they turn out laborers their education will always serve them well."[5] He also loved nature, which is very evident in the construction of the palace gardens (*viridarium*) in Avignon, parts of which are still visible today. When he returned to Rome, Urban also rehabilitated the Vatican gardens, adding fruit trees and a large vineyard. Similarly, when Urban summered in Montefiascone in 1368, he ordered the creation of new gardens and orchards around the *Rocca* (fortress).

A FASTIDIOUS MAN

Urban was a man of integrity, piety, and moral worth. His sole fault, according to Jean Favier, was a detailed, fastidious, and exacting mind that prevented him from delegating tasks and bogged his thoughts down in trivial minutiae. The pope's hand is found on scores of documents that he read and adjudicated himself, where he noted information he had gathered and the decisions he took. Urban oversaw everything, even fashion, going so far as to declare: "It is my intention, and I want, that the indulgence *in mortis articulo* (at the moment of death) be granted only if they [laymen] wear their robe at least to the knee."[6] If the devil is in the details, the pope's personal demon may well have been in his exacting care for matters that could seem trivial for a man of state. In sum, Urban ran the large administrative machine that had developed in Avignon as his personal household, where he involved himself and gave advice on all matters, large and small.

The Avignon registers underscore the energy Urban spent on petitions, a task that other popes often delegated to secretaries. In a single week of November 1363, the pope annotated in his own hand the petitions of an English prince, a Silesian duchess, a poor clerk of Le Puy, an English priest, a Tuscan abbot, Sicilian monks, a York noblewoman, a burgher from Bayeux, and the widow of a Londoner. He confirmed the election of a prior, allowed a deacon to cumulate benefices, and authorized the burial of a priest in consecrated ground. We get a glimpse of his common sense when he authorized Sicilian Benedictines to celebrate holiday masses—exceptionally—regardless of the interdict weighing on the island—because they resided in an isolated location where no one would see and hear them. He simply added that they remain inconspicuous, with their doors locked and bells silenced so as not to raise attention. Last, he authorized a Parisian Franciscan established at Oxford to return to his alma mater if its chancellor and regents authorized him.[7]

Urban was actually so involved in the daily running of the papal court that he is the only pope who left behind clear traces of his own administration and personality. Anne-Marie Hayez has studied the 20,481 petitions scrutinized by the pope and itemized some 5,000 notations from the first year of his rule until November 26, 1366.[8] It is important to note that refused petitions were destroyed, so the exact numbers of these requests that Urban read far outweighed the numbers that he approved or annotated. From these extant documents, Hayez has drawn a picture of Urban's personality. He did not like favors or nepotism. He attempted reforming the mores of the clergy, limited and stigmatized their ambition and greed, and reminded them that their spiritual charges prevailed over their personal interests. To the clergy who cumulated benefices, he

granted new posts only if they let go of others. He enforced an education-
al minimum for clerks, refusing benefices to those who could not demonstrate a university education. The pope also assumed that a priest served
better where he had been born and where he spoke the same language as
his parishioners. Thus, Urban usually granted benefices within the linguistic and geographical limits of petitioners. Urban emphasized that
clerics be of sound mind and good moral standing and (most importantly
in the fashion-conscious Middle Ages!) that they be attired decently for
their vocation. This latter injunction appears many times in his notes, and
it seems that the pope strongly resented the fashions of the day, especially shorter robes for men. Conversely, Urban usually approved the special
dispensations required of illegitimate children to enter regular orders,
and as a rule he mandated that all candidates for benefices first pass
competency examinations and be subject to scrutiny concerning their mo-
rals. The abbot of Montmajour was the usual examiner.

The pope obviously cared about the quality of his clergy. He strove to
maintain a high standard of education and limited the entrance of imma-
ture young people into holy orders. Familial tradition or pressures often
sent young men into the church regardless of their fitness or personal
inclination to that calling; Urban tried to make the selection more rigorous. He reduced the numbers of demands for delayed entrance, allowing,
for example, a clerk to finish his education or take care of other matters,
and he fought arduously against the nonresident clergy. He expelled
from Avignon clergymen who had never resided in their own benefices.
As a monk himself, the pope abhorred idle, rootless, and wandering
monks (*gyrovagues*) subject to little ecclesiastical discipline and unstable
in the religious life, and he seldom approved petitions requesting a move
from one monastery to another or from one religious order to another.
Urban never granted requests to found new orders. He was not an inno-
vator. He rarely granted dispensations to eat meat during a fast and in
one case authorized it only for one meal! He rarely granted a remission of
tithes without full knowledge of the particular conditions and often left
the decisions to local representatives more versed on the matter.

The pope was as strict in secular affairs concerning the laity as he was
in ecclesiastic ones. He granted indulgences only to laypersons who were
not frivolous or secular minded (for example, men who were not slaves
to fashion), and he required women to practice higher forms of penance
than men. Women usually had to fast every Friday for the granting of

absolution in *mortis articulo*, while men were not required to do so. To preserve the holy seclusion of convents, Urban rarely allowed men to visit nunneries, allowing only mature women of ages forty to sixty to visit. There is no doubt that this pope took his temporal and spiritual charges extremely seriously.

HOW TO ELIMINATE THE FREE COMPANIES

In October 1350, ten days after his coronation, King John II of France arrived in Avignon. He had meant to face Innocent but instead found his successor. Froissart again explains,

> The king took with him the lord John of Artois, his cousin, whom he much loved; the earl of Tancarville, the earl of Dampmartin, Boucicault marshal of France, sir Arnold d'Andreghen, the grand prior of France, and several others. He travelled slowly and with much expense, making some stay in all the cities and towns of Burgundy, so that he did not arrive at Villeneuve, until about Michaelmas. It was there that his hôtel was prepared, as well for himself as for his attendants. He was most magnificently received and feasted by the pope and the college at Avignon: the king, pope, and cardinals, visited each other often. The king remained at Villeneuve during the whole time. [9]

The King came to discuss his ransom, raising a crusade, and the possible marriage of Joanna of Naples to his son Philip the Bold. The pope promised to relay the message to Joanna, who had already been promised to her third husband, James of Majorca. The king sojourned close to a year in Villeneuve-lès-Avignon, where he ordered the construction of the fortress of Saint-André. It is still visible today from the balconies of the palace, towering across the right bank of the Rhône.

It is possible that during his sojourn John and Urban discussed the project of a crusade now that the king was somewhat in limbo while awaiting the full payment of his ransom. France would lead a new crusade against the Ottomans, who had just conquered Adrianopolis. By March 1363, Peter of Lusignan, king of Cyprus, and Valdemar of Denmark were present in Avignon; Urban preached the crusade to the three of them. King John was named captain general and the cardinal of Périgord the pope's legate for the venture. Lusignan went on to northern France to garner support and returned to Avignon in July. By then he had convinced King John to abandon the retaking of Adrianopolis for the conquest of Alexandria in Egypt. But John's enthusiasm was cut short when his son Louis of Anjou, a hostage in England since the signing of the Treaty of Brétigny, escaped his captors. John was forced to return to England, where he died in 1364. The Alexandrian crusade nevertheless took place. Peter of Lusignan used the years between 1362 and 1365 to prepare the expedition that led him in October 1365 to take and sack the city. Unable to gather support for an attack on Cairo, he left Alexandria and returned to Cyprus, dreaming until his death of further efforts to take Egypt.

Like his predecessors, Urban kept the crusading ideal a top priority. The crusade also became a motivation to rid France of its companies of roaming mercenaries. For the pope, there was no better way for men-at-arms to atone for their violence than fighting for the cross. Urban attempted to convince them of the rightness of this task. He cajoled the mercenaries for their martial qualities, telling them they were the best-qualified troops for a victorious crusade. He also reminded them that a crusade was the best penance for all their ill deeds. Their departure would free France from their depredations and allow the king to join them instead of fighting them. The companies refused, however, using the great distance as a pretext. Urban's bull *Cogit nos*, published on February 27, 1364, ratified his failure with the mercenaries. He retraced the excesses committed by these arrogant "ferocious animals" who pillaged, robbed, committed arson, murdered, spoiled, and raped and who dared threaten the pontifical court. Offering two years of plenary indulgence to any willing to fight them, he excommunicated the companies and exhorted princes and the Christian faithful to crusade against them. [10]

Urban repeated the bull with slight adaptation in May and July 1364; in January 1365 he also condemned those who joined and supported the mercenary troops. In *Clamat ad nos*, published on April 5, 1365, Urban again excommunicated all guilty of violence and put their lands under interdict, declaring them "ill-famed" for the generations to come. [11] The same injunction appears in a letter dated May 9, 1367, suggesting that the companies stayed on and people supported them, perhaps under duress. [12]

The years 1363–1364 were especially difficult for the pope and Provence. The plague became endemic after 1363, and, beginning in December of that year, our sources insist on a series of climatic events that led to further widespread catastrophes. Initially, the winter between January and March 1364 turned brutally cold, freezing the Rhône to the point that people could cross it on horses and carts; the cold destroyed vineyards and orchards, impeding a successful summer harvest. The free companies simultaneously caused havoc throughout the region, pushing the pope, as we have seen above, to declare a crusade against them. Then the king of France died in April 1364, leading to a war over the succession between his son, Charles V, and Charles the Bad of Navarre, who claimed the French throne with the support of the English. The Battle of Cocherel (May 16, 1364), with Bertrand du Guesclin and Arnaud de Cervole (who eventually deserted) commanding the French troops and the Captal of Buch, Jean de Grailli, leading the Navarrese, ended in a resounding defeat for Navarre. This outcome halted Navarrese pretentions and sent Charles the Bad to Avignon, pleading with the pope to negotiate a truce with Charles V on his behalf. In July, locusts darkened the skies over Provence, feeding on crops until the crops disappeared. This is the first historically documented locust invasion in Provençal history. After two years of such calamitous events, the pope took to heart the words of Roman ambassadors who begged him to return the court to Rome.[13]

THE EMPEROR'S VISIT

Since the twelfth century, the Kingdom of Arles was traditionally attached to the Holy Roman emperor, a vestige of late-Carolingian enterprises and a title reminiscent of Germanic pretensions in Provence. In May 1365, the Holy Roman emperor, Charles IV, made his way to Provence to receive his crown for the kingdom. In Italy, the papacy had simply crowned the emperor, but as a neighbor, the Avignon pope had to do better. The emperor's sojourn in Provence became a spectacular affair. An impressive retinue of Germans, who no doubt relished the charms of the Provençal countryside, accompanied the emperor. According to the bishop of Avignon's secretary, the visit created a shortage of wine for the rest of the year.[14] As protocol required, Anglic Grimoard and the pope's treasurer greeted the emperor and the bishops of Worms and Trier in Valence; from there, they made their way to Pont-de-Sorgues. The pontifical palace of Pont-de-Sorgues was privileged for the residence of eminent guests. The apostolic registers saved scores of entries itemizing the expenses involved with these visits, which usually tallied hundreds of gold florins and pounds for upkeep and provisioning.

The financial burden of such receptions is comparable to today's state budget, and expenses must have taken a toll on the papal treasury. It is important to note that in many cases Jews provided and leased necessities for such occasions, such as the beds that were delivered for the emperor's household.[15] The court also rented dinnerware. The fact that many plates, trenchers, goblets, and cups disappeared in significant numbers suggests that perhaps guests filled their pockets with souvenirs. Among the items used for the emperor's party that disappeared were 1,930 out of 4,200 wooden bowls and 1,030 out of 1,900 plates. Yet these expenses seem minor compared with those of provisioning. For the sole week of May 22–29, 1365, the master cook spent 837 *livres* to feed his guests when he had spent only some 73 the previous weeks.[16] Parting gifts for such honored guests were also expected. For example, in June 1365, the pope offered one hundred florins to the emperor's jugglers for the marriage of their children.[17]

Charles IV entered the city of Avignon and participated in the ceremonies of Pentecost in full regalia. He returned to Prague shortly after, in June 1365. Urban found the presence of Charles IV in Avignon a great respite because the emperor brought with him hope of a crusade, and to Urban a crusade represented the means to rid Provence of the great companies. King and pope agreed on the subsidies they would provide their "crusaders," and Charles granted passage through his northeastern territories to the "crossed" free companies making their way eastward. It was with relief that the pope heard that the archpriest Arnaud de Cervole, a chief of the mercenaries, seemed willing to enlist his outstanding talent for violence and mayhem in the higher cause of the crusade. This crusade, of course, never happened. But Cervole still filled his pockets in Champagne and Lorraine, as he supposedly made his way to Hungary and then turned back toward Alsace, ransoming Metz for some 18,000 florins along the way. Cervole's company controlled the area until Charles and his army intimidated him enough to return to France.[18] Popes and princes opted then to send the mercenaries on another grand crusade, this time toward Spain. The pretext was to attack the Moors; the reality was to dethrone Pedro the Cruel of Castile.

THE CASTILIAN SITUATION

Since 1362, Urban had inherited the Castilian "situation," which Froissart summarizes in these terms in his entry for that year:

> Don Pedro, proud and presumptuous as he was, not only refused to obey the mandate, but even received with insults the ambassadors from the holy father, for which he felt grievously under his indignation. This wicked king still persevered in his sin. It was then considered how or by what means he could be corrected; and it was determined that he was no longer worthy to bear the title of king, or to possess a kingdom. He was therefore publicly excommunicated, in full consistory, held in the apartments of the pope, at Avignon, and declared to be a heretic and infidel. They thought they should be able to punish him by means of the free companies who were in France. They requested the king of Aragon, who hated very much this don Pedro, and Henry the bastard of Spain, to come immediately to Avignon. The Holy Father then legitimated the birth of Henry the bastard, so that he might be in a condition to obtain the kingdom from don Pedro, who had been cursed and condemned by the sentence of the pope. [19]

After the death of Blanche de Bourbon while imprisoned by her husband, Pedro, France supported his half-brother Henry of Trastámara's claim to the throne, while the pope sent Cardinal Guillaume d'Aigrefeuille, the cardinal of Saragossa, to Pedro's court to negotiate the king's abdication. Rumors circulated that the king had ordered his wife's murder. The verdict of historians is still open on this question. Pedro refused to moderate his behavior. Urban then conceived of a plan that would clear Provence, the Comtat Venaissin, and France of the ever-present marauding companies and replace Pedro with his half-brother Henry of Trastámara. Bertrand du Guesclin, famous for his Breton mercenaries, took the lead of the expedition in August 1365; Arnaud de Cervole promised to join him! On their way to Spain, du Guesclin, Trastámara, and their troops managed to ransom Provence for some thirty thousand florins and the Comtat Venaissin for five thousand florins, also claiming a tithe for their "crusade." Following the road to Spain, they ransomed Montpellier for ten thousand francs. By the mid-1360s, the French south had been bled white, and the pope dispatched several missives to princes and kings asking them to lighten the financial burden levied on these territories. While in 1365 du Guesclin and Trastámara passed the Pyrenees and eventually succeeded a few years later in eliminating Pedro the Cruel, some of their troops stopped at the border in Perpignan and made their way back, a final time, to Avignon. The attraction of the capital of Christendom was not easy to let go. In January 1366, Urban decreed another bull of excommunication against these marauding troops. Arnaud de Cervole, who had not yet joined du Guesclin's troops, stayed behind in Burgundy fighting English mercenaries; from there he proposed to join the army of the Count of Savoy, ready to support the Byzantine emperor against the Turks. Urban's joy at the news only increased when one of Cervole's companions subsequently killed him. [20]

The fourteenth century has often been regarded as a calamitous century, marked by famine, plague, war, and schism. Free companies of mercenaries, like a metaphorical pestilence matching the very literal one, burdened the population to extremes. Hired soldiers were numberless and limitless in their depredations. Closer to Avignon, as Trastámara was sacking the French southeast, a war between the Count of Foix (Gaston III of Foix-Béarn, alias Gaston Phoebus) and John of Armagnac erupted, and their mercenary troops ravaged Languedoc. The pope sent Pierre of Clermont, bishop of Cambrai, to mediate in December 1362, but both continued fighting in the vicinity of Toulouse until Gaston Phoebus won. He became one of the greatest barons of France and was tremendously well positioned to bargain with both France and England for the remainder of the Hundred Years' War.

Documents show the frustration that the pope felt toward soldiers, both the rank-and-file and the nobility, who showed only contempt and callousness for civilians. There is no better example than a letter sent to Burgundy by Urban in January 1366, where Urban described a tournament that pitted Burgundian nobles against mercenaries. In summary, when troops did not actually fight, they pretended to yet still marauded the local area, entertaining themselves with bloody "spectacles." The pope excommunicated all involved and asked the bull to be posted on all churches and public offices. [21] Much to Urban's dismay, as if the violence of wars were not sufficient, nobles and mercenaries also needed to fight for sport.

RETURNING TO ROME

Since his encounter with Roman ambassadors in 1363, Urban looked positively on the prospects of a return to Rome. As the episode of Cola di Rienzo demonstrated, the court in Avignon and the pope kept close watch on events happening in Rome. The enduring image of an Avignon papacy utterly detached from Roman politics is inaccurate. On the contrary, the correspondence that the popes maintained with specific individuals in Rome shows that they were well aware of minute political shifts. In his study of the papal letters addressed to the Roman nobility, Jean Coste demonstrates that the papacy was familiar with barons' "death, renewal of best placed familial representatives, or collateral members, and shift in actual center of power."[22] It was this intimate knowledge that allowed Urban to make his decision regarding the continuing location of the papacy. As early as September 1364 the pope asked Cardinal Jean de Blauzac to rule on the status of the Avignonese population, if and when the curia returned to Rome. Inhabitants of the city were divided between citizens (native or naturalized) and courtiers, followers of the Roman court. The pope's departure would have depleted the ranks of the tax-paying citizenry and bankrupted the city unless policies were initiated to soften the change this transition implied. It was needed economically and militarily to support the city after a departure of the court. But at a more theoretical level, the pope who questioned the absenteeism of his clergy could not rationalize a long stay in Avignon, away from the historical location of the papacy. Yves Renouard argues that by the 1360s Rome was actually better suited for Urban's goal of a reunification with the Eastern Church.[23]

The pope could leave Avignon with a certain peace of mind. The truce that followed the Treaty of Brétigny seemed to hold between France and England, and the political situation in Italy had dramatically improved. Albornoz had managed to regain control of the Papal States and of Rome. Albornoz had codified the Roman Statutes in 1363, which excluded the Roman nobility from public offices and, in their absence, radically pacified the city. The death of Giovanni di Vico, the perpetual agitator of the Romagna, facilitated appeasement as Rome itself was under the control of a popular militia, which ruled the commune and managed to frighten away nobles and roving bands of mercenaries. Milan, long the object of many popes' preoccupation, had been subdued with the help of Charles

IV. In 1360, when Bernabò Visconti had sent an army to retake Bologna, Charles had levied a Hungarian army to stop him. Bernabò was again defeated in June 1361 at the Battle of Ponte Rosillo. By then, Albornoz had negotiated an alliance with the Este in Ferrara and the Della Scala in Verona to infringe Visconti's movements, sealed with his excommunication by the pope for his disregard of Emperor Charles IV, his feudal overlord. Following this general offensive, the emperor upped the ante by confiscating the Visconti's lands in Italy.

At that moment, the Visconti's stronghold on Lombardy and Romagna could have been destroyed. The pope hesitated, however, turning face in the name of peace and an eventual crusade. He recalled the efficient Albornoz as papal legate—who opposed any type of settlement with Visconti—in exchange for his promise to return his conquest only to a new legate. Bernabò viewed Albornoz as the impediment to peace. In 1364 a Visconti was again named vicar of Bologna by the new legate, Androin de la Roche, while Albornoz was sent to Naples. Urban realized that he could not trust both de la Roche and Visconti and recalled Albornoz to the north. De la Roche opposed his replacement for a while but eventually moved to Viterbo, where he died in October 1369. Meanwhile, Albornoz continued to pacify the Papal States in order to prepare for the pope's return to Italy. One of his biggest accomplishments was the hiring of John Hawkwood's Company of St. George for the papal army. In the spring of 1367, as Urban was preparing to leave Avignon, Hawkwood defeated the Perugian army, a victory that cleared the way for Albornoz to consolidate his hold on the Romagna.

Urban first communicated his desire to return to Italy in September 1366, much to the dismay of the French court and a French embassy sent to convince the pope of the futility of his plans. But by October, plans were well under way; the pope authorized a tithe to be levied in Germany that would cover the emperor's expenses for accompanying him back to Italy.[24] Urban also ordered the repair and refurbishing of several locales in preparation for his return; orders were sent to make ready the papal city of Viterbo, the Lateran palace, and St. Paul Outside the Walls. Petrarch, who had spent his life penning letters and invectives against the vices of the papal curia in Avignon, reinforced his attacks in order to spur the pope to action. He praised the charms of Italy vis-à-vis Provence, especially its food and wine; but most of all, he reminded the pontiff that one day he would have to answer for his failure to act. Petrarch did not need to prod the pope; Urban stood firm on his decision. His court did not share his enthusiasm, however.

Few members of the curia really knew Italy from direct experience or were deeply acquainted with its politics, and they disagreed in general with the pope's design. The dangers of political strife in Italy and fear of the Visconti added to the French cultural block. French cardinals were also deeply worried about displeasing the king of France. It is striking that the pope, who had the courage to return the curia to Rome, had in actuality better administrative and diplomatic experience with Italy than he had with France. In any case, the pope's plans for a return to Rome failed, no doubt to the pleasure of the French cardinals, but not by their design. Urban V left Avignon on April 30, 1367, and arrived in Rome on October 16. But in 1370, after three short years, Urban decided to return to the safety of Avignon. He entered the city on September 22, 1370, only to die three months later, on December 19, 1370.

Urban organized his departure thoroughly. He first named Philippe de Cabassole as vicar general for Avignon. Cabassole, the former bishop of Cavaillon, had extensive administrative knowledge of the area. He had been nominated rector of the Comtat Venaissin in 1362, and with his nomination to the rectorship Urban efficiently centralized the government of this ultramontane papal territory. This freed Cabassole to deal singlehandedly with emergencies in the area. For example, in 1368 Cabassole bought off Bertrand du Guesclin and thus avoided the renewed incursions of his free companies. In 1368 Urban elevated Cabassole to the title of cardinal of St. Marcelline and in 1369 required his presence in Rome. By then, the rector had inventoried the pope's treasury and investigated two penitentiaries accused of simony and gambling. Urban, already frazzled by the situation in Italy, may have known in 1369 that he would soon return to Avignon. He did not name a new rector; he simply charged the five cardinals who remained behind in Avignon to deal with pressing judicial and administrative matters.

Urban, always a skilled administrator, understood that moving the entire administration from one place to another was close to impossible, if not dangerous. In addition, the administration could not remain vacant during the move. So the pope opted for the safest solution: he divided the administration in half. He left part of the curia's organization in place in Avignon as well as the entire papal treasury. The papal court had been halved, and Avignon retained its centralizing financial role. The treasurer, along with a good number of the Apostolic Chamber and chancery employees, stayed behind in the city. As Yves Renouard explains, the central position of Avignon and decades of financial centralization were habits difficult to break. Thus, it was Avignon that subsidized Rome. [25]

One of Étienne Baluze's sources offers us specific details on Urban's exact itinerary. [26] The pope left Avignon for Pont-de-Sorgues, then Noves, Aix-en-Provence, and Marseille, where he stayed two weeks in his former home, the ancient monastery of Saint-Victor, a site that had been renovated and beautified at his own expense. From Marseille, the pope boarded a galley that brought him to Genoa; he then sailed to Corneto, where Cardinal Albornoz awaited him. There a Roman embassy offered the keys of Castel Sant'Angelo as a sign of the city's submission to its returning ruler. Urban rode to Viterbo, which he entered amid great ceremony on June 9. But while the curia was still in Viterbo, Urban lost a trusted agent of his policy when Cardinal Albornoz died on August 22, 1367.

The events that unfolded after the death of the powerful legate demonstrate how tenuous was the pope's hold on his Italian cities and how volatile the political situation remained on the peninsula. Within a few days of Albornoz's death, on September 5, 1367, the Viterbese rebelled against the curia. They attacked foreigners for some three days and then surrendered to the pope; he severely punished the leaders of the insurrection. The French cardinals, fearing for their lives, had disguised themselves and fled to find refuge in the *Rocca*, the fortress previously strengthened on the order of Albornoz. According to contemporary chronicles, the rebellion started when certain courtiers belonging to the household of the pope's marshal washed a dog in the town's fountain. From there, a maid who rebuked the courtiers for their action may have been killed. The town rose against the pope for the offense committed by his staff.

What is certain is that the insurrectionists' cries, "Long live the pope and death to the foreigners," or "Long live the people and death to the Church," did not bode well for the pope's return to Italy and showed that nationalistic sentiment could mar Italian enthusiasm for the pope. [27] In any case, the pontiff returned to the business of ruling the Church once Viterbo was pacified. He received the Count of Savoy and a delegation, assembling representatives of the patriarch of Constantinople and ambassadors of the Eastern emperor to discuss a return of the Eastern Church to the West. Then, on October 16, the pope left Viterbo and entered Rome in the midst of renewed celebrations. This did not prevent chroniclers from underscoring the decrepit state of the new capital.[28]

As he restored the splendor of the Eternal City physically, Urban also gave it back its liturgical centrality. He commissioned the reconstruction of two of the major basilicas that had been destroyed by earthquake and fire, respectively: St. Paul Outside the Walls and the Lateran. He also ordered two new reliquaries for the heads of St. Paul and St. Peter. Urban celebrated offices at the twin liturgical centers of the city, the basilicas of St. Peter and the Lateran. He revived the civic pride of Rome with public ceremonies, receiving important dignitaries such as St. Bridget of Sweden, who asked permission to found two convents in Rome; Queen Joanna of Naples, to whom he offered the papal Golden Rose as a mark of affection and esteem; and King Peter of Cyprus, who, as he celebrated his victory in Alexandria with the pope, may have recoiled at Urban's presentation of the Golden Rose to a woman. But perhaps by this gesture Urban showed his support for the queen, whose kingdom was then under attack by Louis of Anjou (brother of Charles V) and Bertrand du Guesclin's troops.

In France, alarmed by the threat of so many free companies, the barons had decided to keep these violent mercenaries busy by invading Provence and the Comtat during the pope's absence. The pope railed against the mercenaries with another bull of excommunication, and in Avignon Cabassole negotiated their retreat at the price of some 37,000 florins. This war in Provence affected the region's main cities, dividing constituencies into Angevin and Neapolitan factions as the duke of Anjou and du Guesclin continued their efforts, regardless of the pope's complaints to the king and bulls of excommunication against anyone who helped them. The companies continued to ravage Provence, and their depredations added to the mandatory papal tithes, further exacerbating the population's frustration with their rulers. As in 1358, the peasantry rebelled. If Provençal barons had been ineffective against the well-trained men of Anjou and du Guesclin, they showcased their talent with the repression of the peasantry and laborers. This suppression was violent; in response, Urban excommunicated du Guesclin one more time in September 1368, but to little effect. The king's family was simply untouchable.

Among his more distinguished visitors, Urban again received Emperor Charles IV in September 1368; the imperial "descent" was this time rationalized by the coronation of the emperor's fourth wife. In reality, the journey was a show of force against Bernabò Visconti, who had invaded Tuscany and been excommunicated by the pope. Urban additionally called a crusade against Visconti. Charles's presence held the added advantage of impressing the companies of mercenaries that were now ransacking Italy. Charles met the pope in Viterbo and entered Rome with him, leading the pope's horse through the gate Collina, near Castel Sant'Angelo, to St. Peter. The pope crowned the empress, Elizabeth of Pomerania, in November.

Although protected by Charles, Urban nevertheless second-guessed his decision to return the curia to Rome. He certainly did not ingratiate Romans and Italians to his rule when, in the cardinal promotion of September 1368, he named only one Italian (the Roman Francesco Tebaldeschi) among the eight new cardinals. This promotion signaled to Italians the pope's reliance on France. But Urban was shocked by the situation in Italy and the attacks on Provence and more so by the renewal of hostility between France and England with Charles V's seizure of Aquitaine in 1369. The Perugians' rebellion against Church rule finally enticed Urban to leave Rome in April 1369 for his summer residence at Montefiascone. But the Perugian army commanded by Hawkwood, who had again changed allegiances, threatened the pope's retreat. After excommunicating them in August, the pope moved the court to Viterbo, still surrounded by Hawkwood's troops. Unfortunately, the plague struck Viterbo, and the court was too fearful to exit its walls because of the mercenaries in the surrounding area. Five cardinals died between September and October, including the abbot of Cluny and the intrepid legate Androin de la Roche. Another died as soon as the court returned to Rome. It was at this moment, at the end of October, that the Byzantine emperor, John V Paleologus, arrived in the city to make peace with the West. He submitted his empire to the Western Church in return for aid against the Turks.

In seeming disregard of this spectacular success (the pope had, after all, theoretically reunited Eastern and Western Christianity), Urban decided to return to Provence. The threats of the Hundred Years' War seemed negligible in comparison with Italian instability. He left for Montefiascone and Viterbo in the summer of 1370 and announced to the Romans on June 26, 1370, after having already departed the city, that he would not come back to Rome. He explained that the pacification of Italy allowed him to return to Avignon, where renewed hostilities between France and England required his presence. Urban sailed again from Corneto to Marseille and entered Avignon on September 4, 1370. Fragile, sick, and surely depressed by his failure to stabilize the Church's presence in Rome, he died on December 19, 1370. The body of Urban V rested in Avignon Cathedral for eighteen months before it was transferred to the Abbey of Saint-Victor of Marseille, where he had once been a monk. His body was exhumed on June 1, 1372, placed on a ceremonial bed, and transported to the abbey. During the cortège's first stop at the abbey of St. Ruf, however, Avignonese citizens attacked the bed and shredded its red silk cover to "share it like relics."[29]

Urban had died a good and holy death in the estimation of his contemporaries. His agony was public; he asked to be displayed at his brother Anglic's house with all the gates of the episcopal palace opened "to show that the papacy is immortal even if the pope dies" and to demonstrate to the people "how popes know to die."[30] This good death, taken in combination with his return of the papal court to both Rome and later Avignon, propelled him to quasi-sainthood in these areas. The first inquest for his canonization made him popular in France and Italy. The numerous images and pictures that remain of Urban V in Italian and Roman churches attest to his popularity in Italy. But it is around Marseille and Saint-Victor that his cult became the most active. In 1870 Pius IX declared him "blessed" but not canonized; he could be venerated by local churches but not considered part of the Christian calendar of saints.

In his influential biography, Ludwig Vones retraces the disappointments Urban suffered for Christianity. The pope in some ways failed as a reformer and scuttled the papal return to Italy; even with excellent personal qualities, he remained an uninspiring leader. Still, Urban was a pope in line with the traditions of his Avignonese predecessors. His efforts to raise a crusading army, reform the Church, centralize ecclesiastical governance, and reinforce clerical education were all part of the Avignon papacy's agenda. What distinguished him from other popes was his relationship with his curia and especially with the college of cardinals, from which he was somewhat alienated as an outsider. The personal rivalries of the cardinals, for example, the clash between the Limousins of the Aubert and Roger clans and Albornoz or the factions of Talleyrand of Périgord and Gui of Boulogne, mystified him.[31] But the pope learned and earned their respect. The abbot of Moissac put these words in Talleyrand of Périgord's mouth: "At least we have a pope. We honored the previous ones by duty; this one we must fear and honor because he is powerful in action and words."[32] Urban actually managed to control the college via his close involvement in the collation of benefices, cardinals' nominations, and his reliance on his own family. The pope created his own networks to temper the growing impatience of cardinals looking to increase their power. The next pope elected outside the college, Urban VI, succeeded Gregory XI (Urban V's successor) and followed in the reforming footsteps of his namesake. He failed, opening the doors to cardinals' greater empowerment and the Great Western Schism. Still it remained to reestablish the papacy in Rome. Where Urban failed in that respect, his direct successor, Gregory XI, succeeded, though at a dear price.

THE LAST OF THE AVIGNON POPES: GREGORY XI

Little division was evident within the conclave that elected Gregory XI. The cardinals entered the conclave at the end of the novena (the nine days of devotions and prayers for the soul of the dead pope) and unanimously elected the forty-two-year-old Cardinal Pierre Roger of Beaufort on December 30, 1370. He took the papal name Gregory XI. It is of note that his namesake, Gregory X, had initially created the conclave in 1274 with his bull *Ubi periculum*, a telltale sign that Pierre Roger admired administrators who took charge. Baluze's sources add that Pierre Roger was the son of the Count of Beaufort, that he had been a notary of the Apostolic Chamber in his teens (*adolescentia*), and that he had been named cardinal-deacon of Santa Maria Nuova. They do not highlight that the new pope was only nineteen in 1348 when his uncle Clement VI elevated him to the cardinalate. Pierre studied at Perugia under the tutelage of one of the greatest medieval jurists of the time, Baldo degli Ubaldi, the so-called king of Roman and canon laws. He excelled to such a degree that, according to Ptolemaeus Lucensis, the master often quoted his pupil.[33]

Pierre Roger was calm, humble, pious, and modest. Even his detractors, like the famous Florentine humanist Coluccio Salutati (1331–1406), praised "his prudence and discretion, his modest demeanour, his piety, goodness and affability, the uprightness of his character and his steadfastness of purpose in word and deeds."[34] These qualities should not diminish the fact that Roger was not a pushover and could be obstinate in his anger. Cristoforo da Piacenza, a Mantuan ambassador at the papal court, reported the rage the pope often showed to the Visconti, whom he wanted to see utterly destroyed.[35] Apparently choleric by temperament, he once banished an ambassador of the Visconti, accusing the man of being at the court only to spy.[36]

Gregory represented the traditional and powerful Limousin clan at the curia. He was closely related to some six cardinals and a previous pope. Thanks to his illustrious lineage, Pierre Roger had a splendid career; he rose from deacon to archdeacon and archpriest before being made a very young cardinal in 1348. A prime example of where such a career led, he rose through the Church without ever having been ordained a priest. Roger was only ordained priest and bishop for his papal consecration. He participated in two conclaves before the one that elected him and thus had experience in curial politics. As cardinal he arbitrated several cases of an international nature, and he was also ambassador and negotiator for several affairs in Italy and the Neapolitan court, posts that made him an able diplomat.[37]

Like his uncle Clement VI, Pope Gregory XI was a talented diplomat, but his experience lay more with Italian rather than French affairs. He was at once prudent and daring. Before consulting his consistory on signing a peace treaty with the Visconti, Gregory intercepted all the correspondence sent to the court by the Milanese and the Count of Savoy so that he could decipher the true intentions of his former enemies and investigate whom they were attempting to pay off.[38] The new pope was also a deeply cultured man and an early humanist. He searched for manuscripts of ancient authors but also loved traditional scholastic enterprise. Perhaps his retiring and bookish nature was linked to his fragile health.

As Coluccio Salutati notes, the new pope was modest. But if he disliked luxury for his person, he nevertheless maintained a high conception of his office, keeping up proper appearances and protocol for a person of his lofty rank. He restored the papal coronation cavalcade that Urban V had avoided. The cortège that rode throughout the city was organized around the pope; the closer the person to him, the higher his rank. This procession started with deacons, followed by a large group of clerics carrying the cross, then twelve messengers of the pope with ten red banners and two starred; auditors of the palace and advocates wearing their sacred vestments followed. Then came abbots riding white-blanketed horses, themselves wearing white pluvials (copes) and mitres. Fifty bishops rode along with archbishops and patriarchs, followed by seventeen cardinals in beautiful copes, also riding white-blanketed horses and again wearing white mitres; lastly appeared the pope with the fourth-century crown that Constantine had given Saint Sylvester. The duke of Anjou, brother of the king of France, held the papal horse's bit, with two hundred lances (some six hundred men) and a large group of diverse people finishing the line.[39]

Gregory XI may be the best remembered of the Avignon popes for several reasons. Significantly, he returned the curia to Rome. As we will see in a later chapter, Gregory's death in Rome triggered the events that led to the Great Western Schism. Even more importantly, he fought a war against the Church's most outspoken ally, Florence. The relation between that city and the pope is best epitomized by the words of the Florentine historian and statesman Francesco Guicciardini (1483–1540). Summarizing his views on the Church, he stated, "I don't know anyone who dislikes the ambition, the avarice, and the sensuality of priests more than I do. Nevertheless, the position I have enjoyed with several popes has forced me to love their greatness for my own self-interest. Were it not for this consideration, I would have loved Martin Luther as much as I love myself."[40] Politics was not simple when a city's neighbor was the Roman Catholic Church, the most powerful entity of its time, and when its economic life rested on this neighbor's support.

FLORENCE AND THE POPE: TOWARD THE BREAK

The deterioration of rapport between the papacy and Florence is best placed within the context of the reconquest of the Papal States. Gene A. Brucker, the great historian of Florentine politics, describes the initiation of the break in this way:

> What intensified Florentine fears of the church's temporal power? This question is equally as significant, historically, as that of papal motives and designs. The problem was not simply one of jealousy inspired by the emergence of a strong rival state. One difficulty was the unique character of the papacy's political role in central Italy. In the name of peace and order, church officials could and did intervene in the domestic affairs of the Tuscan communes, seeking to mediate between rival factions, and conceivably giving a decisive advantage to the party which favored the church. Gregory XI contended that the promotion of peace was the objective of Gérard du Puy's intervention in southern Tuscany. The same argument might well have been advanced to justify Pierre d'Estaing's intrusion into the quarrel between Florence and the

Ubaldini. Papal mediation was not a novelty in Tuscany; the innovation was its foundation upon a strong temporal position. The line between arbitration and dictation is particularly narrow when the arbitrator is a powerful neighbor.[41]

The Church's growth in territory alarmed its neighbors and countered the interests of cities like Florence. A papacy in Avignon fitted the designs of Florentines who felt that they could, ironically, better control Guelph support with the pope away from Italy. Similarly, Ghibellines often felt their interests were better preserved as long as the emperor remained on the other side of the Alps. In summary, two allied states striving for expansion, such as Florence and the Church, were bound to clash. It is noteworthy that both states suffered severe internal upheaval from their expansionist policies. The climax of the Otto Santi war led to a schism in the Church and the Ciompi revolt in Florence; both erupting in 1378.

Since the late thirteenth century the Florentine republic was based on a *signoria* government composed of an executive with several elected officials, the priors, headed by a "standard-bearer of Justice" (the *gonfaloniere*). Tenure in this position was changed frequently to account for social mobility and prevent single-family rule. Of course, these measures were in reality only nominal, since magnates did, in fact, control Florentine politics. Many families competed for positions in its government. On the one hand, the ancient patrician families represented old money and the traditional Guelph alliance with the papacy; in contrast, the new rich were associated with *il popolo* (a misnomer since they often did not represent the lower classes but simply other factions of the wealthy, mostly new blood) and Ghibelline leanings.

Politically aligned with the papacy, the ruling Florentine Guelph party often clashed with the powerful merchant guilds that produced the city's wealth, especially when they allowed popes to interfere in internal politics. These Guelph magnates had a long history of banking relations with the popes. Since the end of the thirteenth century they were heavily involved in the collection of papal taxes and finances. This mutual support profited both; patricians received ecclesiastical positions, while popes had their finances in the reliable hands of the Bardi, Peruzzi, Acciaiuoli, Soderini, and Alberti antichi and nuovi banking families, who collected and transferred papal funds. They kept branches in Avignon, and the names of their representatives fill the registers of the Apostolic

Chamber. The Florentine community was heavily represented in Avignon and formed the most important expatriate community of the fourteenth-century Christian capital.

In the late 1330s, however, a series of bankruptcies, most notably of the important Bardi, Peruzzi, and Acciaiuoli houses, destabilized the financial health of the commune, affecting hundreds of subsidiaries. By the early 1340s, Florence found itself seriously indebted after losing a war with Lucca and begged Benedict XII to temporarily give the commune revenues from papal taxation. In spite of their financial relationship, the pope refused, transferring his reliance away from Florentine banks into Sienese firms. By doing so, he further ruined Florentine bankers. To solve this crisis, Florence's magnates endowed full power to one of their commanders in the war against Lucca, Walter of Brienne, Duke of Athens. In 1342, Florence's magnates chose this *signore* (a despot) to rule the commune in this time of emergency, to steer the city toward a sounder fiscal course, and possibly to intervene in their favor with the pope. But Brienne's taxing economic measures failed, and his despotic rule disenchanted both the poor and the rich. He was expelled after only ten months in power.

The Florentines then tried to consolidate the communal public debt with the creation of the Monte in 1345. This was a public saving institution that paid interest regardless of usury regulations. It paid some 5 percent and led speculators to trade Monte's shares as today's stocks. This fresh influx of funds allowed new investors, the *gente nuova*, to acquire financial and political clout in Florence. At this point, more than anything, the members of the rising upper class wanted a relaxation of the Church's moral grip on their commercial activities.

Shortly after the expulsion of Brienne in 1342, the commune found itself at odds with the pope over a debt that the Acciaiuoli owed to one cardinal. Yet the curial agents' aggressive harassment of Florence's bankrupted financiers strained relations between the city and the pope quite severely. To demonstrate its frustration, the *signoria* decided in April 1345 to remove legal cases from ecclesiastical courts; the new law also prevented clerics from escaping local justice by claiming ecclesiastical immunity. The pope's response was swift. He put the city under interdict for disregarding the Church's privileges. In response, the Florentines argued that their city's peace was better served when jurisdiction remained local.

Florence ordered its citizens to ignore the interdict, but the city fractured. *Gente nuova* (the new rich) associated the old aristocracy with the defense of the Church, the institution which in their mind had bankrupted the state. But since the old patrician houses still controlled the bishopric and clergy, Florentine internal struggle reached a stalemate. In any case, both Clement VI and Florence ended up temporizing, and the pope lifted his interdict on the city in February 1347. We can note that afterward, some Florentine banking firms still found their place in papal finances, but they never regained the level of involvement they had attained before the 1340s.

FLORENCE AND THE POPE AT WAR

Relations between the popes and Florence teetered on the brink until a new crisis, the outbreak of the "War of the Eight Saints" (in Italian, Otto Santi, 1375–1378). Gene Brucker blames the "disintegration of the Guelf entente" on many factors: quarrels and misunderstanding, Florence's desire to free itself from the Church's tutelage, and its active sabotage of the Church's diplomacy. When Florence grew strong and controlled Tuscany during the second half of the fourteenth century, it did not require the same level of papal protection that it did earlier in its history. This disengagement was consequential for Florentine life. With its newfound hegemony, the commune complained of curial infringement: in 1364, it protested that Albornoz occupied Florentine territory near Bologna; in 1367, that he was taxing the Apennines district and that Urban V supported a takeover of Tuscany by Emperor Charles IV. Urban V was aware of these protests, and in June 1369 he replied:

> Recently it has come to our attention that the Florentines believed that church troops wished to occupy imperial lands and disturb the status of Tuscan cities. . . . This suspicion is completely false and has no basis in reality. . . . Our intention has never been, nor is it now, to disturb the pacific and tranquil state of Tuscany by means of church forces, nor to occupy imperial territory. We are quite content with the lands, which belong to the church. [42]

Florence riposted by setting itself up as the defender of Tuscan liberties. According to a chronicler, "The Florentines acquired greater honor than they had ever possessed, since they had been confronted by the whole of Italy and the great lords of the world. . . . They sent ambassadors to every part of Tuscany, arranging peace agreements. They assisted the Tuscan cities with troops and money, so that they would remain in peace."[43] Pisa, Lucca, and Siena became Florentine satellites. In Florence, the Albizzi and Corsini best represented the Guelph party, while the Ricci supported their opponents. When the Guelphs succeeded in convincing Florence to support the pope's anti-Milanese efforts, Piero Corsini was elevated to cardinal, a reward for Guelph support. Of course, the Ricci and their Ghibelline lobbyists lost influence in policy making each time they lost patronage.

For his part, Gregory XI (like his predecessors) was intent on recovering Papal States that had fallen into hostile hands, especially territories claimed by the Visconti lords of Milan. Albornoz's campaigns left little doubt as to papal motivations in regaining a foothold on the Italian peninsula; these efforts were, after all, tied to a papal return to Rome. Yet the recovery of those territories encroached upon by the Visconti brought papal diplomacy uncomfortably close to Florentine interests in Tuscany. Perugia, an "independent" Papal State, fell to the papal army in 1371. When Florence wrote to the pope inquiring of his intentions, Gregory again answered that they should not fear. "The Florentines were in error, Gregory insisted, when they criticized the conquest of Perugia. That city was papal territory; it was only natural that the church should seek to recover its own property. The pontiff then broached a subject which appeared with increasing frequency in papal letters to Tuscan communes: 'The clergy are falsely accused of not being satisfied with their possessions, and of seeking to aggrandize themselves at the expense of Tuscany. The popes have always defended the peace and liberty of Italy.'"[44]

From 1372 to 1375, the pope renewed his attacks against the Visconti, buttressed this time by the famous "Green Count," Amadeus VI of Savoy (named after his green livery on tournament fields), and Enguerrand VII, Lord of Coucy, two formidable military leaders. They were supported by papal troops led by the pope's brother Nicolas Roger of Beaufort and his nephew Raymond de Turenne (who became the scourge of Provence during the Schism), all under management of the legate in Italy, Cardinal Pierre d'Estaing. Gregory made his best efforts to present the league as a pact of mutual protection between the pope, the emperor, and the queen of Naples, with the cities of Genoa, Florence, Pisa, Lucca, Siena, and Arezzo. Florence refused to join, however. Three years of military expeditions did not bring any decisive victories. Even though papal troops remained in Milanese territory, they conquered nothing, perhaps because they were paid too irregularly and the papal allies remained half-hearted at best. By 1374, the Green Count had left for Savoy and signed a treaty with the Visconti. These campaigns cost the pope an immense portion of his budget; for example, 218,712 florins were spent for this purpose in 1372. That is half of the Apostolic Chamber's expenses. Another 307,062 florins went to the anti-Visconti campaigns in 1373. [45]

Florence remained neutral when the pope attacked Bernabò Visconti; it refused to help the pope, arguing that wars were expensive and bad for commerce. The *gente nuova* had won, even if by then the Ricci had turned coat and were now supporting papal policies in return for ecclesiastic positions. Florentines eyed the papal troops' progress with suspicion. When papal troops attacked Visconti near Florence's borders and when Siena accused the Church of wanting to overthrow its government, the fears of the Florentines could not be quelled. As tension mounted outside the city, so did internal politics. By 1373, the Florentine regime, attempting to subdue factionalism, enforced a moratorium on the participation of the Albizzi and Ricci families in its governance for the next ten years. Authorities distrusted the magnates' rapprochement with the Church, finding conspiracies everywhere. By 1374, the everlasting wars between the Visconti and the Church had exhausted both parties, and both were ready to enter peace negotiations. Milan requested diplomatic support from the warring parties' neighbors in Siena and Florence; Gregory received the embassies as a courtesy, but lofty in his demeanor, he rejected any assistance, saying dismissively, "In my affairs, I need neither aid nor favor." [46] A treaty was eventually drafted on June 4, 1375. The peace, of course, brought new fears to the surface, including that of the disbanded free companies that would feed on Tuscany while awaiting new contracts.

The early months of 1375 were dire for Florence. The plague of 1374 had weakened the population, and stocks of grain were meager. The Florentines felt disparaged when they were forced to wait for papal permission to import wheat from the Marche and Umbria, as the pope accused the Florentines of secretly negotiating with Milan. In June, a conference gathered papal envoys with the representatives of several Tuscan states, including Florence, Siena, Lucca, and the papacy. The Church required financial help against the Visconti. The Tuscan shareholders promised some 75,000 florins in order to underwrite almost entirely John

Hawkwood's mercenary defense of the Papal States against Milanese incursions. But the events at this conference seemed rather duplicitous to the Tuscans, who feared that Hawkwood's incursion into Tuscany while at the pay of the pope was simply a pretext to attack their cities. In short, many considered the funds either payment supporting an invasion of their own territories or a ransom for protection against this invasion. To Tuscan eyes, both prospects revealed the pope's guile.

By the summer of 1375, all elements were in place for a radical alteration of the Italian political balance. The presence of papal mercenary troops in central Italy, widespread famine, and rumors of anti-Florentine conspiracies as close as nearby Prato combined to push Florence into the arms of Milan. On July 24, 1375, Florence and Bernabò Visconti signed a treaty, joined by the Sienese in November. The recently named priors and *gonfaloniere* made good on their antipapal rhetoric; they named a special commission to deal with the war effort. It was this Otto di Balìa—the governing committee of eight later known as "the Eight Saints" (Otto Santi)—that gave the war its unusual name.

In a letter addressed to the Visconti, the Otto left no doubt as to their intentions: "Since in the pacts of the league no specific mention was made of the pope or the emperor, we declare that this league . . . is to be extended to the pope and the emperor, and against them."[47] The Florentine chancellor Coluccio Salutati, when justifying this revolutionary Florentine defection from the Guelph party to the other European powers, cited the discriminating papal attacks on the Visconti, the pope's refusal to allow grain transport to the city, the plot in Prato, and Hawkwood's incursions into Tuscany. These events demonstrate with little doubt that Urban V and Gregory XI had failed in their administration of the newly conquered Papal States. They had left these territories in the control of French cardinals and bishops. These "foreigners" alienated the Italian people and clergy, who viewed the encroaching French as warmongers. This sentiment echoed in St. Catherine of Siena's words, *"Pace, pace, pace, babbo mio dolce, e non più guerra"* ("peace, peace, peace, my sweet father, and no more war").[48]

Florentine resentment (and to some extent its anticlerical propaganda) against the purported avarice of the Church quickly spread throughout the Papal States, including hard-won Bologna, as the pope raged against Florentine cries of "popular liberty." Most of Albornoz's fortresses, the essential basis of papal military defense in Italy, were totally destroyed.

Gregory had difficulties fighting this insurrection. Financially limited, he could not pay his mercenaries, who responded by ransacking the Italian peninsula. Breton troops were finally hired under the general command of Robert of Geneva (the future Clement VII) to augment the forces of Hawkwood, but the atrocities they committed antagonized the Italians even more and worked against the Church. The slaughter of the population of Cesena, which took place on February 3, 1377, cemented the general mistrust between the Italians and the "French" popes for many years to come.

Although some papal cities eventually rejoined the fold of the Church, including Bologna in 1377, these victories were hard won and only with the skill of violent mercenaries. All negotiations needed to take into consideration the military might of mercenary captains, such as Hawkwood, Landau, and Budes. Their somewhat shifting allegiances directed their strategy and negotiations. The pope's failure at retaining *condottieri* explains in part the failure of his military campaigns, and no action better illustrates this than the changed source of Hawkwood's financial backing, the shift from papal coffers to Florentine and Milanese purses.

But Florence continued to take radical steps. The city refused to negotiate with the pope, thinking that it could bring him to his knees with the strength of its rebellion—especially in 1376, when more than forty cities joined the rebellion. The Florentine *signoria* required the city's clergy to choose sides; then it opted to support its war by selling the Church's property in the city. The pope accepted the challenge; rather than abandon them, Gregory renewed his efforts at reconquering papal lands and decided that the return to Rome would galvanize support behind him. He then put Florence under interdict on March 31, 1376. "Within Florentine territory, all religious services and functions were suspended. Thirty-six citizens who had held important offices since the war's outbreak were excommunicated. The Florentines were declared outlaws of Christendom; no one was permitted to have any dealings or contacts with them. They were to be expelled forthwith from every state; their property could be confiscated, and they could be imprisoned or enslaved."[49] As we will see in chapter 5, the consequences of the interdict were felt in Avignon and all throughout Europe.

THE INTERDICT

Florence's fortune was based on banking and the wool trade; its merchants feared reprisal and confiscation, common "diplomatic" tools used in the Middle Ages. Many European leaders, such as Charles V of France, ignored the pope's interdict, understanding that bringing down Florence would in turn destroy their own economies. This furnishes no better proof of medieval globalization. Throughout Europe, Florence's misfortune was perceived as an opening for profit: local entrepreneurs pressured their authorities to respect the interdict in order to replace Florentine influence in markets where they might now have a chance to compete. Locally raised merchants displaced Florence in the wool trade and in banking. The decline of Florentine commerce eclipsed its fortunes. In the city, economic decline was real; the resulting discontent and unemployment led to the revolt of the Ciompi in 1378. When the Florentines ran short on much-needed cash (to pay mercenaries, for example), they forced loans from the clergy and confiscated ecclesiastical property for resale. In response, the pope did the same, with limited success, on Florentine property in Avignon. In his research, Richard C. Trexler has shown that, while only a few unfortunate residents lost their livelihood, scores of Florentines bought insurance protection to avoid such a fate; they used their networks and relations to buy themselves out of troubles.[50]

Despite this strife between Church and city, on the surface at least, the interdict did not seem to affect the Florentines' spiritual lives very much. Churches remained full and processions multiplied as Florence demonstrated its piety, publicly extolling civic religiosity even as it simultaneously disobeyed the pope. But the psychological damage to Florence's citizens from this conflict was real, in Trexler's estimation. The interdict denied the faithful access to the host, the focal point of medieval piety; and even if they answered, "But we will see it [the host] with our hearts," they keenly felt its absence.[51] In response, the people channeled their religious devotion into other activities. They joined confraternities, practiced flagellation, and listened to apocalyptic sermons preached by Fraticelli (Spiritual Franciscans). This turn to lay forms of spirituality was a harbinger, to a certain extent, of civic cults and public rituals that venerated the state in its various forms. By October 1377, the Florentines decided officially to ignore the interdict; the *signoria* ordered masses and offices to be offered as normal. Still, the interdict produced heated discussion in popular circles and in the end weakened Florentine authorities. Herein lies another cause of the Ciompi revolt.

In 1378, Florence's Otto were branded heretics, and Milan entered negotiations with Gregory, who had by that time returned to Rome. The Roman people had already revolted against the pope when he requested them to disband their militia, forcing him to delay his decisions on the Milanese and Florentine affairs, taking care of pressing matters first. Eventually, both the pope and Florence sued for peace. Negotiations were initiated. Florence had begun to notice the ramifications of three years of war, and in the midst of this confusing situation the reemerging Guelph party strictly opposed the war. Florentine Guelphs managed to stop the nomination of certain members of the *signoria* by nominating some of their own party in the pool of electives. The Guelphs were eventually defeated with the nomination of Salvestro de Medici as *gonfaloniere*. After several skirmishes, grandstanding, and gross manipulation, the Medici won a decree that branded the old patrician magnates and led the lower classes to the revolt of the Ciompi in 1378. The clog-wearing laborers of the wool industry requested and received, for a few years, participation in the government with the formation of their own guilds.

What emerged from the affair is that Gregory was deeply wounded by the Florentines' betrayal; this made him unforgiving. His proceedings against them show an eagerness for Florentine obliteration. The pope forbade the rest of the world to speak, eat, and drink with them or to buy, sell, or in any other way give counsel to, help, or favor the Florentines, directly or indirectly. Gregory XI considered Florence's call for a revolt of Guelph cities atrocious, and he labeled the Florentines schismatic or unfaithful. He expedited their trial, excommunicated them as contumacious, confiscated their movable and immovable goods, imposed a commercial embargo against Florence, and cancelled Florentine credits. He refused Florentines justice, ordered the destruction of their houses, excluded them from receiving ecclesiastical positions, ordered their enslavement for disobedience, placed the city under an interdict, and suppressed all their privileges.[52] The pope's ire was certainly to be feared.

RETURNING TO ROME

As the war with Florence unraveled, Gregory maintained his stance on a papal return to Rome, regardless of the fierce opposition that he encountered from the French court and all of the cardinals.[53] Gregory simply delayed his plans but never cancelled them. King Charles V of France's brother, the duke of Anjou (who eventually played a crucial role during the Schism), warned the pontiff in brutally direct terms: "It will be your fault if the church falls in great tribulations. If you die over there, which is highly probable according to your physicians, the Romans who are bizarre and treacherous will become master of the college and will force a pope of their liking."[54] But the pope was determined. Bernard Guillemain affirms that his resolve was supported by his faith and a certain mystical penchant.[55] The pope fought France, his kin, his court, and the people of Avignon, finally deciding that he would return regardless of what was left of the papal territories in Italy. He silenced criticism with his inner conviction that he had to return the papacy to the place where it belonged; the throne of St. Peter must be in Rome. The Mantuan ambassador at the court reports that the pope even said that he would die if he did not return the court to Rome.[56] Catherine of Siena did not have to encourage him; his decision came from within.

But as Urban V's failure had demonstrated, the papacy's return to Rome was no simple affair. First of all, the pope needed to raise significant funds. A special tax was levied from the clergy. Certain kingdoms, such as England, fought this tax emphatically. Funds were borrowed from willing lenders, and the papal treasury was pawned, not for the first time. While the situation in Italy required the pope's presence, the rest of Europe seemed relatively pacified. Great lords like Emperor Charles IV and Louis of Hungary and the dukes of Bavaria and Savoy were reconciled, and France and England had agreed to the Truce of Bruges on July 1, 1375; it lasted until June 24, 1377.

Since the late 1360s and the end of the Truce of Brétigny, things had not gone well for England, a kingdom more familiar with offensive than defensive wars. Several *chevauchées* were mounted on its French territories, but the English could not dislodge their French reconquerors. England lost most of the territories it had gained during the rule of a younger Edward III with the exception of Calais, Bordeaux, Brest, and Cherbourg. At this juncture, a truce was advantageous to the French, who had been regaining territories (all of Poitou up to Bordeaux) but at great cost. Over the years, Bertrand du Guesclin may have at times been the scourge of the popes when he harassed Provence and the Comtat Venaissin, but his battle tactics regained Brittany for France. He could not clear the Massif Central nor the Limousin of English brigands, however. The campaigns emptied both French and English treasuries, and the papal legates, especially Jean de la Grange, utilized the situation to parlay for peace. They obtained a truce, an act the legates had tried to accomplish since 1369. Discussions took place between the dukes of Lancaster, Anjou, and Berry to secure a lasting agreement; it was unreachable as long as the French sovereignty of the Valois was not accepted by England. Yet the truce satisfied all parties for a while, including the duke of Anjou, who spent a fortune on banquets and tournaments of celebrations.

The pope, reassured that the continental situation was stabilized, followed his heart and left Avignon on September 13, 1376. He labored to avoid the mistakes his predecessor had made by first reestablishing the pope in the Eternal City and then bringing his administration. Gregory did not halve the government of the Church as Urban V had done; he left it in place in Avignon, waiting to transfer the curia whole once he was safely settled in Rome. Gregory's decision demonstrates that he understood his place in the symbolic web of the papacy and the expectations attached to his person. Italians wanted to see the father of the Catholic Church, not the French curial bureaucratic machine behind him.[57] Several cardinals stayed in Avignon, including Jean de Blauzac, who was named vicar general of the Comtat Venaissin, Anglic Grimoard, Gilles Aycelin de Montagut, Pierre de Monteruc, Guillaume de Chanac, and Hugh of Saint-Martial. Gregory did, however, take Pierre de Cros, his camerlengo, with him, leaving his treasurer, Pierre de Vernols, along with most of the treasury and archives secured in Avignon's papal palace.

The papal fleet of some thirty-two ships was commanded by Juan Fernández of Heredia, Grand Master of the Hospitallers. Heredia was a military commander first and foremost, as was Raymond de Turenne, who entered Rome with the pope accompanied by some two thousand troops. Gregory understood well the perils of his voyage. He organized his departure meticulously, producing some twenty-five bulls for Avignon alone. He named Aymar d'Aigrefeuille captain general of Avignon (the man in charge of the city's defense) and maintained his vicar as the city's judge. As will be seen, the pope enacted a series of measures aimed at protecting the status of Avignon's inhabitants and the wealth of the city. To maintain traffic in the area, he offered indulgences to pilgrims visiting the local hospitals of St. James and Roquemaure, the Cathedral of Notre-Dame des Doms, and the Chapel of Notre-Dame la Belle near the Augustinian monastery. He also supported his two favorite almshouses, one for poor orphans and the other for repentant prostitutes, to prevent their decline in his absence.

Baluze's sources retell the pope's return voyage in vivid detail. They all agree that it was a journey plagued by bad weather, delays, food shortages, and disease. Numerous curialists became ill, and the pope's cousin, Cardinal Pierre de la Jugie, died in Pisa. Jean Favier judicially remarks that thanks to his strong morale, although he was the most fragile person among them, the pope fared best.[58] Gregory finally arrived on the banks of the Tiber and entered the city via St. Paul Outside the Walls in January 1377. In the next chapter, we will resume our narrative with the pontiff's entrance into Rome and the initiation of the Western Schism, which would last until 1417. For now, our focus remains on the pope's return and the last months of his life.

Gregory arrived in a city that was ambivalent about his return. On the one hand, the prospect of economic recovery warmed every Roman's heart; yet on the other, they were not keen to surrender their political autonomy to the pope. In her study of the English at the papal court in Rome, Margaret Harvey characterizes the Romans' conflicted feelings in this way: "The city to which the pope returned was turbulent, and although the citizens wanted the papal court, that did not imply cordiality. In theory, Rome was self-governed with its own elected representatives and depended no longer on a rule by either territorial nobility or papal imposed officials. Thus, the *popolo* (the people of Rome) were likely to be uneasy about the return of the pope if that meant replacement of local authority."[59] Issues of nationalism erupted quickly. The French cardinals and court disdained Romans for their general lack of respect for high-ranking officials and for their propensity to walk around armed, while the Romans labeled the cardinals "Limousin robbers."[60]

The Rome to which Gregory returned was caught in a vicious circle of contrary inclinations. The rebellion of the Papal States incited Romans to favor the kind of communal liberty that Florentine banners proclaimed. But the city hesitated in biting the hand that fed it. Florence did its best to pressure the Romans into expelling papal officials. A Roman revolt would effectively shut the pope out of Rome and advance the interests of the league in revolt in the Papal States. Rome was thus a hotbed of spies and double agents. Florentine merchants long established in the city circulated news and planted rumors to agitate the crowd as they paid off whomever was willing to support their cause. Already in 1377 news circulated that the Romans wanted to elect an antipope of Roman extraction. Florence urged the Romans not to disband their militia (the *banderesi*); such an act would leave them powerless once the court arrived in the city. Coluccio Salutati, Florence's chancellor, added:

> While it is possible, while there is still time, while the oppressor of your domestic liberty is not yet served within your walls, we pray you, Roman citizenry, who have your salvation in your hands, to consult your liberty. Even if we are forced to follow, we are ready to lend all our power for your liberty as if it were for our own liberty and health. We are aware that once your citizenry comes under the yoke, although it would seem soft at first, it would be difficult to escape.[61]

Even if overly dramatic and of purely classicist inspiration, these words in themselves were biting. To the Florentines, papal rule equaled the yoke that constricted *libertà*. In the meantime, Florence did its best to disrupt the papal return. It confiscated ecclesiastical property in its territories and spread revolts throughout the Papal States.

Rome's internal fragmentation was aggravated by the assumed alliance between the old Roman nobility and the French curia. Thus, the arrival of the court was assimilated with the assumed Colonna, de Vico, Gaetani, and Orsini's resurgence on the civic stage. This distrust became evident in 1377 when Romans balked at the pope's intention of summering in Anagni, away from prying Roman eyes. The pope needed the permission of city authorities to leave and had to promise to come back! As Gregory negotiated an eventual cease-fire within the Papal States, the disbanded Breton mercenaries ransacked Romagna and territory within Rome's vicinity. Their devastation (which continued even though the pope enlisted them in his own service) exasperated the local population. Rumors flew freely that vengeance might be exacted from the populace, and these were met with calls to violence against the pope himself and his court as the only means of effective self-defense. By January 1378, an extremely sick Gregory was confined to his bed, and new rumors took hold: the cardinals were organizing a coup to ensure the nomination of a

French pope. To ensure the election of a Roman pope, the Romans met, and plans to kill the cardinals were broached.

It was at this juncture that a plot to crush the city's government surfaced, giving credence to these rumors. The pope, in conjunction with several Roman nobles, would have disbanded the militia to seize governance from citizens' hands. The plot issued from certain nobles, and papal responsibility has never been proved. What is certain is that Francisco di Vico, urban prefect and usurper of papal Viterbo, had returned to the pope's fold as early as September 1377, and the populace was more than willing to believe the French court's guilt. The people revolted, forcing the pope and his court to seek refuge at Castel Sant'Angelo. The communal authorities gained the upper hand, executed several plotters, and let the court return to the Vatican. Amid these events, Gregory, feeling his end near, decided to promulgate two new bulls.

Drafted on March 19, 1378, a week before his death, the first bull handed over the guard of Castel Sant'Angelo to a Provençal knight and ordered him to prevent Roman intrusion. The second bull altered the traditional rules of the conclave, allowing cardinals to speed up the election and suspend the traditional nine-day hiatus after the pope's death. This bull also waived nomination by a two-thirds majority. Because of the exceptional circumstances, the pope was in essence empowering cardinals to choose a candidate outside the structure of the conclave. But the second bull was never proclaimed. The eminent papal historian Marc Dykmans discovered and edited its content, suggesting that the papal camerlengo Pierre de Cros hid its contents to facilitate his control over future events.[62] After Urban VI's election, Pierre de Cros went to Castel Sant'Angelo and seized the papal tiara, jewels, and archives—the important symbolic objects of papal sovereignty. He later headed the committee that deposed the elected pope. Eventually, he even handed the pope's regalia to Urban's rival, Clement VII. In any case, Gregory could not know the future, even if he sensed that it was uncertain. The pope died in Rome during the night of March 26–27, 1378, at the relatively young age of forty-nine. He was buried in the Roman Church of Santa Maria Nuova, now known as Santa Francesca Romana.

Anne-Marie Hayez opens her biography of Pope Gregory XI with a short quotation. In his eulogy of the late Urban V, Gui of Boulogne asked that the next pope be one "to put those things that have been changed for no reason back into their original state, one who might make innovations disappear . . . who might not make too many presumptions about himself and who would willingly listen to good advice."[63] For Hayez, these words encapsulate Gregory's papacy well. He satisfied his cardinals with presents and twenty-one promotions, ensuring again the domination of the Limousins. He would have been perfect for French members of the curia but for his steadfast motivation to return the papal court to Rome.

Paul Thibault, Gregory XI's most recent biographer, highlights his failures as pope.[64] Too influenced by his predecessors (especially his uncle, Clement VI), Gregory attempted to replicate their policies and failed. Thibault argues that Gregory's devotion to the crusading ideal was a mistake since carrying such a plan to fruition was simply not viable in the late fourteenth century. His call to put an end to the Turkish threat fell on deaf ears. Most of Europe was too busy fighting its own wars, and Gregory's subsequent reliance on Hungary and Venice for aid in raising a crusade army was a serious misstep. The Venetians promised involvement, but peace in the Levant and a weak Byzantine Empire actually worked to the maritime capital's best interests. As long as the Turks kept trade routes to the East open, Venetians were in no rush to join the melee. Angevin Hungary was little more interested than Venice in crusading. The Hungarians preferred to control the Byzantine Empire, not free it from the threat of Turkish militancy.

Gregory XI also failed to establish control over the Papal States. In that arena he did come close to annihilating the Church's main enemy, the Visconti. But the great expense of these efforts bankrupted his treasury and created Italian resentment toward the pope's relentless fiscal pressures. The pope needed to compromise. By leaving the governance of the conquered states to French curial agents, a more traditional means than Albornoz's bribing and empowerment of local despots, Gregory failed to see the consequences: a general movement of revolt against papal oppression.

If Paul Thibault considers that Gregory XI exhausted the papacy and led it to the Great Schism, Guillaume Mollat is more restrained in his judgment. The historian emphasizes Gregory's moral qualities and his will to reform the Church. He supported Dominican missions in the East and West, fought heresies with the Inquisition, and tried to bring peace to Europe.[65] Despite the disagreement of historians, Gregory is unanimously praised for the energy he spent in returning the papacy to its historic location in the Eternal City. He cannot be wholly blamed for the events following his death, even if his otherwise blameless actions had set the stage.

NOTES

1. John Froissart, *Chronicles of England, France and Spain and the Surrounding Countries*, trans. Thomas Johnes, Esq. (London: William Smith, 1848), chapter 216, 301.

2. Étienne Baluze, *Vitae paparum avenionensium, hoc est, Historia pontificum romanorum qui in Gallia sederunt ab anno Christi MCCCV usque ad annum MCCCXCIV*, ed. Guillaume Mollat (Paris: Letouzey et Ané, 1914), vol. 1, 349–350.

3. Urban (from the Latin *urbanus*) may refer to Matthew 5:14: "You are the light of the world. A town built on a hill cannot be hidden."

4. Elzéar actually led the mission that expelled Emperor Henry VII from Rome. After two canonization attempts led by John XXII and Clement VI failed, Urban canonized his uncle in Rome on April 15, 1369.

5. Bernard Guillemain, *La cour pontificale d'Avignon: Étude d'une société* (Paris: De Boccard, 1962), 142. My translation.

6. Jean Favier, *Les papes d'Avignon* (Paris: Fayard, 2006), 147–148.

7. Favier, *Les papes d'Avignon*, 148.

8. Anne-Marie Hayez, "La personnalité d'Urbain V d'après ses réponses aux suppliques," in *Aux origines de l'État moderne, le fonctionnement administratif de la papauté d'Avignon, actes de la table ronde organisée par l'École française de Rome, Avignon, 23–24 janvier 1988* (Rome: École française de Rome, 1990), 7–31.

9. Froissart, *Chronicles of England*, chapter 216, 301.

10. Heinrich Denifle, *La désolation des églises, monastères et hopitaux en France pendant la guerre de cent ans* (Brussels: Culture et civilisation, 1965), vol. 2, 444–445.

11. Denifle, *La désolation*, vol. 2, 446–452.

12. Urbain V, *Ut per litteras*, no. 020323.

13. Baluze, *Vitae*, vol. 1, 355, 385.

14. Anne-Marie Hayez, "À la cour pontificale d'Urbain V: Réceptions et déplacements," *Annuaire de la Société des amis du Palais des papes* (1986–1987): 16.

15. Hayez, "À la cour pontificale d'Urbain V," 18, 19.

16. Hayez, "À la cour pontificale d'Urbain V," 19.

17. Hayez, "À la cour pontificale d'Urbain V," 20.

18. Denifle, *La désolation*, vol. 2, 478–485.

19. Froissart, *Chronicles of England*, chapter 230, 340.

20. Denifle, *La désolation*, vol. 2, 485–491.

21. Denifle, *La désolation*, vol. 2, 491.

22. Jean Coste, "Les lettres collectives des papes d'Avignon à la noblesse romaine," in *Le Fonctionnement administratif de la papauté d'Avignon: Aux origines de l'État moderne: Actes de la table ronde* (Rome: École Française de Rome, 1990), 165.

23. Yves Renouard, *The Avignon Papacy:The Popes in Exile 1305–1403*, trans. Denis Bethell (New York: Barnes and Noble, 1970), 37.

24. Baluze, *Vitae*, vol. 1, 387.

25. Renouard, *The Avignon Papacy*, 59–61.

26. Baluze, *Vitae*, vol. 1, 361–362.

27. *Chronache e statuti della città di Viterbo*, ed. Ignazio Ciampi (Florence, 1872), 35.

28. Baluze, *Vitae*, vol. 1, 363–365.

29. Jean Baptiste Magnan, *Histoire du bienheureux Urbain V et de son siécle d'aprés les manuscrits du Vatican* (Paris: Retaux-Bray, 1870), 472–473.

30. Baluze, *Vitae*, vol. 1, 393.

31. Ludwig Vones, *Urban V (1362–1370): Kirchenreform zwischen Kardinalkollegium, Kurie, und Klientel* (Stuttgart: Anton Hiersemann, 1998).

32. Baluze, *Vitae*, vol. 1, 413.

33. Baluze, *Vitae*, vol. 1, 415 and 460.

34. As quoted in Guillaume Mollat, *The Popes at Avignon: The "Babylonian Captivity" of the Medieval Church*, trans. Janet Love (New York: Harper & Row, 1965), 59.

35. Arturo Segre, "I dispacci di Cristoforo da Piacenza, procuratore mantuano alla corte pontificia," *Archivio Storico Italiano* 43 (1909): 42.

36. Segre, "I dispacci," 41.

37. Paul R. Thibault, *Pope Gregory XI: The Failure of Tradition* (Lanham, MD: University Press of America, 1986), 24–26.

38. Guillemain, *La cour pontificale*, 145; Segre, "I dispacci," 64–66.

39. Guillaume Mollat, "Relations politiques de Grégoire XI avec les Siennois et les Florentins," *Mélanges d'archéologie et d'histoire* 68 (1956): 359.

40. David S. Peterson, "The War of the Eight Saints in Florentine Memory and Oblivion," in *Society and Individual in Renaissance Florence*, ed. William Connell (Berkeley: University of California Press, 2002), 176.

41. Gene A. Brucker, *Florentine Politics and Society, 1343–1378* (Princeton, NJ: Princeton University Press, 1962), 280.

42. As quoted in Brucker, *Florentine Politics and Society*, 267.

43. As quoted in Brucker, *Florentine Politics and Society*, 268.

44. Brucker, *Florentine Politics and Society*, 271.

45. Galland Bruno, "Le rôle du comte de Savoie dans la ligue de Grégoire XI contre les Visconti (1372–1375)," *Mélanges de l'École française de Rome, moyen-âge-temps modernes* 105.2 (1993): 792.

46. Alison Williams Lewin, *Negotiating Survival: Florence and the Great Schism, 1378–1417* (Madison, NJ: Fairleigh Dickinson University Press, 2003), 42.

47. Brucker, *Florentine Politics and Society*, 294.

48. As quoted in Peter Partner, *The Lands of St. Peter: The Papal State in the Middle Ages and Early Renaissance* (Berkeley: University of California Press, 1972), 361.

49. Brucker, *Florentine Politics and Society*, 294.

50. Richard C. Trexler, *The Spiritual Power: Republican Florence under Interdict* (Leiden: Brill, 1974), 44–54.

51. Trexler, *The Spiritual Power*, 117.

52. Baluze, *Vitae*, vol. 1, 424.

53. With the exception of the Italian Jacopo Orsini.

54. As quoted in Favier, *Les papes d'Avignon*, 540. My translation.

55. Guillemain, *La cour pontificale*, 147–148.

56. Segre, "I dispacci," 70.

57. This situation worked to the advantage of Clement VII in 1379.

58. Favier, *Les papes d'Avignon*, 543.

59. Margaret Harvey, *The English in Rome, 1362–1420: Portrait of an Expatriate Community* (Cambridge: Cambridge University Press, 1999), 31.

60. Richard C. Trexler, "Rome on the Eve of the Great Schism," *Speculum* 42 (1967): 494.

61. As quoted in Trexler, "Rome on the Eve of the Great Schism," 492.

62. Pierre de Cros despised Urban VI. Upon his election, the camerlengo had declared, "This pretentious bloke is no pope and will never be," and labored for his demotion; Marc Dykmans makes him instrumental in the initiation of the Schism. See Marc Dykmans, "La bulle de Grégoire XI à la veille du grand schisme," *Mélanges de l'École française de Rome, moyen-âge–temps modernes* 89 (1977): 494.

63. Anne-Marie Hayez, "Gregory XI," in *The Papacy: An Encyclopedia,* ed. Philippe Levillain (New York: Routledge, 2002), 658.

64. Thibault, *Pope Gregory XI.*

65. Mollat, *The Popes at Avignon,* 59–63.

FOUR

Constructing the Administration

Governance and Personnel

The Avignon popes were administrative innovators, but there is no doubt that their actions were largely directed by the specific conditions in which they found themselves. Their varied adaptations to life in Avignon were part of a concerted effort to carry into France the same mystique that the papacy had enjoyed in the traditional seat of the Church at Rome. Hence they needed to construct—both literally and symbolically—a capital city with a defined architecture, culture, and administration that would leave no ambiguity as to its significance in the mind of their contemporaries. The Avignon popes' institutional legitimacy rested on Christendom's total acceptance of a non-Roman papacy. In their efforts at legitimation, they created what is expected of today's modern states: every pontiff bureaucratized the Church and centralized its government and finances. They occupied a distinct space they had clearly circumscribed. Thus, the papal administration cannot be studied without discussing the imprint it left on Avignon, still visible today in its monumental papal and cardinals' palaces. An intricate hierarchy of papal officials ran what became a well-developed and complicated administrative system, in reality, a government whose administration emphasized efficient productivity rather than the practice of austere spirituality.

One cannot fully gauge the adaptability and creativity of the Avignon popes without glancing backward momentarily to their predecessors. The history of the governance of the Church during the twelfth and thirteenth centuries is framed by the papacy's anti-imperial stance and its correlative will to disentangle the Church from secular influence. This in itself was a continuation of the policies of the great eleventh-century reforming popes of the Gregorian era. In general, popes strengthened their power base by surrounding themselves with politically savvy religious counselors, and over time the administrative role of the cardinals was carved out of their purely Roman liturgical function. The summit of this evolution was in 1274 with the Council of Lyons's elaboration of the conclave, in which the college of cardinals would now hold total responsibility for electing the pope. With this action, the papacy had managed to free itself from secular influence at its most defining moment: the naming of a new pope.

Thirteenth-century popes had initiated a movement of ecclesiastical centralization by expanding the papal court and the administrative layers required to access services from that court. They increased the duties of the Chancery and Apostolic Chamber and added new offices such as the Penitentiary. The papal court became, in the words of Bernhard Schimmelpfennig, the place where a petitioner "received the answers and favors he was looking for."[1] The familiar realities of bureaucracies everywhere—the various offices with their separate procedures, the red tape, and the "greasing of the palms" that went with them—first appeared in the offices of the curia and was devised by thirteenth-century popes. As Schimmelpfennig demonstrates, the tedious process of ecclesiastical petitioning started in the thirteenth century.[2] Similarly, the number of dependent feudatories who owed allegiance to the Church also augmented during the thirteenth century, forcing the organism that operated it, the Apostolic Chamber, to grow with it. Thus, elements were in place for later popes to build on.

The popes understood that the Church's independence rested on its financial autonomy. This financial self-rule was built from and rested on the Church's administrative structure. Since the thirteenth century, taxes had arrived in Rome from the levies imposed on those particular benefices granted by the pope. An ecclesiastical benefice was the equivalent of a salary—one that took the form of a right to receive revenues from property in usufruct. This income supported clergy who did not engage in the pastoral work of "the care of souls" (for this reason, benefices were sometimes called *sinecures*, from the Latin, "without care"). Clerical office and benefice were closely knit by tradition, but over time they separated, leading to a situation where clergy received the income from benefices that they did not occupy. Benefices evolved from salaried posts (with an expectation that the clergy worked in nonpastoral responsibilities) into a system of gifts and rewards (without any expectation of any specific duties in a given post). More taxes were imposed to support both the Church's central administration and clergy who enjoyed the lucrative gains of the benefice system. The genius of the Avignon popes was to reserve for themselves the right to award benefices, thus ensuring that the Church could tax the benefice. For example, by the fourteenth century, the common services (*servitia communia*) were the equivalent of a third of a bishop's or abbot's yearly revenue that an incumbent paid back to the papal treasury after either the pope collated (granted) that benefice to him, approved his nomination or translation, or confirmed his election.

The system of collation, which seems quite obscure to modern readers, revolved around the distribution of benefices and the rewards that the grantor could expect from the beneficiary. Simply stated, until the fourteenth century, popes collated few benefices directly, since secular authorities nominated higher-ranked clergymen and some other offices were elective (abbots, for example). The pope usually approved a choice but did not name him directly. This collation system did not advantage the Church and, ironically, tended to diminish the temporal power that it could exact on what was theoretically its own property. It meant parceling away one's own goods for the sake of governance.

In one of the most notable administrative innovations of the Avignon papacy, the pontiff systematically replaced traditional collators (kings and emperors, bishops, or a monastic community) and assumed to himself this prerogative. This centralization initially led to manifest resentment on the part of former grantors who lost their rights of taxation on these benefices. At the same time, this period saw a tremendous increase in the numbers of petitions and requests arriving at the court from candidates in search of benefices. Significantly, the new and larger role of the Avignon popes in granting these collations sparked an exponential increase in the papal bureaucracy. This very system made the ecclesiastical administration controversial and resented, fostering antipathy for the Avignon papacy! An early-fourteenth-century sermon from the Dominican preacher Guillaume de Sauqueville describes the tedious process put in place by John XXII, the complex protocol a petitioner had to follow punctiliously if he did not want to return home empty-handed. Petitioners or Romipeta (pilgrims to Rome or individuals who appealed to the curia in Rome) had first to access the court, difficult in itself because of physical distance; then to write a proper petition and have it edited, corrected, and inspected to be sure that it contained nothing offensive to the pope; and finally hand the petition, duly written and amended, to a *referendarius* (referee), who presented it to the pope.[3] The process was expensive, with fees collected by the Chamber and Chancery at each level of the process—not to mention traveling, lodging, and miscellaneous expenses.

Bureaucracy also expanded in the collection of taxes. Traditionally, papal revenues came often from afar, with income raised from its temporal (or seignorial) lands, the Papal States, and taxes paid by ecclesiastics. In general, papal income from taxation was irregular with the exception of the common services. In extraordinary circumstances like the crusades, the papacy also levied tithes. The income levied from ecclesiastical seignorial (feudal) rents and the revenues of the Papal States of central Italy were more predictable. But collecting such income brought its own challenges. These states were organized into provinces headed by an ecclesiastical rector and a treasurer, who often faced difficulties meeting their levy. In response to a frequently chaotic political situation, thirteenth-century popes replaced these treasurers with local, powerful lords who earned respect by force and imposed on their people a *census* (a form of lease involving fees that tenants paid in recognition of partial land ownership directly to the papal treasury). Unfortunately for the Church, control of the Papal States quickly became entangled within the networks of allegiance of the secular lords who ruled over them, however poorly, as papal vicars. Popular revolts abounded throughout this region and made papal oversight (and taxation) difficult. This state of affairs weakened centralization and put the Church in a double bind. Wishing to exercise de facto rule in its states, the papacy had to offer a certain level of immunity (if not free rein) to its so-called representatives in exchange for their allegiance to the Church. Yet by the thirteenth century, local powers had come to represent the rule of the popes in their Italian territories, tying the Church's hands and disrupting its politics.

In the early thirteenth century, Innocent III had intended a reorganization of the papal provinces. One means of regaining control over local political forces was to nominate to military command the members of the powerful families of the Roman cardinals, counting on their networks of clientele to support Church policy. The pope hoped that the Orsini, Colonna, Savelli, Caetani, Frangipani, and Conti families could ease the burdensome administration of the States and offer a dedicated elite on whom he could rely. Unfortunately, this plan backfired and eventually familial rivalries came into play, marked most flagrantly by the disastrous alliance of the Colonna with France at the end of the thirteenth century against the Caetani pope, Boniface VIII. Resorting to more drastic measures, the popes decided to allow foreign involvement in order to rein in Italian territorial feuding. At the end of the thirteenth century, the papacy supported Angevin intrusion into southern Italy in exchange for military power—a development that once again left the pope dependent on a temporal power. In sum, the events of the thirteenth century showed that early papal centralization had in turn created new perils. Avignon's popes tried to remedy this situation by developing a system of taxation that could finance wars of reconquest in the Papal States.

Thirteenth-century popes, because of their severely reduced treasuries, also tended to rule by what may loosely be described as "consensus." They employed great councils, gathering a large number of clergymen and lay associates to define guidelines and procedures, deal with specific issues, and reform the Church. Numerous councils worked to define Church policies during the hundred years that preceded the papacy's move to Avignon. The Fourth Lateran Council, called in 1215 by Innocent III, countered heresies, launched European crusades, advanced liturgical life, and promoted ecclesiastical reform. The First Council of Lyons, called by Innocent IV in 1245, dealt with the Holy Roman Empire and Frederick II; the Second Council of Lyons, called by Gregory X in 1274, reformed papal elections and created the conclave. The Council of Vienne, called in 1311 by Clement V (a pope often remembered as the first of the Avignonese line) addressed the Church's rapport with France, the dissolution of the Templars, the reinstatement of Philip the Fair after his excommunication (caused by his attacks against Boniface VIII), and clerical reform. The Council of Vienne remained the one and only Church council of the fourteenth century. The next council, held in Constance, was called a hundred years later, in 1414, as a forum to discuss ending the Schism. This dearth of officially sanctioned councils during the fourteenth century easily demonstrates that the Avignon popes approached their administrative challenges differently: they did not call a single council and relied instead on ecclesiastical support and their own networks of followers.

GOVERNANCE AND FINANCE: AVIGNON

Three generations of Avignon popes learned from papal history and strove to establish a veritable monarchy that could act independently of secular interference. The early Avignon popes understood the power of symbolism and used it to manifest their monarchial pretenses. Between Boniface VIII and John XXII, the papal mitre evolved into a tiara: the red ribbon of the mitre became a gold band, surmounted by a second crown and, finally, a third. John XXII rationalized the transformation of the mitre into a triple crown, explaining that the three crowns represented the three churches: suffering, militant, and triumphant. Symbolism complemented action.

After the Council of Vienne closed in 1312, Clement V centralized his grip on ecclesiastical administration; he used his family and his clients to serve his rule and left lesser autonomy to dioceses and councils. The popes who followed Clement V understood that councils limited centralization and efficient decision making. Ecumenical councils fostered plurality in dealing with Church policy. Councils had been necessary during the century-long centralizing process that had required multilateral negotiations with political powers, but they eventually failed when the papacy was at its most critical moment. Vienne was necessary for Clement V because he needed to address several issues that could not remain ambiguous, especially the relationship between popes and kings, centered on the treatment of Boniface VIII's memory, the Knights Templar, and Church reform. The Avignon popes' approach was markedly different; they acted like temporal princes who designated officials to run their government and staffed their administration according to their wills.

Clement V's successor, John XXII, was an administrative genius who opted for new tools of centralization: he focused on the sound management of revenues collected from taxation. This meant, first, the creation of a dedicated and educated group of efficient fiscal bureaucrats; second, the organization and development of taxable items; and third, the effective collections, recording, and management of these revenues. He can be labeled as the architect of papal centralization. John E. Weakland, discussing John's administrative and fiscal centralization, qualifies it in this way: "Power, centralization, fiscal independence, conformity, political stability, and discipline, were all means to an end—strengthening the Church, maintaining papal primacy, and preserving 'the seamless robe of Christ.'" [4] He continues,

> Everywhere the hand of John XXII was visible: in the complex system of accounts which had to be rendered by the Camera; in the oaths of fidelity to the pontiff required of Curia personnel; in the extensive regulations covering the most minute details of Chancery operations; in the systematization of fees for the expediting of papal correspondence with severe punishment of violators; in the centralization and control of the judicial procedures of the Rota which handled many more benefice cases from all over Christendom than under previous pontificates; and above all in the extensive fiscal activities which became much more intensified. [5]

The evidence for this feverish administrative activity can be found in the usual places; the Apostolic Chancery used some 71,566 pounds of lead to seal its thousands of missives. [6]

The great success of the Avignon popes was to centralize the finances of the Church into their hands, regardless of lingering networks of influence and nepotism. They succeeded where Boniface VIII had failed. Papal political growth was linked to its fiscal growth and to the amount of revenue the pope could collect. Numbers speak volumes: the income of the papacy increased exponentially throughout the Avignonese sojourn. John XXII collected some 228,000 gold florins a year; Benedict XII, 166,000; Clement VI, 188,500; Innocent VI, 253,600; Urban V, 260,000; and Gregory XI, 481,000. At their highest point, under Clement VI, papal expenses covering the administration of the palace and states, the construction of the palace, and the wars in Italy reached some 96,000 gold florins a year. [7] The papal treasury enjoyed a surplus that freed the pontiffs from borrowing and, thus, from external influence.

APOSTOLIC CHAMBER

The cornerstone of the pontifical administration was the Apostolic Chamber (or Camera), in charge of the court's finances. When the papacy settled in Avignon, some four to five hundred officers (papal servants, in comparison to public servants) served the court, which was understood more in terms of the pope's *familia* (household) than as a government of the Church. In Avignon, the finances of popes and cardinals were separated, and under the popes there, the Chamber oversaw pontifical revenues, the court's sustenance, the large group of agents and officers who circulated throughout Christendom, the mint, financial and religious tribunals, papal correspondence, messenger services, and the papal treasury. The chief operator of the Chamber was the camerlengo (chamberlain), who usually was not a cardinal but a bishop or archbishop. Ministers of finance and confidants of the popes, only seven camerlengos assisted the Avignon popes until 1378, with Gasbert de Laval supporting three successive popes between 1319 and 1347. Laval originated, like John XXII, from the Quercy and belonged to the household of the pope before his nomination. He received from the pope several benefices, a parochial church, a canonry, and an archdeaconry. He was named in turn vicar general of the church of Avignon in replacement of its bishop, bishop of Marseille, archbishop of Arles, and eventually treasurer and camerlengo. His well-deserved ascent epitomizes the successful career of a superb administrator. It is worth noting that most of the camerlengos, because of their responsibilities and closeness to the pope, were rarely elevated to the cardinalate. If they did, they had to abandon their post in the Chamber.

Gasbert de Laval and John XXII became instrumental in Avignon's financial centralization. Since Innocent III, popes had actively searched, with little success, to control what was called "the reserve of benefices," until John XXII and his faithful Laval initiated the centralizing momentum that carried the fortunes of the Avignon papacy. They devised means that were rational and efficient, centralizing the various taxes paid directly to the court by increasing the pope's right of reservation, that is, his right to collate benefices directly. John XXII claimed control of the ecclesiastical nominations of major benefices such as bishops and abbots; later popes extended the reserve of collations to minor benefices (priests, canons, deacons, etc.), and all nominations that involved the "care of souls" (that is, not sinecures). Until the fourteenth century, the nomination to benefices was loosely defined by ancient traditions that permitted the nomination of a bishop to the canons of a diocese, that of an abbot to the monks of a monastery, and that of a priest to the lay patrons of a church. The pope only became involved as an arbiter of last resort in cases where the nomination by established custom was inconclusive or challenged. Beginning in the late 1260s, Clement IV had already perceived that this state of affairs should be improved, but it was left to John XXII and Gasbert de Laval to bring these changes to fruition. The pope initially created papal oversight for the nominations of the successors of those clerics who died while at court. From that point forward, each Avignon pope expanded the cases available to his own collation until Urban V finally claimed the right for himself and his successors to collate all benefices as he wished. With each collation, the Chamber received a tax from each new incumbent (called common services), levied on the value of the benefice received. All benefices were assessed for tax purposes, and the tax was valued at one-third to a full year's gross income. Bishops and abbots usually paid their common service over several years to reduce their annual expenses.

John XXII was the first pope to collate successfully an important number of benefices left vacant by death or other reasons: during his reign he collated 455 bishops and abbots.[8] With this development, the pope controlled a large network of ecclesiastical "clients" who waited anxiously for their nominations or advancements. It was a means of rewarding the pope's clients or the clients of monarchs, thus further developing and reinforcing papal networks of power. The ties that bound grantor to grantees ensured their faithfulness as well as the broadening of papal policies supported by officials acting on the Church's behalf. Once appointed, a grantee's interests lay in promoting the politics of the man who had raised him to his position and could still promote him. This movement was quite similar to traditional feudalism, a system in which lords ensured the faithfulness of their vassals through the granting of fiefs.

John also multiplied "expectative" collations; that is, he offered for a future date benefices not yet vacant. Certain benefices might have four or five expectant candidates (who paid their Chancery fees) eagerly awaiting their turn, and in many cases they must have known that their cause was lost. The sheer number of petitioners made the process a lengthy and onerous affair. Vatican registers illustrate a lag of some five years between requests and responses. In addition to Chancery fees, petitioners had to travel to Avignon or send a procurator, who received a fee for his task. The petitioners also needed to befriend the powerful allies who would champion their request, usually through gifts and favors. All of this explains why the Avignon papacy counted a large population of poor "expecting" clerics who were often fed by the papal almshouse, the

Pignotte, and who offered the general population a cheap clerical labor force to attend its liturgical functions.

Petty services were added to the common services described above, tied again directly to the collation of benefices. These burdened the newly collated bishops and abbots with several small fees allocated to members of the court and cardinals' households. Common and petty services were shared between the Apostolic Chamber and the college of cardinals. Several other dues (the *sacra*, the *subdiaconum*, and quittance fees) marked specific moments of a bishop's, abbot's, or subdeacon's career to be shared with other members of the court, like the clerks of the Chamber and its sergeants.

Bishops were not spared from such expenses. Because of persistent dangers, especially with the widespread presence of mercenaries and great chance of highway robberies, they often requested exemption from the visitations they were required to make within their sees. When bishops did visit their sees, they were owed a right of "procuration" that replaced the old *droit de gîte* (right of boarding and lodging). To obtain an exemption from their duties, bishops paid a fee equivalent to one-half or two-thirds of the value of the procuration fee that went to the papal treasury. Similarly, bishops who received their *pallium* and/or visited the curia also paid a fee. In any case, the treasury also received the fees that anyone doing business with the Chancery was required to pay for sending, sealing, and registering letters. These were standardized in the Chancery's *Books of Taxes* established by John XXII in 1316 and 1331. A final kind of tax paid directly to the court was the seignorial dues received from the Church's vassal kingdoms: the Kingdom of Naples, Sicily, Aragon (for Corsica and Sicily), England, Ireland, Avignon, and the Comtat Venaissin. The Church also received donations and gifts, goods from clerics who died at court without a will in place, and the various fines imposed by religious tribunals.

If some of the taxes paid directly to the papal court existed before the curia moved to Avignon, they were never collected as effectively as under the rule of the Avignon popes, who centralized taxation with their rights of reserve on collations. More impressively, what distinguished the Avignon popes from their predecessors was their genius in developing additional means of levying and collecting subsidies and taxes throughout Europe. This resourcefulness culminated in the Church's system of collectors, some of the most powerful but least historically recognized officials of the papacy.

The collection of taxes from all over Europe by agents named collectors, the geographical definition of fiscal regions ("collectorates," from the Latin *collectories*), the creation of adequate administrative personnel to run and collect from these provinces, the transfer of funds to Avignon, the means of currency exchange, the accounting procedure for collecting and spending, the recording and archival procedures—in sum, the creation of an entirely new financial administration for the Church—rested again on the centralizing policies of John XXII and Gasbert de Laval. These policies were refined over time and were finalized by Clement VI in the 1340s.

The principle of sending a special fiscal commissary to collect extraordinary taxes in a defined area at a specific time was certainly not new; nor was the ancient system of asking bishops to collect tithes for the pope. The Avignon popes simply combined the tasks of both special fiscal envoys and bishops into one, made the office permanent rather than periodic, and delineated the boundaries of several collectorates, arriving at thirty-one collectorates for all of Europe, fifteen of which were located in France (a reminder that France was one of the wealthiest European kingdoms at the time). Papal tax collectors were essentially clerics steeped in fiscal matters and legal culture, knowledge that helped them face the myriad legal issues they might encounter. Collectors were charged with collecting taxes and negotiating the amount of their levy with their constituency if disputes arose. They were powerful (perhaps even more so than bishops) since collectors could excommunicate bishops for nonpayment of taxes. The camerlengos chose collectors, and their bulls of appointment officially named them Apostolic nuncios and collectors. They were not paid but all held benefices that provided them with an income. They resided in their collectorate capitals and were seconded by subcollectors, who allowed them to complete the many travels required by their office to receive and transfer funds. There is no doubt that their task was difficult and dangerous; evidence shows that many collectors survived violent robberies, beatings, and torture. They were, however, granted the widest range of action in their duty. Perusing the countless complaints lodged against them in the papal archives, it becomes clear that many collectors abused the trust that had been placed in them.

It seems that their many abuses easily made collectors the most hated pontifical officials of medieval Europe. Of course, complaints against tax collectors are never unusual, and it is highly possible that their numbers are exaggerated in the archives, but the sources do immortalize in a kind of infamy some particularly unsavory types. Jean Bernier, collector for Lyons, Vienne, and Besançon, was poor when first nominated to his charge. Within a few years, he exacted some ten thousand livres from his province in such ways that local officials initiated prosecution, and the camerlengo followed suit. His trial shows that Bernier had robbed the Chamber, cheated on taxation rates, excommunicated both the living and dead, threatened and ransomed, forged fake documents, and practiced usury. Subsequently excommunicated himself, Bernier continued to officiate in his church for four years. Another fellow collector, Jean de Palmis, was charged with thirty-five accusations ranging from raping virgins to collecting from the poor, pimping, notorious adultery (he had a son called Collectoret, "the little collector"), drinking from chalices, forgery, robbery, hoarding, embezzling, usury, and bragging. When his successor, Geraud Mercadier, traveled to Avignon to render account and announce de Palmis's death, he was robbed on the way and stripped of his clothing and two horses.[9]

Collectors stayed busy levying taxes within their collectorates. These included the tithes (*decimae*) levied on benefices, initially for exceptional circumstances, that became a regular source of revenue for the Avignon popes and their reconquest of the Papal States. The value of each benefice was assessed (*taxatus*) in order to identify the share of the levy. Benefices were also renegotiated and reassessed during the vicissitudes of the fourteenth century. The annates (*annatae*), or "first fruits," created by Clement V, were collected from new beneficiaries on their first year of incumbency. The tax originally affected only the limited numbers of collations done by the pope, but the pope's reserve over most collations made this tax apply to most ecclesiastics.

As we have seen, bishops needed to pay their exemption from procuration if they did not visit their see, but the right of spoil (*jus spolii*)—the papal confiscation of goods left by clerics intestate—evolved as a more lucrative affair for the papacy.[10] This right had originally allowed incumbent bishops and abbots to seize the goods (movable property) of their predecessors, the idea being that because they were successors, it rightfully belonged to them. The pope's stranglehold over the collation of benefices changed this state of affairs. Since the pope collated all benefices anyway, the property reverted to him before any of it could be granted to a new occupant. The right of spoil acquired such momentum that in 1362, Urban V made himself heir to the movable property of any dead ecclesiastics. Daniel Williman calculated that between 1316 and 1415, the papacy received the movable property of some 1,200 ecclesiastics.[11] The books of dead prelates were integrated into the popes' libraries, their movable goods sold off, and their jewelry and liturgical ornaments used to enrich the papal treasury. Collectors also levied various "caritative subsidies" charged on exceptional occasions to help the Holy See; *cense*, that is, rentals fees paid for papal lands; vacancies (the income of benefices left vacant or uncollated); Peter's pence (levied on northern Europe); and the papal seignorial revenues from the Papal States, Avignon, and the Comtat Venaissin.

As they gathered their funds, collectors were also charged with spending them properly. Here again, evidence for the administrative genius of the Avignon papacy is noted. Instead of having these funds transported to Avignon, a highly risky and dangerous task, the camerlengo assigned amounts to be paid locally in order to cover various curial expenses. This avoided the logistical nightmare of transportation and redistribution. The Avignonese system lessened risk and promoted efficiency. Such so-called assignations were contracts that named where, why, and to whom the collected funds were to be delivered. The majority of papal expenses during the fourteenth century went directly to Italy for the reconquest of the Papal States.

By the death of Gasbert de Laval in 1347, the financial administration was firmly in place and the camerlengos advised the pope in political, military, financial, and administrative affairs. The organized collection of funds led to systematic expenses ordered around four areas: (1) the court in Avignon with the construction of the palace, the payment of its bureaucrats, and all the expenses tied to curial maintenance, (2) the wars in Italy and elsewhere, (3) the repairs and construction outside Avignon, in Rome and elsewhere, and (4) charity. The role of treasurer evolved from a mere guard of the papal treasury (a store of currencies, prized liturgical objects, and archives) to an officer controlling the revenues and expenses of the Chamber, an aide of the camerlengo in the daily administration of finances. Most treasurers originated from the same geographic area as the pope whom they served and were selected from his group of chaplains;

they had to be his trusted confidants. Clerks of the Chamber acted as the financial bureaucrats who prepared letters and contracts, checked collectors' accounts, and wrote memos at the will of the camerlengo. All were apostolic notaries, and as such, their scripts held public legal value. Clerks of the Chamber were all issued from the financial administration and had previously held the positions of treasurers, collectors, or financial commissaries. This administrative elite was well trained, mainly in the study of canon law, and widely traveled, and they often received prized episcopal sees as rewards for good service.

The camerlengo, treasurers, and clerks of the Chamber regularly met in council to discuss the financial interests of the Church at large, and other counselors could join them, according to need. A staff of lower clerks, including notaries of the Chamber, scribes, scriveners, and servants of the Chamber supported the entire group. This centralization of papal finances was so successful that by the end of the fourteenth century, additional financial servants, cashiers, and money changers lent their services to the Chamber's administration. The success of this financial organization also rested on the many agents sent throughout Europe, the Church's various provincial administrators, and collectors.

Financial centralization could not be sustained without minting a papal coinage, however. And again, the Avignon papacy innovated. Since the early twelfth century, Roman popes had been impeded in the minting of their own coins by the Roman senate, which considered itself the temporal ruler of the city. The coins produced by the senate usually carried inscriptions such as *Roma caput mundi* or the old imperial SPQR (*Senatus Populusque Romanus*) without a single reference to the pontiffs. This situation changed outside Rome. John XXII relied on an existing mint in Pont-de-Sorgues, a few miles from Avignon, to mint the first papal coinages in several centuries. Silver and gold currencies were minted on demand by a master of the money, who was hired for the minting of specific currency. A guard of the money, often Florentine or Tuscan, assisted by a provost, clerks, verifiers, and local laborers constituted this small administration. Of course, John XXII and Gasbert de Laval had rightfully expected that their effective financial governance would create litigation. Hence the Chamber had its own jurisdiction headed by a judge, the auditor of the Chamber, supported by his vice auditor. Fiscal procurators brought cases to the auditor, assisted by fiscal advocates, notaries, a keeper of the seals, and prison guards.

This burgeoning centralization initiated a remarkable growth in the production of official documentation. The early popes of Avignon showed their organizational shrewdness by increasing record-keeping and archival procedures. Thousands of documents were not only mailed but also copied and archived on a yearly basis. Many of those documents are still available for viewing today at the Vatican Archives. The range of information they offer is indeed daunting. Financial records itemize expenses in minute detail. They range from recording the purchase of Burgundy wine to the hiring of mercenary captains; from laundry lists to spices and medicine; from the purchase of fine knives to the making of the pope's red slippers or the embroidery of his chasubles; and the wax, parchment, and ink used by the scribes themselves to write. Letters detail diplomatic and political relations with medieval European "states," the benefices offered to ecclesiastics, both high and low, authorizations to enter convents and monasteries, and individual favors such as the authorization to own a portable altar, to say mass before dawn, to choose a confessor, to deal with "infidels," to travel with safe-passage, and to be promoted. Some focus on spiritual gifts such as indulgences and absolutions, others allow ecclesiastics to draw a last will, and some record complex litigations.

Many of the letters composed by the popes literally passed through the hands of the Chamber's scribes. Documents actually describe them as *litterae que per cameram domini pape transiverunt* ("letters that passed through the Lord Pope's Chamber"). These letters were of two kinds: communal and open, or curial and secret. But the delimitation and boundaries of these two kinds of letters were somewhat fluid. Secret and curial letters covered what could be called the papacy's foreign policy: diplomacy and the administration of the Papal States; the activities of the Chamber, financial and otherwise; the nomination of officers; and any special favor of the pope. Communal letters covered more or less the same subjects but remained tied to internal policy; they responded to individual petitioners and also included the correspondence of the legates. Secretaries sent letters that had been abbreviated (briefs), drafted, and finalized (engrossed) by scores of scribes, both apostolic and papal. There was no state postal service in the modern sense, but the work of the Chamber spanned most of Europe and subsequently needed a comprehensive system of communication. Information was exchanged via a double system of messengers. The official messengers of the pope, under the control of the Chamber, carried missives, dealt with various purchases and their delivery, escorted prisoners and goods, or guarded and arrested whoever faced papal justice, from heretics to poisoners and embezzlers. This multitasking group of some fifty men, employed on a yearly basis, was supplemented by the private messenger services of the Italian merchant companies and a private mail company. We associate courier service with the modern world, but it already was a well-established practice in the Middle Ages. In the mid-1350s the papacy began using the private mail service of the Florentine merchants, the Scarsella, headed first by Piero di Gieri da Scarperia and later by Tomaso Cardini.

Papal secretaries crowned the hierarchy of clerical bureaucrats. They were trusted confidants who took an oath of fealty to the pope. They possessed a deep legal culture that enabled them to mesh with the bureaucracy of the court, and they could often translate and relay on parchment the thoughts and intentions of their superiors. Francesco Bruni (c. 1315–1385), secretary to three popes, is the most notable of the pontiffs' secretaries. The renowned humanist was an official of the Florentine government in the 1350s before he joined the papal court in Avignon in the early 1360s. He assisted Urban V and Gregory XI with their secret correspondence, and the popes used his Florentine experience to send him to Tuscany as an envoy. Bruni defended the interests of the papacy in Italy and the interests of his homeland at the court. He left the papal court of Urban VI, accusing the pope of having cut his salary to such an extent that he was starving. He returned to the government of the *signoria* in the 1380s and was named Florence's *gonfaloniere* of Justice (*gonfaloniere di Giustizia*) in 1383. Bruni's private letters describe a world of stiff competition for these bureaucratic positions at the papal court, where networks of influence each tried to advance candidates who competed intensely for promotions. The selection process was complex, and the Church, aware of the issue of pluralism (individuals who collected multiple benefices and offices as sinecures), tried to limit the selection to candidates who were actually qualified for the job. [12]

In total, the Chamber was the largest employer of the Avignonese papal court, constituting between five hundred and six hundred bureaucrats. But it was not solely the papal administration that was centralized and enlarged in the fourteenth century. When the papacy reserved the collation of most benefices into the hands of the pope, it required a well-organized administration to record who went where and when, in replacement of whom, and so forth. This administration was the Chancery.

CHANCERY

The Chancery dealt with the hundreds of petitions to higher and lower benefices that the pope received daily, as well as any other business that required the pope's written response, like special privileges, dispensations, excommunications, absolutions, and indulgences. Once again, numbers best demonstrate its productivity. The Apostolic Chancery produced some 300,000 documents from 1305 to 1378 and some 500,000 by the end of the fourteenth century. [13] It had produced some 50,000 documents in the thirteenth century. [14] The Chancery also kept records of all present and past documents, which could be reproduced for a fee when need arose. The Vatican registers list some 550 curialists who were employed in the Chancery from 1305 to 1378, evidence enough that this was an important service. More importantly, the staff of the Chancery improved socially throughout the fourteenth century, as in many cases office assistants advanced to become the personal assistants of high-ranking dignitaries. This promotion in status is a sign of the growing importance of the administration and of a related trend that saw the Chancery's personnel hiring assistants to do their jobs. In sum, many of these positions became sinecures.

The Chancery, charged with the publication of papal records, already existed in the thirteenth century, but its procedure was reorganized and extended by John XXII in 1331. The Chancery also dealt with the two forms of letters: the secret letters, regarding political and administrative business, also called curial letters; and the communal letters, sent to individual petitioners who requested waivers for movable altars, masses before dawn, absolutions, marriages within prohibited degrees of consanguinity, or benefices. Most documents, if not every single step in a document's production and delivery, required a fee that went to papal coffers. Hence, the rise of the Chancery is also linked to the growing monetization of the Avignon papacy. [15] In the large majority of cases, documents responded to petitions. First, the requests were referred to the pope by the *referendarius* (referee), who suggested an answer (his *fiat* of approval). The petition was then registered, and the answer briefed and sketched out in the form of minutes (abstracts) prepared by abbreviators. Once corrected, the abstracts were passed to scribes who "engrossed," or developed, them in longer form; they were then checked by correctors, who reviewed their form and content, making sure that the response matched the petition. They were then sealed by *bullatores* (the *bulla* was the pope's metal seal), registered by registrars, and indexed (with a synopsis of the letter's content) for the rubrics that headed the registers where they were recorded.[16] It should be noted that the *bullatores* were all illiterate Cistercians from the Abbey of Fontfroide in the diocese of Narbonne. Their illiteracy safeguarded and prevented the dissemination of private material. In order to maintain their privacy, the monks actually resided in some undisclosed area of Avignon outside the papal palace with their own cooks, sergeants, valets, and scribes.

The Avignon papacy also transformed the administration of the Church by developing archives and recording procedures. This once more demonstrates the efficiency of its leadership. Registrars copied all letters in ledgers. Those made out of paper remained in Avignon until 1784, when they were shipped to Rome; they are commonly named the Avignon registers. Others were recopied on parchment. They were labeled "Vatican registers" and sent to Rome in the 1430s. But efficiency had its limitations. It has been calculated that the court produced some 70,000 bulls (sealed letters) per year, but the Avignon and Vatican registers only account for some 2,000 of them, indicating that a choice was made to either save and archive or not. It is possible that some petitioners actually paid an extra fee to see their scripts recorded, as an added safeguard that ensured a paper trace in case of litigation. In any case, the bureaucracy was tedious and heavy. A single bull traversed seven offices and went through the hands of twelve officers, with a system of fees or taxes paid to segments of the administration at every step of the way. There is no doubt that the fees imposed by this administrative machine gave a bad name to the Avignon papacy.

The Chancery employed scores of scribes and secretaries all working within a defined and complex hierarchy. In many cases, high-ranking positions were truly sinecures, administered by teams of assistants. The titles "apostolic secretary" and "engrosser" were in some cases rewards granted for previous service, given to individuals clearly not directly involved in the secretarial functions of the administration, such as physicians or the director of the palace's construction. These officers belonged to the entourage of high secular or religious dignitaries who collected offices and were often exempted from residency in the place of their titles. Abbreviators had been originally Italians, but in Avignon, more often than not, they originated from the same area as the pope. Scribes of apostolic letters were also Italian and French. Notaries of the pope issued from the great French and Italian aristocratic families. Achieving the position of notary was seen as a great step up the ladder of church preferment since many cardinals had held that title before their elevation.

A vice-chancellor, either a friend of the pope or a relative, headed the Chancery. Most secretaries were trained in civil and ecclesiastical law and eventually moved up to the cardinalate. In difficult cases brought before the vice-chancellor, a corrector or the auditor of the Chancery determined which procedure to follow; issues were solved preemptively to minimize aggravation. A *referendarius* (referee) decided which petitions would be brought to the attention of the pope. It should be noted that by the sixteenth century, many offices of the Chancery became *vacabili*, meaning that they were sold to the highest bidder, evidence enough that the revenues this administration produced were extremely attractive to the many candidates who bid on positions.

PENITENTIARY AND ROTA

Two more offices had belonged to the Roman court: the Penitentiary, and the Apostolic Court of Audience, renamed in Avignon the Rota (or "wheel" in Latin, perhaps from the circular arrangement of its benches in the meeting room). The Grand Penitentiary headed the Penitentiary and heard the confession of ecclesiastics who required the pope's absolution. He was thus the cardinal confessor of the court. The office dealt with spiritual jurisdiction. Sixteen to eighteen minor penitentiaries chosen by the pope (usually multilingual mendicant brothers) also dispensed spiritual justice and heard confessions. Some forty scribes answered petitions for waivers (dispenses), excommunications, and interdicts. As in the Chancery, the office of Scribes of the Penitentiary became a sinecure, handled by an assisting staff. Again, fees and fines were attached to this jurisdiction, which also included a staff of correctors and an auditor for difficult cases.

The Rota was the Audience of Apostolic Causes, the permanent judiciary unit of the papal court. It grouped together various auditors or judges who sat on a round, padded bench, hence the name of *rota* (wheel). The

Rota was, again, a foundation of John XXII (in 1331). The auditors acted as the pope's chaplains and confidants. Ten to twelve auditors were assisted by four notaries. They served some five years and could be sent on diplomatic missions during their tenure. Medieval law required knowledge but little creativity, and subsequently, auditors tended to regroup commentaries and compile, classify, and index them, but rarely did they innovate. Each auditor held his own caseload, heard witnesses, examined evidence, and wrote conclusions to each case. These he shared with his colleagues, who, within twelve days, had to sign onto or refute the sentence. Case results were then passed on to notaries, who recorded and notified the concerned parties. Litigations were numerous and procedures lengthy.

In addition to meting out justice for the Latin Church as a whole, the Rota also identified and directed cases to local tribunals. In Avignon, this was no simple affair. Before the arrival of the Roman court in the city, the legal process had carefully distinguished between layfolk and clergy. The Temporal Court, headed by a vicar and two judges, administered justice to lay citizens, both Christian and Jewish, while secular clergy (priests) were subject to episcopal justice. The orders of monks, friars, and nuns obeyed their abbots, generals, or abbesses, and—as the last resort—were referred to the pope.

Created long before the papal move to Avignon, the Court of the Marshal of Justice existed to remove the followers of the Roman court, the so-called curialists (the staff of religious and lay papal officers and servants) from the jurisdiction of the many cities the pope visited, in order to judge them without the intervention of local authorities. Once in Avignon, the organization of the Court of the Marshal of Justice was finalized between 1335 and 1337. The Avignon papacy extended its authority not only to the lay curialists of the court but also to all immigrants who came to reside in the city. Considering the tremendous growth of the city during the fourteenth century, the Court of the Marshal dealt with an important share of Avignon's population. The leader of the court, the marshal, was charged with law and order and the general security of the city, organizing the pope's defense and supplementing the pope's household guard. Because the pontiff relied on the marshal for his personal safety, he personally filled appointments to this position from his own homeland, if not from the members of his own family. To assist him in the administration of justice, the marshal also appointed two judges, who conducted civil and criminal cases. A fiscal procurator represented the pontifical administration, assisted by a treasurer who received fees and fines. A captain headed a company of forty sergeants, which policed the city along with the sergeants of the Temporal Court. The Avignon popes excelled in administrative efficiency. The sheer detail with which these popes addressed both internal affairs and public administration proves the wide extent of their oversight and regulation.

THE POPE'S HOUSEHOLD

The "household of the pope" is the last papal administrative unit to be defined in this short survey of the pontifical bureaucracy. The English word "household" best translates in Latin as *familia* (and a member of the household, *familiaris*). These included the kitchen and stable staff, notaries, domestic servants, almoners, chaplains, sergeants, and officers of the Chamber and Bull's Office who received food, lodging, clothing, and gifts from the pope.[17] Members of the pope's household took care of his person; they were his private staff, separate from the small army of administrators and civil servants whose purpose was the administration of the Church. Note, however, that medieval people did not clearly separate personal and administrative services performed for a sovereign, and one finds in ecclesiastical careers some fluidity of movement between both services individual and personal due to the pope himself and otherwise general administrative responsibilities.

The papal institution, and monarchies in general, strove to create political stability and continuity throughout the Middle Ages. Quite often, the transitional periods that followed the death of a secular or religious leader were rife with intrigue and challenges to the status quo. Institutions responded by creating mechanisms of continuity—a king naming his successor during his lifetime, the creation of an electoral college, or the conclave, for example. This concern for the continuity of sovereignty, for the stable and uninterrupted exercise of personal power even after a monarch's death, led Ernst Kantorowicz to theorize the dual nature of the king. For the king was at once a physical body (that needed care and honor) yet was also the embodiment of the enduring monarchical institution itself. The king's physical body eventually perished, but his institutional body endured through the life of his kingdom.[18] Building on Kantorowicz, Agostino Paravicini Bagliani demonstrates in his seminal work,

The Pope's Body, how the Church also represented its own institutional continuity in the dual nature of the pope, who simultaneously embodied a transient, mortal man yet also personified the Church's institutional continuity. [19] Hence, the protection and prolongation of the pope's body became a pressing focus. Starting in the thirteenth century, the papal court maintained physicians whose sole task was to preserve the physical body of the pope and in sum, the institution.

More specifically, the entire personal staff of the pope, consisting of chamberlains, physicians, cooks, and sommeliers was devoted to his physical welfare. Originally assigned to the pontiff's domestic service, the chamberlains (who knew the pope intimately because of their required tasks) grew in importance and became confidants to whom the popes could turn for various missions. Between the pontificates of Clement V and Gregory XI, some forty-four medical doctors surrounded the popes, with each pope keeping one to four physicians on call at his court at all times. [20] Most popes were older, frail men who necessitated constant care (with the exception of the highly energetic John XXII), so they surrounded themselves with physicians who were either renowned for their successful practice or academic knowledge. Their names are among the most famous of their time, including Arnaud de Villanova (who died before getting to Avignon in 1313), Guy of Chauliac, and Jean de Tornamira. [21] A few barbers (who also treated fractures), and apothecaries (who dispensed medicines) aided and complemented these specialists. Spice merchants, who sold the spices needed to flavor food (or to make it digestible), also provisioned the court with the various waxes and ink products needed for lighting and writing.

Feeding the pope and his household was the task of the "pope's kitchen," staffed by cooks but also by the food-purchasing and storing administration, a group that included buyers, scribes, and pantry guards. A "small" kitchen prepared the pope's meals while the "big" kitchen operated for staff and guests. Kitchen extras were hired locally when required by necessity. A *maître d'hôtel*, called master of the room (*magister aulae*), usually a sergeant, oversaw the observance of dining etiquette and ordered space and people during the pope's meals. The pope's bakery delivered bread to the court without making it in the palace; it was bought from Avignon's bakers. The bottle office bought and distributed pitchers, cups, and drinks, usually wines bought locally but also some imported from Bordeaux or Burgundy. Water was carried, sometimes from afar, to the pope's kitchen by the officer in charge of water provisioning.

The pope received many guests, and his domestic administration must have been constantly busy. Papal dinners were gigantic affairs. For example, the dinner offered by John XXII for the marriage of his niece required 4,012 loaves of bread, 8 steers, 55 sheep, 8 pigs, 4 boars, innumerable fishes, 200 roosters, 690 chickens, 580 partridges, 270 rabbits, 77 ducks, 50 doves, 4 cranes, 2 pheasants, 2 peacocks, 292 birds, 33 quintals of cheese, 250 dozen eggs, and 11 carts of wine. Clement VI's coronation meal counted 118 steers, 1,023 sheep, 101 calves, 914 kids, 60 pigs, 6,900 kilograms of lard, 15 sturgeons, 300 pikes, 1,500 roosters, 3,043 chickens, 1,446 geese, 12 mortars for aioli, 3,250 dozen eggs, 50,000 tarts or little cakes, 36,100 apples, 400 pears, fresh almonds, 5,875 pitchers, 200 flasks, 5,000 glasses, 26,000 platters, and wines from Provence, La Rochelle, Beaume, and the Rhine.[22] Granted, not all meals at the papal court were of such magnitude, but given these examples we can still envision the energy expended to coordinate such events. Stefan Weiss's publication of the dinner guest lists of John XXII, Benedict XII, Clement VI, and Innocent VI and his subsequent tabulations of large purchases for the Avignon popes and the Apostolic Chamber demonstrates the array, variety, geographic range, and expenses involved in feeding the papal court and its guests.[23]

All services ancillary to the pope and curia's living conditions were also established within the pope's household. These comprised the various officers in charge of lodging, decoration, and maintenance according to the changing seasons; the tailors who manufactured the pope and court officers' garments and liveries; and the laundresses, sweepers, bell ringers, gardeners, architects, and masons who were constantly employed for the upkeep or new construction of the buildings that sheltered this important court.

The staff of the Pope's Chapel, consisting of his confessors, almoners, and theologians, handled the pope's spiritual welfare. It has been accurately suggested that the growth of the papal court mirrored contemporary princely courts, and as most medieval dignitaries and magnates did, the popes maintained their own "chapels," naming almoners (to assist in the distribution of charity) and personal confessors. The Pope's Chapel was the administrative unit charged with the performance of the liturgy, of which singing and chanting were an essential part. Benedict XII organized a new *schola cantorum,* a choir especially dedicated to the singing of the canonical hours, often in the new polyphonic fashion from the north that eventually replaced plainchant. Other chaplains were necessary to the performance of the offices, which Benedict XII also reformed by assigning the purely liturgical tasks to chaplains of the chapel (*capellani capelle*). These chaplains were headed by a master of the chapel, while commensal chaplains (*capellani commensales*) became honorific titles with vaguely identified liturgical functions.

Public religious worship also entailed pious works of charity. The papal almshouse focused on three tasks: the daily distribution of food, clothes, and shoes to the indigent poor in Avignon at the Almshouse of the Pignotte; the occasional tossing of coins and food during the pope's coronation ceremony, or on holy days, or when the pope entered or exited cities; and the distribution of specifically targeted alms. The pope also supported Avignon's many hospices and hospitals. While perhaps negligible as a specific contribution to a poor person, in the aggregate, the sums spent on relief of the poor could be significant. For example, in 1375 a scribe of the Apostolic Chamber recorded that on Easter, almoners distributed some 880 florins, giving 680 florins to the religious and charitable establishments of the city and 200 florins to Avignon's poor and its hospitals.[24] It is estimated that the "charitable" budget ranged between 12,000 and 25,000 florins per year, and in times of crisis, like the years 1346–1348, it reached 46,500 and 52,000 florins. These sums fluctuated between 2.34 percent and 19.4 percent of the papal yearly budget.[25]

Within the realm of papal charity, the "secret almonry" was yet another innovation of the Avignon popes, more specifically of Clement VI, who consolidated the various alms distributed to numerous institutions and individuals into the hands of a "secret almoner." Still, trustworthy persons continued to be charged with distributing various alms to a wide array of beneficiaries. Convents and monasteries were often the recipients of alms, in turn allowing them to donate directly to their own crowd of indigent persons. While these sums were important, they were not as large as those reserved for the Almshouse of the Poor. For example, in 1364, Guidonus de Podiovallis, a squire of the pope, donated to eight girls ("named in the 'big book' for special alms") the sum of 253 florins for their dowry funds. Who were these women, and what decided their selection? Certainly someone at the court had personal knowledge of their cases, as with Johannetta, a poor orphan, daughter of the late Theobaldus Alegre, who was promised to a certain youth; she received twenty florins for her dowry and ten florins for her wedding gown (*vestibus nuptialibus*). Another recipient, Jacometa de Aquis, was promised to Guillemus Guillemi, a servant of the cardinal of Saint-Martial, and received twenty florins for her dowry and ten florins for her wedding gown. Another, Marguerite, daughter of the late Burdolfi, silversmith of Avignon, promised to Johanneto, notary of the Papal Court of the Marshal, was given thirty florins. It is not difficult to imagine some cardinals or courtiers petitioning the pope for the grant of alms for these specific cases.[26]

The papal Almshouse of the Poor, also known as the Pignotte, took its name from the Italian word *pagnotta*, meaning "little bread." Its budget was twice that of the secret almonry, meaning that it needed to receive a regular source of income budgeted from the Chamber's expenses, in this case taken out of assignations from collectorates. Its name indicates clearly the nutritional staple of the Middle Ages and the Pignotte's main function: the distribution of bread. In the fourteenth century, the name designated not only the almshouse staff with its administrator, chaplains, cooks, and sergeants but also the building where the alms were distributed. Records show that papal almoners distributed hundreds of bread loaves and sometimes other food items, clothes, and shoes to the poor of Avignon daily, dedicating enormous sums (up to 3,000 to 4,000 florins per single order of wheat) to the task. The Pignotte's administrators bought the grain used daily by local bakers to bake six thousand to ten thousand or so "little loaves," composed of two-thirds wheat and one-third barley or rye.[27] Bernard Guillemain estimates that some 1,200 individuals each received seven small loaves weighing some sixty grams, accompanied by a ration of wine each day.[28] We can note that roughly a pound of bread was considered sufficient nutrition for basic human survival. Usually, one-third of the daily bread recipients (some 350 individuals) were allowed a full meal, consisting of wine, porridge of peas and beans, cheese, mutton, or fish.[29] Because of the gargantuan task of feeding Avignon's poor, the Pignotte required a competent administration, and its administrators, suppliers, cooks, sergeants, and ushers (to contain the crowd) may have been some of the most efficient and capable members of the entire curia. In any case, this quick survey of the papal almonry testifies to the care with which the pope took his charitable obligations.

Another Avignonese innovation in the spiritual realm was Clement VI's creation of the post of papal confessor in 1342. Again, the pope's confessors and "secret" almoners emulated positions already well established at the court of the king of France. Like other high-ranking curial posts, papal confessors usually originated from the same provinces as the popes. They ordered liturgical life for the pope, deciding the themes of the sermons that were to be preached in his presence and assisting vespers, solemn masses, and other special services. Papal confessors also prepared liturgical ornaments for ceremonies, safeguarded sacred jewelry and the papal tiara, presented the pope with ritual objects in the course of divine services, and served at the pope's altar. A sacristan relieved the confessor of most mundane tasks. When the pope traveled, his confessor followed him on a mule carrying the Blessed Sacrament with him. The confessor's role was precise and clearly enunciated in ceremonial books, where he is described assisting the pope during the mass ritual of ablution. But his most important task was to attend the pontiff through the last hours before his death, hearing his final confession and offering the sacrament of the last rites.

The papal court attracted and necessitated an educated elite that could effectively manage its growing administration. To facilitate recruitment, the pope kept a school that also belonged to his household. In Avignon, the curriculum focused on theology, since civil and canon law were taught at the recently founded university. Some of the school's masters had careers that led to the highest ecclesiastical positions like auditors, cardinals, and even pope, as in the case of Urban V. These masters formed students for their special teaching degree, the *licencia ubique docendi*. The masters produced sermons and preached before the pope and his entourage; they also advised him on difficult spiritual and doctrinal questions. Most of the professors, however, were Dominicans who seem to have followed closely the teaching of Saint Thomas Aquinas without much originality. Because this institution seldom challenged its students to step beyond the conventional, its general lack of brilliance has led the great historian of papal Avignon, Bernard Guillemain, to comment that "speculative and doctrinal issues did not garner much attention" in a court where jurists and administrators made their careers. [30] It seems that the school indeed epitomized the character of this Avignon papacy; there was first and foremost a down-to-earth pragmatism at the curia, and administrators had little patience for hypothetical and theoretical abstractions.

In the papacy's continued efforts to protect the pontiff's soul and body, an honor guard supervised his personal and palace security and also belonged to his household. But this guard cannot be considered solely protective; among the 125 ushers, sergeants, and squires maintained yearly by the popes, some held their office purely on honorific terms while others actually worked for them. The facts that their names can be traced on the Apostolic Chamber registers and that they received liveries and payments does not substantiate their actions. Registers show that movement was fluid between one rank and the next. Positions were often rewarded to deserving servants of the pope, and many accumulated posts in this manner. Giovanni Bruni, for example, appears as sweeper of the palace from 1343 until 1347, when he was promoted to messenger. He was named usher in 1351.[31] Roberto di Sangallo was a barber and sergeant of the pope from the 1360s until the 1380s.[32] He belonged to the large group of messengers, sweepers, cooks, goldsmiths, apothecaries, furriers, wax purveyors, and other workers who rendered enough service to the pope and his court to be promoted as members of the papal guard. It is difficult to ascertain whether or not these men actually held two positions at one time. Still, the pope needed real protection and received it, at least from the marshal and from a portion of his guard. Ushers, sergeants, and squires multitasked at the court. They could escort and defend people and convoys but also relay messages and act as purchasers. Ushers (*hostiarii* and *porterii*), as their name indicates, guarded the doors of all palace rooms. Sergeants (*servientes armorum* and *masserii*) escorted and guarded the pope, his staff, and papal convoys. They also arrested clerics or guarded jails and could be dispatched as special envoys, or nuncios. The squires of the pope (*scutiferi* and *domicelli*) represented an underemployed elite or parade corps. The pope rewarded his family and friends or high-ranking petitioners with these sinecures. They were all nominal titles, and sergeants usually replaced them in their actual functions.

All in all, the papal curia of the late Middle Ages owed much to the administrative genius of John XXII. He multiplied the personnel in each of the curial offices (Apostolic Chamber, Chancery, Penitentiary, and Rota) and as such extended his control over the administration. This increase in the papal workforce also meant an increase in the amount of money that had to be reserved for salaries, but fees attached to the administration compensated and paid for the enlarged expenses. The multiplication of sinecures in most of the offices indicates that these were valuable positions worth competing for. They were cozy posts that, for their owners, raised enough income to hire a parallel staff to actually complete expected duties. As they centralized the administration of the court, the Avignon popes raised revenues and extended their control over the Church and its administration.

THE ADMINISTRATION'S MARK ON AVIGNON

It is evident that the papal administration left its imprint on Avignon, first, in physically reshaping it by adding new buildings and neighborhoods but also in the way the massive influx of curialists transformed how the Avignonese occupied their own territory. It is possible to locate in Avignon the site of the various apostolic services. Before the construction of the papal palace, the Chamber and the treasury were divided between an almshouse next to the Gate Notre-Dame and a building south of the episcopal palace that the registers call the "old treasury." Starting in 1316, John XXII enlarged his papal residence, the episcopal palace. He bought or annexed most of the houses that surrounded the palace in order to increase his space. He then rearranged the episcopal palace to fit its new function as a papal residence, dedicating for this task the enormous sum of 48,413 florins between 1316 and 1334.[33] The parochial church of Saint-Étienne was transformed into the pope's chapel, and older and newer buildings were linked with eastern, western, and southern wings, thus enclosing a courtyard and a cloister and sheltering the various offices of the court. John XXII resided in a tower with his treasury. After his death, his successor, Benedict XII, continued to reshape the old episcopal residence.

Benedict decided on residing in his predecessor's residence and literally remaking it as his own. On June 5, 1336, he bought a group of houses (now called the Petit-Palais) that formally belonged to Cardinal Arnaud de Via and reassigned them to the current bishop, Jean de Cojordan, while Benedict assumed full ownership of the episcopal palace for himself. The transfer of ownership was ritually sealed on June 27, when each new owner opened and locked each door of his new residence as a sign of full possession. Benedict was then free to improve his lodging and transform his palace into an administrative and liturgical center, a fortress that would at once serve as shelter to the popes and as the symbolic locus of Christianity.

Benedict first ordered the construction of a great chapel truly worthy of a pope (this Grande Chapelle is now a depository for the archives of Avignon), and he moved into a new forty-six meter (six-floor) tower known at the time as the Big Tower (*magna turris*), the Tower of the Treasury, or the Tower of the Pope. This tower formed the pope's treasury (above and below his apartments), the pope's residence, and the apartments of his camerlengo (located below his). Over time, additional wings and towers grew around several cloisters and formed what is called today the Old Palace. It included a tower for study, with chambers for secret meetings, a kitchen and a latrine tower, papal dressing rooms, big and small dining rooms (the pope usually ate in the Petit Tinel with his officers and special guests; the Grand Tinel was reserved for special occasions), conclave and consistory wings, a great cellar, and apartments for visiting dignitaries that were refurbished for each new guest. The palace's construction offered some interesting moments. The Tower of Trouillas was built by Saracen prisoners offered to the pope by the king of Spain; it became the papal prison. During the construction of the Tower of the Bell (Campane) a laborer fell to his death; in compensation, Benedict provided his sisters with dowries. [34]

When Benedict died in 1342, the next conclave elected Clement VI, a brilliant man and a true Renaissance cardinal skillful in diplomacy and a patron of the arts. His ties to Avignon were unambiguous; he bought the city from the Countess of Provence in 1348 and built what is now called the New Palace (*palais neuf*). Influenced by northern Gothic architecture, the creation of the new palace initiated with the construction of the Tower of the Wardrobe, south of the Tower of the Pope, an edifice that displaced Benedict's kitchens and required the construction of a new Tower of the Kitchen. The latter, rather unfortunately, shared walls with the Tower of the Latrines and Benedict's former Tower of the Kitchen. (Incidentally, kitchen waste and palace sewers emptied into the Rhône River.) The further creation of the Tower of the Wardrobe added space to the pope's apartments, with a floor dedicated to bathing (with some sort of wood-boiler to warm up the water), several wardrobes for the pope's linen, the Chambre du Cerf (a study cabinet exquisitely decorated with hunting scenes), and the Chapel of Saint Michael. The unidentified French and Italian painters who decorated these rooms brought with them a new artistic movement to Avignon, naturalism. Clement chose to adorn the rooms of his new palace with secular and aristocratic motifs that depicted forests, vegetation, men, and animals in their natural environment. His choice matched the sensibility of the time when authors like Jean de Jandun and Petrarch sang the praises of nature.[35]

Clement's next project was to enlarge the Audience, a building dedicated to hearing judicial cases. He ordered the construction of the Grande Audience, the first floor of which was reserved for officials' apartments and which contained a basement that served as a theological study room. The *cour d'honneur* (Courtyard of Honor) allowed access to the Audience. Attached to the Audience, the Grande Chapelle became Clement's private chapel, comparable in size to some of Rome's basilicas.

Once finished, the palace physically centralized the administration, containing the staff of the Chamber, treasury, and Chancery, the camerlengo, and the Rota. Their offices were located to the southeast of today's palace and in the Tower of the Pope with the pope's and camerlengo's apartments and the treasury. A record of 1343 estimates the treasury's content at forty coffers and six bags containing some 600,000 gold florins. The treasury's rooms also contained armoires for books and important ledgers, several hideouts, and a secret meeting room. They were staffed with the Chamber's scribes, notaries, accountants, and some of the Chancery personnel. We learn from the expense registers that all of these rooms were swept daily. Certain staff members actually slept on site, maybe as a means of protection. But their proximity to the papal riches may have also been irresistibly tempting. On October 23, 1343, Clement VI asked his treasurer to investigate the robbery of certain sums from his treasury.[36] In that same vein, we read that on March 30, 1360, a requisition was made to fix the locks of the treasury's door that had been broken by robbers.[37]

The modernization of the palace ordered by Clement VI widened palace rooms and eased the working conditions of the camerlengo, treasurer, auditors, and their staffs. Their apartments were expanded and made airier and sunnier, and their access to the pope improved. The Rota's benches took on their circular shape, with seats and desks behind them for the auditors' scribes and notaries. A guardroom was attached to the audience hall, where guards, judges, and notaries shared common latrines. Little is known on the location of the bulla's office and Chancery.

Most historians suggest that given their diligent work ethic, the exemplary bureaucrats of papal Avignon brought their work home.

CARDINALS

The pope and his administration were not alone in needing shelter in the new papal city. Cardinals expected homes appropriate to their rank. Yet unlike the pope, in most cases they did not build new residences but instead rehabilitated preexisting buildings. In general, the higher one's social rank, the closer one's lodging stood to the pope's. Cardinals set up housing clusters (called *librata* in Latin, from *liberate*, or "freed" [that is, "freed for the pope's needs"], *livrées* in French) where they resided with their staffs. The English "liveries" brings to mind notions of uniforms worn by officials and servants and does not fit the profile of these housing clusters. These were not new constructions but simply the appropriation of a number of residences (sometimes up to fifty) that were nominally united to form a single residence while materially circumscribed with barricades and chains. The latter feature often hampered commuting, and the city quickly ordered their removal when the pope left Avignon in 1376. [38]

Tradition dictated that *livrées* carry the name of their last, and sometimes penultimate, owner. But in the Middle Ages, naming a cardinal was not a straightforward affair. Cardinals were designated either by their last name, such as Saluces, or their title as cardinal, such as "the cardinal of Sant-Angelo." Finally and most often, they were named after the episcopal see they occupied before their elevation to the cardinalate, such as the cardinal of Florence.

Livrées spread throughout Avignon's territory during the fourteenth century, and their presence is still palpable in the modern city. The Parish of Saint-Étienne, close to the palace of the pope, held the Small Palace, or Petit Palais, as a *livrée*. Today a museum, it was initially occupied by an uncle and nephew both named Bérenger Frédol, who both died in 1323. The parish also regrouped the *livrées* Sant-Angelo (not identifiable today), Mirault, whose tower is still visible today between the Palace's *place* and the Rue de la monnaie, and Auch, between today's streets Petite-Fusterie, Saint-Étienne, and Racine and the Saint-Agricol Church.

The Parish of Saint-Agricol included the Albano *livrée*, which stood roughly on the location of today's town hall, the bell tower of which is a fourteenth-century vestige; the *livrée* Amiens, between today's Impasse de l'Oratoire, Rue Joseph-Vernet, and Rue Plaisance; the *livrée* Poitiers, quite large, extending to today's streets Saint-Agricol, Bouquerie, Plan de Lunel, Petite Calade, and Felix Gras; the *livrée* Cambrai, on the location of today's Calvet Museum; the *livrée* of Naples (now gone, but extending from today's Rue Théodore-Aubanel to Rue Bouquerie); and the *livrée* Dax, close to today's Place de l'Horloge.

The Parish of Saint-Didier encompassed the *livrée* Vergne or Ceccano, which today serves as Avignon's magnificent municipal library; the *livrée* Venice, near Ceccano, on today's Rue Laboureur; and the *livrée* Giffon, on the southern limits of today's Rue des Lices. The Parish of Notre-Dame la Principale held the *livrée* Pétramale, on the location of today's namesake street; the *livrée* Viviers, near Pétramale (it was located between the streets Bonneterie, Collège de la Croix, de la Masse, and Grivolas); the *livrée* du Puy, located on today's Rue du Collège de la Croix; the *livrée* Principale or Pampelune, on today's Rue des Fourbisseurs; and the *livrée* Garlanderie, on today's Rue Galante.

The Parish of Saint-Geniès tallied the short-lived *livrée* "at or near the Dominicans," which was made up of a building owned by the Franciscans; and the *livrée* Saint-Geniès (where the old parochial church, Rue Bonneterie, stood). The Parish of Saint-Pierre counted the *livrée* Thury, the vestiges of which can be found in the cellar of a hotel located on the Rue de Mons; the *livrée* of Florence, on today's Place Pie; and the *livrée* Neuchâtel, which housed the auditor of the Apostolic Chamber and his jail, the tower of which can be seen today in Rue du Chapeau Rouge. The Parish of Saint-Symphorien held the *livrée* Saunerie, with its surviving tower in today's Rue Carnot; the *livrée* Saluces, north of the previous one, running from the Rue de la Croix to Rue Sainte-Catherine; the *livrée* "Old" Viviers, north of the Rue Banasterie; and south of the same street, the *livrée* Auxerre. Last, the *livrée* Saint-Martial stood on today's Rue Peyrolerie and Rue Taulignan.

The construction of the palace and the delimitation of *livrées* altered the fabric of Avignon's urban landscape. Houses were bought or rented by the court to be assigned to curialists and administrative departments, while others were destroyed in order to make way for new construction projects. When space eventually ran out within Avignon's city center, the cardinals moved across the bridge to Villeneuve. From 1316 on, faced with a housing shortage, civil and religious authorities set up a system of assignation. *Assignatores* (assignation officers), after having inventoried all available lodgings, allotted houses at fixed rents to newly arrived curialists. In this way, the papacy devised some form of rent-control practice. Once a house was selected, the owners were mandated to leave it after receiving fair compensation. The system was not perfect, though. In 1346, for example, the cardinal of Autun evicted from his house the representative in court of the city of Hamburg, claiming that the residence belonged to his *livrée*. Tenacious, the German representative complained to the pope and received *gain de cause*.[39] In 1364, Bishop Anglic Grimoard of Avignon, Urban V's brother, could not take possession of his episcopal palace because a cardinal, Talleyrand of Périgord, considered it his instead.[40]

Still, all parties tried to take advantage of the situation. The Avignonese, who carried the burden of this housing crisis, demanded exorbitant rents and selling prices. They rationalized their claims by stating that homes requisitioned by *assignatores* could not be sold or bequeathed at will, since they had to be rented or sold to curialists. Because they were hampered in their rights of ownership, the Avignonese instead tried to charge whatever they wanted in this buyers' market. The situation became so dire that John XXII devised a new system of home taxation wherein each homeowner contented himself with the minimum rooms necessary to his rank and allowed available space to be offered to curialists. *Assignatores* and *taxatores domorum* (home-tax officers) formed a commission that inventoried all available space, assigned a tax rate to rentals, and distributed available lodging according to necessity and rank. To forestall eventual discontent, Clement VI declared the area outside the city walls free from the *"livrée* burden"; there, all new construction could be permitted without restriction.[41] This regulation created a large flux toward the city suburbs.

Cardinals were not shy in claiming their territory. Often at the expense of others, they (or, rather, their staff) preemptively branded their coat of arms on houses belonging to others, forcing the unlucky owners to drag cardinals to court for their removal. We know, for example, that in 1357, Cardinal Nicolas Rosell branded the house of the sergeant at arms Giraud de Beaupuits. Papal officers subsequently ordered the removal of the coat of arms, much to the cardinal's annoyance.

Another housing problem surfaces frequently in Avignonese records: rental evasion. This was so pervasive that the popes intervened on several occasions, issuing numerous bulls in response to the problem. In July 1311 the camerlengo requested that the followers of the Roman court pay their rents within nine days of arrival. [42] On April 10, 1367, at the request of the Avignonese citizenry, Urban V, on leaving Avignon for Rome, commanded under the threat of excommunication that all followers of the Roman curia—regardless of rank, ecclesiastic or monk, religious or layman—pay their rents. Urban did clarify that expenses incurred from repairs done to the rentals could be deducted from the total sum, as long as lessors and lessees agreed on the terms. [43] After his return to Avignon, Gregory XI reiterated the same injunction on December 1, 1373, in his own words to satisfy the Avignonese people, and he did so again in 1376 on leaving for Rome. [44]

The recurrence of these issues points to a specific mind-set. Cardinals and other curialists showed a remarkable detachment toward Avignon and its people, an attitude perhaps revealing their sense of the unnatural and transitory character of the Avignon papacy. They refused to pay rent because they were not engaged with their community; Avignon was just a means to an end. The court's presence in itself economically benefited the city, and to much of the curia this alone sufficed; with that, their involvement with Avignon ended. Even when they died, most cardinals chose to be buried in their homelands, sometimes electing to leave a portion of their remains entombed in a monument in the papal city, if only to keep with the papal tradition of double burial.

After the pontiff, cardinals were the most important members of the Church. Like the pope, they were named for life. Most of them had long careers at the court, which perhaps led them to create partisan factions, to lead networks of clients, and to practice nepotism. The "princes of the Church" were the pope's electors when meeting in conclave and his advisors when meeting in consistory. Cardinals led the pope's executive branch of government. They often headed the Chancery, Penitentiary, and special tribunals set up to resolve difficult ecclesiastical cases. They drafted reports and appeals; they were sent on legations abroad, specifically to pacify the Italian Papal States while serving as vicar-general; they might broker peace between France and England or travel generally throughout Europe to defend the interests of the Church. Some twenty of them supported each Avignon pope, and their numbers varied slightly, according to papal promotions. Clement V and John XXII each named twenty-eight cardinals; Benedict XII, seven; Clement VI, twenty-five; Innocent VI, fifteen; Urban V, fourteen; and Gregory XI, twenty-one.[45] The numbers of Italian cardinals decreased exponentially with the election of southern French popes (all together, ninety-five cardinals were southern-French between 1316 and 1375), and of the fourteen Italians who remained, three were of the Orsini family, two were Colonnas, and two were Caetanis, evidence that the turbulent Roman aristocracy was still welcomed at the court.[46] As will be discussed later, this French majority became pivotal in the initiation of the Great Western Schism. Of the 134 Avignon cardinals, 91 were members of the secular clergy, and 43 belonged to the regular orders. In general, the majority of them were promoted because they were either relatives or compatriots of the pope, high-ranking curial servants, or officers of kings or great magnates.[47]

The "princes of the Church" were funded in part by the Apostolic Chamber, in part by the income of the many benefices they held, and by generous gifts from popes and kings. They usually supplemented their ecclesiastical income with their own private fortunes, which were usually quite large since most cardinals issued from the aristocracy. They kept households that mimicked the pope's in composition, with a staff of around fifty; this explains their demanding need for space.[48] Their households included a chapel with chaplains and cantors, an almoner, physicians, apothecaries, barbers, sergeants, squires, a kitchen, officers, scribes, secretaries, and a judicial team led by an auditor; the whole lot was headed by the cardinals' chamberlains.

Cardinals were arrogant, ostentatious, and vain. As such, they followed the lifestyle of magnates and aristocrats, men who considered magnificence their duty. The most obvious example is Cardinals Annibal Ceccano and Pedro Gomez and the infamous banquet they offered in honor of Clement VI in April–May 1343. Cardinal Ceccano was widely known for such an extravagant and refined lifestyle, it led Saint Bridget of Sweden to promise him eternal life in hell (this could explain why he chose to be buried in Franciscan garb).[49] He and Cardinal Gomez fed the pope, his entire retinue (with a large contingent of the pope's family), and some additional cardinals nine courses comprising three dishes each. These included a castle constructed from "hairy" game with a huge stag, boar, roe deer, and hares, which, even when roasted, were arranged to look alive! Trees covered with silver held apples, pears, figs, peaches, raisins, and candied fruits. Wines came from the best regions: Greece, La Rochelle, Beaune, and Saint Pourçaint. The rooms of the cardinal's palace were decorated with exquisite cloths, furs, covers, and tapestries. The entertainment consisted of a choir of young boys, tableaux vivants, jousting and hand-to-hand combats, music, and dancing. In addition to this feast, the attendants received sumptuous gifts: the cardinals offered the pope two rings of sapphire and topaz and a racehorse, while the pope's knights and squires received new coats and silver belts holding florin-filled purses; all in attendance received gifts of money and jewelry.[50]

In spite of their efforts to flatter the popes, John XXII in 1316 and Innocent VI in 1357 rebuffed cardinals by promulgating sumptuary regulations aimed at limiting their extravagant behavior. The popes attempted to limit the size of the cardinals' entourages, the quality and quantity of the food they ate, and the lavishness of their entertainment. The cardinals responded mostly by ignoring papal regulations until the pope died. After all, as papal designators they had the upper hand in choosing a pope whom they felt would give them wider berth. If a pope became insistent on these measures, some cardinals rebelled openly against what they considered papal infringement on their lives. As we saw earlier, before the cardinals agreed to confirm Innocent VI's election in December 1352, they coerced him into a "capitulation" that freed them from papal interference. Innocent VI agreed to the amendments for his election, but he repudiated them quietly in June 1354.[51] Of course, the most flagrant act of rebellion against the pope arose in 1378, when the cardinals' rebellion against their pope initiated the Great Western Schism.[52]

When summarizing the general and specific traits of the Avignon papacy, Jean Favier insists on differentiating between royal and ecclesial administrations.[53] In the case of monarchies, by the fourteenth century, royal domains and realms tended to coincide, while for the papacy, the Papal States did not actually coincide with the Church. The pope's spiritual kingdom was much larger than his temporal one. This major difference led to unique attributes in the development of the papacy's judicial and financial administrations. For example, the pope did not feel the need to judge a large group of subjects and, as such, did not develop an administration centered on imposing justice on people, as kings did. Rather, the pope's justice went to litigation centered on curial benefices and collations. In practice, this meant that papal justice could not borrow administrative procedures from secular states, as European states did, and was bound to innovate. The papacy had to stand alone and negotiate its rights with secular states. This position led to a strengthening of papal diplomacy that gave the Church an advantage in European politics. Papal diplomacy cost the pope very little. Legates and nuncios did not receive salaries from the Chamber but incomes from their benefices; the only caveat was for the pope to ensure that his staff was well trained and competent. Because of its unique status in Europe, the Church created a specific legal system with its own personnel tied to its distinct needs; this is why popes created a university in Avignon that specialized in the study of law. But ironically, secular and clerical states recruited for their bureaucracies in similar fashion: once established, personnel invited family and friends to join them, and nepotism was widely encountered in both.

All in all, the greatest originality of the Avignon papacy was its archiving and financial capability. Jean Favier states, "The Avignon Papacy constantly made an effort comparable to that of England at the time of Domesday Book."[54] It may have been the sole Western state to ever preserve its documents with such a level of detail and meticulousness. The abundance of material found in the Vatican Secret Archives is a testament to the Avignon papacy's foresight. In addition to their penchant for thorough record keeping, the popes understood that the Church needed a well-qualified administration. As it centralized documentation, the papacy's financial centralization also quickly made Avignon a business capital of Europe, concentrating funds, business elite, and spending in one location. This elite altered the fabric of the city. Some of the beautiful cardinal *livrées* still stand today, like Avignon's Bibliothèque Ceccano, former home of Cardinal Annibaldo Ceccano between 1329 and 1350, serving as reminders of the city's glorious medieval past.

NOTES

1. Bernhard Schimmelpfennig, *The Papacy*, trans. James Sievert (New York: Columbia University Press, 1992), 188.

2. See Schimmelpfennig, *The Papacy*, 188–197, where he itemizes the function of the court.

3. Guillaume de Sauqueville, Paris, BnF, lat. 16495 f. sermon 24 (f. 66rb–66vb), in Christine Chevalier Boyer, *Les sermons de Guillaume de Sauqueville: L'activité d'un prédicateur dominicain à la fin du règne de Philippe le Bel* (Thèse de doctorat d'Histoire, Lyon 2: Lumières, 2007), http://theses.univ-lyon2.fr/documents/lyon2/2007/chevalier_c#p=0&a=top.

4. John E. Weakland, "Administrative and Fiscal Centralization under Pope John XXII, 1316–1334," *Catholic Historical Review* 54.1 (1968): 43.

5. Weakland, "Administrative and Fiscal Centralization," 54.

6. Weakland, "Administrative and Fiscal Centralization," 51; Sebastian Zanke itemized some 67,000 letters for John XXII's pontificate; see "Imagined Spaces? The Papal Registers in the Pontificate of John XXII (1316–1334)," in *Images and Words in Exile: Avignon and Italy in the First Half of the Fourteenth Century (ca. 1310–1352)*, ed. Elisa Brilli, Laura Fenelli, and Gerhard Wolf (Florence, Italy: SISMEL-Edizioni del Galluzzo, forthcoming).

7. These numbers come from Jean Favier, *Les papes d'Avignon* (Paris: Fayard, 2006), 251–252. Favier was the great specialist on the finances of the Avignon papacy.

8. Favier, *Les papes d'Avignon*, 229.

9. See Charles Samaran and Guillaume Mollat, *La fiscalité pontificale en France au XIVe siècle: Période d'Avignon et Grand Schisme d'Occident* (Paris: Fontemoing, 1905), 116–119, 211–220.

10. It was, in fact, so lucrative that it was condemned by the Council of Constance in 1417.

11. Daniel Williman, *The Right of Spoil of the Popes of Avignon, 1316–1415* (Philadelphia: American Philosophical Society, 1988), 1; and Joëlle Rollo-Koster, *Raiding Saint Peter: Empty Sees, Violence, and the Initiation of the Great Western Schism (1378)* (Leiden and Boston: Brill, 2008), 107–166.

12. See Gene Brucker, " An Unpublished Source on the Avignon Papacy: The Letters of Francesco Bruni," *Traditio* 19 (1963): 351–370.

13. Irena Sulkowska-Kuras and Slanislaw Kuras, "Suppliques, brouillons, lettres et registres de la Chancellerie apostoloque relatifs à la Pologne à l'époque d'Avignon (1305–1378)," *Mélanges de l'École française de Rome, moyen-âge-temps modernes* 96.2 (1984): 721.

14. Walter Ullman, *A Short History of the Papacy in the Middle Ages* (London: Methuen, 1972), 248.

15. Michael Tangl, *Die päpstlichen Kanzleiordnungen von 1200–1500* (Innsbruck: Wagner, 1894), published the medieval popes' regulations for the Chancery, updated at the beginning of their taking office. They itemized the fees charged for each imaginable letter the Chancery possibly sent and the remuneration that the various scribes, notaries, correctors, abbreviators, and others received for their tasks.

16. The seal held Peter and Paul on one side, Peter recognizable by his curly beard and Paul by his pointy one, and the name and number of the pope on the other. It was tied to the parchment with a yellow or red ribbon or hemp.

17. Bernard Guillemain, *La cour pontificale d'Avignon: Étude d'une société* (Paris: De Boccard, 1962), 42.

18. Ernst Kantorowicz, *Laudes Regiae: A Study in Liturgical Acclamations and Mediaeval Ruler Worship* (Berkeley: University of California Press, 1946); and *The King's Two Bodies* (Berkeley: University of California Press, 1957).

19. Agostino Paravicini Bagliani, *The Pope's Body*, trans. D. S. Peterson (Chicago: University of Chicago Press, 2000).

20. Guillemain, *La cour pontificale*, 376–382.

21. See Thomas F. Glick, Steven J. Livesey, and Faith Wallis, eds., *Medieval Science, Technology and Medicine: An Encyclopedia* (London: Routledge, 2005), 51–53, 213–214, and 85 for, respectively, Villanova, Chauliac, and Tornamira.

22. Robert Brun, *Avignon au temps des papes* (Brionné: Gérard Monfort, 1983), 220.

23. Stefan Weiss, *Die Versorgung des päpstlichen Hofes in Avignon mit Lebensmitteln (1316–1378): Studien zur Sozial- und Wirtschaftsgeschichte eines mittelalterlichen Hofes* (Berlin: Akademie, 2002), is a monumental study of the food supply and provisioning at the court of Avignon; see, specifically, 449–515 for the papal guest list and 516–652 for the tables of purchase organized by pontificate.

24. Karl Heinrich Schäfer, *Die Ausgaben der apostolischen Kammer unter den Päpsten Urban V und Gregor XI (1316–1378)* (Paderborn: Ferdinand Shöningen Verlag, 1937), 582.

25. Guillemain, *La cour pontificale*, 409.

26. Schäfer, *Die Ausgaben der apostolischen Kammer unter den Päpsten Urban V und Gregor XI*, 326.

27. Guillemain, *La cour pontificale*, 412.

28. Guillemain, *La cour pontificale*, 413.

29. Schäfer, *Die Ausgaben der apostolischen Kammer unter den Päpsten Urban V und Gregor XI*, 584.

30. Guillemain, *La cour pontificale*, 391.

31. Guillemain, *La cour pontificale*, 426. I describe some of the careers in *The People of Curial Avignon: A Critical Edition of the Liber Divisionis and the Matriculae of Notre Dame la Majour* (Lampeter, GB, and Lewiston, NY: Edwin Mellen Press, 2009), 146–147.

32. On Roberto di Sangallo, see Guillemain, *La cour pontificale*, 382; Anne-Marie Hayez and Michel Hayez, "Les saints honorés à Avignon au XIVe siècle," *Mémoires de l'académie de Vaucluse*, series 7, 6 (1985): 200; Pierre Pansier, "Les médecins des papes d'Avignon (1308–1403)," *Janus* (1909): 405, 432; Schäfer, *Die ausgaben der Apostolischen kammer unter Benedikt XII, Klemens VI und Innocenz VI (1335–1362)*, 809; and Schäfer, *Die Ausgaben der apostolischen Kammer unter den Päpsten Urban V und Gregor XI*, 72, 207, 221, 254, 517, 542, and 602.

33. Dominique Vingtain, *Avignon: Le palais des papes* (Saint-Léger-Vauban: Zodiaque, 1998), 72.

34. Vingtain, *Avignon: Le palais des papes*, 168–171.

35. Vingtain, *Avignon: Le palais des papes*, 254–84.

36. Clément VI, *Ut per literas apostolicas*, no. 000480.

37. Roberte Lentsch, "La localisation et l'organisation matérielle des services administratifs au palais des Papes," in *Aux origines de l'État moderne: Le fonctionnement administratif de la papauté d'Avignon: Actes de la table ronde d'Avignon (23–24 janvier 1988)* (Rome: École française de Rome, 1990), 299.

38. August 25, 1376, Archives départementales de Vaucluse (henceforth ADV), *Archives communales d'Avignon*, boîte 77, no. 2251.

39. Joseph Girard, *Évocation du vieil Avignon* (Paris: Les éditions de minuit, 1958), 50.

40. Anne-Marie Hayez, "L'entourage d'Urbain V: Parents, amis et familiers," *Annuaire de la Société des amis du Palais des papes* (1988–1989): 38.

41. ADV, *Archives communales d'Avignon*, boîte 18, no. 574.

42. ADV, *Archives communales d'Avignon*, boîte 18, no. 581.

43. Urbain V, *Ut per litteras apostolicas*, no. 019752.

44. Grégoire XI, *Ut per litteras apostolicas*, no. 027351; and ADV, *Archives communales d'Avignon*, boîte 77, no. 2551.

45. Guillemain, *La cour pontificale*, 184.

46. At their origins, cardinals were the administrators of Rome: cardinal-deacons administered Rome's oldest churches; cardinal-priests were the priests of Rome's greatest parishes; and cardinal-bishops were bishops of the Latium sees.

47. Guillemain, *La cour pontificale*, 183–276 remains the best thorough study of the Avignon cardinals.

48. Guillemain, *La cour pontificale*, 252, emphasizes this "mimicking" characteristic.

49. See Marc Dykmans, "Le cardinal Annibal de Ceccano (vers 1282–1350): Étude biographique et testament du 17 juin 1348," *Bulletin de l'institut historique belge de Rome* 43 (1973): 145–344.

50. George de Loye, "Réceptions du pape Clément VI par les cardinaux Annibal Ceccano et Pedro Gomez à Gentilly et Montfavet (30 avril–1ier mai 1343)," in *Avignon au moyen âge: Textes et documents*, ed. I.R.E.B.M.A. et alii (Avignon: Aubanel, 1988), 81–92.

51. The text is published in Pierre Gasnault and M. H. Laurent, *Innocent VI (1352–1362): Lettres secrètes et curiales* (Paris, 1960), vol. 1, fasc. 2, 137, no. 435.

52. Stefan Weiss, "Luxury and Extravagance at the Papal Court in Avignon and the Outbreak of the Great Western Schism," in *A Companion to the Great Western Schism (1378–1417)*, ed. Joëlle Rollo-Koster and Thomas Izbicki (Leiden: Brill, 2009), 67–87.

53. Jean Favier, "Traits généraux et traits spécifiques de l'administration pontificale," in *Aux origines de l'État moderne: Le fonctionnement administratif de la papauté d'Avignon: Actes de la table ronde d'Avignon (23–24 janvier 1988)* (Rome: École Française de Rome, 1990), 1–4.

54. Jean Favier, "Traits généraux et traits spécifiques de l'administration pontificale," 3.

FIVE

Avignon

The Capital and Its Population

It is a matter of course that the settling of the papacy at Avignon transformed what was then little more than a Provençal village into a vibrant cosmopolitan city, a true Christian capital. This transformation was the result of various related events. The papacy did not control the flow of immigrants who constantly populated the city in its footsteps, but its presence, its administration, and its ordinances encouraged this movement. The fourteenth-century population boom redefined habitable space in the city. In addition to this marked increase in Avignon's residents, the popes installed themselves in a new palace at the center of the old town, expanding service buildings nearby, and all crowded within the old twelfth-century walls. Following the construction of the palace, the city arranged itself concentrically, placing, with great symbolic importance, the head of Christianity at its ancient center and his administration around the Rocher des Doms (Rock of the Domes), sanctified by the city's cathedral and the papal palace. When space became scarce, papal services spread outward and around the city, toward the boundaries of its urban limits.

A new Avignon, segmented topographically and socially, grew from the inside out, with the papal administration and wealthy citizens at the center and the poorer population on the margins of its territory, in the new *bourgs* (suburbs) that sprang up outside the old walls. Despite this separation, the new fourteenth-century walls, built in the late 1350s, en-

189

circled Avignon's old and new quarters, integrating to some extent the wealthy and poor. All in all, the city acclimated to these changes well. In truth, the commune did not have much choice after the pope bought Avignon from Joanna of Naples in 1348, legally binding the fate of the city to that of the papacy. Given this unique arrangement, what surprises historians of the city the most is fourteenth-century Avignon's relative cultural modernity. Avignon was far quieter than Rome with its turbulent politics, and its aristocracy never reached the level of violence and aggression found among the Roman clans. Papal civic legislation managed and satisfied Avignon's population, which was diverse and relatively tolerant for the time. The city accepted all newcomers without stigmatizing the poor or foreigners. Contrary to popular assumption, medieval urban life did not differ dramatically from its modern counterpart. Cities have always attracted people in search of opportunities to better their lives, and medieval Avignon serves as a paradigm for the study of the social-cultural effect of immigration on urban growth. Avignon's residents endured a rapid population increase, overcrowded streets, noise, poor sanitation, and scarce shelter, mainly as a result of the mass of urban poor who arrived in the footsteps of the popes.

At Avignon, the municipal and papal authorities responded quite wisely to demographic expansion. They regarded immigrants as legal agents having specific rights and duties, who eventually formed a new population combining natives of the city and immigrants—a rather multicultural society, redefining and pioneering a new urban space. Meanwhile, the native-born moved out of the urban center to make room for the papacy's new demand for real estate, and Avignon's ancient core became the administrative center of Christianity. Still, in fourteenth-century Avignon, as in many settings throughout history, people living in very close quarters tended to get anxious and aggressive; fierce demand for housing created sharp price increases, and the government in turn attempted to regulate the resulting social chaos.

Set within the wider context of our general understanding of medieval urban society, this chapter attempts to recover something of the texture and flavor specific to medieval Avignon. Several mitigating factors are analyzed in order to reconstruct the city's life. First, we discuss the city's governance and regulations, leading to an examination of the various categories of urban dwellers among the citizens and courtiers. Even though the focus of the chapter lies with Avignon's people, certain institutional practices also need explanation, especially when they affected those people. A tour and history of the urban landscape and architecture then introduces a presentation of Avignon's social topography based on its seven parishes. The chapter ends with vignettes touching on everyday life in the capital of Christianity.

AVIGNON'S GOVERNANCE AND ADMINISTRATION

The struggle for power among religious and secular authorities shaped life and politics in western Europe in the Early Middle Ages. Popes, kings and nobles, magistrates and burghers: all negotiated, schemed, manipulated, and openly fought for control over medieval cities and the wealth they generated. In the 1120s, the free male citizens of Avignon agreed to make Avignon a commune—a sworn association of free men for their own protection and self-governance. The city's multiple overlords, the bishop of the city and the counts of Forcalquier, Provence, and Toulouse, allowed the commune to form because they understood the financial advantages they gained from such a venture. The commune assumed its own defense, and its self-regulation increased prosperity. What the lords lost in prestige they gained in taxes.

The commune chose to form a consular government with eight consuls, four members of the nobility and four burghers, elected by a small group of men who had been drawn by lot and approved by the bishop. Some hundred years later, during the Albigensian crusade in the 1220s, Avignon sided with the Count of Toulouse and lost against the papacy and its French crusaders. The Venaissin (the western part of Provence) was punished for its unfortunate alliance, and in 1229 the region passed from the rule of Toulouse to that of the papacy.

At the beginning of the fourteenth century, Pope Clement V (1305–1314) promoted the Venaissin to the status of county or comtat, establishing what is still known today as Comtat Venaissin. Until 1791, the popes retained control over the area and directly named its rector (*recteur*), an official who held jurisdiction over the land and ran its general administration. He appointed all magistrates, presided over the county's council, confirmed the statutes of the Venaissin's towns, received homage from feudal lords, and led the army.

Avignon itself escaped the 1229 papal annexation of the Comtat, however, and the city remained the property of Raymond VII of Toulouse until his death in 1249. By then, the Capetians' territorial ambitions to exert control over the south led them to pursue a clear strategy: a matrimonial policy that gained them a large portion of the Midi when their sons married the daughters of southern nobles. At his death, Raymond's land passed to his daughter Jeanne of Toulouse, wife of Alphonse of Poitiers (Louis IX's brother). When the couple died childless, the French crown co-opted their patrimony, with the exception of the Comtat Venaissin, which Jeanne had bequeathed to the papacy. Avignon was allowed to continue its self-governance under the lordship of the Capetian Count of Provence.

In 1251, Charles of Anjou, husband of Beatrice of Provence (younger daughter of Raymond Berenger V, Count of Provence and Forcalquier), and Alphonse of Poitiers, each of them respectively the counts of Provence and Toulouse, reorganized Avignon's institutions. On May 11, they decreed that from that day forward a vicar (*viguier*) would govern the city on their behalf and would annually appoint two judges to head the seignorial Temporal Court of Justice. The Avignonese, though now limited in their right of assembly, were still allowed to try criminal and civil cases in situ, claim damages against foreigners, and refuse to pay new taxes (e.g., taillage, forced taxes, new tolls).

Starting in 1290, a seneschal (an agent of the Count of Provence) began annually appointing Avignon's vicar and both its judges. The vicar and judges controlled all political and judicial institutions within the city. A subvicar supervised the municipal police, with ten soldiers serving as his personal guard and thirty-two sergeants headed by a captain maintaining public order. The vicar in turn chose the city council, which elected a few officials as his permanent representatives in municipal affairs. The role of the bishop of Avignon was maintained in that he never lost his right of supervision; he oversaw the vicar, examined him to ensure that he conformed to Christian doctrine, and received his oath in the presence of the city council.

French dominion did not affect Avignonese citizenship and the rights it entailed. In the 1240s, the city's consuls had negotiated special commercial treaties with other cities that favored the native inhabitants of Avignon and, more specifically, those who claimed an Avignonese father or grandfather (it is obvious that this limitation curtailed female kinship and reinforced agnatic ties). Citizens descending from Avignonese males were exempt from paying certain tolls and taxes. But the Avignonese never granted any special privileges or exemptions for the resident aliens who lived in their city. Throughout the thirteenth century, the Temporal Court administered lay citizens and the Jewish population. Except for the poor (the ill-defined *vilissimi*), who were not recognized as citizens but still placed under the authority of the vicar of the Temporal Court, the counts' legislation of 1251 had not considered any noncitizen residents. We must assume that at the time they were few in number and quickly assimilated with the citizenry.

Resident aliens were able to apply for citizenship when they lived within the walls of the city (*intra muros*) and when they held at least one-third of all their real estate within the city.[1] The naturalization ceremony required candidates to take a special oath and pay a small fee of one *obol* to formalize entry into the civic rank. Again, their low numbers signify that it was not a pressing issue for anyone before the fourteenth century.

In 1316, when Pope John XXII established his residence in Avignon, he became a guest of the Count of Provence, sole lord of the city since 1290. The status between Avignon and its pope changed from guest to lord in 1348, when Pope Clement VI bought Avignon for 80,000 florins from Joanna of Naples, the Countess of Provence. The Avignonese citizens, obviously forewarned of the acquisition in 1347, petitioned the queen not to sell their city. Their reasoning remains uncertain and opaque. It seems that the Avignonese feared an alteration of their status and privileges, and their petition reflects fear of a change in leadership. Their meeting with the queen resulted in a public instrument (*publicum instrumentum*), authenticated by Pierre Guiramand of Aix, notary of Avignon.[2] The document explains that on February 13, 1347, the knight Jean d'Aurons, syndic of Avignon, and the burgess Dalmas Brotinel, ambassador of the council of the city, met with Queen Joanna in the royal chamber of her palace in Aix-en-Provence. After kissing the ground at her feet in a sign of peace, they formally petitioned the queen not to sell, exchange, mortgage, or transfer the city to any person, entity, college, or community. The queen promised that she would not, but in case she changed her mind, she guaranteed the Avignonese that they would not be coerced into paying homage or swearing fealty to another political entity. The syndics and the queen solemnly swore on the Gospels to maintain the liberties, immunities, franchises, privileges, and conventions previously ratified in 1251.

This meeting was to no avail, since the queen sold Avignon to the pope just over a year later. Respectful of local sensibilities, however, the papacy waited ten years before it required the Avignonese to formalize the transfer of property with an oath of fealty to the pope, by then Innocent VI. The ceremony started on April 10, 1358, and continued over several days, with some 780 citizens and 200 Jews promising their fealty to the pope and the Church.[3] A 1363 document shows that the community of Avignon (*universitas civitatis Avinionensis*) renewed its allegiance with the next pope when it petitioned the newly elected Urban V to confirm the 1251 conventions.[4]

The purchase of the city put the Comtat Venaissin and Avignon solely in the hands of the papacy. Rather than joining both administrations into one, the papacy chose to keep them separate. They ran parallel to each other until the papacy's second attempt at returning to Rome. On leaving in 1367, Urban had required that resident aliens who stayed in Avignon be de facto naturalized.[5] In 1370, when the pope came back to Avignon after a three-year absence, he did not challenge the administration of Avignon. The vicar had maintained continuity, and the papal presence or absence was largely incidental. In 1376, when Gregory XI returned to Rome, he joined the two positions of vicar and rector into a single post, to which he appointed Jean de Blauzac. The office of vicar survived throughout the Great Schism, but in 1434, after the Council of Basel took over the papal possessions in southern France, a papal legate replaced the vicar in governing the city; he did so until the French Revolution. In 1790, Avignon and the Comtat proclaimed their union with France, finally ending papal control over the region.

CITIZENS AND COURTIERS

The arrival of the Roman court in Avignon and the mass of people attending it (the so-called *curiam romanam sequentes,* or "followers of the Roman court") challenged local institutions not only by their sheer numbers but also by their uncertain legal status. It is estimated that thirteenth-century Avignon counted some five thousand inhabitants, and most historians agree that the fixed population climbed to approximately thirty thousand by the 1370s, a number swelled by thousands of uncounted visitors (lay and religious petitioners at court, students, beggars, and officials) who escape our statistics. This demographic boom created a pressing need in Avignon for social organization and control but most of all for justice. Which law and authority were these people supposed to follow? The papacy settled that question.

Avignon was not the first city besides Rome where a pope had resided. Between the pontificates of Innocent III (1198–1216) and Benedict XI (1303–1304), the popes sojourned in Viterbo for a total of 3,319 days; another 3,216 days were spent in Anagni; 2,806 days in Orvieto; and 1,770 days in Perugia. By the time John XXII arrived in Avignon, a system adapted to the pope's itinerant ways was already in place with the Court of the Marshal of Justice. Any newcomer to the city obtained the qualifier of courtier (*cortisianus/a*) when he or she presented the Marshal with the documents or witnesses justifying his or her motivations to be in court. Fourteenth-century documents immediately tried to differentiate the large crowd of immigrants who came to Avignon from the actual followers of the court who traded directly with the curia, but before long the terms "curialist," "courtier," "resident," and "follower" were used interchangeably.

Fourteenth-century records aggregated curialists (*curiales*), followers of the Roman court (*curiam romanam sequentes*), and inhabitants of Avignon (*habitatores Avinionensis*) into a larger group generically labeled courtiers (*cortisiani, cortesiani, cortesani*) and sometimes citizens of the Roman Court (*cives romane curie*). For example, a papal bull dated August 1373 that reviews the status of natives and nonnatives of the city refers to the latter as *omnes curiales* in its third paragraph and then switches to *dilectos filios cortesanos* in the following paragraph.[6] In summary, the variety of descriptions attached to Avignon's nonnatives, whether *curiales, cortisiani, curiam romanam sequentes*, or *habitatores Avinionensis* indicates that no clear distinction separated curialists from immigrants; they all served the popes and their courts one way or the other. By enlarging its definition of resident status and lumping into one large category all the nonnatives, the papacy effectively legitimized the presence of any transients within the city: they were all the pope's followers. At a time when most governments restricted and condemned "vagrancy," "transiency," or the presence of anyone who had no specific ties to a location, the papacy proved most generous (and relatively modern) in its views. In fact, this open mind-set remained with Avignon for some time after the papacy returned to Rome; scholars must look at the mid-fifteenth century (1458, precisely) to see the first Avignonese regulation targeting foreigners and vagabonds who did not exercise an "art" or profession in the city.

Even then, offenders were simply asked to leave and were condemned to a fine if they returned without a working permit.[7]

This somewhat dry discussion of jurisdictional language should not obscure a social reality. Avignon was crowded with people from all over western Europe, and justice needed to be served within the narrow confines of its walls; perhaps the papacy attempted to level the field by treating all residents equally. No evidence indicates social or professional favoritism for either citizens or courtiers. No restrictions limited either group from participating in professional activities, possessing real estate, or paying taxes. As we will see later, there were no clearly demarcated national or professional neighborhoods within the city. National discrimination only surfaced in a few cases: when Gregory XI levied extra funds to ransom back a number of castles held by mercenaries in his native province of Limoges, for example, he asked the Limousins in Avignon for contributions. In 1376, to take revenge on Florence during the War of the Otto Santi, he expelled the Florentine courtiers from the city.

Avignon attracted large numbers of people who followed opportunity to the city, and if some like Francesco di Marco Datini were resounding successes, the livelihood of most resident aliens was fragile at best.[8] The main threat to resident aliens was the right of reprisal that punished foreign nationals for the actions committed by their homeland. In times of political hostilities, medieval governments imprisoned any foreign nationals they found on their territories and froze and confiscated foreign assets (the latter action is still practiced today). The papacy wielded this diplomatic tool expertly, as a Florentine merchant, Buonaccorso Pitti, explained in 1375:

> Being young, inexperienced, and eager to see something of the world, I joined forces with Matteo dello Scelto Tinghi, a merchant and a great gambler. We went to Genoa, Pavia, back to Genoa and on to Nice and then Avignon, which we reached at Christmas time and where we were seized and thrown into the prison of the Pope's marshall. When we had been a week in prison, they had us up for questioning and accused us of being spies for the commune of Florence. They produced a letter to Matteo from a brother of his in Florence telling him that Florence had instigated Bologna's rebellion against the pope. After examining us closely, the court recognized our innocence but insisted nonetheless on our furnishing a bail of 3,000 *fl.* lest we leave the city without the marshal's permission. Matteo found someone to put up the bail, and once we were out of prison, sagely decided that it would be

dangerous to stay on here while our Commune was waging war in the territories of the papacy. . . . [After returning to Florence, he heard that] the Pope had caused all Florentine citizens to be arrested and their records and possessions seized.[9]

As we have seen, the war between the papacy and Florence had dramatic consequences for the Florentines established in Avignon. In March 1376 the pope expelled them and seized their goods. But in a bitterly ironic twist, the people who lost the most were those who had the least connections with the court: the common folk. Among those spared were the great number of international traders who had dealt with the curia for decades and who had literally bought their security from officials, as were those who, in anticipation of the papal interdict, had been wealthy enough to part with their Avignonese goods in quick sales or consignments with their compatriots. Their losses, if and when they materialized, were largely incidental. For example, the pope actually allowed his corsairs to seize Florentine goods that left from the southern French ports of Aigues-Mortes and Montpellier.

A witness to the events of 1376 states that some Florentines were expelled "like dogs."[10] A banker who eventually left Avignon of his own free will describes the events in these words: "Upon the delivery of the said sentence [the March 31, 1376, expulsion], all Florentines and other people of Florence were expelled of the city of Avignon, and they were robbed, and all what they had in the city of Avignon was taken by the pope's officials and the rectors of the said city."[11] After a stalemate of a few months, in October 1376 the curia proceeded to auction off all Florentine property in Avignon. The Chamber received some 30,000 florins from sales, a substantial but not enormous amount, proof enough that the very wealthy had escaped with their capital (in cloth, spices, and weapons, for example). The items that sold were the household goods and the belongings of the common folk who made a good living in the city but not a fortune. They had no wealth to protect them. In one instance, the curia seized the wine stock of Cardinale di ser Neri from Carmignano, an innkeeper who had resided in the city since the 1330s. The auction brought some 500 florins to the Apostolic Chamber, plus some 2,000 florins for his real estate.[12]

The legal distinction between citizen and courtier could also become of utmost importance when facing trial; it could mean the difference between life and death. Any medieval person knew that religious justice was more lenient than a noble lord's secular justice (as long as one considers excommunication milder than beheading or hanging). And luckily for its residents, religious justice abounded in Avignon. The Court of the Marshal took care of lay courtiers at large because of their connection to the papal court. Cardinals and their respective auditors prosecuted cases regarding their own household staffs. The auditor of the Apostolic Chamber took charge of cases regarding religious courtiers and religious petitioners. Finally, the bishop's justice controlled the Avignonese secular clergy. The Temporal Court administered justice only to lay citizens and the Jews. Jacques Chiffoleau, in his study of papal justices, *Les justices du pape*, found evidence that religious justice effectively prevailed in Avignon, where he counts only fifteen to thirty public executions per year—a number which he considers very low in comparison with other medieval cities. [13]

Often a tonsure (a special haircut that identified clerical status in the minor or major holy orders) proved one's membership in the clerical ranks and, as such, suggested the legal status of a courtier since the demarcation between lay courtier and religious curialist was very fluid. Since wearing a tonsure moved a defendant from the realm of lay to religious justice, it is easy to understand why many laypersons adopted the tonsure in phony imitation of their religious neighbors in order to escape the rigors of the temporal judicial system. False clerics flourished in papal Avignon. In 1356, the mother of a young delinquent led the defense of her son to prove that he indeed had attended school and, because of that, his tonsure was real. Her argument won; he was transferred from the Temporal Court to the Court of the Marshal. Others did not hesitate to get tonsured in jail in order to avoid secular justice. Obviously, a tonsure could bring complexity to a legal case. For example, in May 1336 the marshal's sergeants arrested the Florentine Lorenzo Burbaci for the presumed robbery and murder of several merchants. In August of the same year, the court of the bishop demanded to try Lorenzo because he claimed to be tonsured. His legal odyssey did not end there. His complicated status of courtier-tonsured-cleric led the pope to withdraw the case from the bishop's tribunal and assign him to a special commission led by the inquisitor! After a two-year trial, Lorenzo was proved innocent and freed.

In general, Avignon's civil and criminal courts handed out fines and avoided the death penalty. Because medieval justice was a means of raising revenue, Avignon followed the letter of medieval law and typically allowed the permutation in kind of most offenses (even when accompanied by serious harm). Torture or incarceration were used only in the case of unpaid fines, so we can assume that the poorest paid dearly with their bodies. The death sentence was pronounced only in cases of homicide *sine justa causa* and treason.

AVIGNON'S URBAN LANDSCAPE

Since the early Middle Ages, Avignon counted seven parishes: Saint-Étienne, Saint-Symphorien, Saint-Pierre, Saint-Geniès, Notre-Dame-la-Principale, Saint-Didier, and Saint-Agricol. Since the twelfth century, the city was wealthy enough to enclose those parishes within formidable walls. In 1226, in the course of the Albigensian Crusade, these ramparts offered strong resistance to the invading French army of Louis VIII but not strong enough to prevent Avignon's eventual capitulation. When Avignon fell to these northern invaders, Occitania, or the Midi, lost its independence and was absorbed into the royal kingdom of France.

After 1316, the perimeter area around the outer walls evolved into new neighborhoods grouped into fifty or so *bourgs*, districts generally named after the owner of the land on which they developed. These may perhaps be defined as medieval suburban neighborhoods. Most often, the impoverished nobility led the development of these *bourgs* as a means of raising revenue and profit from the land. Proprietors leased parcels long term and allowed the construction of houses, sometimes a few, sometimes a hundred, within each area. Since rents were generally lower outside the walls of the city, the inhabitants of Avignon's *bourgs* were mostly a working-class hodgepodge of citizens and immigrants alike, while the wealthy lived within the protection of the city's walls. *Bourgs* developed in higher numbers where space permitted, that is, to the east, west, and south of the city; the Rhône River and the surrounding rocky terrain to the north precluded new construction. These *bourgs* allowed the civic territory to expand and relieved the demographic pressure inside the old walls. Eventually in the mid-1350s, however, the *bourgs* were incorporated into the city with the construction of new surrounding walls.

Religious houses were likewise positioned throughout the city. The orders of men (principally the mendicants) occupied the exterior periphery of the old walls. The mendicants' location was not accidental.

Throughout the thirteenth century, when these orders started to prolife-
rate, their arrival posed a threat to the city's existing religious orders.
Rectors of parochial churches saw mendicants as direct competition for
souls and gifts and asked them to move away from the parochial boundaries, toward the city's outskirts close to the old walls. In Avignon, the
mendicants divided three large zones of influence. Thus the religious
orders were symmetrically opposed in the east, south, and west of the
city: Dominicans in Saint-Agricol, Franciscans in Saint-Geniès, Carmelites
in Saint-Symphorien, and Augustinians in Saint-Pierre. The male Benedictines were of little importance in Avignon; their small community
resided in the college of Saint-Martial, in the parish of Saint-Didier, to the
south. Alone among the new orders of warrior-monks, within the old
walls was the Order of Saint John of Jerusalem, with its temple to the
west and *Commanderie* to the east.

Within the ambit of the old walls of Avignon were closely enclosed
female institutions as well, with the Benedictines of Saint-Laurent to the
northwest, Benedictines of Notre-Dame-des-Fours to the southwest, Cistercians of Sainte-Claire to the northeast, and Franciscan Clarisses to the
southeast. The symmetrical disposition of these four *intramuros* convents
is remarkable. There can be no doubt that these religious communities
traced some form of symbolic boundaries for the city and that the nuns'
prayers rose from the center inscribed by the sacred space of this circle.
The *Repenties*, a convent for repentant prostitutes, was unsurprisingly
located outside this symbolic area on the city's southern margin.

The original episcopal residence, a small fortress with several towers,
stood on the Rocher des Doms, a rocky promontory that sits on the western bank of the Rhône facing Villeneuve-lez-Avignon. Avignon's cathedral of Notre-Dame des Doms was the parochial church of Saint-Étienne,
with a campanile, baptistery, and cemetery as its neighbors. The first of
the so-called Avignon popes, Clement V, was in reality an itinerant who
resided in the city only sporadically between 1309 and 1314. When
present there, he was installed in the largest space that could accommodate him and his staff, the Dominican convent. His successor, John XXII,
elected in 1316, had been bishop of Avignon between 1310 and 1312 and
opted to return to his former city and palace. The arrival of the pope and
his court of some five hundred curialists in Avignon immediately meant
that space for work and lodging was at a premium. John's solution was to
share the episcopal palace with the bishop and acquire various properties

in Avignon's surroundings and the Comtat Venaissin to accommodate his large staff. He initiated a beautification and construction campaign, adding chapels to the cathedral but also installing parochial and conventual churches; in addition, he founded the Chapel of Notre-Dame des Miracles in the southwestern section of the city.

By 1350 the construction of the new palace had ended. It was a massive and imposing fortress that ensured defense from any threats outside, yet it was also an exquisitely decorated, functional palace on the inside. Built on high terrain, the palace was a place designed to see and be seen. Following in the footsteps of his predecessor John XXII, Clement VI had more or less bankrupted his court for the construction of the papal palace. By the time of Clement VI's death, the palace had more or less taken its present-day shape. His successors in turn satisfied themselves with smaller projects, including the planting of a large garden during Urban V's papacy.

From their palace, the popes could gaze on one of Avignon's greatest landmarks: its bridge, the Pont d'Avignon or the Pont Saint-Bénézet (a nickname for Benedict). Local tradition held that God commanded Bénézet, a young shepherd of the Vivarais area, to build in Avignon a bridge by which to cross the turbulent Rhône River. The 915-meter-long bridge, graced by twenty-four arches, was built in the 1160s and refurbished in the 1230s. The small Chapel Saint Nicolas, still visible today, adorned its eastern bank. The bridge became the natural border between France, on the western bank of the Rhône in Villeneuve-lez-Avignon, and the city of Avignon on the eastern side. One of the very few spots that crossed the Rhône, it was a continual point of contention between the papacy and France.

We learn from the many legal records that this rivalry produced that, for several decades, the Avignonese controlled the entire length of the bridge to the doors of Villeneuve and that they actually set their gallows on the Villeneuve side, at a place named Les fourches de Montault.[14] In 1365, several witnesses came forward to declare that for the previous sixty or so years they had seen executions there, sometimes with thirty men hanged at once.[15] Regardless, in 1368 King Charles V declared that the pope controlled only the portion of the bridge that ran from the walls of Avignon to the Chapel Saint Nicolas; France controlled the rest.[16] But Avignon did not rest on this claim. When in 1379 a prisoner of Avignon, condemned to death, was thrown into the Rhône from a section of the

bridge that belonged to France, Pope Clement VII was forced to acknowledge the deed and renounce any future executions from that spot. [17] In a
gruesome effort at collaboration between the pope and France, one Marie
de Roussiac was condemned by a judge of Villeneuve to be flogged at the
hand of Avignon's executioner from the gates of Villeneuve across the
bridge, past the chapel, and into Avignon. [18] We unfortunately do not
know what the poor woman did to deserve such a treatment; the only
information given is that she was a widow.

Of course, the discussion over control of the bridge was not simply an
issue of justice; it was first and foremost a question of money. Who was
supposed to receive the tolls and taxes charged on merchandise passing
across the bridge, and who was to pay for the bridge's maintenance? Its
upkeep was such a pressing concern that many individuals made bequests in their wills for the bridge's "works" or repairs, testimony to the
constant care it required. Among many such examples was Barthelemie
Tortose, who in 1317 left ten *sous* for the repair of the Pont Saint Bénézet,
and another two *sous* for the construction of a new bridge whenever it
should need to be built. [19] This preoccupation remained in the minds of
the Avignonese, since in 1386, Jacoba Heymerice left six *deniers* for the
"works of the bridge." [20]

Before turning to an overview of the city and its parishes and inhabitants, a few words should be said about its protective ramparts. In the
1350s and 1360s, Avignon and the Comtat Venaissin suffered from various incursions of mercenary bands, the so-called companies made up of
soldiers of fortune who descended on the south, attracted by the presence
of the pope and his wealth. These were the men who had fought the
battles of the Hundred Years' War and the Italian Wars of Cardinal Albornoz. In times of peace, when their income disappeared, they made a
living harassing the population at large wherever they suspected an opportunity for gain. Some of these mercenaries are well known, such as
John Hawkwood, Arnaud de Cervoles, and Bertrand du Guesclin. Specialists in plunder and rapine, they devised ingenious ways to ransom
entire cities from their eventual attacks.

The presence of these gangs in Provence alarmed the pope, and Innocent VI with the city council decided that Avignon needed reinforced
protection and the construction of new ramparts. The old thirteenth-
century walls, even if repaired, were deemed insufficient. The city had
simply grown too much throughout the century, and it largely exceeded

the limits of the old walls. The new ramparts, still visible today, counted some twenty towers and ten gates with their respective drawbridges when completed.

Pope Innocent VI first suggested constructing the new ramparts, but he funded the enterprise only partially, and begrudgingly at that. Quickly, communal authorities were pressed to devise a new scheme to pay for the project and decided to implement a new form of taxation, the *gabelles*, levied on wine, merchandise, and salt. These taxes, auctioned (that is, "farmed") to the highest bidder for the first time in January 1358, were collected at the gates of the city from citizens and courtiers (one-third from citizens and two-thirds from courtiers) as foodstuffs came in. The *gabelles* ended up paying not only for the new walls but also for the entire defense and guard of the city.

The Vatican Archives still preserve some of the registers that detailed the deposits and expenses incurred for the ramparts' construction between roughly 1356 and 1372.[21] According to these registers, on average between 1366 and 1372 (at the height of construction), some 23,500 florins were levied per year on the wine *gabelle*, 7,600 on merchandise, and 3,400 on salt. Only the very wealthy did not pay. Twelve teams of masons and laborers built the walls within approximately ten years, using large quantities of stone and lime from Villeneuve or Châteauneuf, on the other side of the Rhône, and wood from Savoy.

According to the registers, work started with trenches dug around a newly designed periphery that was ample enough to cover large gardens and edifices such as all the mendicant convents, the Hospital Bernard Rascas, the Chapel of Notre-Dame des Miracles, and the Convent for Repentant Prostitutes. Next, they set the gates, and finally, they raised the walls. The new construction led to a few expropriations; most notably, the *livrée* of Cardinal Gui of Boulogne was shorn of a few houses, and a few inside traders profited from their resale.

If they were never overly concerned, the popes were certainly solicitous of Avignon's future welfare in some of their decisions, especially when they decided to leave the city. Urban V's failed return to Rome lasted from April 30, 1367, to September 27, 1370, while Gregory XI left on September 13, 1376, with well-known and far-reaching consequences. The pope of true Avignonese obedience, Clement VII, entered the city on June 20, 1379. In the case of both Urban and Gregory, their respective camerlengos followed them back to Rome, but the treasurers, along with the papal treasury and archives, stayed behind in Avignon. For the Avignonese these repeated divided administrations afforded a slight hope that the papacy might someday return, especially with the papal treasury still housed within their walls. The idea was reinforced by the lingering presence of certain cardinals. Five of Urban's cardinals stayed in Avignon, while six of Gregory's also remained. They assured a minimum of continuity in the administration of the Church during the pope's displacement.

In general, the popes chose talented officers to rule the city in their absence. Urban V named the capable Philippe de Cabassole, former bishop of Cavaillon, as rector of the city and of the Comtat Venaissin. He eventually left in February 1369 to help the pope in Rome. His position was not refilled, but Urban asked Jean de Blauzac to deal with all pressing matters, like the status of the city's inhabitants once the papacy left. When Gregory left, the previous experience of Jean de Blauzac marked him as an ideal candidate to oversee the city in the pope's absence. De Blauzac had experience with both the logistics of curial moves and the administration of Avignon.

The popes took further care to promote several bulls for Avignon's economic survival after their departure. In 1368 Urban allowed the city's council to devise the best ways to establish a wool industry in the city, granting it the right to negotiate financial privileges and stimuli. Gregory extended these privileges in 1376. Specialists were required to define the dimensions, quality, and finish of the cloth produced.[22] Likewise, the popes waived tolls and taxes and allowed the settlement of capable specialists in the city, the construction of windmills on the Sorgue and Durance Rivers, and the alteration of their riverbeds if need be, as long as it did not prejudice others.

The pope continued to support the defense of the city in a period marred by the ravaging by free companies of mercenaries. Both vicars and captains handled municipal defense by calling on the city's council some fifteen to twenty-five times a year to deal with these issues. In addition, the papacy made sure that the city's administration functioned continuously. The mint kept operating, multiple justices still functioned, and a special commission headed by Jean de Blauzac resolved the issues created by the papal departure, usually concerning housing assessments and taxations, as well as the legal status of the population. Urban V mandated all followers of the Roman court to pay their rents and debts before they left the city, under the threat of excommunication.[23] Gregory repeated the injunction. A month or so before his departure, Urban decreed that all secular courtiers (*omnes curiales*) remaining in Avignon after his departure would be automatically considered citizens. That bull of March 26, 1367, is well known among historians of Avignon and was repeated by his successor when he, too, later left.[24] This question of citizenship was so essential to the demographic and economic survival of the city that it reemerged with the return of Clement VII. In April 1383 and again in May 1388, the pope repeated that even though the court had returned to Rome, followers of the court in Avignon would be considered inhabitants and citizens of Avignon.[25]

All in all, the popes showed more care for the economic survival of Avignon when they left than they ever did during their tenure in the city. In addition to the previous legislation, they facilitated recruitment for Avignon University by allowing masters and students to receive the revenue of their benefices even when not in residence. This allowed the maintenance of the university in the city with all the benefits that it brought. The Avignonese also received the special privilege to trade with Alexandria in Egypt, to receive wheat from Italy, and to fund the maintenance and construction of more defensive walls and towers. The pope also financially supported several religious houses and foundations like the orphan hospitals and the House for Repentant Prostitutes, institutions that indirectly benefited the city's population.

One of the defining events of the fourteenth century, the Black Death of 1348, is, rather ironically, poorly documented for Avignon. The attack of the plague cut short the vibrant era of Clement VI's papacy. Bernard Guillemain measured the town's demographic and economic growth during roughly 1342–1346 by surveying interventions of the town's assessors aimed at preventing real estate speculation.[26] These interventions by papal authorities bear witness to their efforts to tame unruly urban development based on fraudulent real estate transactions, a trend brought on by quick economic expansion. But suddenly, a "huge mortality and pestilence started in September 1347" that halted this growth.[27] Still, the constant flow of human traffic reaching Avignon mitigated the disease's effects on the social and economic life of the city. Immigration spurred by the presence of the court hid some of the consequences of the first epidemic, as new residents quickly arrived to replace those who had died in the first wave of the disease.

According to contemporary author Louis Heyligen, several portents akin to the apocalyptic plagues of the scriptures announced the arrival of the Black Death: on the first day, it rained frogs, snakes, lizards, and scorpions; on the second, it thundered and hailed; on the third, fire descended from the sky and burned all. Then, according to the author, the "calamity" spread quickly via the "stinking breath of the wind" taking various forms. Sometimes it infected the lungs and breathing, leading to a rapid death within two days—this form was highly contagious. Alternatively, it sometimes killed via the sudden appearance of boils or "buboes" under the armpits or in the groin areas. In each instance, death followed quickly, leaving people too traumatized or too afraid to care for the dying and dead. Heyligen offers staggering numbers: seven thousand houses were emptied of their inhabitants, and no survivors were left in the suburbs; some eleven thousand were buried in the city's new cemetery, without counting those interred elsewhere.[28] Heyligen estimates that between January and March 1348 some 62,000 dead were buried in Avignon.[29] Bernard Guillemain suggests losses reaching half of the general population—about one-fifth of all curial personnel—many of whom, by escaping the city, minimized their losses.

It is certain that after the first epidemic, even though reduced in population size, Avignon still attracted newcomers. The flow of immigrants and visitors did not dry up, and the economic profile of the city did not change. Avignon presented the same pattern of occupation, the same geographical origins of its residents that it did before the epidemic. Taxation and assignation registers demonstrate the continuing need for shelter and space, in fact, with an increase in the size of the city's occupied space after the first epidemic.[30]

However, the plague did not stop in 1349; it continued and became endemic. The renowned physician Guy de Chauliac remarks in his *Chirurgia Magna* that the plague of 1361 varied from the first outbreak, for while more commoners and large numbers of women died in 1348, the wealthy, the nobility, and children were more affected by the latter.[31] By the 1380s, the plague had become almost continuous, and it was a frightening part of daily life. The remedies proposed by spiritual and medical healers seem bizarre quackery to us today; they included the usual prescriptions of masses, prayers, penitential processions, fasts, and indulgences, together with the more medically effective strategies of sequestration or flight. Still, some Avignonese had recourse to physicians who

prescribed special diets, fumigations, and cauterizations, which sometimes healed them.[32]

In the midst of these decades of plague, the departure of the curia may
also have felt like a catastrophe for some inhabitants. Not all Avignonese
dreaded seeing the papacy leave, however, since its absence freed the
city's real estate from all the lodging obligations attached to the court's
presence. Houses were released from the right of *livrées*, and the chains
and barriers that demarcated the cardinals' quarters were removed.[33]
Some of the freed space was used to enlarge the university quarters.

AVIGNON'S PARISHES AND THEIR SOCIAL TOPOGRAPHY

All in all, regardless of their differences in social composition, Avignon's
parishes were organized on a similar twin pattern. The wealthy classes
belonged to the "old city" close to its center, within the old ramparts,
while the poorer classes were located in *bourgs* within the old and newly
constructed walls. The parish of Saint-Étienne could be considered Avignon's crown jewel since it held the Rocher des Doms (Rock of the
Domes), with its original episcopal-turned-papal palace, the cathedral
Notre-Dame des Doms, and the bridge. Limited to the north and west by
the rock and the Rhône River, Saint-Étienne never grew like Avignon's
other parishes. Defended by the rock's height, it was easily accessible
from the Rhône, and geography dictated its evolution. As the cradle of
Avignon, it quickly became the court's parish, housing prelates and curial servants while its western boundaries hosted goods and newcomers
arriving down the river or across the bridge. Originally, the parochial
church was adjacent to the cathedral, but in 1316, John XXII took ownership of the church for his private service and transferred the parochial
title to a chapel named after Saint Mary Magdalene. Hence, throughout
the fourteenth century, references to the parish usually named both
saints, as in *parrochia Sancti Stephani alias Magdalene*. Benedict XII demol-
ished the old church in Saint-Étienne to rebuild a new grand chapel on its
grounds, a sanctuary subsequently incorporated into his palace. Today it
is a repository for the departmental archives of the Vaucluse department.

Avignon's cathedral grew during the papal sojourn. It was endowed
by several dignitaries who added chapels around its apse. The cathedral
served as the ceremonial hub for the funerals of popes and cardinals and
other high dignitaries. Benedict XII chose to be buried in one of its chap-

els, and his tomb is a beautiful example of the fourteenth-century Gothic style. The large *place* (town square) that stands today below the cathedral, accessible by a flight of stairs, was covered with dwellings in the Middle Ages. As early as 1316, mercers were allowed to trade there in front of the bishop's palace, certainly in recognition of the importance of their trade.

Saint-Étienne was obviously a prime location for the city's inhabitants, and its real estate was expensive. The original inhabitants were often *domicelli* (sons of nobles), or patricians, who quickly sold or rented their "mansions" to eminent courtiers. Papal registers show well-known Avignonese names like Faraud, Flamenc, Matheron, Morières, Hugues, Vayran, and de Sade leasing to cardinals, camerlengos, apostolic nuncios, auditors of the Chamber, chaplains, scribes, and other curial servants. Avignon's traditional elite engaged in brisk commerce, and we find *domicelli*, for example, involved in the rental of mixed-gender bathhouses, establishments quite often used as brothels. One of the parish streets, the Grande Fusterie or Fusterie Vieille (named after the wood, *fusta*, that was shipped down the Rhône), was the seat of the episcopal tribunal. The Fusterie was the city sector devoted to temporary lodging. Visitors arriving by land via the bridge or by river could find a variety of inns and hostels here, with names like the Inns of the White Horse, the Iron Crown, the Wood Crown, the hostels Saint-James, the Red Hat, the Peacock, the Lilly, the Saint-George, the Saracen, the Golden Lion, the Black Peacock, the Griffon, the Star, the Golden Bowl, and Saint-Martin. In our age of bland uniformity, of the predictable chain names of Marriott and Holiday Inn, it is quite interesting to read the diverse selection of popular names for inns preferred by medieval people! Even if highly lucrative, this location was at high risk because of its proximity to the Rhône and its violent floods. Finally, close to the Gate Eyguière we find the pope's barns (for the court's cereal, wine, and fodder) and the hospital Bénézet for poor pilgrims, founded in the twelfth century.

The parish of Saint-Symphorien is the best documented of all Avignonese parishes, simply because several religious houses within its bounds left records pertaining to parochial life.[34] Saint-Symphorien's Church was already decrepit in the fourteenth century, and a 1374 papal bull explains that, in a kind of negative competition, neither citizens nor courtiers would spend anything on its repair, thus leaving the church to collapse.[35] The bull makes clear that in general, the obligation to maintain churches fell on parishioners, and their refusal to fulfill their Christian duty enlightens us on the limits of medieval urban piety. In Avignon, many parishioners were immigrants who may have felt no particular ties to their new residence and church. Indeed, their wills frequently show foreigners leaving bequests to their home parish, evidence how much more their homelands counted in their hearts than Avignon. Our sources also note the important economic role that Saint-Symphorien cemetery played because of its Saturday market. Initially on the cemetery's outskirts, the fresh produce market kept expanding into neighboring streets. The bustling market testifies how the urgent, basic needs of a living population jostled against the resting place of the dead.

As was quite common in the Middle Ages, the prior of the church of Saint-Symphorien did not attend to the duties of his benefice directly; rather, he "leased" the charge to secular priests, who "farmed" the revenue of the church. This meant that priests paid a lump sum to the prior to minister at the church; over time, they expected to recover their initial investment directly from the donations of their parishioners. Sometimes priests were not above suspicion, and we read in the ledgers of the diocese that a certain Hugh, priest of Saint-Symphorien, committed adultery, violence, and robbed a breviary.[36]

From the early years of the papacy's tenure in Avignon, Saint-Symphorien attracted an inexhaustible stream of new parishioners who enjoyed proximity to the pope's residence. Curial servants, ambassadors, high prelates, and jurists displaced native inhabitants, who took advantage of the real estate boom. Not long after the papacy moved to the city, the curial "nobility" replaced Avignon's traditional knightly class. By the time of Urban V and Gregory XI, the parish was still the residence of many curial servants, bull officers, papal guards, and messengers, but many had by then spread to the other parishes. In return, artisans and merchants moved in, and the parish became something of a hub for the housing industry, with plasterers, carpenters, stonecutters, masons, and roofers lodging within its limits. Only the jurists seem to have remained grounded in this parish, maybe because of the closeness of several legal "schools."

Because the parochial area circumscribed by the city walls was so large, it allowed several suburbs to develop within the boundary of Saint-Symphorien. A well-known Avignonese family, the Cabassole, founded a few of these suburban areas. In spite of this growth, the size of the parish allowed for open spaces and gardens, with enough room left in between to house the pope's stables and most of the city's smiths and farriers. The presence of the fresh produce market on the perimeters of Saint-Symphorien's cemetery was a reminder of the parish's agricultural character. Aside from its wealth of green space, however, the parish was also defined by the presence of the important Cistercian Convent of Saint Catherine.

The convent moved inside the old walls for protection sometime during the 1250s and became a haven for the daughters of patricians and nobles, who in turn endowed the convent with substantial property. It is remarkable that a single abbess, Aygline de Blauzac, led the house as its head for some forty years, between 1356 and 1399. Saint Catherine's nuns were women of high standing, and one wonders whether their social station gave them self-confidence to fight abusive neighbors. For several decades the nuns complained of their lack of privacy and initiated several procedures. They sued most of their neighbors, who between 1327 and 1405 kept building extremely tall houses that enabled their inhabitants to look down on the sisters inside their convent.[37] We also find them fighting a procurator who claimed access to their well. A squabble between neighbors has become a treasure for historians; all in all, Saint-Symphorien offers testimony concerning such a representative cross-section of residents that a prominent historian of papal Avignon has called it "a window into the pontifical court."[38]

Located to the southeast of Saint-Symphorien, the parish of Saint-Pierre was a thriving commercial and institutional center, sheltering the papal justices, the Jewish quarter, the Augustinian convent, the Hospital Sainte-Marthe (founded by Bernard Rascas and today's Avignon University), and scores of shops and artisan stalls. It was an important parish, and its real estate was in high demand.

The collegiate church of Saint-Pierre remains one of Avignon's most beautiful monuments to this day, but without a doubt its cemetery attracts the largest share of our notice. Saint-Pierre's cemetery was not walled in, and it seems that in a medieval city tight for space, opportunities to make use of the burial grounds were not missed. Already in 1306 a cattle market used the space, and although it was eventually displaced toward the old ramparts, various commercial activities continued in advance of Clement V's entry in 1309. Trading in the cemetery went on for decades; in fact, a complaint from 1359 states that there were still merchants, public meetings, fights, and all sorts of crimes committed on its hallowed ground, including fornication, debauchery, adultery, homicide, and other "abominable" things. [39] Supporting these charges, in 1347 Saint-Michel, another of Avignon's cemeteries, was described as a bordello. [40]

Cemeteries in medieval Avignon were well integrated into the fabric of urban life. Avignon counted some twenty parochial, conventual, and hospital cemeteries, a Jewish cemetery, and Champfleury (flower field) south of the old walls, created to bury the dead of the 1348 plague. Traditionally, urban cemeteries were open spaces, and as the population grew, so did the demand for their space. Medieval cemeteries hosted many economic and social activities, an uncomfortable thought for our modern Western society, so sheltered from the sight of death. Court records make mention of the many crimes that took place within their boundaries, but also of communal meetings like those of the Masters of the Streets, who met in Saint-Pierre. [41]

Saint-Pierre also counted several religious establishments, including the house of the Hospitallers of Saint-John, the Trinitarian order, and the mendicant brothers of Saint-Augustine. These three orders were in constant litigation with the parochial canons and priors over their share of the offerings. The parish expected a share from all donations made to the various orders established within its boundaries.

It was no coincidence that the Augustinians had settled at the limits of the city by the old walls, as far away as possible from the parochial church. The front of their conventual church sheltered an image of the Virgin (Notre-Dame la Belle) that was quite popular with the Avignonese, but the building was difficult to access because of the rubbish that seeped from the neighboring inns, bathhouses, and houses. The stench was intolerable, and it inconvenienced visitors. To solve the issue, the Augustinians developed the area commercially. They installed a subfloor and merchant stalls that eased access to the church and sanitized the area. [42] The Augustinians also allowed the meetings of the confraternity of Notre-Dame la Majour within their walls. Notre-Dame was a kind of community center and support association for the Italians resident at Avignon. They met regularly to organize social and religious events. The association also supported poor pilgrims in their nearby hospital.

The Trinitarian brothers had spiritual charge of the patients of the Hospital of Sainte-Marthe, founded in 1353 by Bernard Rascas and his wife. An eminent Avignonese, Rascas issued from the old knightly class but studied law to become a professor. He was at the time Avignon's ambassador to the court of Queen Joanna of Naples and marshal of the Roman court from 1353 to 1354. Needless to say, as often happened in large cities, competition was stiff among the many religious orders, and Sainte-Marthe and the Trinitarians were sued by the parish for a portion of the offerings they received from pious almsgivers.

The western limits of the parish abutted the Rock and the twelfth-century communal palace. With the papacy's arrival, the area became the residence of vicars, judges, and sergeants of both the Temporal and Marshal Courts, accompanied by their prisons, tribunals, and archives. The courts explain the location of the pillory and the presence of many notaries in their vicinity. The same neighborhood also sheltered the clothes-resellers and (hemp) rope-making streets. Hemp dressing was a lucrative profession, and Avignon's archives have kept some 184 documents belonging to its most famous representative, Jean Teisseire. [43] Married and widowed three times, two of his wives were daughters of hemp dressers, evidence of intermarriage within the profession. The children born of his unions all predeceased him, and in 1384 Teisseire bequeathed all of his patrimony to the city council. A good portion of Teisseire's real estate was located within the parish, counting four houses in front of the church and cemetery, a house with the inn "of the drink," three shops (combined with apartments) near the inn, and seven merchant stalls for vegetables, bread, and meat. Even if he owned real estate in the other parishes, Teisseire invested heavily in Saint-Pierre because of its rich commercial character.

The parish also accommodated the *Payrolerie*, named after the cauldron/stove makers that also housed the furriers, pitcher makers, clog makers, and salt workers/merchants. A small square in the latter street served daily as an open labor fair. One of its main avenues was the Street of the Spice Merchants (at once spice merchants, wax sellers, and apothecaries). The profession actually defined the street quite well, as most of its residents were Tuscans or Avignonese spicers. Intermarriage homogenized this class, and we often find daughters of spicers marrying other spice traders or merchants. Exacting in the quality of the service they provided, in 1376 spicers who met in the fraternity of the spice traders paid three laborers to sweep the street daily and wash it twice a week.

The Jewish quarter moved to Saint-Pierre in the 1230s. Jews lived in an enclosed area of some two and a half acres, secured (or rather contained) by three gates. Avignonese Jews were at the mercy of the popes in residence there, and their protection fluctuated with the personality of each pope. Early in his rule, John XXII projected his twin fears of magic and antipapal conspiracies onto the Jews. He persecuted the Jewish communities of the Comtat, expelling them in 1322; they were readmitted in the 1340s. Several authors have even linked the pope's anti-Judaism to French monarchical policies during the same time.[44] Conversely, Clement VI showed relative tolerance toward Avignonese Jews during the horrors of the Black Death and defended their community. Within this flimsy bubble of papal protection, the Jewish community elected its own representatives, who dealt with civic and papal authorities and negotiated the many small taxes imposed on the community.

If Jews were traditionally allowed to engage in lending with interest, this activity was limited to short-term consumer loans; Italian merchants controlled the larger international financial market. Jewish pawnbroking led to reselling and retailing, and Jews specialized in the general resale of various objects ranging from furniture to cloth. As was the custom generally in western Europe at that time, Jews were forced to wear a yellow badge of recognition and forbidden to circulate after sunset and during Easter week, while Christians were allowed free access to the Jewish quarter. Christians could possess real estate in the quarter, and so many did that in 1379 Clement VII granted Avignon's Jews the freedom to control their own streets, prohibiting Christians from living in the Jewish quarter and renting or owning houses.[45] The Jewish community of the fourteenth century also counted several medical doctors renowned for their scientific knowledge, two surgeons, and some artisans, including several weavers, binders, and parchment sellers.[46] In 1358, 215 Jewish heads of household gave their oath to Pope Innocent VI, suggesting the presence of a community that must have ranged in the thousands. Their meeting place, Avignon's synagogue, was called "the Jews' School," and it supported an almshouse for the poorest members of their community. The Jewish cemetery was located near the old walls and the Pignotte, the papal almshouse.

Records of the Temporal Court allow a glimpse into the daily lives of Avignon's Jewry. By a large majority, the registers mention civil cases punishable by fines. For example, Vicia de Chambayrino and Nathan Roussel attacked and beat the porter Aymon Teissier for no apparent reason and then paid a sergeant to keep the affair quiet. Abraham Bonaqui of Saint-Rémy carried a knife into the city, the length of which exceeded the allowed dimensions; and Donette, wife of Astruguet Sartre, abused Jeannette la Bugadière with insults (she was accused of saying, "*Tu mentes per la gola,*" which translates into "You lie through your face"). In each case, a fine resolved the issue. Likewise, when the Christian Raymond Chaput fought with the Jew Ferrier Escale, both were fined. But religious tolerance was limited; Samuel Cohen, a Jew from Aix, was arrested and fined for not wearing his *rota* ("the wheel badge") the moment he arrived in Avignon. Bellicadra, Bonafes of Agde, and Abraham Achier were also fined for leaving the Jewish quarter after curfew. One of the biggest court cases on record pitted Aginet, son of Jacob Bendich, against his brother-in-law Salon Fournier and his brother David, accused of having led the wealthy and elderly Jacob to Barcelona to eventually seize his fortune after his natural death. The case highlights the precarious nature of medieval Jewish life. Three years after the 1348 arrival of the Black Death, servants of Cardinal Nicholas de Besse instigated "reprisals" against Avignon's Jews, accusing them of causing the epidemic. [47] Several members of Avignon's Jewish community escaped to Cataluña; they eventually returned to Avignon after facing more epidemics, famine, and reprisals in Iberia. Yet the Jews were but one group in the large parish of Saint-Pierre in Avignon. From its religious pluralism to its economic and multiethnic diversity, it is obvious that fourteenth-century Saint-Pierre was a thriving community that mixed agriculture, commerce, and administration within the wide ambit of its boundaries.

The parish of Saint-Geniès was by far the most humble of Avignon's districts. Little is known about the state of its church during the papal sojourn except for the familiar squabbles between citizens and courtiers regarding the funding of its repairs. A 1374 letter of Gregory XI reiterates that it was the duty of citizens and courtiers to maintain the parochial church, which the pope labeled as "in ruin." [48] The parish was largely dedicated to the leather, skin, and fur industry, and it is highly probable that the stench produced by the treatment of animal skins made it undesirable as a place of residence. Every Tuesday the parish hosted a leather market, first in the street Pelleterie, then on the square of the Curaterie (both names indicate skin or leatherwork). Leatherworkers joined an almonry (the fraternity of the leatherworkers) that distributed alms but also regulated leatherworks, since we find this group suing a worker for disregarding the city's weights and measures regulations. [49]

The parish counted a large *livrée* (traditionally labeled de Viviers) formed by scores of houses. For some thirty years it was assigned to Cardinal Pierre de Monteruc. His position of vice-chancellor may explain why several jurists (judges, notaries, or professors of law), protonotaries of the popes, scribes, and correctors of apostolic letters resided in the vicinity. Historians have had difficulty identifying a single location for the papal chancellery, and it is highly probable that papal scribes and copiers worked from their homes within the parish.[50] A few more curial servants, such as ushers and sergeants of the pope, seem to have resided in the parish, but their persistence in declaring their wives as proprietors suggests that they were scamming the court. Ushers, sergeants, and curriers received a lodging indemnity, and a common real estate scam consisted of entering their wives' names so that they could claim their indemnity while residing someplace else and subletting the tenements.

Saint-Geniès also boasted some well-known residents such as Gandulphus de Cremona, master surgeon of the Court of the Marshal. Gandulphus was also some sort of coroner or expert witness, since in 1366 he was paid to examine murder victims for the court. Adding to the diversity of its residents, the parish counted several individuals in the music trade, including Brocardo di Campanino, a maker of musical instruments, a trumpet maker, and several minstrels.

The horse market was located outside the old walls, and after the 1340s, scores of *bourgs* grew farther east toward the new walls, amid large tracts of land occupied by orchards and gardens. All kinds of small artisans moved in, often renting from the more well-to-do who lived in the city's center, making Saint-Geniès a true working-class neighborhood.

In contrast to Saint-Geniès, Notre-Dame la Principale was small but nevertheless rich, the economic hub of the city. Much of its territory rested within the old walls, and most of its inhabitants were wealthy enough to afford its high rents. According to tradition, Notre-Dame la Principale's church was named after the "church of the prince" (*principale*), but we do not know who this prince was. One of the church's chapels, Notre-Dame d'Espérance, was dedicated to a miraculous image located outside the church, facing the street (the image had started bleeding after a drunk threw a rock at it). This wonder-working image became so popular and received so many rich donations that it sparked a rivalry between the diocese and the church's dean, a veritable tug-of-war over its custody. Eventually, both were required to share the collected revenues it generated that, incidentally, were so high that they needed to be managed by an Italian broker.

Just as in other parishes, Notre-Dame la Principale's cemetery again attracted the attention of the authorities, and in a letter of 1373 the pope ordered its enclosure, along with the cemetery of Saint-Didier. The pope lambasted the profane actions, like dicing and fighting to the point of bloodshed, that took place on public hallowed grounds, and he required the parishioners to pay for the labor required to properly secure it.[51]

The Franciscan Clarisses, or Poor Clares, possessed the sole convent founded in the parish. Even though small in number, they received preferential treatment among the city's religious orders. Ill-acquired goods that had been confiscated by the Marshal Court reverted to their order, and the papacy waived their tax payments to the parish. In general, the Avignon popes showered them with gifts, paying for the construction of their kitchen and dormitory, granting them indulgences, and bestowing many presents in the form of clothing and liturgical objects. Lovers of Petrarch will know that he said he had first met his Laura in this church of the Franciscan Sisters on Good Friday in 1327, which was (according to him) exactly twenty-one years to the day before her death.

Notre-Dame was a commercial hub, tightly knit and overcrowded. Its heart was the Place des Changes, a town square dedicated to banking and money changing. Of course, Avignon had no stock exchange, but this square was the closest thing to one. Money changing and banking in papal Avignon is well documented because, as seen earlier, the papal administration developed a thriving financial market. Avignon bankers operated from shops and stalls facing onto the streets and kept a *nummularius* (a strong room) in their basements. The Italians, who traditionally dominated the medieval banking industry, lived in this expensive neighborhood. Notre-Dame la Principale was best defined by its population of Florentines. Well aware of the frequency of rights of reprisal, a form of economic warfare where authorities imprisoned or confiscated alien persons and merchandise, these wealthy merchants, bankers, and silver and goldsmiths never assimilated or settled permanently in the area. Specialized butcher shops and luxury boutiques were intermixed with the banking stalls. The parish also sheltered herb and oil markets. Every Tuesday the leather market operated in this sector until it moved to Saint-Geniès, where circulation was easier.

The parish of Saint-Didier was heavily remodeled during the papal sojourn, starting with the 1355 reconstruction of its modest church, elevated to the rank of collegial church by Cardinal Bertrand de Déaulx. It is still one of Avignon's prettiest churches. Once inside, one can still visit the tomb of the Cardini brothers, Florentine master messengers of the pope and developers of the private courier service of the *scarsella*.

The parochial cemetery of Saint-Didier has already been mentioned, along with Notre-Dame la Principale's, for its many infractions. Still another cemetery is worth noting because it shows an unusual side of charity. In 1341, a naturalized Florentine bought a piece of land in front of the cemetery of the Hospital Pont-Frac in order to bury the dead of Avignon's hospitals, all the deceased, both rich and poor. This was a generous action, as offering proper burial is one of the Christian works of mercy. Originally named Saint-Antoine, the cemetery was simultaneously labeled Saint-Michel after a small chapel of the same name and Pont-Frac after the hospital. This cemetery gained fame when two recluses (the recluse of Saint-Michel from 1330 to 1348, and Marie Robine in the 1390s) lived there, enclosed in an oratory, and when the miracle-working Cardinal Peter of Luxembourg also chose to be buried there as a sign of humility. Eventually, in the 1380s Pope Clement VII charged the new convents of the Celestine and Saint-Martial Benedictines to manage the collection of funds and the various chapels founded on its grounds.

The parish also contained several hospitals extremely active during the fourteenth century, Pont-Frac and Saint-Antoine, dedicated to the care of poor courtiers. The Hospital of Pont-Frac had been founded in the thirteenth century and was made famous by a miracle-producing image painted on one of its exterior walls. The offerings it produced allowed the construction of a new building dedicated to the care of orphans and the poor. Created during the thirteenth century, the hospital of Saint-Antoine moved with the popes and took care of poor pilgrims and curialists who followed the popes, including during their Avignon exile. Finally, a smaller hospital, founded by the Italian confraternity of Notre-Dame la Majour, also supported poor pilgrims. All in all, these charitable institutions testify to the power the papacy exerted on believers and also their willingness to accommodate and support the growing number of newcomers arriving in Avignon. It is truly remarkable that private individuals and institutions were so compassionate in the care of these unfortunate or needy persons.

To a certain extent, these hospitals were born from the unique social mix and mutual solidarity of the parish. Inhabitants of Saint-Didier covered a wide range of occupations, from nobles to jurists, merchants, bankers, farmers, and skilled artisans (including parchment makers, who took advantage of the brook running alongside the old walls to clean their skins). The parish also included large gardens tended by those who lived in the parish's *bourgs* and probably served the needs of the wealthy population within the city walls. The parish also comprised many inhabitants involved in the garment industry, such as tailors, underskirt makers, and silk workers.

A 1380 tax document offers a quick snapshot of the social composition of Saint-Didier. According to that source, the wealthiest members, who were required to pay a defense tax, included a Florentine noble who had escaped the 1376 expulsion and was worth some 10,000 florins, a blacksmith from Turin worth 6,000 florins, several Italian money changers and a few Avignonese nobles worth between 1,000 and 2,500 florins, as well as a few hemp merchants, spicers, and market gardeners, all worth more than 1,000 florins.[52] This data demonstrates how much and in what ways papal Avignon allowed commoners the opportunity for relative financial success and social mobility.

The parish of Saint-Agricol, named after one of the earliest bishops of the city, boasted Avignon's oldest church. John XXII cared specifically for this church, endowing it with revenues, chapels, and bells.[53] By Gregory XI's era, however, it was so run down that the pope granted an indulgence to those who contributed toward its repair.[54] Within the church and among the many chapels founded by both popes and parishioners, the Almshouse of the Petite Fusterie stood out. It was founded by the carpenters and wood merchants of the city in order to succor the poor and indigent; it remained throughout the fourteenth century one of Avignon's most active confraternities. As with many of the city's churches, the bourgeoisie of Avignon often requested to be buried within its walls, while common folk were buried outside in its cemetery's tombs or in mass graves.

The cemetery attached to the church retained portions of its enclosing walls, but an interesting tradition allowed burials outside the walls as well, a sign that being "near" consecrated ground was often good enough for parishioners. An inquest on the matter interviewed scores of inhabitants to establish whether the practice was sound, and as a result, the body of a suicide victim was disinterred from consecrated ground to be reburied next to the Durance River.[55] Christian practice did not allow suicide victims to be buried in consecrated ground.

The Dominican convent, the largest of the religious buildings in Avignon prior to the completion of the papal palace, also stood in the parish of Saint-Agricol. Its size made the convent an ideal location for various grand occasions. In the early fourteenth century, it lodged Pope Clement V and his court, as well as high-ranking visitors like Queen Dowager Clemencia of Hungary, widow of Louis X. The convent also served as the site for grand liturgical ceremonies like the canonization of St. Thomas Aquinas and the coronations of Benedict XII and Clement VII. The convent was also the site of large processions and sermons that attracted widespread attendance from the Avignonese populace.

Notre-Dame des Miracles, founded by John XXII, sat directly south of the convent on a location that was usually attributed to the gallows. The chapel was built in the 1320s to commemorate a miracle of the Virgin that freed from the stake a young man accused of lewdness toward his mother. For the medieval Avignonese, such a place of redemptive deliverance was a worthy and fitting site on which to establish a convent for repentant prostitutes (Repenties). It should be noted that if traditionally the gallows were located outside the boundaries of cities, pillories were usually located at their centers. Thus in Avignon, after the foundation of Notre-Dame des Miracles, the gallows moved from the south to the north—on the bridge—while the pillory remained in the center, next to the church of Saint-Pierre. The "theater" of medieval justice moralized offenses; it is clear that hanging, often reserved for lower classes and outsiders, polluted the symbolic territory of the city while the pillory, reserved for citizens and residents, was there to edify its audience and thus deserved a place within the city.

Saint-Agricol included a few more religious institutions. The Templars built a church here in the 1280s, the possession of which passed to the Hospitallers of Saint John after their dissolution by Clement V in 1312. Both orders have unfortunately left few traces of their presence in Avignon. Female religious orders also found safety in the parish. The aristocratic Benedictines of Saint Laurent may have been the parish's oldest foundation (from about 1100), but the nuns' observance of their holy rule was lax enough for Pope Innocent VI to reinforce their enclosure "because of the many disorders and troublesome lives they led there."[56] In contrast, the poor and unwelcome Benedictine ladies of No-tre-Dame des Fours moved inside the city walls only when bands of mercenaries threatened their safety. Once reinstalled in the parish, a new menace threatened them in the form of the local rector who claimed all of their revenues, leaving them destitute. The nuns reached a settlement in 1376 when they agreed to pay a percentage of their income to the parish.

Saint-Agricol was one of Avignon's largest parishes, divided between an older section within the old walls that had been long occupied (it was close to the episcopal/papal palace) and an *intermuros* section that was populated largely during the sojourn of the papacy in the city. In the old section, streets leading to the palace specialized in commerce and luxury crafts. The meat, tripe, and fish markets were located between the palace and the church, where sellers rented stalls from wealthy bourgeois. The northwest section housed a socially diverse group of carpenters and woodworkers, merchants, nobles, and court officers. The newly devel-oped *intermuros* section was also divided between an urbanized northern area and gardens to the south, where the popes kept their fish ponds. It should be noted that the fourteenth-century capital of Christianity was a great consumer of fish, the quintessential fasting food associated with Lent. Saltwater fishes arrived in plenty from the Mediterranean coast, while freshwater fishes were transported down the Rhône from Bur-gundy to fill the pope's ponds. Finally, Saint-Agricol counted some fif-teen *bourgs*, mostly inhabited by the papal court's civil servants.

The large-scale approach that I have undertaken up to this point does not preclude a more intimate knowledge of the city's population. The *Liber Divisionis*, a document that lists some 3,800 heads of household who resided in the city in 1371, offers one of the best social portraits of the city. In addition to names and legal status (either citizen or courtier), the docu-ment notes the parish of residence and sometimes an occupation and town or region of origin—most of the individuals listed are not Avi-gnonese natives. The document allows the historian to gain a quite accu-rate picture of the Avignonese population at its second-highest point—that is, after the initial losses of the 1348 epidemic and after the second return of the papacy to the city.

In general, immigrants outnumbered citizens in all parishes, with a few clusters of citizens in the parishes of Saint-Didier, Saint-Symphorien, and Saint-Pierre. Citizens had lost control of the traditional heart of the city as delineated by the old walls in the parishes of Saint-Pierre and

Notre-Dame-La-Principale. They faced stiff professional and social competition from newcomers who were employed in the skilled occupations necessary to the papal court. Rental prices and real estate values increased closer to the palace and decreased toward the *bourgs*, making it more expensive for citizens to reside in the more bustling, profitable areas of Avignon.

According to the *Liber Divisionis*'s data, the service industries employed a large percentile of the Avignonese population. Metrics on the forty or so most common occupations offer the following results: the garment and shoe industry represented 21 percent of the working population expressed in the *Liber*; occupations related to agriculture employed 19 percent; merchants, 16 percent; preparation and sale of food, 14 percent; hostelry, tavern, and innkeeping, 10 percent; construction and home equipment, 8 percent; stevedores, 3 percent; barbers, 2 percent; occupations related to horses, 2 percent; notaries, 2 percent; procurators, 2 percent; and weavers, 1 percent. Interestingly enough, these numbers come close to statistics related to modern Western economies that employ a large segment of their working force in the tertiary sector.

In general, occupations correlated with geographical origins. Usually lower-skilled workers came from a fifty-kilometer radius around Avignon, while high-skilled occupations, like international commerce and finance, attracted immigrants from regions as far away as Italy. Geography dictated residence in something close to socionational neighborhoods. For example, the southern French lived in Saint-Didier, Saint-Symphorien, and Saint-Agricol parishes, while Tuscans and northern Italians resided principally in Notre-Dame-La-Principale, Saint-Pierre, and Saint-Agricol parishes.

Papal Avignon attracted a large number of immigrants, and while many came from Italy, a significant portion also hailed from what is today France's northeastern region: Toul, Metz, Besançon, the Alps (most specifically, Gap and Grenoble), the Limousin, and Paris. The document shows that the immigration radius correlated with occupations. Thus, workers in the garment and food industries came mainly from the northeast, and farmers and stevedores from Avignon and its hinterlands. Italy sent merchants, innkeepers, notaries, and procurators to Avignon, while construction workers and barbers descended from the mountains. The weavers, saddlers, and blacksmiths came from the north of France. The large pool of immigrants stemming from the north and northeast also explains why it was the place of origin of 49 percent of the bakers, 57 percent of the butchers, 37.5 percent of the carters, 35 percent of the stonecutters, 40 percent of saddlers, 36 percent of blacksmiths, and 43 percent of pie makers. But this argument fails to explain why the little-represented southwest was the home of 45 percent of candle makers.

In spite of the influx of northern French immigrants, the Italian community had the most significant presence in the city, the majority of them being Florentines and lower numbers coming from Turin, Milan, Lucca, Asti, Piacenza, Siena, Carmignano, Bologna, Prato, Rome, Pistoia, and Bergamo. It was a skilled community with merchants, bankers and money changers, innkeepers, and haberdashers but also artisans such as carpenters, waistcoat makers, barbers, armorers, tailors, silversmiths, and goldsmiths. Most often, men arrived alone, grouped themselves within certain streets and neighborhoods, and joined religious associations or confraternities that met to honor a particular saint or a chapel. These associations also facilitated social networking.

The Italian merchant class rarely intermarried with the Avignonese. Their social alliances remained Italian. We know, for example, that an Avignonese Italian, Piero di Lorenzo, found his wife and most importantly, her dowry, in Florence. Unfortunately, he was robbed of the latter when making his way back to Avignon alone. He states, "I went to Florence to fetch a wife, got a few penny for her [he never names her]; lost half of it and spent the rest. Between one thing and the other, this has brought me nothing good."[57] On the other hand, another Florentine, Tieri di Benci, married a Florentine and brought her back to Avignon,[58] while Andrea Rapondi married the daughter of Helena de Plaisance (another Italian) and received a dowry of 3,000 florins. A merchant's letter commenting on the latter marriage adds, "And this is without counting what he can expect from the mother," proof enough that good deals could still be made in the city.[59]

In the Central Middle Ages, confraternities—religious societies devoted to prayer, the practice of spiritual discipline, charitable works, and artistic patronage—were a common feature of urban life, seen everywhere in the large trading centers of Europe and offering adherents material and spiritual protection, support, social networks, and communication. In papal Avignon, their membership largely consisted of foreigners. For example, the large confraternity of Notre-Dame la Majour integrated Italian immigrants into the city by facilitating networking horizontally with their native and foreign peers and vertically with their socially superior brothers who remained at the court, such as curial servants and cardinals. Later in the century the records mention a confraternity of Saint John the Baptist strictly for Florentines, which acted as a lobby to the papacy and king of France.

Notre-Dame la Majour was a confraternity for the merchants, followers of the Roman curia (the *curiam romanam sequentes*) who were purveyors of the many services needed by the papal court. Proof of its social utility, most Italians who arrived in the city joined its ranks immediately. When, for example, Matteo Benini arrived in Avignon in 1360, he joined the association. He left soon afterward for Arles, where he became a trading partner of the Avignonese Florentines. Still, even though in Arles, he remained a member of the organization and retained his membership as long as he remained active in his trade. Maybe Notre-Dame la Majour served as a reference for good social and commercial practices. Ronald Weissman explains that "in a society where patronage, recommendation, and personal ties were of primary importance, the confraternity was a vehicle for expanding personal networks and gaining access to patronage chains throughout the city and, thus, for exercising patronage and organizing factions on a citywide . . . basis."[60]

Members of Notre-Dame met periodically and practiced what can be loosely defined as the seven corporal and spiritual works of mercy. They attended Mass twice per month, recited the Our Father and Hail Mary daily, distributed alms regularly, buried their dead, and offered prayer for the souls in Purgatory. According to the association's statutes, members had to lead respectable lives, avoid blasphemy, murder, and concubines, and keep the peace. In Avignon, the association funded two hospitals for poor pilgrims (the Lombards' Hospital and the Hospital of Notre-Dame), evidence again that pilgrims massed to the city.

Immigration inevitably affects the position of women in any particular society, and in papal Avignon, a woman's status was to some extent dictated by the demographic evolution of the city. The traditional weight of that society's expectations that a woman would either marry or retire to a cloister (and in either event largely disappear) was lighter in the face of immigration and the unusually high rates of death and disease in that era. The large extended family was scarce in this unusual urban setting; most families were small and often went extinct after a couple of generations. The number of testamentary bequests that ended up in the possession of charitable institutions is the best evidence for the testators' lack of successors. Legally, small families favored women's patrimonial accumulation, and with these legal rights they became more socially visible. Women inherited houses, lands, shops, and cash, and they could officially assume the title of head of household—since often no men were left to claim it. The traditional exclusion of dowered daughters from any rights of succession often vanished, and women were designated inheritors in more than 24 percent of the wills of the period.

During the fourteenth century, widows and older daughters often bypassed their *alieni juris* status (this was, under Roman law, their incapacity to act legally without male guardianship) and acted in legal matters with or without the authorization of a guardian. Records also mention married women acting with or without their husband's permission.

Our sources also indicate that some women worked, mainly in the lodging industry as innkeepers or hoteliers; they sold foodstuffs and unspecified articles; they manufactured and sold textiles, shoes, and clothing. And a few Avignonese women were unskilled laborers or skilled artisans. Of course, the presence of the court and masses of immigrants, including large numbers of unmarried men, also led to the presence of a substantial number of prostitutes in the city. Brothels spread throughout Avignon, often near entrance gates and public "baths," with an area specialized in the sex trade in the "New Bourg," next to the Franciscans. Prostitutes were tolerated as an evil necessary in order to avoid the greater evils that would ensue without them. Males without access to sex were assumed to be by nature sexually aggressive, inclined to rape, incest, and sodomy. But we must take care in considering the many hidden assumptions behind these conclusions.

When discussing women, Avignonese records usually identify them as mothers, wives, or daughters. A lack of affiliation identifiers or of titles specifying the men to whom they were related often indicates a single person. By this standard, papal Avignon held a large percentage of single women in its population. A generation of historians assumed that when medieval women were identified as single, their lack of affiliation indicated vagrancy and prostitution. Granted, the large number of unmarried men living in Avignon offered a ready clientele; nevertheless, these women may still have been employed in some form of ancillary services. They could have been maids or servants rather than career prostitutes, strictly speaking. The frequent mention of "maids" (*ancillae*) in single men's testaments points to this, even if at times these maids could also have been their concubines.

Yet the large number of single women in Avignon's records does not necessarily mean that prostitution was rampant and endemic throughout the city; on the contrary, other sources lead us to think it was controlled and regulated. Prostitutes were not overwhelmingly stigmatized, since a few of them owned property. A 1366–1368 tabulation of leases held by the bishop of Avignon names "public women" who owned properties under the episcopal lordship: Mingette of Narbonne, Jeanette of Mers, alias of Lorraine, and Marguerite La Porcelude owned tenements in the *bourg* of Guimet Abbert. Mingette of Narbonne, a "common woman," paid nine sous every Easter for a house neighboring the two houses of the said Jean Tesseire, the public street, and the house of Simonette, wife of William the Taylor. Her neighbor was Jeanette of Mers, another "common and public woman" who held a house that also neighbored with the public street and the houses of Peter Barneri of Montpellier and Nicholas Raymond. She paid ten sous at Easter. In the same neighborhood, Marguerite La Porcelude (alias De La Casserra) paid six sous and nine deniers for her house. [61]

Statistical data on medieval Avignon's labor force shows that single women were far more active in their communities than married women, and often they practiced a wider range of activities which both required better skills and offered better compensation. In the absence of wide networks of kinship, women had to work to survive, and spinsterhood and widowhood sometimes favored women's social and occupational gains.

Like any capital bustling with people, medieval Avignon posed as many dangers as it did opportunities. Jacques Chiffoleau, in his study of criminality, considers certain districts of the city more prone to violence than others. [62] His data shows that most criminals condemned by the Temporal Court were not transients but actually integrated in the city's labor force and resided on the margins of the city. They lived in the new, affordable *bourgs* that developed outside the twelfth-century town, especially close to the Gates of Saint-Michel, Imbert, and Lazare. In 1387, for a total of 174 criminals, only 33 lived within the walls; the rest were in the *bourgs*. Chiffoleau argues for a spatial and social segregation that pinned the social classes perceived to be dangerous to the good order of the city into the new neighborhoods near the inns, bordellos, and taverns that skirted the old gates close to the mendicant orders.

As often is the case, close quarters incited violence. Noise, such as the music of minstrels going late into the night, led to verbal jousting, aggression, and physical violence. Study of court records shows that in Avignon violent incidents were, in the majority of cases, spontaneous acts linked to domestic disputes, gambling, and drinking. Homes, brothels, taverns, and the streets themselves were the main sites of this violence. People cursed each other for what seem to the modern reader trivial matters and then punched and kicked if they did not also unsheathe their knives. Violence was random and impulsive, and most crimes were not premeditated; death usually happened by accident when a sword or knife was drawn too quickly. The Italians also brought their crimes of vengeance or "honor" with them, and we find in Datini's letters many examples of Florentines arriving in Avignon to avenge the death of a relative, sometimes targeting people who may have been related by blood to the guilty party but not at all related to the affair in question. As in any case of vendetta, vengeance took years to be appeased. On October 30, 1399, Tieri di Benci wrote to Francesco Datini that three days earlier, the streets of Avignon witnessed a vendetta. Figlono, son of Nicolo Alamani, arrived in Avignon from Florence to avenge the death of his brother, killed four years earlier by the son of Jacopo Vivoli. Vivoli's son was caught on his doorstep and was struck twelve times; his sister was also wounded. His deed accomplished, Figlono had dinner and found refuge at the palace of the cardinal of Florence, Piero Corsini.[63]

As a deterrent to these kinds of crimes, justice was served in the form of fines, maimings, and executions, always carried out publicly. Records at the municipal archives show that the executioner (*carnifex*, or "butcher") threw prisoners from the bridge down into the Rhône.[64] Between June 1328 and February 1329, records of the Temporal Court show that the *carnifex* performed sentences that called for the cutting of hands, feet, tongues, and ears.[65] In addition, decrees were enacted in order to contain what society thought were instigating conditions for crime: open spaces. Medieval authorities linked openness to gambling, drinking, prostitution, and circulation at night. Hence, these "deviations" were institutionalized within the closed walls of inns and bordellos as curfews limited circulation and all open spaces were walled in. Most of these regulations failed. According to papal letters, even enclosed monks gambled.[66] Gambling prohibitions were readily ignored, even when linked directly to the sins of blasphemy and lust,[67] and no better proof can be offered of their failure than the continual repetition of such crimes across the centuries.[68]

Xenophobia was another marker of the city's violence. It was closely linked to immigration and the perception of vagrancy. Avignon received immigrants and visitors from a large portion of Europe. People came for specific callings or simply with the hope of finding a job. In spite of this diversity, parochialism was prevalent. Marseillais despised Normans, Avignonnais hated Florentines, and so on. Language barriers and a general lack of communication may have been at the root of the situation, but even in an urban setting, transients were perceived as threats to local peace. The fear of robbery, the most prevalent crime of the era, also added to general feelings of insecurity.

The papal city also offered a form of class warfare mixed with the presence of what may be described as "clerical gangs." Ecclesiastics of high rank, such as abbots, bishops, and cardinals, were patrons of a wide network of clients who often lived within their quarters (*livrées*) and caused trouble with other grandees' clients or the natives. For example, in 1331 a fight erupted between the "people" of the abbot of Saint-Victor and those of the bishop of Castres, and Catalan knights caused the death of one of them. The reason for the altercation epitomizes Avignon's situation in the fourteenth century. The Catalans had found rooms in an inn close to the abbot's and bishop's quarters. The smoke emanating from the inn's kitchen inconvenienced the southern French who, through a hole in the wall, "tainted" the roasting meat. The Catalans retaliated with a fight. The offense that started the whole affair is not described. Was it the smell or smoke emanating from the roasting meat, fear of fire, a dislike of foreigners, or lack of communication?[69] As this example demonstrates, the presence of armed guards, those knights attached to ecclesiastics' households, may have added an element of instability in the city. They were men of war, quick to start a fight or draw their weapons, but evidence shows that there was little correlation between, for example, the cardinals' *livrées* and criminality. Data provided by Chiffoleau for criminals' residences in 1387, when correlated to maps of *bourgs* and *livrées*, suggests no specific results that would indicate such a connection.[70] The only trait that emerges is that certain *bourgs'* residents received the most sentences, with Saint-Pierre ranking first with forty, Saint-Didier second with thirty-one, and Saint-Agricol third with twenty-six convicts.

TO LIVE IN A MEDIEVAL CAPITAL CITY

Regardless of the information available to us, it remains difficult to perceive what life was like for the common people of Avignon. Historians can only imagine and infer from whatever documentation is left. In addition to the multitude of services that an urban setting offered, there is no doubt that Avignon must have been a noisy, vibrant city with many things to see and experience. A capital city offered entertainment that country folks and the residents of other cities rarely saw, like jousting, minstrel shows, ceremonial entries, grand funerals, and coronations. Two papal letters, respectively dated from 1328 and 1348, prohibit tournaments and jousting in the city and its suburbs, evidence enough that they took place.[71]

Many guests visited the papal court during its Avignonese sojourn, and their entries offered a grand spectacle for the populace. For example, Pope Urban V received the king of France John the Good in November 1362, followed a few days later by the Count of Savoy and the king of Cyprus. In 1363 Waldemar, king of Denmark, arrived, as did the Holy Roman emperor Charles IV. The Duke of Anjou, second son of John the Good, visited Avignon in December 1364 and July 1366, the Duke of Berry in May–June 1365, and the Duchess of Anjou in January 1366. For each grandee, the ceremony of entry began a few miles outside the city so that the entire region, attracted by the pomp and circumstance, profited from the occasion.[72]

Various civic religious organizations celebrated feast days throughout each year, and Avignon must have witnessed many grand liturgical parades and processions. For example, the confraternity of Notre-Dame la Majour participated in the procession of the Assumption every August. On August 15 at six o'clock, the brothers paraded throughout the city accompanied by civic authorities. They always stopped at the great courtyard of the palace, where they received the pontiff's benediction.

The pope's movements were also a motive for ceremonies and monetary gain. Popes traveled in cortege and usually rode under a canopy with their banner displayed. An almoner throwing coins to spectators always accompanied them, as tradition dictated. Of course, the funerals and elections of new popes were also cause for revelry, looting, and violence. On the death of popes, mobs sacked the property of the deceased and of any potential candidates to the papacy. The coronation ceremonies of a pope (and of other claimants) offered pomp, pageantry, and more alms. During the coronation of Clement VI on the Sunday of Pentecost 1342, the most ostentatious of the Avignon popes proceeded through the town with pennons, banners, a menagerie, and attendants who sprinkled pennies on the crowd like holy water. At his death, the papal almshouse distributed 400 livres to the poor of the city; an additional 40 livres were distributed to onlookers during the funeral cortege. The pope also bequeathed 400 florins to the mendicants of Avignon, 300 florins to female religious orders, and 425 florins to local hospitals.[73]

We can also assume that, like most large medieval cities, Avignon was unhygienic and polluted. When Petrarch complained about the stench of the city, he was not only using a rhetorical artifice, he was telling the truth. Raymond Chalmel, a doctor who wrote a treatise on the plague, argues that poor hygiene in Avignon and in Paris influenced the propagation of the epidemic.[74] Louis Heyligen, a Flemish cleric who resided in Avignon in 1348, describes the infection that spread "by means of the stinking breath of the wind," adding that "sea fish are now not generally eaten, men holding that they have been infected by the infected air."[75] Masters of the Streets were engaged to try to organize and improve hygiene, traffic, and circulation, but the growing number of inhabitants made their tasks nearly impossible. Circulation throughout the city was difficult, forcing the Temporal Court in 1377 to stop carters from remaining on their mounts while traversing the city. This precaution was intended to slow down their movements within the city and the dangers they presented to pedestrians. This legislation was unfair, however, since courtiers escaped the jurisdiction of the temporal court and could indeed ride at their convenience.

Papal Avignon did not invent urban public administration—what is called in French *l'hygiène des rues* (street hygiene). As early as 1233 an officer existed in Rome to inspect and maintain its streets, fountains, aqueducts, and sewers.[76] Similarly, in thirteenth-century Avignon, three officers were in charge of the streets' cleanliness: they prohibited littering and throwing any kind of used water into the street and disposing of dead animals and other carcasses in any locations other than the Rhône and Durance rivers. They forbade diverting the course of public water ditches, mandated that outhouses be carefully enclosed, and asked the public not to use public roads as latrines.[77] Statute forty, entitled "of not purging one's belly in the street," reminded residents that no men or women older than twelve and fourteen could "purge" themselves into the street, gardens, or vineyards that carried fruits.[78] Emptying oneself was allowed only in the ditches of the city. Human manure (*fimoratium*) could not be stored in homes nor piled in narrow public streets nor any confined space made out of walls or hedges, and no one was allowed to use an already existing pile for "purging their bellies" or to add anything to an existing pile that already stank.[79]

One of the basic principles of medieval hygiene linked noxious smells with corruption and disease.[80] Hence, many regulations tried to entice citizens to keep the streets clean, and often Avignonese authorities led the way. The *mandats de gabelles*, or receipts of expenses paid by the treasurers on the *gabelles* taxes on wine and merchandise, show that in October 1376 the *gabelle* treasurers paid for the cleaning (*purgacione*) of the street located between the back of the palace and the court of the Marshal of Justice. It required the work of two carts, two horses, and three men for three days.[81]

As seen previously, the frequent grand ceremonies that took place in the city offered a hidden advantage to life in Avignon: the cleaning and rehabilitation of certain streets and quarters that were on the routes of festivities. The more visitors came, the cleaner Avignon got. For example, a 1380 payment warrant indicates that the drawbridge of the Gate of Saint James was repaired, this time for the exit of the Duke of Anjou. The warrant insists that the bridge was in such poor condition that no animal could cross it.[82] Extant receipts saved from the 1389 visit of the king of France display the works initiated for the visit of a magnate. The bridge was repaired and covered with mulch; torches lit the town, streets were paved and dressed with colorful banners and cloths, and town magistrates, sergeants, and councilmen received new clothes.[83] In December, repairs and cleaning were done on the Rue Carreterie in front of the Augustinian church and the Chapel of Notre-Dame la Belle and then again on the street in the back of the Augustinian church. The *mandats* also paid for paving the front of the Augustinian church and chapel of Notre-Dame la Belle.[84] This area had been a sore spot for a long time. It existed as of 1328, when a certain Petrus de Mascone was whipped for having stolen a large quantity of candles burning in front of the image in the Chapel of Notre-Dame la Belle.[85] In March 1390 the port of the Rhône and other places near it were dredged. The city paid seventy men to clean the Rue Palafrenerie. Trash was in such quantity that merchants could not unload their wood. [86] Cleaning projects like this one could be of large scale. In June 1406 the waters of the Sorgue were diverted so that the riverbed could be dredged, forcing an anonymous chronicler to state that the Sorgue had never been so beautiful. The work lasted two months. [87]

It seems that in many cases, paving streets was often considered a better option than systematically draining them. We must assume that paving also allowed cart traffic and circulation in general to flow more smoothly. The *Mandats de Gabelles* offer several examples. In March 1376 the treasurer paid the laborers who had covered the bridge of the Rhône with some sort of ballast. [88] A year later, in September 1377, the treasurer released funds for paving the bridge (the arches of the bridge were also repaired and marked with the pope's coat of arms). [89] In 1388 the Rue Carreterie was paved. [90] In June 1390 the treasurers paid for paving the *lissiis (lices*, the walkway that followed the ramparts) toward the Moulin de Pertus, the gate of Aquerie, the Place Saint-Didier, and the Place des Corps-Saint.

If draining was not done systematically, controlling the flow of Avignon's three rivers (the Rhône, Durance, and Sorgue) was considered. In March 1376, the city council ordered the construction of a protecting ditch to divert the flow of the Durance as a means of impeding floodwaters. Floods plagued Avignon throughout the latter part of the fourteenth century. We find records of flooding in 1353, 1358, 1362, and then eight more times in the next twenty years, counting 1384, 1396, 1408, and 1433. [91] In October 1376, the treasurer paid to repair the fishpond of the pope in order to prevent water from draining into the new ditches that ran along the ramparts. [92]

The *gabelles* registers also demonstrate that not only the palace but also the city of Avignon contained sewers (*aygueria seu conductus*), vestiges of ancient Roman construction. They were roughly one meter by one meter and emptied into the Rhône. In 1382, the treasurer paid workers to purge sewers next to the Tower of Saint-Jacques, next to the residence of the cardinal of Urgell, and next to the Tower of Mal-Conseil. In 1386, a grid was placed on a sewer next to the pope's attic and the Sewers of the Stew. The chronicle of Martin de Alpartil, a secretary of Pope Benedict XIII who recounted the siege of the palace during the 1398 subtraction of obedience during the Great Western Schism, records the failed attempt by mercenaries to enter the palace via its kitchen sewers. The description of the events indicates that besiegers cleaned the sewer that served the common kitchen and certain other parts of the palace that ran through a stone column into the garden.[93] The system had the advantage of both irrigating and fertilizing the garden. In any case, their attempt at penetrating the palace failed when guards sounded the alarm as they reached the kitchen and captured the mercenaries.

It is evident that the medieval Rhône and Durance Rivers were as polluted as, maybe even more than, they are today. Indirect evidence for their foul state appears in the canonization procedure of Saint Peter of Luxembourg. Many depositions describe rescue and reanimation after individuals (adults and children) had drowned in either the Durance or Rhône. In one case, Bertrand Calneti, a salt merchant, spent up to an hour under the Rhône's waters. Knowing how to swim, in his own words, "as well as a stone," he ingurgitated much water but managed to survive, by miracle, without getting sick. Still, for eight days he felt "the stench of the Rhône on and in him."[94] I would argue that modern-day Avignon, during its summer festival, brings us closest to the crowds, smells, and sounds of the medieval city.

Finally, another pressing issue remained for medieval Avignon: the pervasiveness of urban fires. Fires were even more devastating in an age that lacked any efficient means of extinguishing them, so strict regulations attempted to prevent them. Citizens were asked to keep their chimneys clean, to cover their hearths, and to keep plenty of water on hand. Storing straw and hay within the walls of the city was also forbidden.[95] Once fires started, the local parish bell rang to alert certain corporations that held a monopoly on firefighting: the porters, carpenters, plasterers, well clearers, and delegates of the mendicant orders.[96] No one else was supposed to help with dousing the fire, with the exception of the twenty-four nearest relatives and neighbors of the fire victims. Vicars, sergeants, and the city's militia secured order and safety.[97] A miracle from Peter of Luxembourg describes a huge fire in Avignon at the *hostellaria ad signum leonis* (Inn at the sign of the lion) in the Grande Fusterie. The fire started during the night by accident and, fueled by a strong mistral wind, consumed everything, including the house and five horses. It became unstoppable. The owner of the house, Richardona de Carmiliano, a female spice merchant and innkeeper, prayed to the cardinal of Luxembourg asking for his help in stopping the wind and fire; and he did, in her own words, "as if all the water of Rhône had been thrown on it."[98] One of the most terrible Avignonese fires, however, was one that destroyed a good section of the papal palace on May 7, 1413. According to a chronicler, the fire burned the consistory, great kitchen, and wine cellar.[99]

At another canonization, more evidence was offered of the compelling need for an adequate alarm system. Pons Joannis was a fishmonger whose lips were so swollen that he had not been able to eat for eight days. He was miserable and promised Peter of Luxembourg that he would visit his tomb naked and as a penitent if the cardinal fulfilled his wish. Joannis fell asleep and had a compelling dream in which the cardinal asked him to tell the Avignonnese to build a bell tower over his tomb, in which tower they would put a big bell, nice and clear, that would ring for the elevation (offertory) but also sound the alarm for storms, thunder, and lightning (another cause of fires) to save the "fruits of the land."[100]

We will never know how happy Avignon's residents were compared with other people of the late Middle Ages, but historians can ascertain that they lived and died no worse than most medieval urban dwellers. Unlike many other Europeans of the age, however, the Avignonese had access to more goods, charitable help, and services. After the papacy returned to Rome, Avignon remained for a few decades a vibrant cultural center and a relatively comfortable place to live, within the parameters set by the Middle Ages, of course. As Ronald Musto states so eloquently,

> But nothing compared to its [Avignon] court spectacles, its lavish feasts, or the annual awarding of the Golden Rose. This prize—worth over 100 florins and created by Tuscan craftsmen from sapphire, pearl, garnet, and gold—was bestowed by the pope on the fourth Sunday of Lent to the prince of the pope's choosing and would often climax the arrival of a great, and politically important, visitor. It was, in 1368, even granted to a woman, Queen Giovanna I of Naples. Yet cultural life in this papal city naturally went deeper than spectacle and ceremony. The home of some of the brightest and most influential men in Europe, the Curia was a center of intellectual creativity and exchange: in law and theology for the most part, but from an early date the new international humanism pioneered by Petrarch. Poetry, letter writing, history, and classical literature found avid supporters. While there is no record of grammar schools in Avignon, the substantial number of educated heads of households—lawyers, notaries, advocates, diplomats, and others of every type—made the presence of several schools indispensable. A university had existed since 1303, and this soon specialized in what best served the needs of the Avignon papacy: law.[101]

NOTES

1. The walls enclosed the ancient episcopal city and were composed of a double stockade complemented by ditches and a canal that ran along its route.

2. The petition is transcribed by Anne-Marie Hayez in "Le conseil de la ville supplie la reine Jeanne de ne pas vendre Avignon," in *Avignon au moyen âge: Textes et documents* (Avignon: Aubanel, 1988), 97–102.

3. The document is discussed by Bernard Guillemain, *La cour pontificale d'Avignon: Étude d'une société* (Paris: de Boccard, 1962), 628–642, and Anne-Marie Hayez, "Citoyens et notables Avignonnais au milieu du XIVe siècle," *Bulletin philologique et historique du comité des travaux historiques* (1982–1984): 199–219.

4. Urbain V, *Ut per litteras apostolicas*, no. 005447 (May 5, 1363). This letter states that Urban followed in the footsteps of Innocent VI, who had renewed the 1251 conventions on March 28, 1358, a few days before the oath of allegiance of the city to its pope.

5. Urbain V, *Ut per litteras apostolicas*, no. 019710 (March 26, 1367). Urban specified that he was approving this request from the community of Avignon to allow for its defense. The court's departure depleted its population, and the city needed men for its defense. Urban also proceeded to remove Avignonese citizens from external jurisdiction; see Urbain V, *Ut per litteras apostolicas*, nos. 019711 and 019712.

6. This bull is transcribed by Anne-Marie Hayez, Jeanine Mathieu, and Marie-France Yvan in Grégoire XI, *Ut per litteras apostolicas*, no. 026855; and Marc Dykmans, "La fin du séjour des papes en Avignon d'après quelques documents inédits sur les habitations," *Mémoires de l'academie de Vaucluse* 4 (1983): 45–46.

7. Joseph Girard and Pierre Pansier, *La cour temporelle d'Avignon au XIVme et XVme siècles* (Paris: Champion, 1909), 150.

8. Born into a humble background in Prato, Italy, fifteen-year-old Francesco di Marco Datini left his hometown for Avignon sometime around 1335. He made a fortune in trading (mainly weapons) and returned to Tuscany in December 1382, a very rich and influential man. He died on August 16, 1410.

9. Gene Brucker, *Two Memoirs of Renaissance Florence: The Diaries of Buonaccorso Pitti and Gregorio Dati* (New York: Harper & Row, 1967), 25.

10. Arturo Segre, "I dispacci di Christoforo da Piacenza, procuratore mantuano alla corte pontificia," *Archivio Storico Italiano* 43 (1909): 86.

11. Richard C. Trexler, *The Spiritual Power: Republican Florence under Interdict* (Leiden: Brill, 1974), 46 (my translation).

12. Trexler, *The Spiritual Power*, 51–52.

13. Jacques Chiffoleau, *Les justices du pape* (Paris: Publications de la Sorbonne, 1984), 235.

14. See, for example, ADV, *Archives communales d'Avignon*, FF4, 5, 21, and 25–26.

15. ADV, *Archives communales d'Avignon*, boîte 64, no. 2205.

16. ADV, *Archives communales d'Avignon*, boîte 68, no. 2230.

17. ADV, *Archives communales d'Avignon*, boîte 68, no. 2231.

18. ADV, *Archives communales d'Avignon*, boîte 68, no. 2233.

19. September 16, 1317, ADV, *H Sainte Praxède* 52, no. 39.

20. December 3, 1386, ADV, *H Cordeliers* 14, no. 15.

21. Archivio Segreto Vaticano (henceforth ASV), *Collectoriae*, ff. 47–49.

22. See Michel Hayez, "Éviter la recession économique, souci des papes Urbain V et Grégoire XI, au départ d'Avignon," in *Avignon au moyen âge: Textes et documents* (Avignon: Aubanel, 1988), 149–152, for a French translation of these bulls.

23. Urbain V, *Ut per litteras apostolicas*, no. 19711 (March 26, 1367); no. 019752 (April 10, 1367).

24. It is partially quoted in Guillemain, *La cour pontificale*, 653 n. 140. Guillemain states that the pope ordered this radical solution because there were not enough citizens for the defense of the city. This seems to be an exaggeration since mercenaries were in charge of the defense of the town. See Anne-Marie Hayez, "Travaux à l'enceinte d'Avignon sous les pontificats d'Urbain V et de Gregoire XI," *Actes du 101ème congrès national des sociétés savantes* (Paris, 1978), 195; and Guillemain, *La cour pontificale*, 619–625. On the delicate issue of citizens and followers of the Roman court, see Joëlle Rollo-Koster, *The People of Curial Avignon: A Critical Edition of the Liber Divisionis and the Matriculae of Notre-Dame la Majour* (Lampeter, GB, and Lewiston, NY: Edwin Mellen, 2009).

25. ADV, *Archives communales d'Avignon*, Boîte Pintat 18, nos. 575, 582.

26. Guillemain, *La cour pontificale*, 555.

27. Rosemary Horrox, *The Black Death* (Manchester: Manchester University Press, 1994), 41.

28. Horrox, *The Black Death*, 42–43. The disease attacked humans and also animals. A writer of the life of Clement VI mentions that dogs, cats, roosters, chickens, and all kinds of animals also died during the plague; see Jacques Chiffoleau, *La comptabilité de l'au-delà: Les hommes, la mort et la religion dans la région d'Avignon à la fin du Moyen Age (vers 1320–vers 1480)* (Rome: École française de Rome, 1980), 95–101.

29. Horrox, *The Black Death*, 44.

30. Guillemain, *La cour pontificale*, 558–559.

31. Guy de Chauliac, *La grande chirurgie*, ed. E. Nicaise (Paris: Alcan, 1890), 173.

32. Chiffoleau, *La comptabilité de l'au-delà*, 95–101.

33. ADV, *Archives communales d'Avignon*, Boîte Pintat 77, no. 2251, and Pierre Pansier, "Annales Avignonnaises de 1370–1382 d'après le livre des mandats de la gabelle," *Annales d'Avignon et du Comtat Venaissin* 3 (1914–1915): 36–37.

34. They were the Chapels of Saint Perpetua, Notre-Dame de Fenouillet, and Sainte-Croix, the highly endowed Cistercian convent of Saint-Catherine, and the convent of the Carmelites.

35. ASV, *Registra Avenionensia* (henceforth *Reg. Aven.*), 193, f. 304.

36. ADV, *Archives communales d'Avignon*, G9, F 129.

37. ADV, *H Sainte Catherine*, 30, 52, 54.

38. The original reads "Une vitrine de la cour pontificale," in Anne-Marie Hayez, "La paroisse Saint-Symphorien au temps des papes d'Avignon," *Annuaire de la Société des amis du Palais des papes et des monuments d'Avignon* 74 (1997): 50.

39. See ADV, *Archives communales d'Avignon*, 9G7, 22, 23, 24, 28, and 34.

40. See ADV, *H Célestins* 5.

41. ADV, *H Augustins d'Avignon*, 22 mi 693 bis (1395).

42. ADV, *H Augustins d'Avignon*, 22 mi 693 bis (1395).

43. ADV, *Archives municipales d'Avignon*, Boîte 96.

44. Kenneth R. Stow, *Popes, Church, and Jews in the Middle Ages: Confrontation and Response* (Aldershot: Ashgate, 2007), 296. In his chapter on the Avignon papacy, Stow details the inconsistencies of Jewish papal policies.

45. ASV, *Reg. Aven.* 215, f. 158v.

46. See Irven M. Resnick, *Marks of Distinctions: Christian Perceptions of Jews in the High Middle Ages* (Washington, DC: Catholic Press of America, 2012), 138; and Danielle Iancu-Agou, "Avignon," in *Medieval Jewish Civilization: An Encyclopedia*, ed. Norman Roth (New York City: Routledge, 2003), 63–66.

47. The cases are found in Michel and Anne-Marie Hayez, "Juifs d'Avignon au tribunal de la cour temporelle sous Urbain V," *Provence historique* 23 (1973): 165–173.

48. Grégoire XI, *Ut per literas apostolicas*, no. 033602.

49. ADV, *Archives municipales d'Avignon*, HH 141.

50. Brigide Schwarz, *Die Organisation kurialer Schreiberkollegien* (Tübingen: Niemeyer, 1972), 67–71.

51. Grégoire XI, *Ut per literas apostolicas*, no. 028339.

52. ADV, *Archives communales d'Avignon*, CC 21.

53. Jean XXII, *Ut per litteras apostolicas*, no. 14634.

54. Grégoire XI, *Ut per litteras apostolicas*, no. 20352.

55. ADV, *Archives communales d'Avignon*, 8G4.

56. Hermann Hoberg, *Die Einnahmen der apostolischen Kammer unter Innozenz VI* (Paderborn: F. Schöningh, 1955), 63.

57. Robert Brun, "Annales Avignonnaises de 1382 à 1410: Extraites des archives Datini," *Mémoires de l'institut historique de Provence* 13 (1936): 73.

58. Brun, "Annales," 12 (1935): 26.

59. Brun, "Annales," 12 (1935): 4.

60. Ronald Weissman, *Ritual Brotherhood in Renaissance Florence* (New York: Academic, 1982), 80.

61. Anne-Marie Hayez, *Le terrier Avignonnais de l'évêque Anglic Grimoard: 1366–1368* (Paris: CTHS, 1993), 314–315.

62. Chiffoleau, *Les justices du pape*, 254–255.

63. Brun, "Annales," 14 (1937): 14. He was eventually expelled from the palace and caught by the Avignonese authorities.

64. ADV, *Archives communales d'Avignon*, boîte 68, no. 2231.

65. Girard and Pansier, *La cour temporelle*, 57–60.

66. See, for example, Nicolas IV, *Ut per litteras*, no. 003297 (April 9, 1290); Innocent VI, *Ut per litteras*, no. 000459 (July 29, 1353); and Urbain V, *Ut per litteras*, no. 000349 (August 19, 1363) and 001461 (July 29, 1365).

67. Innocent VI, *Lettres secrètes et curiales*, no. 000459 (July 29, 1353), where officials of the provinces and cities of the Roman Church prohibit their immediate subjects from cheating at dice games and procuring or pandering prostitutes.

68. The 1243 statutes established a curfew, prevented citizens of all status from circulating without a light or from drinking, gambling, and patronizing inns, taverns, and prostitutes after the toll of the night bell; see statutes 76 and 77 in René Maulde-La-Clavière, *Coutumes et règlements de la république d'Avignon au treizième siècle* (Paris: L. Larose, 1879), 166.

69. Anne-Marie Hayez, "Familiers de prélats contre catalans: Un 'tumulte' à Avignon au temps de Jean XXII," *Annuaire de la Société des amis du Palais des papes et des monuments d'Avignon* 75 (1998): 149–155.

70. Chiffoleau, *Les justices du pape*, 255.

71. Tournaments were prohibited under sentence of excommunication because they were considered dangerous for body and soul; see Jean XXII, *Ut per litteras apostolicas*, no. 003543; and Clément VI, *Ut per litteras apostolicas*, no. 004197.

72. The 1379 entrance of Clement VII had the pope enter the city via the eastern route from the direction of Carpentras, initiating some five kilometers from the city, near the monasteries of Montfavet and St. Praxède; see Pansier, "Annales Avignonnaises," 51.

73. Eugène Déprez, "Les funérailles de Clément VI et d'Innocent VI d'après les comptes de la cour pontificale," *Mélanges d'archéologie et d'histoire* 20 (1900): 237.

74. Joseph Girard, *Évocation du vieil Avignon* (Paris: Les éditions de minuit, 1958), 54.

75. See Horrox, *The Black Death*, 42, 45.

76. Jacques Heers, "Les villes d'Italie centrale et l'urbanisme: Origines et affirmation d'une politique (environ 1200–1350)," *Mélanges de l'École française de Rome, moyen-âge-temps modernes* 101.1 (1989): 69.

77. Maulde-La-Clavière, *Coutumes et règlements de la république d'Avignon*, 168.

78. Maulde-La-Clavière, *Coutumes et règlements de la république d'Avignon*, 146.

79. Maulde-La-Clavière, *Coutumes et règlements de la république d'Avignon*, 201.

80. I find no better evidence than the letter of Louis Heyligen.

81. Pansier, "Annales Avignonnaises," 28.

82. Pansier, "Annales Avignonnaises," 55.

83. Pansier, "Annales Avignonnaises," 64–67.

84. Pansier, "Annales Avignonnaises," 69.

85. Girard and Pansier, *La cour temporelle d'Avignon*, 57.

86. Pansier, "Annales Avignonnaises," 69.

87. François Charles Carreri, "Chronicon parvum Avinionense de schismate et bello (1397–1416)," *Annales d'Avignon et du Comtat Venaissin* (1916): 166.

88. Pansier, "Annales Avignonnaises," 12–13.

89. Pansier, "Annales Avignonnaises," 14.

90. Pansier, "Annales Avignonnaises," 63.

91. See Jacques Rossiaud, *Le Rhône au moyen âge* (Paris: Aubier, 2007), 131, 134–135. There is evidence that during floods, the water unearthed buried corpses that could then be seen floating downstream. See Rossiaud, *Le Rhône*, 348.

92. Pansier, "Annales Avignonnaises," 29.

93. Martin de Alpartil, *Chronica actitarum temporibus domini Benedicti XIII*, ed. J. Angel Sesma Muñoz and M. Mar Agudo Romeo (Saragossa: Centro de Documentación Bibliográfica Aragonesa, 1994), 46.

94. See *Acta Sanctorum: Secunda dies julii, de B. Petro de Luxemburgo S. R. E. Cardinali, Ep. Metensi. Avenione in Gallia: [230] [Depositiones de mercatore in Rhodanum lapso,]* Testis XLIII, Col. 0566F.

95. Girard and Pansier, *La cour temporelle d'Avignon*, 167; regulations about the storage of hay are found on pages 174–175 under the rubric *Igne* (fire).

96. Girard and Pansier, *La cour temporelle d'Avignon*, 175.

97. Girard and Pansier, *La cour temporelle d'Avignon*, 28–29.

98. *Acta Sanctorum*, CCLV, 584.

99. Carreri, "Chronicon parvum avinionense," 171.

100. See also *Acta Sanctorum*, CCLV, 585.

101. Ronald Musto, *Apocalypse in Rome: Cola Di Rienzo and the Politics of the New Age* (Berkeley: University of California Press, 2003), 64.

SIX

The Great Western Schism and Avignon

The preceding chapters have argued that the Avignon papacy strove to establish institutional and administrative legitimacy as it developed an acceptable capital away from Rome, one with a vibrant international society and culture. This chapter, which focuses on the Schism, returns to the issue of legitimacy at the core of the double papal election that initiated the crisis in 1378. One of the lessons the Schism offers institutional historians is that two papal capitals could compete in advancing the legitimacy of their respective claimants and both be successful. Two papal courts could not only survive but flourish. If Rome and Avignon had not been thriving Christian cities, they would not have rivaled each other for papal supremacy for close to two generations without instigating major social upheavals. The Church's administration had been so well defined by the Avignon popes and was so innovative and efficient that it could be cut in half and still function quite effectively.

The Great Western Schism (1378–1417), approximately forty years that witnessed a double and sometimes triple papacy, belongs with the Black Death and the Hundred Years' War as one of the threefold calamities that plagued the fourteenth century. The Schism shattered Western Christian unity, the ideological touchstone of the Middle Ages, literally dividing western Europe into two camps that each obeyed their respective popes. It diminished the aura of the Catholic Church, raised doubts about papal authority and the advance of conciliarism, and saw the emergence of national churches. While many historians have discussed the Schism's religious, political, and economic consequences, few have focused on its social effects on both capital cities of Christianity. With that in mind, this chapter reviews the main events of the Schism, removing the emphasis from institutional issues to reset it within a sociocultural historical context. Presently, we will examine the Avignonese's understanding and perception of the crisis and, in more general terms, its repercussions on the population.

WHY A SCHISM?

Upon his election in Avignon, Pope Gregory XI (like his predecessor, Urban V) made a point to voice his wish to return the papacy to Rome. Politics prevented Gregory from acting quickly on his desire, but he eventually put a plan into action and embarked for Rome on September 13, 1376, arriving four months later on January 17, 1377. Later naysayers, with the advantage of hindsight, of course, emphasized the many bad omens attached to Gregory's departure: in Avignon, his horse refused to be mounted; en route, weather played havoc with the pope's flotilla, scattering ships with strong winds or stopping its progress when the gales died.[1] Human intervention also slowed down the pope's progress. Gregory had to wait some five weeks in Corneto, on the Italian Mediterranean coast, for his Avignonese and Roman representatives to reach an agreement on his ceremonial entry into the city. In the Middle Ages, the official entry (or *adventus*) of an important personage into a city was a significant event among the rituals of social communication. The pageant displayed social and political harmony for both audience and participants and needed to be carefully articulated and negotiated by all parties before its enactment.

For the Romans, the *adventus* symbolized the balance between independence and obedience. The Romans' joy at the papal return reflected the heightened status and economic advantages that the city would regain. Still, the Romans balked at their loss of independence, which they had enjoyed during some seventy years of papal absence. The pope was the lord of Rome, and the city needed to renew its acknowledgment of his lordship, both symbolically and persuasively, as it simultaneously strove to maintain a semblance of autonomy. The entrance of the pontiff ceremonially displayed his political dominance over Rome and provided a suitable spectacle for his receiving the keys of Castel Sant'Angelo, the fortress that protected the Borgo—the Vatican's Leonine city, where the ancient basilica of Saint Peter stood—together with Rome's cathedral, the basilica of St. John Lateran, and the complex of its buildings and palace. To reassert his presence, a magnificent procession paraded down the Via Papalis that meandered through the ancient city, by the Capitol Hill and the Colosseum.

The *adventus* held for Gregory in January 1377 was remarkable in the sense that it ratified an implicit victory for the Romans. The Romans altered tradition by leading the pope from the basilicas of Saint Paul to Saint Peter, in the opposite direction of the traditional Vatican-Lateran route. During their negotiations over the pope's homecoming celebration, the Romans signaled a subtle and symbolic rebuke, arranging for the pontiff to enter the city via the traditional route of the Roman carnival! A population attuned to communication through ceremony must not have missed the message signaled by this change in protocol. In any case, Gregory settled in Rome only to die a few months later, on March 27, 1378, tired but certainly satisfied with his return of the papacy to its traditional home.

Following canon law, on the night of April 7, 1378, the sixteen cardinals present in Rome entered into conclave (by nationality, they were eleven French, four Italian, and a single Spanish cardinal). The following day, despite internal divisions between Limousins and northern French and a boisterous Roman crowd chanting at their windows, the college elevated Bartolomeo Prignano, archbishop of Bari, as Pope Urban VI. He was crowned on April 10 and, after a reign of eleven years, died on October 15, 1389. Significantly, Urban VI was not a cardinal, and he has the distinction of being the last pontiff elected from outside the college of cardinals. He was, however, a well-qualified curial servant, praised for his rigor and moral integrity; but he was also temperamental and intense. It did not take long for dissatisfaction about the new pontiff to surface. By June, unhappy French cardinals began abandoning Rome for Anagni, and on August 9, 1378, they posted their *Declaratio* on the gates of Anagni's cathedral, denouncing Urban's election as fraudulent because it had taken place under duress and violence. The cardinals justified their abandonment of Urban by asserting the illegality of an election in which the Roman mob had subjected them to a "fear of the kind that can conquer even a steadfast man" (*metus qui potest cadere in constantem virum*). The dissenting cardinals cited the Romans' threats: "We want a Roman pope—or at least an Italian. If not, we'll cut you to pieces!" They argued that their decision to elect Urban was invalid because it had been a desperate act of self-defense, exacted from them under extreme pressure. During the months of July and August 1378, both parties initiated talks in an attempt to avoid a break between the pope and his cardinals, but positions soon hardened. Twelve French cardinals required Urban's unconditional abdication; others advised the pope to rule with the aid of a council. The idea of a general council also circulated, but with one important caveat: only a legitimate pope could call one. The French cardinals agreed early on to the *via facti*, meaning the "way of force," or removal of the pope by military means. On July 20, 1378, emboldened by their troops' recent defeat of Roman soldiers at Ponte Salario, they declared their election of Urban null and void. Positions on all sides remained firm, however, and on August 2, 1378, the cardinals again invalidated their election and urged Urban to step down.

A week later their declaration became an encyclical letter denouncing Urban as *intrusus* (intruder) and anathematizing him. They followed their declaration by physically distancing themselves from the pope's reach, settling at the court of Onorato Caetani in Fondi, in the Kingdom of Naples. On September 21, a conclave of all thirteen rebellious cardinals elected Robert of Geneva as Pope Clement VII. The three Italian cardinals present abstained from voting. Clement was crowned in Fondi a month later on October 31, with the papal tiara brought from Castel Sant'Angelo by Gregory XI's former camerlengo, Pierre de Cros, who had joined the French party. At Rome in September 1378, Urban VI learned of the election of his rival. In response, he expanded his power base by completely renewing the college of cardinals, elevating twenty-five new candidates. With this action, he officially confirmed the Schism. None of his cardinals had participated in his election to the papal throne. All the electors in his own election in April had abandoned him. From the outbreak of the Schism in late 1378, tradition assigned the partisan supporters of each of these two pope into two rival factions; even after the deaths of Clement VII and Urban VI, their followers were still labeled Clementists or Urbanists.

Previous schisms had usually been political in origin and caused by the intense rivalry between popes and Roman emperors. In contrast, this new Schism divided Christianity between two popes, two courts, two loyalties, each one directing all of his energy at proving his own legitimacy and robbing his opponent of supporters. The crisis was essentially an electoral dispute, and the equal strength of both sides ensured that this division would take a long time to heal.

After the initial events of 1378, politics played a large part in the allegiances garnered by either pope. Clement VII gained the support of the king of France, Charles V, his brother Louis of Anjou, and to a lesser degree the kings of Castile, Aragon, and Navarre. Most of Gregory XI's former administration also stood by Clement, while Urban had more or less to staff his entire government. To re-create an efficient papal administration on the fly was a daunting task that Urban tackled pragmatically. He did have the support of Portugal, the Holy Roman Empire, Rome, the Italian city-states, and England and its territories in France. Internal European politics also dictated allegiances. Because England opted to support Urban, Scotland chose Clement. The Holy Roman emperor, Charles IV, and the king of Hungary chose Urban, leading the Dukes of Luxembourg, Lorraine, and Austria to support Clement in turn.

The financial assets of the Clementist obedience rested on its well-run collector system. Again, Urban VI had to start anew, as only a single collector chose his camp after 1378. As these officials continued to collect and pay assignations for Clement VII, Urban had to keep improvising, often changing his staff and the size of his collectorates. The system largely failed Urban, for the collections from the Papal States and the pontifical vicars from this region could often be unreliable. The rival popes were intent on financially sapping their opponents, going so far as allowing theft if it increased their own incomes. Put in the same predicament, both popes minimized the always perilous movement of funds and relied on local assignations, as often as possible spending funds exactly where they received them. In Avignon, Clement's camerlengos controlled assignations; after deducting their personal expenses, collectors sent their surplus on to the treasury. Urban and his Chamber, on the contrary, held little control over their revenues and expenses. They replaced the traditional system of assignation with rectors and temporal vicars who were given direct financial control over their posted locations. Often abusive, their monetary exactions in the Papal States led to numerous popular revolts. On a day-to-day basis, Urbanists borrowed from bankers to survive.

Banking grew equally in importance for both parties. Even if by different means, merchant-bankers coordinated the transport of funds and supported both popes financially. The Avignon popes employed several small firms that received letters of change in their various European agencies and in the capital city. In general, the Avignon papacy used its resources well, free from bankers' pressure. In contrast, the Roman papacy handed its financial control over to bankers who responded by granting generous credit that supported the pontiffs. This reliance on external funds led the Roman popes to choose expedient and unsavory means to replenish their treasury. Under the guise of promoting Christian spirituality, they really advanced their own material interests—like the calling of two Jubilee Years within ten years, in 1390 and 1400, to fill their coffers.

As years went by, popes died, and with each new election, any hope for the reunion of the Latin Church vanished. First, the popes tried to defeat each other through the use of force. When this failed, each camp suggested its rival's abdication (willingly or coerced) or perhaps the withdrawal of secular support from papal obedience (self-serving arguments with dangerous future implications). After years of stalemate, the much-debated proposal to call a council to reconcile the Urbanist and Clementist parties eventually became the accepted solution. The first general council, held in Pisa in 1409, succeeded in befuddling the situation even more. Called to Pisa to participate, both popes refused to attend; in response, the council tried them, declared them disobedient and contumacious, and deposed them both. The council then elected a third pope, Alexander V, who added a third line of claimants to the papacy since the two other popes rejected the authority of the council to depose them. In 1413, both the Holy Roman emperor, Sigismund, and Alexander's successor, John XXIII, broke ground by calling the next council. They used their collaboration to unite all papal factions around a single goal: reunion. The Avignonese and Roman obedience could not refuse this summons, since the call came from the emperor and not from an illegitimate pope. The Council of Constance, held between 1414 and 1417, effectively ended the crisis by accepting the resignation of the Pisan claimant, John XXIII, and the Roman claimant, Gregory XII, deposing the Avignonese claimant, Benedict XIII, and electing Martin V as singular pope of Western Christendom.

Historians who have tried to understand the causes of the Schism have largely benefited from hindsight. The council simultaneously solved the Schism and sapped at least two centuries of papal efforts at gaining political and religious supremacy. In their words, the fathers of the council put the common good (*bonum commune*) of the Church before the claims of either pope.[2] The Council of Constance's decree, *Haec sancta synodus*, asserted the legitimacy of the council as representative of the Church and posited the authority of a Church council above that of the popes, thus defining "conciliarism." A subsequent decree, *Frequens*, organized a regular pattern of council meetings as "an especial means for cultivating the field of the Lord and effecting the destruction of briars, thorns, and thistles, to wit, heresies, errors, and schism, and of bringing forth a most abundant harvest."[3] The negative implications of these decrees for the monarchical papacy sent shockwaves through the camp of those defending papal primacy. But perhaps they also revealed the hidden motives of those who had always opposed papal supremacy and who had helped their cause by generating the Schism in the first place. The Schism was narrowly about a legal issue attached to the validity of an election; disputed papal elections were not infrequent in the Middle Ages for the simple reason that they involved multiple, competing interests. But the implications of that one contested election in 1378 were far reaching for the general theory of the papal fullness of power (*plenitudo potestatis*).

Papal nominations or elections were a variance of the episcopal nomination, since the pontiff was essentially the bishop of Rome. The momentous election of a pope inevitably evolved through the ages, but its most significant development was perhaps the notion of a conclave—an independent, secret election held by a group of special electors (the cardinals) in a reserved, private space (in Latin, *cum clave* means "with a key," hence "locked")—which lessened some of the concerns repeatedly raised across the centuries. The main issue was ridding the vote of secular interference and conflicts, whether from crowds of Roman clerics, aristocratic families, Holy Roman emperors, or, more simply, from human ambition. Until the time of Gratian's *Decretum* in the twelfth century, Rome's clergy had elected the pope, upon some general approbation of the people. At a Lateran synod in April 1059, Pope Nicholas II created the first independent ecclesiastic electoral college, giving cardinal-bishops first choice in naming a pope, seconded by cardinal-deacons, the rest of the clergy, and the Roman people. To prevent certain abuses, the Third Lateran Council of 1179 gave a single vote to each cardinal and required an electoral majority of two-thirds. This legislation proved to be contentious and troublesome; in many instances, the majority was not attained, and the vacant see or interregnum lasted up to several years. Tebaldo Visconti, taking the name of Pope Gregory X, was elected in 1271 after a three-year papal vacancy and, to prevent another such impasse, he decreed the revolutionary innovation of the conclave in 1274 with his bull *Ubi periculum*. In his own words,

> Where there is greater danger, there must certainly be greater foresight. We learn from the past how heavy are the losses sustained by the Roman church in a long vacancy, how perilous it is; we see this all too clearly when we wisely consider the crises undergone. . . . We judge therefore that everything wisely instituted by our predecessors and especially by Pope Alexander III of happy memory, for avoiding discord in the election of the Roman pontiff, should remain altogether intact. We intend in no way to detract from this legislation, but to supply by the present constitution what experience has shown to be missing.[4]

From then on, the conclave's regulations strictly enclosed the College of Cardinals to prevent electoral interference. If cardinals took too long to reach a decision, they were subjected to fasting after their third day of enclosure.

According to the cardinals, in 1378 violence and external interference marred the election, making it noncanonical. The cardinal of Mende emphasized the threat he felt when he heard Romans chanting: "We want a Roman, or at least an Italian or by the keys of S. Peter we will kill and cut to pieces these French and foreigners, starting first with the cardinals!"[5] According to their depositions, bands of armed men roamed the city as the crowd occupied and invaded the Vatican on the conclave's opening and closing days.

On the other hand, violence was expected during and after the election. Dietrich of Niem, a papal notary residing at court, states, "After the cardinals had elected him [Prignano] pope unanimously, they sent for him and other prelates on Friday, at the third hour. He immediately moved his books and other valuables into a safe place, so that they would not be stolen, *as is the Roman tradition* [author's emphasis] if the rumor were spread abroad that he had been elected."[6]

As they later asserted, the cardinals deemed the violence so insidious that it nullified their decision. Still, they refrained from mentioning that such violence was traditional and that they had witnessed it on previous occasions and (more importantly) in Avignon. How could they not have seen this, when Bartolomeo de Zabrici, Bishop of Recanati and Macerata, testified, "*As it was customary* [author's emphasis] and as I witnessed in Avignon when the Lord of Beaufort had been made pope, back then, they [the crowd] had pillaged the house [of the elected] *as was customary* with all of his predecessors."[7]

The simple fact that no one doubted the validity of the election in the days immediately following it offers further evidence that the cardinals might very well have expected this violence. In their depositions against the pope, cardinals simply refrained from mentioning that they were familiar with "electoral violence." The carnivalesque behavior surrounding the election and the plunder of ecclesiastical property, accompanied by the pillaging of cardinals' residences and the cells of the conclave, are well documented from the third to the eighteenth centuries. Such mob-like disorder was commonplace by the fourteenth century.[8] Yet only in 1378 was such a claim of duress used to invalidate an election.

In the main, modern students of papal history decline to blame the Schism on a single party; rather, it seems wiser to enumerate the several circumstances whose convergence produced the crisis. All agree that the French cardinals were largely instrumental at its inception. It was they, after all, who repudiated their own initial judgment that the election was canonical. It is obvious that the cardinals regretted their choice of Urban soon after electing him, especially when he turned imperious, reproving, and erratic. By electing a bureaucrat, they attempted to supplant him, proposing instead an innovative scheme in which they shared in a limited fashion in the pope's rule; but Urban resisted, determined to maintain the absolute supremacy of the papacy.

Throughout the Middle Ages, the pope's growing assertion of his plenitude of power went hand in hand with a metaphorical construction that conflated the pope's body with the Church's (in medieval parlance, the pope was head *and* body of the Church). This vision barred cardinals from participating fully (literally and metaphorically) in the life of the Church. By their own vision, the cardinals saw the pope at the head of the Church and themselves as its trunk and limbs, directly challenging the papal understanding of the intimate relationship between man and institution. Even if today this debate seems lofty and idealistic, it had real implications for medieval papal governance and finance. Cardinals wanted participation in decision making and their own share of the Church's revenue because they saw themselves as fully integrated within the Church's body. They resented that the pontiff reserved to himself various taxes (like the *annates*) and did not share this bounty with them. If it can be claimed that the pope aimed for an absolute monarchy, it must also be acknowledged that at the same time, the cardinals were pulling toward a constitutional one. That the pope and his cardinals clashed over what may be regarded as "lifestyle questions"—for example, the personal observance of standards of apostolic life (*vita apostolica*) appropriate to their positions as church leaders—perhaps also fueled the break. The pope was intent on fighting simony and other abuses, and some cardinals no doubt resented Urban's reform agenda and his pressing summons to religious discipline and austerity.

Another factor contributing to the crisis was the conflict between Urban's personality and the motivations of Charles V of France. The French king obviously regretted Gregory's departure to Rome and favored returning the papacy to Avignon, where the pontiff would once more reside in his territorial and political sphere of interest. Predictably, the French cardinals supported the king; they, too, expected a return to Avignon and begrudged Urban for his refusal to do so. The personality of Urban was also at fault. The pope acted independently in his nominations to major and minor offices, bypassing the counsel of his court and thus further curbing the cardinals' influence. He may have simply been too rigid and unbending for a position that required the ability to compromise. The cardinals had elected a man they knew to be prudent and modest; he had been an effective administrator of the Chancery with little political clout. Once pope, however, the man's personal strengths became for the cardinals a serious political obstacle. The administrator felt no esprit de corps with the princes of the Church. In fact, Urban's attitude toward his cardinals was downright demeaning. He was inflexible, arrogant, unrestrained in his reproach, and abusive. The office had changed the man. Cardinal Robert of Geneva ominously warned Urban, "Holy Father, you have not treated the cardinals with the honour due to us and that your predecessors used to show us, but you are diminishing our honour. I tell you in all earnest that the cardinals will work to diminish your honour too," but his advice went unheeded.[9]

As historians have scoured archives to pin down a single or multiple factors responsible for the origin and continuation of the crisis, they have also laid much of the blame on the papal institution itself. For Howard Kaminsky, the institutional culture that grew from the Avignon papacy was directly responsible for the break. Essentially, the Schism was a consequence of the Avignon papacy. His judgment is harsh; while labeling the Avignon papacy a "triumphant construction of papal monarchy," he accuses it of "reifying the ecclesiastical institution into a system of benefices apprehended as property rights, acquisition and preservation of which were the primary objects of clerical interest."[10] The consequence of such an attitude was a general disinterest in things "papal." In the minds of the silent majority of Christians in the Latin West, the survival of the institution became largely detached from the issue of salvation. That disconnect explains why no widespread and general movement to end the Schism emerged. As Robert Norman Swanson states, "The schism was not, therefore, a matter of belief, but of administration; this explains why the response on the ground was 'cavalier.'"[11] The Schism was primarily a dispute of succession irrelevant to the quality of the religious lives of the individuals involved or of the laity at large. Thus, it did not create a confessional crisis in the larger Church, nor did it provoke religious wars more widely in Europe.

THE EARLY YEARS

Initially, both Clement and Urban resorted to force to defeat his rival. Clement's hopes to seize Rome and its pope vanished when Urban's Company of Saint George, led by the famous *condottiere* Alberico da Barbiano, defeated Clement's mercenaries at Marino on April 29, 1379. The best of the *condottieri* of his time, Jean de Malestroit, Sylvestre de Budes, Louis de Montjoie, and Bernardon de la Salle, led Clement's Breton and Gascon mercenary troops. In spite of their fame and skill, these mercenaries could not prevent Castel Sant'Angelo from capitulating to Urban's forces. With this defeat, Clement lost his foothold in Rome. As for Urban, he had achieved one of his two goals: he had prevented his opponent from seizing Rome. His next move was to force Clement out of Italy entirely.

Urban's second goal in fact mirrored Clement's strategy. Both popes' foreign policies relied on control of the Kingdom of Naples. At that time, Queen Joanna, granddaughter of Robert, late king of Naples, and daughter of Marie of Valois, sister of the late King Philip VI of France, ruled Naples. She was countess of Provence and Forcalquier and titular queen of Jerusalem and Sicily. After some brief hesitation, Joanna nominally opted for Clement, and the pope relied heavily on the foothold she provided in Italy. Unfortunately for Clement, the Neapolitans did not support their queen's choice, and any hope he may have had of initiating a conquest of the papal territories via Naples vanished quickly. He had to retreat from southern Italy. Clement eventually left his unsustainable position in Italy and retreated to the former papal city; he entered Avignon on June 20, 1379, relying on the experienced administration that had supported the Avignon papacy.

Back in Avignon, Clement resettled his court with some five hundred papal servants. Although fifty of them were from his native Geneva, he is not generally accused of having widely practiced nepotism. As shown by his policy in the distribution of benefices, Clement was not a pawn of France. Rather, he distributed (or collated) ecclesiastical, spiritual, and temporal benefices across a geographically wide diversity of clergy, independent of French influence. Still, he faced French pressure throughout his rule. The king, the bishops, and the University of Paris attempted to sway him from the traditional right of reserve, a right that the Avignon popes had long fought for and gained. This right of reserve allowed the pope (and no one else) to collate benefices. Such control over who received benefices allowed Clement to widen his influence by choosing his own nominees to church posts and to receive income from the *annates*, the tax on the first year's revenue of a benefice. Clement needed these funds to fight his "way of force," but like most aristocrats, Clement also proved to be generous. By generously funding scholarships for French clerics to attend universities, he tamped down discontent. His magnanimity also extended to the city of Avignon, where he agreed to support the Pignotte almshouse.

Clement's return to the city also occasioned municipal improvements. Two weeks before his arrival in Avignon, officials inspected the roads the papal cortege was to follow and decreed the traditional route via the Gate Saint-Michel unusable. They rerouted the pope via the Gate Saint-Lazarus, next to the Perron, site of public executions. Once again, the *adventus*'s change of route may have been totally necessary, but it is probable that residents were communicating a message to their returned leader. Such a route change may have been a subtle way of demonstrating to the pope the city's mitigated satisfaction at seeing him back. The Italian conquest, with its diplomatic ramifications and endless financial levies, became the central preoccupation of the pope, and in turn, of Avignon.

Of course, Avignon rejoiced at the prospect of regaining its status as the capital of Christianity; but it also paid a high price in supporting the pope. By the time Clement entered the city under his golden-embroidered canopy, he had already taxed the city council a subsidy of 3,000 florins, levied to help the war effort while in Italy. Clement's financial reliance on his city continued after his return; he required of them some 10,000 florins in January 1379 and 5,000 florins in 1380. [12]

After arriving in Avignon, Clement's rapport with his capital remained distant and driven by financial self-interest. In November 1379, the pope ratified the old and unpopular convention of 1251, which had ended the city's political autonomy. For Avignon, it was easier to revert to a familiar status quo than languish without a formal agreement with its suzerain. Extending slight grace and favor to a few prominent citizens (permitting the enclosure of their daughters in convents), Clement otherwise showed little concern for the city where he set his throne. The local *gabelle* taxes, levied on salt, wine, and merchandise, and which had been initially created to fund the defense of the city, became the pope's indirect taxes instead.

After his failure to gain Neapolitan allies, Clement's hopes turned to Duke Louis of Anjou, brother of Charles V of France, to whom he proposed the conquest of the fictive Kingdom of Adria, which would regroup all the Papal States, minus the Latium. Regretting and later refuting this decision, Clement found a comfortable alternative in asking the childless Queen Joanna to adopt the same Louis. The French duke thus became de facto heir to the Neapolitan throne. Since the County of Provence and Forcalquier were attached to the Kingdom of Naples, the leaders of both were involved in the recovery of the kingdom. Provence and the Comtat Venaissin were either physically or financially implicated along with big players such as Milan and its ruling family, the Visconti, and the house of Savoy. The journal of Jean Le Fèvre, bishop of Chartres and chancellor to Louis I and II of Anjou between 1380 and 1388, offers a glimpse into these intense diplomatic relations. Le Fèvre recorded in his journal the correspondence he received and dispatched between February and July 1382 as well as the flow of eminent visitors who followed the Duke of Anjou to Avignon, including the Count of Savoy, the Duke of Berry, the Marquis of Montferrat, the Viscount of Rhodes, and many more ambassadors whom the cardinals and the pope hosted. [13]

Avignon became a diplomatic hub that hosted foreign officials as the pope dispatched legates and ambassadors all over Europe. The financial support of the Clementist curia fell on French clergy and the capital city. Le Fèvre itemizes countless meetings, always around meals, reminding us how important the act of eating together was to medieval society. These various assemblies promoted the local economy, if only by the amount of resources needed to feed and equip the various parties. It may have been with mixed feelings that on May 30, 1382, the Avignonese sent the Duke of Anjou on his way. In a grand public display, the duke received the banners of the Kingdom of Sicily and Jerusalem from the hands of the pope, performed his feudal obeisance by kissing the pope's slipper, and in a sign of peace kissed all the cardinals present on the mouth. [14] The income the duke generated while in Avignon was lost, but the cost of his wars remained Avignon's burden. [15]

Meanwhile, Urban VI responded to the situation by supporting Charles of Durazzo's claim to the Neapolitan title. [16] This cousin of the queen conquered the kingdom of Naples over the summer of 1381. Durazzo captured Joanna, imprisoned her, and eventually ordered her death by suffocation in May 1382 when Louis initiated a rescue mission to liberate his "mother." After her demise, Louis moved to reclaim Naples. His campaign was a difficult one, with Durazzo proving a brilliant strategist who starved and harassed the French army. Louis's death in 1384 ended all hope for the French until Urban's actions turned the situation around.

Shortly before Louis of Anjou's death, Urban VI had severed his ties with Charles of Durazzo when the latter refused to hand over conquests (and some hard cash) to Urban's nephew, an adventurer named Butillo Prignano. Their argument escalated when Durazzo also refused to give up his hard-won crown. Urban was left with no choice but to look for the protection of Butillo in Nocera. Life in Nocera was dismal, and many at the court used any opportunity to escape it. During the summer of 1384, the plague stalled the triple contest of Louis of Anjou versus Durazzo, Durazzo versus Urban, and Urban versus Louis of Anjou. Louis died, and the crown passed to his oldest son, Louis II (then quite young and under the regency of his mother, Marie of Blois). His troops started their journey home, freeing a convalescent Durazzo to deal with the pope. The argument between Urban and Durazzo reached its climax when they declared war against each other. Some of Urban's cardinals sided with

Durazzo, however, suggesting that a council should assist the pope in ruling. Livid by reports of this treachery, Urban called the offending cardinals into consistory, imprisoned and tortured them, and ultimately ordered their death; he simultaneously excommunicated Durazzo and his entire court. In reply, Durazzo sent Alberico da Barbiano, now in his pay, to take Nocera and besiege the castle where the pope had found refuge. The death of Charles of Durazzo in February 1386 allowed the Angevins to reclaim the Neapolitan throne, relying this time on the leadership of Otto of Brunswick, the late Queen Joanna's fourth husband. Otto entered Naples in 1387; the young Louis II of Anjou, proclaimed king of Naples in 1389, took possession of his kingdom a year later.

In an ironic turn of events, mercenaries in the pay of Anjou delivered Urban from Nocera's siege, freeing him only after he agreed to pay a hefty ransom. Urban then fled to Benevento and Genoa, this time rewarding his Genoese rescuers with the papal town of Corneto. After a year in Genoa, Urban journeyed through Lucca and Perugia, and eventually regained Rome, where he died on October 15, 1389, though not before proclaiming 1390 a Jubilee Year.

Meanwhile, in these early years of the Schism, Avignon faced tremendous threats, beginning with the constant incursions of the so-called Union of Aix (1382–1387) and, throughout the Schism, the constant attacks of Roger Raymond de Turenne (1352–1413). Louis of Anjou created the Union in the early 1380s, when he journeyed south to Provence to receive the crown of the Kingdom of Naples that he had inherited from Queen Joanna. In 1382, the duke-turned-king accepted the lordship of many Provençal towns, except Aix-en-Provence, which refused to bow to the northern lord. Aix assumed the leadership of the union against the Angevin house and chose instead to support its dynastic enemy, the house of Durazzo. Politics mingled with religion when the duchy of Anjou sided with Clement VII, and Durazzo with the union of Aix and Urban VI. This rivalry brought war to the gates of Avignon. Roads were unsafe, and travelers were often attacked by unpaid troops. This basic insecurity remained a scourge during most of the Schism since funds were often lacking on all sides and soldiers felt entitled to exact some form of payment, even if nothing more than highway robbery. As a merchant stated so callously, "If they [meaning Clementists] had money, it would be a good war for our pockets."[17] But "they" did not, and insecurity prevailed, hampering the travel of goods and men.[18] Unpaid soldiers pillaged the Avignonese countryside, leaving the city's inhabitants confined within the safety of its walls, fearful they would be robbed the moment they ventured outside.[19] The arms dealers who equipped the citizen-conscripts for the siege of Aix (who did receive a small wage for their pains) were among the few Avignonese who profited from the war in Provence.[20]

During this period, Viscount Raymond de Turenne (the so-called scourge of Provence), a brilliant military commander and negotiator, chose to exact a heavy toll from the pope and Avignon. Heir to the late Pope Gregory XI as his nephew, of the lineage of Roger de Beaufort, and former captain of the Comtat Venaissin, Raymond eventually turned against his employers. He is frequently mentioned in the contemporary writings of his time, which describe his unceasing attacks on Avignon's environs in search of cattle to carry off and wealthy victims to kidnap.[21] Raymond initially became an archenemy of the count of Anjou when the latter seized several territories attached to his patrimony, including the town of Pertuis, capital of Raymond's viscounty. Seeing the Clementist-Angevin alliance gaining ground, Raymond then accused Pope Clement VII of defaulting on the loans his late father had granted his brother, the late Pope Gregory XI. Finally, Raymond grew impatient and, aggravated by the pope's slow payment of his wages, recovered his losses during several campaigns for the papacy and the king of France. (Stalling payments was actually a familiar strategy for the cash-strapped papacy, well known from several campaigns.) Raymond hesitated in deciding which camp to join in the war of the union of Aix, but he finally offered homage to Marie of Blois, mother and regent of Louis II of Anjou. Despite his support of the Angevins, the viscount spent his life fighting Clement VII, Benedict XIII, and the Angevins, going so far as refusing to allow the marriage of his only daughter, Antoinette, into the Angevin dynasty. Instead, Antoinette married the renowned man-at-arms, Marshal Bouci-caut. Raymond preferred to defend his choice by stating that the House of Anjou was far too high for his own, and he certainly did not want to bow to his in-laws.

The significance of these events for the population of Avignon is more difficult to assess. Reviewing the contemporary sources, Philip Daileader concludes that people adjusted as best they could and learned to live with the Schism.[22] The case study of the Italian bankers, however, shows a somewhat different result. The letters exchanged between one of the most successful Italian merchants in Avignon, Francesco di Marco Datini, and his agent and associate Boninsegna di Matteo offer a glimpse into the life of Avignon in the era of the Schism.[23] As direct witnesses of these events, the sources offer historians invaluable information. Sadness and frustration emerge from their exchanges. They clearly gauged the failure of institutional Catholicism in quite remarkable terms for a period that is often characterized by pious submission to authority.

In his letters, Boninsegna di Matteo shows no real attachment to the Roman pope of his native Tuscany; he never calls him "Holy Father," for example. When Urban VI died in Rome on October 15, 1389, Boninsegna remains laconic on the topic, mentioning that nothing will change in Avignon and that the Italians in the city have nothing to fear.[24] Ironically, in his letters Boninsegna usually speaks of Clement VII as "Our Pope."[25] When the latter's brother died, Boninsegna commiserates with the now "orphaned" Clement. Boninsegna treats Clement as a man, showing a human compassion rarely found in descriptions of Christ's Vicar.[26]

The 1376 expulsion of the Florentines from Avignon as well as the absence of courtiers who had sided with Urban created an opportunity that tempted economic risk takers. During the Schism, Italian residents were scattered throughout the seven parishes of the city, with the bulk still residing in the three parishes of Notre-Dame la Principale, Saint-Pierre, and Saint-Agricol. These districts comprised the southern, wealthier section of the city, where residents specialized in skilled crafts, trade, and commerce. The Italians still met in two confraternities, Notre Dame la Majour and Saint John the Baptist (Boninsegna was elected master of Saint John in 1394). The latter association played a "legal" role in various deals. The masters of Saint John lobbied the curia for the Florentine Office of the Merchants (*mercanzia*) and Priors.[27] When the Lieutenant of Beaucaire (representing the king of France) charged the Avignonese Florentines with reprisal and condemned Florentines on French soil for the supposed embezzlement of French funds, he also settled scores with the masters of the confraternity "of the community of Florentines in Avignon."[28]

The confraternity of Notre Dame la Majour played an essential role in the socialization of the Italians with the Avignonese merchant class and the papal bureaucracy, all joining under its banner to celebrate the living and the dead.[29] An analysis of the matriculation lists of the association allows historians to follow the ebb and flow of this Italian population.

Although the tables below highlight those who left rather than those who remained in the city, they still provide an accurate portrayal of the Italian population at an instant in time. Italians represent 80 percent of the lists' membership, and Florentines represent 71 percent of the Italians. The inflation of numbers for 1373 and 1374 found in table 6.1 represents the endemic ravages of the plague. But interestingly enough, the Florentine expulsion from the city in 1376 does not appear to be reflected in the numbers. As we have seen, most wealthy Florentines were exempt from harsh papal legislation because they were able to buy protection. In addition, the bull released from its condemnation those who were younger than nine years old or were seventy and older, those who were without relatives or property, and those who owed no taxes and had not visited Florence in at least ten years.[30] In addition, some could claim they were from the Florentine suburb of Prato; the curia seems to have accepted this subterfuge. Table 6.1 reveals a surge in numbers for the years attached to the return of the papacy to Rome (between 1367–1370 and 1376–1379), certainly linked to the departure of "followers of the Roman court." Table 6.1 also underscores a minor Italian exodus at the onset of the Schism, but it halted in 1381 when Clement VII reauthorized Florentine residency in Avignon.

On October 8, 1381, Clement permitted Urbanist Florentines—who were largely merchants and bankers—to travel and reside on Clementist lands for five years. He also suspended the effects of the 1376 condemnation. In 1385, Florentine merchants began to contemplate their options. In October of that year, Boninsegna wrote to Datini: "As you know the Florentine received grace from the pope through the intervention of the Cardinal of Florence; for five years they were allowed to remain and circulate freely, as usual, and it was such until the fourth year passed in August, and next August will bring a term to the deal. The cardinal has already been contacted but he has not yet done a thing. They wrote to Florence, but supposedly the commune does not want to hear a thing from Avignon."[31] Thus, in 1386 Florentine merchants still felt nervous about their future in the city and were proactive in buying their protection from a court that was always willing to sell. They used traditional networking means: influence and cash. Merchants' letters are blunt, "regarding what you are telling me, concerning your intentions to deal with messires d'Aigrefeuille and Naples [both cardinals] in order to be spared by the pope. . . . It seems to me that 300 or 400 florins or more would be

Table 6.1.   Notre Dame: Table of Payments

Year	ND1	Only in ND1	ND2	Only in ND2
1367	17	9	10	2
1368	14	6	5	
1369	10	6		
1370	49	24		
1371	36	22		
1372	51	37	2	
1373	102	71	1	
1374	90	73		
1375	56	50		
1376	29	18		
1377	19	14	5	
1378	36	31		
1379	41	34		
1380	82	60		
1381	63	50		
1382	7	5		
1383	5	4		
1384	5	4		

The two lists of matriculations (ND1 and ND2) range from 1364 to 1384, well into the Schism years. They record thousands of names along with dates of payments. Dues were paid in advance, and the number attached to each name indicates the year up to which a member had paid. After the stated year passed, and if no arrears were collected for three to five years, the association added a cross to the entry and removed the name from the next list (see table 6.2). Based on the assumption that as long as they resided in the city members continued to join the association, the crosses and Roman numbers allow historians to infer when individuals left Avignon or died.

good."[32] Boninsegna leaves no doubt that the merchants purchased their protection at a high price. The same idea is echoed further when he says, "I do not believe that the people of the pope will cause you harm because you have lent money to the pope and you are not badly seen here."[33]

The papacy's pressing and endless need for funds made it the ideal client for a banker but also an unreliable patron. While the prospect of immense gain was attractive to merchants, the papacy's habit of default-

Table 6.2.   Individuals with Crosses

1358: 1	1363: 1	1369: 0	1375: 5	1381: 3
1359: 0	1365: 6	1370: 5	1376: 3	
1360: 0	1366: 0	1372: 0	1377: 0	
1361: 3	1367: 0	1373:12	1379: 0	
1362: 0	1368: 0	1374:10	1380: 1	

ing on loans was far less appreciated. Boninsegna regularly complains of this state of affairs in his letters: "We cannot get anything from Monseigneur d'Amiens [Cardinal Jean de la Grange]; Amiens's chamberlain keeps promising us some funds coming from a clerical benefice, but that is all he can do." Boninsegna mentions further:

> We cannot get back the money you loaned Monseigneur de Macôn [Jean de Boissy, bishop of Macôn]. He says that he will repay us at Saint-Michael when he gets income from his benefices. We will pester him and see if we can get it sooner. We cannot get anything from Andrea Tici [a renowned merchant of the city] because lately, he has lots of issues with the Apostolic Chamber; they found him guilty and jailed him for fifteen days at the request of the Auditor. We still cannot get anything from messire Guy de Saint-Marcel [Knight and Lord of Lercio], and not for lack of trying! He only pays us with his words. We will hassle him. We cannot get anything from the marshal's lieutenant, and Andrea da Siena goes there often. It seems to me that *you* should write to all these lords, and when they are willing to pay, we will visit them and get the funds. This will help us greatly.[34]

If moneylending did not fill merchants' purses, still the popes' expenditures on war invigorated the sale of weapons, a brisk business that pleased them. Boninsegna reports: "For this expedition [the 1384 war against Aix and the taking of the Castle of Lançon] we sold bassinets, harnesses and other weapons for some 1000 *fl.* of the Queen";[35] and "Even though we take pretty high risks here . . . this place is a good place especially for our trade."[36] Still, wars entailed great risk, and merchants were often captured and ransomed as a means of impeding the circulation of merchandise, thus increasing the odds for losses.[37] On April 6, 1384, Boninsegna writes, "The land is filled with mercenaries, many coming from France. We expect the arrival of the Duke of Berry any day now. During this month we estimate that some ten to twelve galleys at the pay of the pope will arrive from France and Marseilles, and four from Finale to cross to Naples. Thus, be more cautious than ever when you ship your merchandise. Send small quantity and insure your stock until the galleys are far at sea because they will hunt anybody since they need money."[38]

Disruptions like these could at times seem catastrophic and insurmountable. The sad tale of Filippo, a young Florentine broker in the pay of Datini, is a telling example.[39] A September 24, 1389, letter explains how in the city of Pertuis, Raymond de Turenne had confiscated for toll evasion some merchandise that Filippo transported for Datini. Young Filippo was so disconcerted that he locked himself in a room he was renting from a Jewish broker and killed himself. Medieval society considered suicide a grave sin, and Raymond further threatened to hang Filippo's body in disgrace and confiscate his goods and funds if tolls and fines were not paid. Luckily for Datini and for Filippo's body, the unnamed Jewish broker took charge, a touching example of Jewish-Christian rapport in medieval Europe. Having discovered Filippo's body, he called a barber to clean and treat it and a priest to administer confession and last rites. He then told two Italian pilgrims (Chiario and Puccio) who were passing through Pertuis to warn Boninsegna in Avignon of Filippo's death and the confiscation of his goods. Boninsegna, once aware of the situation, bought a safe-conduct to retrieve the merchandise. Meanwhile in Pertuis, Chiario and Puccio paid for Filippo's honorable funeral. The tale is a marvelous example of the Schism's toughest years but also one of human kindness and resourcefulness. Raymond de Turenne received sixty florins, but most importantly for Boninsegna and those who knew the young merchant, Filippo's soul was saved.

Urban VI's Avignonese supporters sometimes also lost their possessions in Avignon with rights of reprisal, but there was no systematic persecution. The registers for "reprisal" name only twenty-four individuals who lost property because of their allegiance to Urban.[40] In some cases, however, the pope's expedient decisions did fall on unfortunate Italians. A July 1387 letter describes the misery of Lorenzo di Buto, a Florentine resident of Avignon who lost his life savings. According to Boninsegna, Datini financially supported the ailing Lorenzo with two florins per month. Boninsegna adds,

> As I believe you already know, the pope has given his [Lorenzo's] house, the one where he has been living for the past 36 years, to one of his squires, a German named Tibutto; the house is considered property of Matteo, the dead brother of Lorenzo and it has been confiscated as

Florentine goods. [We have to assume that the squire had eyes on that house to argue that Lorenzo's house was in fact not his, but his dead Florentine brother's.] And, because this squire has great influence over the pope, he is suing Lorenzo and has done so well that he has three injunctions against him; Lorenzo has not found a procurator, lawyer, cardinal or a bishop who will speak for him, and on July 13, Lorenzo, his wife and family were evicted. To add harm to injury, they have confiscated all his rags that are not even ten gold florins. Here is mercy and justice![41]

Through these experiences merchants developed, if not a moral conscience, then at least a political consciousness, self-aware of their own interests and prompting their tendency to express political criticism when things were not going their way. They wrote, "The people of the pope afflict merchants and commoners, and they are advised by people who only think of themselves, and who do not pay attention to the ills they're causing us, merchants and little people."[42] As Boninsegna liked to repeat, "Provence is a brigand's den," and the "people of the pope want all the fat for themselves."[43] These words resonate in the writing of the *Anonimo fiorentino* (1382–1401), a man of roughly the same social background who vehemently argues that peace is essential for business. For the *Anonimo fiorentino*, peace is a vital element of economic success, and he lambasts the *antipapa da Vignone* and his *antipapisti* supporters, arguing that violence and political confusion have worsened the economic situation of the "city dwellers, merchants, good men."[44]

CONTINUATION

When Urban VI died in October 1389, all hope for a solution to the crisis vanished, as fourteen of his cardinals quickly elected his successor, Boniface IX, on November 2. This hasty election demonstrates that an end to the Schism was not yet attainable. Clement's response to Boniface's election was to put his rival on trial and forbid his followers from attending the Jubilee that he initiated in December 1389—an event that was quite successful regardless. Clement continued to defend what he considered his rightful claim to the papacy, increasingly supported by his own personal wealth. In 1392 his brother died, and Clement became sole heir of the wealthy county of Geneva. Clement was still actively championing his "way of force" when he died on September 16, 1394.

When the news of Clement's death reached Paris on September 22, the king took the advice of his *conseil*, made up of the Dukes of Bourbon, Orléans, Berry, and Burgundy, and drafted a letter to the cardinals in Avignon, asking them to wait for the arrival of his embassy before opening the conclave.[45] But the missive arrived as the gates of the conclave were closing, and it remained unread. On September 28, 1394, the twenty-one cardinals present in Avignon elected Clement VII's successor, the Aragonese Pedro de Luna. He took the name of Benedict XIII. Clement VII had named Pedro legate to Castile, Aragon, Navarre, and Portugal and had sent him in 1393 to France, Brabant, Flanders, Scotland, England, and Ireland. Pedro resided in Paris when not traveling. In general, his wide European experience and connections made him well suited to forge a solution to the crisis.

By 1394, the "way of force" was failing, and other alternative solutions began to emerge, such as the "way of cession" or the "way of council." Influential authors like Philippe de Mézières recommended that councils and kings spearhead ecclesiastical reform and unite the Church. Jean Gerson, speaker for the University of Paris, put forward his theologians' and jurists' suggestions: the Church's unity was possible if either pope abdicated willingly (*cessio*); if a commission selected by both popes reached a conclusion (*compromissio*); or if a general council was convened (*concilium pacis*). Numerous renowned intellectuals of the time, such as Jean Petit, Pierre d'Ailly, Simon de Cramaud, Nicholas de Clamanges, Gilles Deschamps, and Honoré Bonnet, participated in something akin to a propaganda campaign aimed at ending the Schism. They all wrote pamphlets calling for its end. Benedict XIII agreed in theory to the idea of abdicating, but refusing to submit to secular pressure, he presented "discussion" between the two popes (*via discussionis*) as his solution to bolster negotiations.

Benedict's proposal led to several French embassies. In May 1395, Charles VI sent his uncles, the Dukes of Berry and Burgundy, and his brother, the Duke of Orléans, to Avignon to persuade the pope to abdicate. This was to no avail. Gontier Col, a secretary of the king of France, kept a journal that informs his readers on the day-to-day conduct of the negotiations. Gontier explains that the pope habitually offered dinner to the emissaries, after which he systematically refused any of their proposals. On July 7, the French ambassadors told Benedict that they had eaten enough! Frustrated, they left Avignon.[46] The embassy nevertheless benefited the city's merchants. Boninsegna relished the spending of the four thousand men who arrived with the Dukes of Berry, Burgundy, and Orléans.[47] Discussions continued for three years after their departure, until July 1398, when the French king and clergy voted for the "way of cession," also called the "subtraction of obedience."

The royal ordinance forbade anyone to obey Benedict's commands or send any tax revenues to his court. The king deprived the pope of his right of collation and decreed the loss of benefices for any of his followers. This legislation favored a French (or Gallican) church financially and administratively independent from the papacy. The resolution reached Avignon in early September 1398, and most of Benedict's cardinals left for Villeneuve, directly across the bridge on French soil. They supported an Avignon pope whom (ideally) they could influence, as opposed to the Roman intruder, but not their current, inflexible pope. Benedict found refuge in his palatial fortress with some Spanish troops and five cardinals. The subtraction quickly led to war.

Martin de Alpartil, Benedict's chamberlain, wrote a chronicle that elaborates on this momentous event.[48] He explains how king and cardinals decided that the capture of the pope would be the best means of softening his resolve and how they hired the *condottiere* Boucicaut to take the palace and its pope. Once in Avignon, Boucicaut bragged to anyone listening that he would drag the pope back to Paris in chains. But, confounding his plans, the pope did not give in. The siege lasted almost a year, until May 1399, and actually worked to Benedict's advantage. Louis of Orléans (Charles VI's brother) admired the pontiff's stubbornness and resilience and became his protector. Louis negotiated an end to the siege, by whose terms the pope was required to remain isolated in his palace. Benedict submitted to this mandate, but only until he escaped the palace on March 12, 1403. The pope's evasion precipitated the end of the subtraction, and France quickly restored its obedience to Benedict XIII in May 1403.

The French subtraction put Avignon in a difficult situation. The city became the focal point of a complex mesh of factions that forced its citizens to join a camp. Rumors of the expulsion of Benedict's Spanish troops circulated, and letters were posted on the palace gates urging the pope to abdicate and the town to disavow him. In September 1398, after meeting with the cardinals, the city council decided just that and gave Boucicaut's men their support. Lobbies were divided territorially: Benedict's supporters favored the old town within the twelfth-century walls, the palace, and its surroundings, while his enemies distanced themselves both politically and physically from the palace. Some cardinals settled in Villeneuve, French lands on the other side of the Rhône, and antipapal meetings took place on the city's outskirts, away from the palace: at the Franciscan convent in the southeast, and at the Church of Saint-Didier to the south. The 1398–1399 siege inflicted much damage on the city, especially in its expensive northern neighborhoods. Boucicaut bombarded and mined the palace, and Benedict retaliated by aiming his own bombards and crossbows at the city, greatly damaging the area directly around the palace.

The siege of the palace led to a stalemate, and time favored the pope, even if the besieged had to resort to eating cats, rats, and sparrows (which Benedict supposedly relished). The papal fortress was impregnable; military failure led to Boucicaut's dismissal and his replacement by the Sénéchal of Provence, an agent of the king of France. Propaganda permeated this urban space. In December 1399, a sermon preached at the city's Carmelite convent renounced a return of obedience to Pope Benedict. In February 1400, Benedict's supporters then preached sermons at the Church of Saint-Geniès. In response, the cardinals forbade calling the pope by anything else but his secular name, Pedro de Luna.

The sense of loss of control felt by the Avignonese appeared incongruously in spectacles that symbolized their position. In April 1400, craftsmen supporting the pope appropriately chose to reenact the Trojan War in the city's streets. We can imagine Benedict as the heroic Hector, fighting to defend the homeland of his Trojans, while the French were presented as the invading and besieging Greeks. A few months later, in June 1400, craftsmen organized a passion play at the Dominican convent during Pentecost. It is hard to tell whom the crucified Jesus symbolized: the pope, the city, or the state of the Church. When, in October 1400, the king ordered his brother Louis to protect the pope, two factions took over: one pro-cardinal group supporting papal abdication, and the other pro-Orléans group supporting the reinstatement of France's obedience to Benedict. Both factions posted letters throughout the city to advance their cause.

Eventually Benedict capitulated to these demands, assured of the Duke of Orléans's protection. The pope was assigned to mandatory confinement in his palace for the next three years while his enemies debated whether or not to restore their obedience to him as leader of the Church.

In May 1401, Provence returned its obedience to Benedict, and events took a dramatic turn for the worse. The French cardinals, feeling their control of the situation loosening, heightened the antipapal rhetoric. Mobs searched the town to expel any Catalans and Spaniards, whom, as the pope's compatriots, the mobs considered to be traitors by association, and such murky politics led to spectacularly gruesome executions. Compelled by the cardinals, Avignon's authorities accused a few men of treason because they had publicly shown their support for Benedict. Condemned as traitors, they were beheaded, eviscerated, and quartered. As a deterrent to others in the city who might sympathize with Benedict, their limbs were hung on the gates of the city and remained there for several months. [49]

The cardinals chose this moment—surely to distance themselves from the extreme violence and to legitimate their own position in the cause of the Avignon papacy—to honor the late Clement VII and Peter of Luxembourg, a local saint. On September 18, 1401, the body of Clement VII was transferred with great pomp from the Cathedral of Notre-Dame des Doms to his final resting place at the newly built Convent of Celestines, founded to honor Cardinal Peter of Luxembourg. The cardinals used this ceremony to communicate with the population in the familiar medieval language of ritual; they were making clear to their audience that they supported the schismatic Avignon papacy but not Benedict himself. By the end of November, the limbs of the pseudotraitors still hung at the Gates Saint-Lazare, Imbert Neuve, Saint-Michel, and des Miracles to remind the Avignonese that the cardinals would not relinquish their hold on the city. The crisis had reached a climax.

The political situation stabilized in Avignon only when powerful actors outside the immediate theater of the conflict compromised in their politics and came to an agreement. In Paris, Isabeau, King Charles's wife, negotiated a truce between the Dukes of Orléans, Berry, and Burgundy. She charged the Duke of Orléans with special responsibility for the pontiff's personal protection as well as safeguarding the cardinals, while she assigned the protection of Avignon itself to the Duke of Berry. But the key to the restoration of peace was Benedict XIII's escape from the palace during the night of March 12, 1403, in the disguise of a Carthusian monk. According to a receipt found at the Vatican Archives, Benedict left the palace at three in the morning and reached the Inn of Saint-Antoine, where several knights belonging to Louis of Orléans's household and the constable of Aragon were waiting for him.[50] The group embarked, sailing down the Rhône and up the Durance toward Châteaurenard, in Provençal territory.

Although Benedict's departure left Avignon without its pope, the city still remained a papal seat. Benedict appointed his nephew, Rodrigo de Luna, as rector of Avignon and the Venaissin, but never again did a pope rule the Latin Church from the city's magnificent palace. On March 29, 1403, Avignon offered the pope the keys of the city in a sign of submission. Celebrations marked the end of the crisis, including feasts and a procession led by children. But Avignon's return to papal obedience, soon followed by France and Castile, still did not solve the Schism.

The result of the subtraction was total failure. Both popes continued to control their individual camps, but no more than that. Boniface IX in Italy had also refused to abdicate and still ruled as rival to Benedict XIII. Indeed, the subtraction had created in France an administrative mess when royal collectors replaced papal officers, leaving ecclesiastical benefices mere pawns in secular hands. The French clergy who had so vehemently supported the subtraction soon realized that the king's authority was no better than the pope's. By 1403, two of the three proposed solutions, the ways of force and cession, had utterly failed, and the University of Paris worked feverishly to formulate new options.

In 1381, Pierre d'Ailly, a young *docteur* of the University of Paris, had proposed to the Duke of Anjou the calling of a general council. But because only a legitimate pope could summon a council, the proposal was not considered feasible. Ironically, the very act of summoning a church council presupposed the legitimacy as pope of the one who convened it; in an era when two popes simultaneously asserted their legitimacy, the calling of a council to determine legitimacy was itself problematic. In addition, in order to mediate this conflict effectively, both parties needed to participate in the council, and neither side was willing to defer and allow a common meeting. However, there were signs of hope; after all, after years of failure, the initial options pursued at the beginning of the Schism—physical aggression, double resignation, and cession—were finally dropped by 1403. The return to Christian unity was an imperative, and kings and courts spent the five years that followed the restoration of obedience negotiating the feasibility of a council at which both popes met and mediated their differences.

Ironically, the difficulties the Schism created for both popes did not alter their resolve. In Rome, Boniface constantly faced threats from his enemies, mostly led by the Colonna family. Boniface exerted little control over the Italian Papal States, which gained politically by constantly repositioning themselves vis-à-vis both popes. On the Clementist side, the subtraction and restitution had only managed to buttress Benedict's resolve to remain in power. His main enemy, Philip the Bold, Duke of Burgundy, died in April 1404. The duke's rivalry with his nephew, Louis of Orléans, had fueled most of the events of the subtraction. The death of his enemy, however, did not bring much relief to Benedict.

After the 1403 restitution of French obedience, Benedict proclaimed his willingness to meet his papal competitor face to face. He promised to step down if the Roman pope did also or if he died; and he promised to attend a council if he could be convinced that it truly aimed to reunite the Church. Many thinkers of that time, like Jean Gerson, assumed that Benedict's strategy to cast his actions as a goodwill effort to reestablish the Church's unity was a delaying tactic devised to maintain the status quo. For Gerson, a council was the sole viable solution to the Schism. At Marseille in November 1403, Gerson met Benedict. As the French ambassador delegated to negotiate with the pontiff, he preached a sermon insisting that a good shepherd sacrifices his life for his lambs.[51] The half-hidden allusion hit its mark and shamed Benedict into action, as he then agreed to negotiate directly with Boniface. He deployed ambassadors to Rome, who reached the city at the end of September 1404. The chronicler of Saint-Denis recounts the contentious meeting that took place between the envoys of Benedict and Boniface, followed by the Roman pope's death a mere three days later on October 1, 1404. Alarmed by the coincidental timing of Boniface's death, the Roman population imprisoned Benedict's envoys until the end of the conclave that elected his successor, Innocent VII.[52]

As at earlier times, the death of a pope initiated a flow of declarations from all sides intended to delay the opening the conclave; they were largely ignored. The Roman cardinals elected Boniface's successor and swore that they and the new pope would work toward unity. Their choice of Cosimo de' Migliorati, who took the name of Innocent VII, was based on his reputed honesty. The new pope continued negotiating with the now-freed Avignonese envoys, who remained in the city to continue their task. Discussions eventually stalled, and in February 1405 the ambassadors returned home when Benedict excommunicated his new rival. Benedict chose this moment to march toward Rome, intent on forcing unity. It seemed no secret to anyone that, supported by Louis of Orléans, the pope was reverting to the "way of force." He traveled from Marseille to Nice and entered Genoa in May 1405. He remained in the city for a year, waiting for support from the king of France that never materialized.

This incursion on Italian soil naturally alarmed Pope Innocent, even more so because it emboldened his archenemy, the Colonna clan. In Rome, the Colonna continued instigating the city's population to revolt. Innocent charged his nephew Ludovico Migliorati, a *condottiere* whom he had named cardinal, to defend his position. But Migliorati's heavy-handed response fueled the uprising even further, forcing the pope and his court to escape to Viterbo and to dismiss his nephew (whom he later made a marquis and count). But again, behind all Roman political intrigues of the early fifteenth century stood a familiar antagonist: Ladislaus Durazzo, son of Charles of Durazzo, the sometime king of Naples, archenemy of Louis II of Anjou, and supporter of the Colonnas. Papal policies were again enmeshed with the disputed Kingdom of Naples and the claims of its rulers to papal territories. Like his father Charles, Ladislaus had inherited the contested Angevin Kingdom of Naples and defended it against the son of Louis I of Anjou. The Roman papacy backed Durazzo, but their relations were tense, as illustrated by Durazzo's actions against Innocent. The pope realized that Durazzo's ambition did not stop at the defense of his southern kingdom of Naples; he knew that Durazzo also plotted to conquer Rome and other Papal States. Innocent's response was to keep troops of mercenaries readily available in Rome.

Innocent's rival, Pope Benedict, was also wary of his own situation. Even though he had left his capital city of Avignon, he made sure to repair his palace-fortress from the damage it had sustained during the subtraction, and he kept a garrison of Catalan mercenaries stationed there. In December 1403 he ordered the razing of several houses that faced the palace, partially opening the square that still exists today, the Place du Palais. He then initiated work on the ramparts that protected the palace, the cathedral, the episcopal palace, and the Rock. He filled the palace's towers with provisions and weapons, obviously preparing for a possible attack. His actions were not lost on the French court. The chronicler of Saint-Denis reports, not without exaggeration, that "Our Lordship Benedict kept busy restoring his palace of Avignon, and he fortified its ramparts by razing to the ground the Church of Notre-Dame, tomb of his predecessors, and several other solid edifices."[53] But it was clear that while Paris paid attention, Benedict, unabashed in his resolve, was far from ready to give up the papal throne.

Financial support for rival candidates from interested parties prolonged the Schism, making it last as long as it did. Resourceful measures, more or less successful, met the financial crises of the two campaigns for Naples in 1382–1384 and 1389–1399 and the French subtraction. The Avignon popes increased their taxation of the French clergy, who returned the favor by subjecting the pope to similar financial pressure when they withdrew their payments during the subtraction of obedience. Resolved to maintain his power, Benedict ordered the French clergy to pay back its arrears after the 1403 restitution of obedience, and in this fashion he managed to fund his travels by dividing his court. The camerlengo and treasurers remained with the pope, while the fiscal administration stayed in Avignon to collect the necessary funds. These administrators then supplied the pope with letters of exchange to be paid in Perpignan, Genoa, or Savona. This sophisticated system allowed the pope and his court to survive via the cashing of "checks," the letters of exchange. The system had the advantage of minimizing risks by eliminating the physical movement of funds.

Financial matters also precipitated the second break with France and what is called the second subtraction. Benedict required the French clergy to pay all ecclesiastical arrears that had lagged since 1398. The French clergy and the University of Paris, spurred on by the Dukes of Burgundy and Berry, opposed the idea and decided to meet in council. Discussions started in November 1406, continued through 1407, and evolved into a division between an old-school partisan of an absolutist papacy that could not envision limits to its power (represented by Pierre d'Ailly) and the reformers who pleaded for limiting papal powers (represented by Simon de Cramaud, Jean Petit, and Pierre Leroy). On January 3, 1407, France declared its independence from the papacy. Gallicanism thus emerged from the Schism; it was born at this specific historical moment when local French authorities decided on certain temporal matters independently from the papacy. The assembly of 1407 took the bold step of declaring the Church ill governed and in need of major reform.

TOWARD A SOLUTION

By early 1407, the crisis had partially abated for both parties. Innocent had died in November 1406, and his successor Gregory XII was open to negotiations. Most of the cardinals in both colleges were too young to have participated in the original break of 1378, and both colleges were also willing to open serious discussions. They convinced both popes to meet in Savona, near Genoa, at the end of October 1407. Benedict arrived early in September, but Gregory, limited financially, advanced only with great difficulty. In the end, both popes remained some thirty miles away from each other, one in Portovenere and one in Lucca, never to meet face to face. Events external to this meeting sealed its fate. In November 1407, men of John the Fearless, Duke of Burgundy, assassinated the Duke of Orléans, John's nephew and Benedict's strongest supporter. The Duke of Burgundy now equally controlled Parisian and papal politics. Benedict, realizing that he had lost his most influential advocate, excommunicated King Charles VI and put France under interdict. This news precipitated the second French subtraction of obedience declared on May 25, 1408. The French crown reestablished the French church's liberty to act independently from the pope and declared its neutrality.

After losing French support, in August 1408 Benedict found refuge in Aragon, settling in Perpignan, on what is modern France's southwestern coast. It was from there that he decided to call his own council, attended mainly by Castilians and Aragonese, now his sole base of support. In Italy, Gregory's response was to call his own council in June 1409, an event joined by even fewer participants.

By the summer of 1409, both colleges had reached the limit of their patience with their respective popes, and groups of dissidents from both sides met in Livorno, deciding to call a Church council in Pisa. Their call rallied most of the European kingdoms, which approved of "rebellion" when facing "tyranny." Both colleges agreed on advancing the theory of the Church's universality to solve the council's deadlock. Even without the presence of a pope, a council summoned by an entity outside the papacy was legitimate because in some instances an assembly representing the universal Church was legitimate and surpassed the pope's authority.

In April 1409, some five hundred representatives attended the Council of Pisa, proof of the cardinals' power of persuasion. The council opened with the trial of both popes, both accused of heresy and witchcraft, evident from the fact that they had not tried to find a solution to the division. On June 5, Simon de Cramaud read the unanimous sentence. The council, in the name of the universal Church, pronounced both popes notoriously schismatic and deposed them from office. De Cramaud declared the papal see vacant. The council allowed the cardinals present to choose a new pope, an interesting situation since they had all been appointed by popes now declared schismatic; their decision could be considered illegitimate. On June 26 they elected Peter Philarges, Pope Alexander V. The council ended in August after announcing the news of "union" to most of Europe while Alexander settled his court in Bologna. But Pope Alexander, a Franciscan monk, managed to quickly arouse widespread clerical discontent when he allowed the mendicant orders to preach and confess wherever they wished, setting them in direct competition with secular clergymen. This radical novelty was strongly criticized, especially by the University of Paris, which labeled it "intolerable."

The crisis was far from over. Benedict and Gregory rejected the decisions of the Council of Pisa, and Alexander died within a year of his nomination. The cardinals of the new Pisan obedience then elected a third pope, Baldassare Cossa, John XXIII. All three popes continued to receive various levels of support as internal and external politics fueled disunity, now between three papal courts. Each court offered financial advantages to its followers that led to a chaotic race for ecclesiastical benefices. Pisa's union was unraveling at a fast pace. The solution rested in the call of another council.

Avignon followed this news closely. A chronicler of the time had remained silent on the second subtraction.[54] But the situation changed in 1409 after the Council of Pisa condemned both popes and elected a third one: the chronicler then writes that "the said pope [Alexander V] was crowned on 7 July. It is to note that there is a Schism, that is to say we have three popes. Benedict XIII done in Avignon, Boniface done in Rome, and the said Alexander, who is Greek." He was not aware (or at least pretended not to be) that Benedict had been deposed. He follows with a description of Notre-Dame des Doms's evacuation of its monks and deacons by the garrison of Catalans.[55] In January 1409, Benedict took the bold step of excommunicating all the cardinals, patriarchs, and the University of Paris as "schismatic" heretics. The bull was posted on all the churches of Avignon. A propaganda war thus raged again. In March, the

French lobby ordered the execution of a prisoner and left him hanging on the Rocher des Doms to impress the population. In early April, a king's representative paraded on the Bridge Saint-Bénézet to remind Avignon that the city needed to heed his orders and those of France.[56] In spite of these threats, the "War of Catalans" officially erupted on April 29, 1410, when the captain of the palace, the pope's nephew Rodrigo de Luna, captured twelve eminent citizens and held them as prisoners. Some one thousand French-paid knights and troops arrived to free them, besieging the palace while supported by a massive *bombarde* (an early cannon) that required thirty-six horses to draw it. The palace was well defended by Benedict's Catalan troops; it suffered damage but did not fall.[57] The war dragged on, causing more harm when both sides aimed their trebuchets and *bombardes* at each other. The artifice of a crusade, called by John XXIII to boost morale and hasten a dénouement to the conflict, did little to lessen the captain's resolve. Rodrigo de Luna's heroic defense of the besieged palace lasted close to eighteen months; he finally surrendered in November 1411. Casualties were high on both sides. The anonymous chronicler lists the death of most captives and the public displays of several executed prisoners; he lists some four thousand losses for a single assault in February 1411.[58]

John XXIII ordered repairs for some of the damage at the end of 1412, when he anticipated moving into the papal fortress. Lacking funds, John followed the well-established custom that required the Avignonese to finance the pope's expenses in their city. In the name of the Church he took over incomes produced by the unclaimed succession of Avignonese citizens, taxed Jewish moneylenders, and pocketed bequests made to "pious institutions." This significant repair and construction campaign certainly brought some work back to the city, as well as a few pilgrims. Holy Roman Emperor Sigismund, on hearing praises of the refurbished palace's majesty, spent some twenty-three days between December 1415 and January 1416 visiting the area. He was so impressed that he bought two paintings of the palace.

Pisa and the second subtraction demonstrated a dire need for ecclesiastical reform, and John XXIII, eventually expelled from Rome, turned to the Holy Roman emperor for a solution. As a new Constantine, Sigismund, King of the Romans and, as such, defender of the Church since 1411, called a meeting by general edict in Constance for November 1, 1414. Ecclesiastical delegates (abbots, bishops, cardinals) and representatives of all states arrived at a slow pace, beginning with the French in March 1415. For voting purposes, organizers divided the attendance into linguistic communities, or nations, based on the model found in European universities, with French, German, English, and Italian nations and the cardinals. Nations voted in a block with a single vote each. It is important to note that Benedict XIII's Spanish nation was absent early on as Spain's national organization remained fragmentary and insular, working against the desired universality of the council.

The council's first order of business was clearly to reconcile the Church. Moved by the spirit of reform, delegates launched violent diatribes attacking the avaricious, luxurious, and simoniac practices of the curia, pressuring John XXIII to abdicate. Worried for his safety, the pope escaped to Schaffhausen with the help of the Duke of Austria, still protected by Emperor Sigismund. After a month-long negotiation, John XXIII resigned without conditions, and the council deposed him. The pope who had taken the first vital step toward union was the first one the council dealt with; two other popes were left. On April 5, 1415, the decree *Haec sancta* paved the way toward a radical solution by legitimizing all decisions taken by the council. The council claimed its power directly from Christ and ordered all men, regardless of office, to abide by its decisions as a matter of faith, for the extirpation of the Schism. This radical declaration nullified the powers of the Catholic Church's hierarchy and of the pope, replacing hierarchical authority with the congregation of the faithful. The many replaced the one.

Events accelerated quickly after the council made this groundbreaking decision. Gregory XII abdicated, and in July 1415, as a reward for his gesture, the council ratified all the decisions he had made. Matters were not so simple with Benedict XIII, however, who rejected any type of compromise. The pope argued that as the sole survivor of all the cardinals nominated before the Schism, he held the right to choose a new pope. He was the unique legitimate elector. Stubborn in this belief until the end, Benedict's Spanish supporters abandoned him for his inflexibility, and he eventually left Perpignan for his fortress of Peñiscola, which he nicknamed his Noah's ark.

Benedict's retreat allowed the Spanish nation to join the council at the point when his trial opened. Benedict's obstinacy earned him the epithets "disturber of the peace and Church's union, schismatic, heretic"; and as such the council deposed him on July 27, 1417. With this action, all contenders for papal supremacy had been eliminated. The slate was wiped clean to elect a new pope once the assembly agreed on the modalities. The council articulated voting procedures that all members agreed on, leaving the election to fifty-three electors (six representatives for each nation) and twenty-three cardinals, with a majority of two-thirds required for each nation and the college of cardinals. After a three-day-long conclave, on November 11, 1417, the nations and cardinals picked Oddone Colonna as the sole pontiff ruling the Church. He took the name of Martin V. With Martin's ascension, the Schism was officially over. In Avignon, the anonymous chronicler who remains the main source for the period relates how the news of the election reached the city on November 20 among general celebrations. Avignon, relieved to be left with no more than one pope, hosted festivities that lasted a week.

EFFECTS AND RESULTS

It is clear that this lengthy division within the Church lasted as long as it did because it benefited the private interests of many parties. Both sides perpetuated the Schism, even if through different means. The simple fact that the financial records of the Avignon papacy survived the Schism and the Roman records did not has led many historians to suggest Roman incompetence. Unable to support the accounting procedures so dear to its predecessors, the Roman administration simply faltered. On the contrary, the Avignon popes benefited from a real advantage when Gregory XI's camerlengo chose to serve Clement VII, thereby bringing to him the support of most of the Chamber's staff. The treasurer's decision to follow Clement with most of the papal treasury consolidated Avignon's finances and organization. Avignon kept the Chamber's personnel along with its experience.

Avignon's central location relative to those subject to its obedience—in and around the city and more generally in France—made the collection of taxes steady and regular. Ecclesiastical and seignorial revenues (a few thousand florins per year) levied from the Comtat Venaissin and Avignon were not as widespread as Urban's and easily reached Clement's treasury. They were also far less important than the one million or so florins Urban received from the Roman Papal States. But Urban's obedience was large and dispersed throughout Europe, making it more difficult to control. Ireland, Scandinavia, and Hungary were far away from

Rome, while the closer kingdoms of Germany and Italy could be at time uncooperative. If not because of distance, politics made the collection of taxes laborious for the Roman popes. Papal rectors and vicars collected ecclesiastical and seignorial revenues and spent funds according to papal needs. The Roman popes were at the mercy of their administrators, who could sometimes be members of rival political entities. In addition, Urban's newly formed Chamber and Treasury lacked experience, and this complicated the administration of his court. But regardless of their differences, by the late 1380s both administrations collected roughly the same amount of revenues from direct taxation—some 250,000 florins yearly, enabling the Schism to last because each side could literally afford it.

As Avignon's residents suffered the prolonged effects of local warfare, the depredations of the marauding companies, and Raymond de Turenne's troops, as their economy inevitably faltered and they bore the brunt of so many exactions committed in the name of Church unity, it is difficult to assess how the people really perceived the events of the Schism, but we may hazard a guess, perhaps. The lack of widespread literacy prevents historians from properly gauging how people felt, at least based on what may have been preserved in written sources, and whether they cared about these lofty political and religious issues or not. Jean Favier, in the introduction to his book *Genèse et débuts du Grand Schisme d'Occident*, maintains that continuity in the parochial infrastructure of both papal parties made the Schism an elite, academic debate that did not concern average people. The common folk were not overly worried since their priests still maintained the familiar sacramental and liturgical continuities that lay at the heart of their religious lives.[59] Most people followed their political and religious leaders, and as long as priests delivered the sacraments in their local communities, they did not worry. Thus for Favier, the Schism was not a spiritual crisis for Europe's population. Following Favier, in his own recent discussion of this question, Philip Daileader calls the response to the Schism "muted." The crisis created changes and complicated lives, but people learned to adjust: "As long as masses were said, confessions heard, baptisms administered, and burials conducted as they had always been—as long as the means of salvation remained unchallenged—then the Schism's local consequences could only be minimal."[60]

On the other hand, in her study of the diocese of Cambrai during the Great Western Schism, Monique Maillard-Luypaert has argued to the contrary, suggesting that since the crisis touched important matters of faith, it was a daily preoccupation for all levels of society.[61] But her information comes from the written sources of a literate class that may have been more engaged in the crisis and understood its implications than common laborers and peasants. Renate Blumenfeld-Kosinski, in *Poets, Saints, and Visionaries of the Great Schism*, similarly tries to assess the level of anxiety produced by the crisis in a group study comprising saints, visionaries, poets, and prophets. She suggests that their literary and iconographic responses, laden with apocalyptic themes, indicate deep malaise.[62] As with the study of Maillard-Luypaert, her data is not truly representative of the attitudes of the common folk.

Sources available for late medieval Avignon offer a modicum of information that may afford us a glance into popular reactions to the crisis. They range from legal documents like final wills to chronicles and canonization dossiers. Because of the papal court's presence and the early deployment of Roman law in the French south, Avignon boasted a high number of lawyers and notaries who spread their legal culture to all levels of society. Most all classes recorded deeds, marriage contracts, donations, and wills. The last wills, or testaments, of hundreds of people offer an indirect way by which to gauge the impact of the crisis on the population. Testators dictated their final wishes to notaries, who first hand-drafted "minutes" in their notebooks and later recast them as a formal document, usually a thick piece of parchment that they eventually delivered to the testator for safekeeping. Wills are formulaic, but they are sometimes a historian's sole entry into the minds of people dead centuries ago. They offer snapshots into emotional lives, familial connections, and relations with institutions.

All medieval wills started with the same formula: *"In nomine domini. Amen"* ("In the name of the Lord. Amen"), followed by the date and a preamble on the certainty of death and the necessity to draft a will. Testators then revoked past wills and dedicated their souls to God, the Virgin, and the celestial Court. The choice of the place of burial followed, with the list of pious bequests, usually monetary gifts to religious institutions in exchange for masses and prayers. Then came bequests and legacies to a wide array of named individuals, relatives, kin, friends, acquaintances, neighbors, and servants, and to specific religious institutions that testators wished to endow (such as churches, convents, confraternities, and

hospitals). Gifts most often came in the form of money, products, uten-
sils, and often, clothing.

In his study of Avignonese testaments, Jacques Chiffoleau draws few
conclusions about the impact of the Schism on individuals' inner lives.
First of all, he finds in the extant wills no echoes of the eschatological
crisis that marked the literary treatises of the time. He notes an increase in
alms and donations from 1380 to 1420, indicating that the population was
looking for intercessory prayers. But he also observes that testators were
keenly aware of the financial burden the Schism imposed on churches
and monasteries and chose to lighten it by compensating some of those
losses with their private donations. The personal engagement of testators
compensates them for the lack of institutional support. In a similar vein,
it is worth noticing that Avignon's mass of unemployed poor clerics,
losers in the quest for benefices between the two competing papacies,
created a "liturgical proletariat," as it were, readily available to support
the heavenly aspirations of commoners by praying on their behalf. Testators asked and paid for these clerics' attendance in funeral corteges, processions, and masses. In short, testamentary bequests prove that the
circumstances of the Schism actually empowered the lower classes to
copy the liturgical practices of their wealthy contemporaries. Commoners
expected, much like their wealthy neighbors, rather flamboyant and
spectacular funerals that featured supernumerary torch-bearing clergy,
who would (for a fee) be engaged to offer countless masses ensuring their
benefit in the afterlife. In this manner, to a certain extent the Schism
democratized access to a complex array of socially important liturgical
practices.

Finally, Jacques Chiffoleau suggests that the high incidence of requests for burials within mendicant cemeteries (Franciscans, Dominicans,
Augustinian, and Carmelites) could suggest a certain mistrust of traditional parochial institutions. Still, he recognizes that this trend could simply be a response to a local situation. During the Schism, money shortages led to the quick degradation of many parochial churches, forcing
testators to choose burial elsewhere, most of all in convents. [63]

Because of its sweeping chronological scope, Chiffoleau's study
underscores large movements and not subtler shifts in popular mentalities. My own analysis of some eighty testaments of middle-class Avignonese women offers a different approach. These sources permit the
possibility of weighing data from a discrete sample, divided chronologi-

cally between a pre- and post-Schism sample (see table 6.3). They are divided almost equally between thirty-three testaments for the forty years that preceded 1378 and thirty-two for the following years until 1446. Using these sources to test hypothetical attitudes toward the Church as these are revealed in bequests, I chose to consider only instances of legacies to institutions, not those to individuals. Contrary to Chiffoleau's conclusions, these women did not differentiate between burials in parochial or conventual churches, and they donated equally to their parochial churches and to their favorite convents and monasteries. In sum, this discrete sample suggests that at the local level, the Schism did not alter how women viewed, related to, and supported their local institutions.

Table 6.3.   Testamentary Donations by Instances

	Before 1378	After 1378
Church burial	17	20
Convent burial	16	12
Total	**33**	**32**
Buried with father	2	7
Buried with mother	1	2
Buried with husband	9	6
Buried with children	3	5
Buried with other	1	2
To Franciscans	9	9
To Dominicans	15	7
To Augustinians	11	6
To Carmelites	6	7
To Benedictines	3	0
To parish	25	26
To nuns	11	6
To confraternities	20	8
To bridge	8	5
To hospitals for poor	20	4
Marriage poor girls	5	1
Inscription in obituary/necrology	0	6

Indeed, a close reading of the data actually shows a very slight decrease in bequests to conventual and monastic institutions, confraternities, and hospitals after the Schism. This decline may simply represent the lower wealth of testatrices rather than an overall shift in mentality. The bequests aimed at repairing the St. Bénézet Bridge remained stable over time, as did the alms for the marriages of poor girls.

Only one notable testamentary change stands out in the wake of the Schism. It is the injunction by testatrices to see their names written down in conventual and parochial necrologies or obituaries. These liturgical "books of the dead," created in the early Middle Ages for memorializing the death of monks, quickly grew into lists of benefactors that recorded names and dates of a benefactor's passing. By the end of the Middle Ages, most parochial, confraternal, and monastic institutions kept necrologies where they recorded the names of their members and the dates of their deaths. These books of remembrance prompted the liturgical staff to pray and celebrate the anniversary days of the dead. This Avignonese practice of citing the names of the dead suggests a desire to remember the deceased as still living by annually invoking their names; although they are dead, yet still they live in remembrance—an important and consoling act during the unstable and dangerous years of the Schism. The act of writing a name down secured a place in Heaven by reminding intercessors to do their job in prayer. This also represents another instance of liturgical democratization. Obituaries and necrologies started with monks and nuns, spread to the aristocracy and patrician families, and finally reached all social classes by the end of the Middle Ages.

Extraordinary circumstances led to exceptional events, and their occurrence provides a window into the mentality of the era. The few "spontaneous" pilgrimages encountered during the Schism also reflect how contemporaries internalized the crisis. Nicolas di Bonaccorso, a merchant-banker located in Avignon, corresponded frequently with his Florentine employer Francesco di Marco Datini. Starting in September 1393, Nicolas began to write about groups of youths taking off from France and Avignon for the Mont Saint-Michel. A letter dated September 16, 1393, mentions that starting in July of that year, some young boys from France led by the banners of Saint Michael, the fleur-de-lys, and Brittany abruptly left their families with no provisions (the letter notes that they had no bread or wine). Several groups made their way to Mont Saint-Michel, prayed, and returned home. The movement spread to Avignon, and Nicolas states that in the past three days from the date of his letter, at least two hundred children of diverse ages left with their banners. He states:

If only you could see them run! Happy is the one who can escape and follow them! They say that big miracles have occurred; that fathers and mothers who did not let their children go saw them dying on the spot. They say that they will find enough provision to eat and drink on their way, and that people give them enough alms. In Brittany and on the lands of the duke of Berry, lords have decreed that they should be fed. By God, these are great lords! We heard that thousands of children have gone there from several countries.[64]

Records of the Apostolic Chamber support the merchant's account. On September 18, the almoner of the pope sailed to Mont Saint-Michel "by way of the dangerous sea" to bring aid to the poor children and pilgrims of Avignon and its surroundings, who had just reached their destination.[65] This spontaneous movement lasted into October, when Nicolas remarked that by October 4, some one thousand Avignonese had left the city. Their departure stunned its residents. Nicolas insists again on how young the children were, most between the ages of eight and fifteen, and that they broke natural bonds by escaping their mothers and fathers. This pilgrimage was for him truly miraculous, especially when innocent children disobeyed their parents for the love of God. In his eyes, the pilgrims were truly carried by supernatural fervor. Their youth and, as such, purity added an intercessory quality to their task. Nicolas adds, "This is for our sins since it started with the little children."[66] For him, the Schism was the affair of corrupted, selfish adults whose sinful intransigence could be washed away only by the purity of children. The merchant thus reflects a familiar topos in medieval reasoning: the sacrifices of children to remit the sins of their elders.

This pilgrimage to Mont Saint-Michel had all the elements of an expiatory voyage. The distance covered to reach Brittany was significant enough to give real intercessory value to the trip; and Saint Michael's stewardship and leadership was traditionally believed to protect pilgrims from evil. He was the leader of God's army, the protector of believers who felt lost and powerless. This pilgrimage shows that the faithful understood their lack of control and remedied it by showing their unadulterated devotion. Indeed, such pilgrims may have been somewhat comforted by the continuity of ritual observance, but the Schism still affected them. Frustrated by the church hierarchy's indifference to their spiritual welfare, they seized control of the situation by either leaving or supporting and admiring those pilgrims who did travel to faraway Brittany. Many Christians were waiting for Saint Michael to end the crisis.

But the archangel was not the only saint asked to intervene. The cult of a new saint appears to have been directly linked to the Schism. As Robert Norman Swanson states, "When the church was split, the official stance on canonization could raise serious issues. During the Great Schism of 1378–1417, for instance, the separate lines of pontiffs created their own saints. Both successions sought support by offering the carrot of canonizations to their adherents."[67] Saints legitimated popes. Pope Urban counted on Catherine of Siena, while Clement advanced the support of Peter of Luxembourg and Vincent Ferrer. In general, each camp was not afraid to use verbal and visual propaganda that included sermons, processions, pamphlets, executions, and religious architecture as a way to argue its pope's legitimacy. The case of Peter of Luxembourg illustrates this development.

A cousin of the king of France, Peter of Luxembourg received the bishopric of Metz at age fifteen, in 1384; he died a cardinal three years later, on July 2, 1387, just shy of his eighteenth birthday. Peter quickly became a popular intercessor, his high rank and youth making his tomb the center of a cult that attracted hundreds of pilgrims. Mystics like Marie Robine also moved close to his remains. She set up residence in a small oratory in the cemetery of Saint-Michel.[68] The combined presence of Luxembourg's tomb and Robine's residence made Avignon an attractive destination for traveling pilgrims.

Realizing how popular he was with the people, the executors of Luxembourg's will denied his original wishes to be buried in the humble cemetery for poor immigrants. Luxembourg's canonization procedure (preserved in volume 27 of the *Acta Sanctorum*) records the cardinal's notoriety and his miracles. Interestingly enough, the procedure that led to his beatification started shortly after his death; proof alone of his immense popularity. Secretaries recorded a first set of testimonies between July and December 1387. The formal process of canonization that began three years later shows signs of extensive manipulation, emphasizing a politicization of his miracles that supported the Clementist obedience.[69] The earlier set of testimonies makes it obvious that Peter's remains caused a prodigious enthusiasm in the city. His following was local and urban, and maybe because of his age Peter was soon perceived as a protector of sick children and youth. Testimonies mentioning Peter of Luxembourg offer a window into the religious practices of late medieval Avignon. For example, during the vigil that preceded his burial, a mass of people came to kiss his hands and feet, so many, in fact, that the doors of the Church of Saint-Antoine could not be shut. Women brought jewelry and rosaries that they rubbed on his head, hands, and feet, presumably to save as personal relics.[70] Devotees assailed his coffin, ripping the shroud that covered it and cutting it to pieces, along with the pillows and cushions that supported his head. Then they broke through the bier and hacked it to pieces in order to distribute as many shards as possible.

After witnessing such violent enthusiasm, the authorities decided to fence off the site of his burial behind a wooden barricade. This did not stop numbers of devotees from bringing pounds of wax and images (ex-votos) to his tomb. Boninsegna di Matteo, a Florentine residing in Avignon whom we encountered earlier in the chapter, marveled at the devotion surrounding Peter of Luxembourg and used him as a catalyst to discuss what was wrong with the Church of his time. He may not have realized how much promoting the veneration of local saints legitimated popes and secured for themselves the grateful loyalty of large numbers of devotees.

Discussing the fervor surrounding the saint and his tomb, Boninsegna writes to his interlocutor,

> the learned, the ignorant, the idiot, and the poor go there as they would for a Great Pardon (a form of pilgrimage), and this, morning, afternoon and night. Think that every single night 300 people remain there in vigil. Many of the sick people who come for their novena end up cured. . . . People arrive from everywhere, lame, crippled, one-armed, and paralytic, and they are cured by the grace of God and of this saintly cardinal. . . . This seems to be a great lesson, about real faith in the Holy Church, and about those who want to live honestly in the world. When you see the miracles that a young man of 24 [*sic*] operates, all the faithful should thank God and behave well.[71]

Like Nicolas before him, Boninsegna sharply takes the church to task for its institutional defects. The faithful throng of pilgrims are for him the honest ones, the true believers, and as such, these pilgrims are rewarded by miracles. God recognizes his own. If the Schism is allowed to last, it is because God chooses not to heal the wound. It is the Church's just punishment for its sins.

Proof that there was a great need for healing and that the Schism affected Christian believers, the saint's fame quickly spread far and wide. He became a favorite intercessor for thousands of pilgrims from all over

France, who brought wax images to his tomb in thanks for fulfilling their wishes. According to canonization procedures, Peter resurrected children, saved the young and old from drowning in the Rhône and Durance Rivers, healed the sick, cured the lame, doused fires, and found and returned lost or stolen goods (even a mule). Pilgrims who visited his tomb usually kissed the fence that protected the site and took some of the soil from around the tomb to use in miraculous unguents.[72]

Still, people did not systematically link the saint with the legitimacy of the Avignon papacy, a trope that, as we will see below, ecclesiastics favored. Boninsegna's previous comments are the extent of his criticism when discussing the crisis. The merchant's correspondence does not dwell on the Schism and usually avoids discussing it directly. It was, to him and many people of his day, a jinx. In July 1394, Boninsegna states: "They say that sometimes, the ones who discuss the schism become mute by virtue of Saint John Golden Mouthed. If a bigger principle does not intervene in this business [the Schism] things will remain the same, because the world goes toward evil, everyone works against their own interest, simony rules, and they want more money without thinking of their souls."[73]

The statement seems a clear attack on the church hierarchy, which seemed unwilling to solve the crisis. St. John Chrysostom was the patriarch of Constantinople in the late fourth century. At the imperial capital, he earned for himself the surname "golden-mouthed" (*chrysostomos*) on account of his eloquence, but he also made himself an exile from the Byzantine court by his impolitic denunciation of all kinds of abuses, both civil and religious. How appropriate, then, that the golden-mouthed saint's reputation for eloquence and truth rendered mute those who discussed the Schism. Simply naming the schismatic popes carried negative associations. For example, the *Anonimo fiorentino* utilized the generic *antipapa* for Clement, never naming him directly, as if this simple act would legitimize his existence.[74]

The Schism's prolonged continuation diminished the credibility and international status of the papacy, promoting the emergence of national churches that centuries of deliberate papal policy had smothered but never totally eliminated. The old idea, fatal to papal pretensions of overlordship, that a king or emperor was in fact more fit than the pope to defend the Christian faith, once more resurfaced. The Schism also promoted conciliarism, a far more dangerous movement and one that Renaissance popes eliminated quickly. As for Avignon and its people, the end of the Schism in Constance and the election of a "Roman" pope must have stung, particularly when they saw their last hopes of retaining the papacy vanish. The Schismatic papacy had been an ambiguous blessing for the city, which had remained a truncated capital of Christianity, but a capital nonetheless.

NOTES

1. Étienne Baluze, *Vitae paparum avenionensium, hoc est, Historia pontificum romanorum qui in Gallia sederunt ab anno Christi MCCCV usque ad annum MCCCXCIV*, ed. Guillaume Mollat (Paris: Letouzey et Ané, 1914), vol. 1, 427, 440–441.

2. See Phillip H. Stump, *The Reforms of the Council of Constance, 1414–1418* (Leiden: Brill, 1994), for a thorough discussion of the council and common good.

3. *Decrees of the Ecumenical Councils*, ed. N. P. Tanner, S.J. (London: Shed and Ward, 1990), vol. 1, 438–442. The text is also available online at http://www.fordham.edu/halsall/source/constance2.asp or http://www.papalencyclicals.net/Councils/ecum16.htm (session 39).

4. *Decrees of the Ecumenical Councils*, ed. N. P. Tanner, S.J. (London: Shed and Ward, 1990), vol. 1, 314.

5. Noël Valois, *La France et le grand schisme d'occident* (Paris: A. Picard et fils, 1896–1902), vol. 1, 12.

6. *Annales ecclesiastici*, ed. Cesare Baronio, Odorico Rinaldi, Giacomo Laderchi, Augustin Theiner, Antoine Pagi, and Giovan Domenico Mansi (Barri-Ducis: L. Guerin, 1864–1883), vol. 26, 288–289.

7. Louis Gayet, *Le grand schisme d'occident d'après les documents contemporains déposés aux archives secrètes du Vatican* (Florence: Loescher et Seeber, 1889), *Pièces justificatives*, 100.

8. This violence is the subject of my *Raiding Saint Peter: Empty Sees, Violence, and the Initiation of the Great Western Schism (1378)* (Leiden and Boston: Brill, 2008).

9. Howard Kaminsky, "The Great Schism," in *The New Cambridge Medieval History*, ed. Michael Jones (Cambridge: Cambridge University Press, 2000), vol. 6, 676.

10. Kaminsky, "The Great Schism," 679.

11. Robert Norman Swanson, "Obedient and Disobedient in the Great Schism," *Archivum historiae pontificiae* 22 (1984): 377–378.

12. Anne-Marie Hayez, "Clément VII et Avignon," in *Genèse et début du grand schisme d'occident*, ed. Jean Favier (Paris: Éditions du CNRS, 1980), 126, 136.

13. See Henri Moranvillé, ed., *Journal de Jean Le Fèvre, évêque de Chartres, chancelier des rois de Sicile Louis I et Louis II d'Anjou* (Paris: Picard, 1887).

14. The events are also recounted in *Thalamus parvus: Le petit thalamus de Montpellier publié pour la première fois d'après les manuscrits originaux*, ed. Ferdinand Pégat and Eugène Thomas (Montpellier: J. Martel ainé, 1836–1840), 405.

15. According to the Florentine merchants, in periods of pressing financial needs, the Chamber increased minting and devalued money to inflate its revenues and be solvent; see Robert Brun, "Annales Avignonnaises de 1382 à 1410 extraites des

archives Datini," *Mémoires de l'institut historique de Provence* 12 (1935): 54, 72, 78, 85, 108.

16. Charles of Durazzo was one of the sons of Robert of Anjou's youngest brother, John of Gravina, Duke of Durazzo.

17. Brun, "Annales" 12 (1935): 36.

18. Capturing and ransoming merchants were also lucrative activities; see Brun, "Annales" 12 (1935): 81.

19. Brun, "Annales" 12 (1935): 78.

20. Brun, "Annales" 12 (1935): 39.

21. Brun, "Annales" 12 (1935): 92, 111.

22. Philip Daileader, "Local Experiences of the Great Western Schism," in *A Companion to the Great Western Schism (1378–1417)*, ed. Joëlle Rollo-Koster and Thomas Izbicki (Leiden and Boston: Brill, 2009), 89–121.

23. See Robert Brun, "A Fourteenth-Century Merchant of Italy: Francesco Datini of Prato," *Journal of Economic and Business History* 2 (1930): 451–466; Brun, "Annales" 12 (1935): 17–142; 13 (1936): 58–105; 14 (1937): 5–57; 15 (1938): 21–52, 154–192. The translation is mine in all instances. See also Iris Origo, *The Merchant of Prato: Francesco di Marco Datini* (New York: Knopf, 1957).

24. Brun, "Annales" 12 (1935): 119.

25. Brun, "Annales" 13 (1936): 96.

26. Brun, "Annales" 12 (1935): 135.

27. Brun, "Annales" 12 (1935): 94–95.

28. See two different cases in Brun, "Annales" 13 (1936): 7–9, 37–38.

29. Bernard Guillemain, *La cour pontificale d'Avignon: Étude d'une société* (Paris: De Boccard, 1962), 596–605, summarily analyzes this document. I edited and analyzed its content in detail in *The People of Curial Avignon: A Critical Edition of the Liber Divisionis and the Matriculae of Notre Dame la Majour* (Lampeter, GB, and Lewiston, NY: Edwin Mellen, 2009).

30. Richard C. Trexler, *The Spiritual Power: Republican Florence under Interdict* (Leiden: Brill, 1974), 46.

31. Brun, "Annales" 12 (1935): 88.

32. Brun, "Annales" 12 (1935): 87.

33. Brun, "Annales" 12 (1935): 89.

34. Letter dated July 1383; Brun, "Annales" 12 (1935): 42.

35. Brun, "Annales" 12 (1935): 55.

36. Brun, "Annales" 12 (1935): 56.

37. For example, in April 1385, see Brun, "Annales" 12 (1935): 81.

38. Brun, "Annales" 12 (1935): 56.

39. Brun, "Annales" 12 (1935): 114–117.

40. Hayez, "Clément VII et Avignon," 130.

41. Brun, "Annales" 12 (1935): 113.

42. Brun, "Annales" 12 (1935): 75.

43. Brun, "Annales" 12 (1935): 111.

44. *Alle bocche della piazza: Diario di Anonimo fiorentino: BNF, Panciatichiano 158*, ed. Anthony Molho (Florence: L. S. Olschki, 1986), il. My translation.

45. It should be noted that since 1392, Charles VI had suffered fits of madness that left him unable to rule. From then on, French politics became intertwined with the influence wielded by Charles's entourage, starting with his uncles, the Dukes of Berry

and Burgundy, his brother, the Duke of Orléans, his wife, Isabeau, and his many counselors.

46. Edmond Martène and Ursin Durand, *Veterum scriptorum et monumentorum historicorum, dogmaticorum, moralium, amplissima collectio* (1724), vol. 7, 479–525.

47. Brun, "Annales" 14 (1937): 17.

48. Martin de Alpartil, *Cronica actitatorum temporibus Benedicti XIII Pape*, ed. and trans. José Angel Sesma Muñoz and María del Mar Agudo Romeo (Zaragoza: Centro de Documentación Bibliográfica Aragonesa, 1994).

49. See Joëlle Rollo-Koster, "The Politics of Body Parts: Contested Topographies in Late Medieval Avignon," *Speculum: A Journal of Medieval Studies* 78 (January 2003): 66–98, where I detail the episode.

50. ASV, *Reg. Aven.*, 348, f. 671.

51. Guillaume Henri Marie Posthumus Meyjes, *Jean Gerson, Apostle of Unity: His Church Politics and Ecclesiology* (Leiden: Brill, 1999), 99–101.

52. Louis Bellaguet, *Chronique du religieux de Saint-Denys contenant le règne de Charles VI, de 1380 à 1422, publiée en latin pour la première fois et traduite* (Paris: L'imprimerie de Crapelet, 1839), vol. 3, 217–218.

53. Bellaguet, *Chronique du religieux de Saint-Denys*, vol. 3, 219.

54. François Charles Carreri, "Chronicon parvum Avinionense de Schimate et bello," *Annales d'Avignon et du Comtat Venaissin* (1916): 166. All translations are mine.

55. Carreri, "Chronicon parvum Avinionense," 166.

56. Carreri, "Chronicon parvum Avinionense," 167.

57. Carreri, "Chronicon parvum Avinionense," 167–174.

58. Carreri, "Chronicon parvum Avinionense," 169.

59. Jean Favier, "Le Grand Schisme dans l'histoire de France," in *Genèse et débuts du Grand Schisme d'Occident: Avignon, 25–28 septembre 1978* (Paris: Editions du Centre National de la Recherche Scientifique, 1980), 7–16.

60. Philip Daileader, "Local Experience of the Great Western Schism," in *A Companion to the Great Western Schism*, ed. Joëlle Rollo-Koster and Thomas Izbicki (Leiden: Brill, 2009), 121.

61. Monique Maillard-Luypaert, *Papauté, clercs, et laics: Le diocese de Cambrai à l'épreuve du Grand Schisme d'Occident (1378–1417)* (Brussels: Publications des Facultés universitaires Saint-Louis, 2001).

62. Renate Blumenfeld-Kosinski, *Poets, Saints, and Visionaries of the Great Schism, 1378–1417* (University Park: Pennsylvania State University Press, 2006).

63. Jacques Chiffoleau, *La comptabilité de l'au-delà: Les hommes, la mort et la religion dans la région d'Avignon à la fin du moyen-âge* (Rome: École française de Rome, 1980), 110, 237, 243, 251, 260.

64. Brun, "Annales" 13 (1936): 78–79.

65. ASV, *Intr. et exit.*, 370, fol. 152.

66. Brun, "Annales" 13 (1936): 80.

67. Robert Norman Swanson, *Religion and Devotion in Europe: C. 1215–1515* (Cambridge: Cambridge University Press, 1995), 149.

68. See Matthew Tobin, "Le 'livre des révélations' de Marie Robine (+1399): Étude et édition," *Mélanges de l'École française de Rome: Moyen-âge, temps modernes* 98 (1986): 229–264; and Blumenfeld-Kosinski, *Poets, Saints, and Visionaries of the Great Schism*, 29, 35, 81–85, 93.

69. See the study of Yveline Prouvost, "Les miracles de Pierre de Luxembourg (1387–1390)," in *Hagiographie et culte des saints en France méridionale (Xiiie–Xve siècle)* (Toulouse: Privat, 2002), 481–506.

70. *Acta Sanctorum*, vol. 27, 562.

71. Brun, "Annales" 12 (1935): 100.

72. See *Acta Sanctorum*, vol. 27, 486–628.

73. Brun, "Annales Avignonaises," 13 (1936): 93.

74. *Alle bocche della piazza*, 208.

Conclusion

This book has endeavored to tell the story of the popes and their people in Avignon. I have not lingered very long on passing visitors who, like Petrarch, are commonly associated with the city. Readers especially interested in him will find information in the Petrarchian literature below.[1] Petrarch is considered the father of humanism; and even if he railed against Avignon, his name and eloquence are part of the city's story, regardless. Poetry and rhetoric shone in Avignon, and Petrarch was not the sole humanist or protohumanist who found fame in the city. After him, authors like Giovanni Moccia and Jean Muret also left their mark on the rebirth of the study of the classics.[2] Even though mere sojourners there, these men found themselves woven into the historical fabric of Avignon.

I have also left to specialists of the field a detailed discussion of the many artists who, like Matteo Giovanetti or Simone Martini, embellished the Avignonese monuments built by the popes and their courts. Cathleen Fleck has recently surveyed art in the capital (despite her work's title) in the pre- and post-Schism periods.[3] A recent publication of the *Société des amis du Palais des papes et des monuments d'Avignon* highlights the cultural contribution of the Avignon popes. In the year 2000, Avignon was named the European capital of culture to acknowledge not only the city's present but also its past. The vibrant theater and opera festival that brings legions of visitors every summer is well known all over the world, as are Avignon's imposing medieval papal palace and bridge.

The Avignon popes were cultivated, educated, capable administrators and politicians who enriched their court and environment. They studied civil and canon law and theology, and a few of them taught these subjects. As in today's governments, heads of services and popes were doctors of law, showing again how modern was the papal administration in this era, staffed as it was with an educated elite. The popes kept up with education and ordered the copying of manuscripts and the building of an important library, in large part through their use of the right of spoils.[4] Some 2,045 volumes were collected between 1342 and 1352.[5] Books were essentially academic, organized around the liberal arts, medicine, law, and theology.[6] The popes are known to have specifically decentralized the study of theology (taught mainly in Paris), bringing faculty in theology to the universities they supported. This academic culture was buttressed by the need to form an administrative elite to serve the court; the foundation of universities assuaged this need.[7]

Between 1305 and 1378, several universities appeared throughout Europe, in Orléans, Angers, Valladolid, Prague, and Perugia, all with pontifical confirmation. The Avignon popes also founded colleges within existing universities. In 1359, Innocent VI created the College of Saint-Martial in Toulouse; in 1368–1369, Urban V founded in Montpellier the Colleges of St. Germain, St. Benedict, and the Twelve Doctors. Gregory XI chose Bologna in 1371 for his foundation of a college named after him.[8] Cardinals followed suit, founding colleges in Paris, Toulouse, Montpellier, Bologna, and Perugia. But, as Jacques Verger duly notes, the greatest success of the Avignon papacy in regard to universities was its unconditional support of students. The Avignon popes distributed thousands of benefices to support students, waiving for them the requirement of residence to allow them full dedication to their studies. Last, it is possible to speak of an intentional policy to promote education when popes founded provincial boarding schools in the south of France to recruit and train talented young students who would pursue their studies in universities.

Music also interested the papal court, though not all popes were enthusiastic about musical innovations. John XXII, who, as we have seen, micromanaged his court, legislated on musical developments in one of his *Extravagantes* decretals. He condemned motets as profane, menacing with spiritual punishment anyone who would use them in liturgy. But specialists of the fourteenth-century musical culture consider John's analysis revolutionary. In condemning some forms and allowing others, the pope advanced polyphony and defined the stylistic traits specific to religious music and separated them from profane music. He made plainchant the musical expression of liturgy, allowing several voices to improvise at once, leading thus to polyphony.[9] The papal chapel adopted the new polyphonic chant (the *ars nova* or new art) and hired northern cantors to embellish worship. Benedict XII was the first to organize a *capella intrinseca* ("chapel of the interior") that focused essentially on the celebration of the divine offices, music included. Clement VI transformed it into a college of singers, engaging qualified cantors from all over Europe.[10]

Taste for music spread from the papacy to southern towns. Gretchen Peters has recently documented the activities of minstrels in the south of France. Many were freelance musicians who made a living cobbling together part-time contracts with cities, confraternities, and individuals. In Avignon, the pope was one of their employers. He patronized a watchman who sounded his trumpet from the top of the Bell Tower of Notre-Dame des Doms, and he financially supported musicians who served his guests. Music went out from behind the walls of the papal palace to fill the streets of the city during various papal and communal celebrations.[11]

It has been the intent of this book to rehabilitate for the English-speaking reader the Avignon papacy from its "black legend." As the previous pages have shown, the Avignon popes were certainly no more venal nor less worthy to claim the papal office than their predecessors and successors. As southwestern Frenchmen, their mental apparatus and reflexes were not that different from their contemporaries; venality and nepotism were rampant among all members of the high society. The popes simply acted like men of their times. We find in the Avignon popes a common, relentless insistence on crusading, reforming the Church, centralizing the Church's administration and finance, and more generally, on asserting their authority over their court and lands. The well-established practice of excommunicating insolvent creditors and the financial harassment of the Church tax collectors did not ingratiate the papal court to the secular rulers and ecclesiastics who participated in the construction of the Avignon papacy's enduring negative legend.[12] Most of these popes were lawyers, and their legal thinking may have at times clouded their spirituality; but men like Urban V and Gregory XI show that they could prioritize spirituality before convenience. There is little doubt that all of Avignon's popes understood their city to be a temporary residence. We have seen that their attachment to the city was limited. To a large extent, Avignon provided the popes with a base, with funds and bodies. When they created something at Avignon, as with the construction of the palace, for example, the popes attempted to remake Rome rather than work from something new.

One way to prove their successful centralization is to return to the resentment they created with the members of the court who saw their chances at governing the papacy diminish with each new pope. As curial life grew and centralized, so did the pretensions of the cardinals, who claimed a more central role in the governance of the Church. Their hopes

were high with the election of Innocent VI, who, even as he paid them
dutiful lip service, quickly deflated the cardinals' pretensions. The Great
Western Schism marked the culmination of their demands. It sealed, at
least for a few years, the cardinals' hopes to govern with the pope as an
elite spiritual oligarchy. They had attained the ultimate responsibility: the
making and unmaking of popes. Conciliar rule lasted but a few years,
and the first assertion of the Renaissance papacy was to repeal Constance's regulations.

The little city of Avignon gained recognition during the papal sojourn.
The large burg grew into a capital, supporting within its ramparts an
ever-renewing population. Its walls encompassed wide social and ethnic
variety. We can note that the Provençal shores of the Rhône did not
witness social movements and rebellions to the extent that they arose
throughout the rest of Europe during the fourteenth century. Avignon
witnessed panic during the plague and the assaults of the free companies,
but nothing like the French Peasants' Revolt of 1358, for example. Socially
the capital allowed for individual promotion, and although conditions
were far from idyllic, social improvements were definitely permitted, if
only in the scores of occupations and professions that the papacy and its
court supported. The popes also left their physical mark on the city's
streets and neighborhoods as Avignon shared their successes and failures. The wide ramparts that protected the population are the best example of the popes' care for their new residence; the scars left by both
subtractions of obedience showed the price to pay. To travelers visiting
the area today, the Avignon popes' presence can still be felt acutely in the
many monuments they have left us and in the vineyards they planted,
like the renowned Châteauneuf-du-Pape. As for us *Provençaux*, they also
left us legends like the good mule of the pope. [13] After being dragged up
the bell tower of the palace by a mischievous Tistet Védène, the mule of
the pope waited seven years for his return from Queen Joanna's court to
exact her revenge. She kicked him to death the day of his induction into
the ranks of spicers of the pope. Alphonse Daudet's tale of vengeance is
framed by the popular vision of Avignon at the time of the popes: a city
of sycophants searching favors from a good pope who loved his wine
and his mule.

NOTES

1. Victoria Kirkham and Armando Maggi, *Petrarch: A Critical Guide to the Complete Works* (Chicago: University of Chicago Press, 2009); and, among many other valuable works, Harold Bloom, *Petrarch* (New York: Chelsea House, 1989); David Thompson, *Petrarch: A Humanist among Princes: An Anthology of Petrarch's Letters and of Selections from His Other Works* (New York: Harper & Row, 1971).

2. Ezio Ornato, "L'humanisme à la cour pontificale Avignonnaise," *Annuaire de la Société des amis du Palais des papes et des monuments d'Avignon* 77 (2000): 51–67.

3. Cathleen Fleck, "Seeking Legitimacy: Art and Manuscripts for the Popes in Avignon from 1378 to 1417," in *A Companion to the Great Western Schism (1378–1417)*, ed. Joëlle Rollo-Koster and Thomas Izbicki (Leiden: Brill, 2009), 239–302.

4. See Daniel Williman, Marie-Henriette Jullien de Pommerol, and Jacques Monfrin, *Bibliothèques ecclésiastiques au temps de la papauté d'Avignon* (Paris: Editions du CNRS, 1980); Daniel Williman, *The Right of Spoil of the Popes of Avignon, 1316–1415* (Philadelphia: American Philosophical Society, 1988).

5. Bernard Guillemain, "La formation, la culture et les gouts des papes d'Avignon," *Annuaire de la Société des amis du Palais des papes et des monuments d'Avignon* 77 (2000): 14.

6. Jacques Verger, "La politique universitaire des papes d'Avignon," *Annuaire de la Société des amis du Palais des papes et des monuments d'Avignon* 77 (2000): 18.

7. Hilde de Ridder-Symoens, ed., *Universities in the Middle Ages* (Cambridge: Cambridge University Press, 1992) offers the most recent treatment on medieval universities.

8. Verger, "La politique universitaire des papes d'Avignon," 23.

9. Gunther Morche, "L'ars nova et la musique liturgique au temps des papes d'Avignon," *Annuaire de la Société des amis du Palais des papes et des monuments d'Avignon* 77 (2000): 132.

10. Morche, "L'ars nova et la musique liturgique au temps des papes d'Avignon," 137.

11. See Gretchen Peters, "Urban Musical Culture in Late Medieval Southern France: Evidence from Private Notarial," *Early Music* 25 (1997): 403–410; "Urban Minstrels in Late Medieval Southern France: Opportunities, Status and Professional Relationships," *Early Music History* 19 (2000): 201–235; *The Musical Sounds of Medieval French Cities: Players, Patrons, and Politics* (Cambridge: Cambridge University Press, 2012).

12. As illustrated, for example, in Daniel Williman, *Calendar of the Letters of Arnaud Aubert, Camerarius Apostolicus 1361–1371* (Toronto: Pontifical Institute of Mediaeval Studies, 1992).

13. Alphonse Daudet, *Letters from My Windmill*, ed. Mireille Harmelin and Keith Adams (Auckland: Floating Press, 2013).

Additional Bibliography

1: EARLY POPES

In addition to Guillaume Mollat, *The Popes at Avignon: The "Babylonian Captivity" of the Medieval Church*, trans. Janet Love (New York: Harper & Row, 1965); Bernard Guillemain, *La cour pontificale d'Avignon: Étude d'une société* (Paris, 1962); Yves Renouard, *The Avignon Papacy: The Popes in Exile 1305–1403*, trans. Denis Bethell (New York: Barnes and Noble, 1970); and Jean Favier, *Les papes d'Avignon* (Paris: Fayard, 2006), used extensively throughout the book, this chapter has relied on the following studies. On Boniface VIII, see T. S. R. Boase, *Boniface VIII* (London: Constable, 1933); Charles T. Wood, *Philip the Fair and Boniface VIII: State vs. Papacy* (New York: Holt, Rinehart and Winston, 1967); and, more recently, Agostino Paravicini Bagliani, *Boniface VIII: Un pape hérétique?* (Paris: Payot & Rivages, 2003). For his trial, see Jean Coste, *Boniface VIII en procès: Articles d'accusation et dépositions des témoins, 1303–1311* (Rome: L'Erma di Bretschneider, 1995). Regarding the first jubilee, see Herbert L. Kessler and Johanna Zacharias, *Rome 1300: On the Path of the Pilgrim* (New Haven, CT: Yale University Press, 2000). On Clement V's early career, see J. H. Denton, "Pope Clement V's Early Career as a Royal Clerk," *English Historical Review* 83.327 (1968): 303–314. The Templars have become victims of their historical success. Publications abound, but many are fantasies far removed from reality. I am listing here some of the best and most recent historians who have worked on the topic: Helen Nicholson, *The Knights Templar: A New History* (Thrupp, Stroud: Sutton, 2001); Malcolm Barber, *The Trial of the Templars* (Cambridge: Cambridge University Press, 1978, reprint 2006); Malcolm Barber, *The New Knighthood: A History of the Order of the Temple* (Cambridge: Cambridge University Press, 1994); Malcolm Barber, *The Crusader States* (New Haven, CT: Yale University Press, 2012); Malcolm Barber and A. K. Bate, *The Templars: Selected Sources* (Manchester: Manchester University Press, 2002); Norman Housley and Malcolm Barber, *Knighthoods of Christ: Essays on the History of the Crusades and the Knights Templar Presented to Malcolm Barber* (Aldershot: Ashgate, 2007);

Alan Forey, *Military Orders and Crusades* (Aldershot: Variorum, 1994); Alan Forey, *The Military Orders from the Twelfth to the Early Fourteenth Centuries* (Toronto: University of Toronto Press, 1992); Alain Demurger, *The Last Templar: The Tragedy of Jacques de Molay, Last Grand Master of the Temple* (London: Profile, 2004); Jochen Burgtorf, Paul Crawford, and Helen Nicholson, eds., *The Debate on the Trial of the Templars: 1307–1314* (Franham: Ashgate, 2010). On Vienne and other medieval Church councils, see Norman P. Tanner, ed., *Decrees of the Ecumenical Councils* (Washington, DC: Georgetown University Press, 1990), vol. 1. For a thorough discussion of the Papal States, see Peter Partner, *The Lands of St. Peter: The Papal State in the Middle Ages and Early Renaissance* (Berkeley: University of California Press, 1972). Regarding Napoleone Orsini, see the only biography available, by Carl A. Willemsen, *Kardinal Napoleon Orsini, 1263–1342* (Berlin: E. Ebering, 1928); Guillemain, *La cour pontificale*, 241–244; and Emily E. Graham, "Reconsidering Reputation through Patronage: Cardinal Napoleone Orsini and Angelo Clareno at the Avignonese Papal Court," *Journal of Medieval History* 39:3 (2013): 357–375. On Robert of Anjou, King of Naples, see Samantha Kelly, *The New Solomon: Robert of Naples (1309–1343) and Fourteenth-Century Kingship* (Leiden: Brill, 2003); and Ronald G. Musto, ed., *Medieval Naples, a Documentary History: Historical Texts, 400–1400* (New York: Italica, 2012), 192–223. On the conclave that followed Clement V's death, see my *Raiding Saint Peter: Empty Sees, Violence, and the Initiation of the Great Western Schism (1378)* (Leiden: Brill, 2008), 138–145. The ceremony that marked the coronation of John XXII is detailed in Marc Dykmans, *Le cérémonial papal de la fin du moyen âge à la renaissance: De Rome en Avignon ou le cérémonial de Jacques Stefaneschi* (Brussels: Institut historique belge de Rome, 1981). A biography of John XXII is found in Louis Duval-Arnould, "John XXII," in *The Papacy: An Encyclopedia*, ed. Philippe Levillain and John W. O'Malley (New York: Routledge, 2001), 847–851. John's poisoning is discussed in Franck Collard, "*Horrendum Scelus*: Recherches sur le statut juridique du crime d'empoisonnement au Moyen Age" *Revue historique* 300.4 (1998): 737–764; and Edmond Albe, *Autour de Jean XXII: Hugues Géraud, évêque de Cahors: L'affaire des poisons et des envoûtements en 1317* (Cahors: Girma, 1904). Valérie Theis, "Jean XXII et l'expulsion des juifs du Comtat Venaissin," *Annales, histoire, sciences sociales* 67 (2012): 41–77 discusses John's expulsion of Jews. See Robert André-Michel, *Avignon, les fresques du Palais des Papes, le procès des Visconti* (Paris: Colin, 1926), 146–206 for the accusations against the Visconti. For a transcript of the commission John set up against witchcraft, see Alain Boureau, *Le Pape et les sorciers: Une consultation de Jean XXII sur la magie en 1320 (manuscrit B.A.V. Borghese 348)* (Rome: École française de Rome, 2004). For a discussion of all the ramifications of this commission, see Isabel Iribarren, "From Black Magic to Heresy: A Doctrinal Leap in the Pontificate of John XXII," *Church History*, 76.1 (2007): 32–60. For a gendered analysis of the phenomenon, see Nancy Caciola, *Discerning Spirits: Divine and Demonic Possession in the Middle Ages* (Ithaca, NY: Cornell University Press, 2003); and Dyan Elliott, *Proving Woman: Female Spirituality and Inquisitional Culture in the Later Middle Ages* (Princeton, NJ: Princeton University Press, 2004). The Franciscan poverty discussion is the background of Umberto Eco's popular *Name of the Rose* (*Il nome della rosa*, 1980). For a full discussion of the topic, see Decima L. Douie, *The Nature and the Effect of the Heresy of the Fraticelli* (New York: AMS, 1978); Malcolm Lambert, "The Franciscan Crisis under John XXII," *Franciscan Studies* 32 (1972): 123–43; Malcolm Lambert, *Franciscan Poverty: The Doctrine of the Absolute Poverty of Christ and the Apostles in the Franciscan Order 1210–1323* (St. Bonaventure, NY: Franciscan Institute, 1998); John Oakley, "John XXII and Franciscan Innocence," *Franciscan Studies* 46 (1986): 217–226; Thomas Turley, "John XXII and the Franciscans: A Reappraisal," in *Popes, Teachers, and Canon Law in the Middle Ages*, ed. James Ross Sweeney and Stanley Chodorow (Ithaca, NY: Cornell University Press, 1989), 74–88; David Burr, *The Spiritual Franciscans: From Protest to Persecution in the Century after Saint Francis* (University Park: Pennsylvania State University Press, 2001); Takashi Shōgimen, *Ockham and Political Discourse in the Late Middle Ages* (Cambridge: Cambridge University Press, 2007); John V. Fleming, Michael F. Cusato, and Guy Geltner, *Defenders and Critics of Franciscan Life: Essays in Honor of John V. Fleming* (Leiden: Brill, 2009); and Michael J. P. Robson, *The Cambridge Companion to Francis of Assisi* (Cambridge: Cambridge University Press, 2012). For an in-depth discussion of property, see Virpi Mäkinen, *Property Rights in the Late Medieval Discussion on Franciscan Poverty* (Leuven, Belgium: Peeters, 2001). Bernard Délicieux was a tremendously charismatic preacher; he has recently received the attention of historians and journalists; see Alan Friedlander, *The Hammer of the Inquisitors: Brother Bernard Délicieux and the Struggle against the Inquisition in Fourteenth-Century France* (Leiden: Brill, 2000); Stephen O'Shea, *The Friar of Carcassonne: Revolt against the Inquisition in the Last Days of the Cathars* (Toronto: Douglas

& McIntyre, 2011). For testamentary bequests to Franciscans, see Anne-Marie Hayez, "Clauses pieuses de testaments Avignonnais du XIVe siècle," in *Actes du 99ième congrés national des sociétés savants* (Paris: Bibliothèque nationale, 1977), 129–159. Thomas Frank, "Exploring the Boundaries of Law in the Middle Ages: Franciscan Debates on Poverty, Property, and Inheritance," *Law and Literature* 20. 2 (2008): 243–260, highlights and discusses the legal quandary between donations and poverty. On Franciscan theology, see, for example, Kenan B. Osborne, *The History of Franciscan Theology* (St. Bonaventure, NY: Franciscan Institute, St. Bonaventure University, 1994); Marsilius de Padua and Annabel S. Brett, *The Defender of the Peace* (Cambridge: Cambridge University Press, 2005); Gerson Moreno-Riaño, ed., *The World of Marsilius of Padua* (Turnhout: Brepols, 2006); George Garnett, *Marsilius of Padua and 'the Truth of History'* (Oxford: Oxford University Press, 2006); Hwa-Yong Lee, *Political Representation in the Later Middle Ages: Marsilius in Context* (New York: P. Lang, 2008); Joseph Canning, *Ideas of Power in the Late Middle Ages, 1296–1417* (Cambridge: Cambridge University Press, 2011); Arthur Stephen McGrade, *The Political Thought of William of Ockham: Personal and Institutional Principles* (London: Cambridge University Press, 1974); Paul Vincent Spade, *The Cambridge Companion to Ockham* (Cambridge: Cambridge University Press, 1999); Eva Luise Wittneben, *Bonagratia von Bergamo: Franziskanerjurist und Wortführer seines Ordens im Streit mit Papst Johannes XXII* (Leiden: Brill, 2003). See Blake R. Beattie, *Angelus Pacis: The Legation of Cardinal Giovanni Gaetano Orsini, 1326–1334* (Boston: Brill, 2007) on the imperial-papal rivalry. Additional information on the northern Italian situation can be found in H. S. Offler, "Empire and Papacy: The Last Struggle," *Transactions of the Royal Historical Society*, Fifth Series, 6 (1956): 21–47; Sharon Dale, "The Avignon Papacy and the Creation of the Visconti Myth," in *La vie culturelle, intellectuelle et scientifique à la cour des papes d'Avignon*, ed. Jacqueline Hamesse (Turnhout: Brepols, 2005), 333–366; "Contra Damnationis Filios: The Visconti in Fourteenth-Century Papal Diplomacy," *Journal of Medieval History* 33 (2007): 1–32; and "Fourteenth Century Lombard Chroniclers," in *Chroniclers and Historians in Medieval and Renaissance Italy*, ed. Sharon Dale, Alison Williams Lewin, and Duane J. Osheim (University Park: Pennsylvania State University Press, 2007), 171–195. On William of Ockham's *Defensor pacis*, see William of Ockham, *On the Powers of Emperors and Popes*, trans. and ed. Annabel S. Brett (Bristol: Thoemmes, 1998). See Blake Beattie, "The Antipope Who Wasn't

There: Three Formal Submissions to Pope John XXII," in *La vie culturelle, intellectuelle et scientifique à la cour des papes d'Avignon*, ed. Jacqueline Hamesse (Turnhout: Brepols, 2006), 197–236, on Louis's antipope. For the beatific vision controversy, see Decima Langworthy Douie, "John XXII and the Beatific Vision," *Dominican Studies* 3 (1950): 154–174; Marc Dykmans, *Les sermons de Jean XXII sur la vision béatifique: Texte précédé d'une introduction et suivi d'une chronologie de la controverse avec la liste des écrits pour et contre le pape* (Rome: Presse de l'Université Grégorienne, 1973); Christian Trottmann, *La vision béatifique des disputes scolastiques à sa définition par Bénoît XII* (Rome: École française de Rome, 1995); and Isabel Iribarren, "Theological Authority at the Papal Court in Avignon: The Beatific Vision Controversy," in *La vie culturelle, intellectuelle et scientifique à la cour des papes d'Avignon*, ed. Jacqueline Hamesse (Turnhout: Brepols, 2006), 277–301. Jacques Fournier's Latin registers have been edited and translated into French; see Jacques Fournier, *Le registre d'inquisition de Jacques Fournier, evêque de Pamiers (1318–1325)*, ed. Jean Duvernoy (Toulouse: Privat, 1965), 3 vols.; and Jacques Fournier, *Le registre d'inquisition de Jacques Fournier (Evêque de Pamiers) 1318–1325*, trans. and ed. Jean Duvernoy (Paris: Mouton, 1978), 3 vols. See also René Weis, *The Yellow Cross* (New York: Penguin, 2001). On Benedict XII's reforming zeal, see Peter McDonald, "The Papacy and Monastic Observance in the Later Middle Ages: The Benedictines in England," *Journal of Religious History* 14.2 (1986): 117–132.

2: PAPAL MONARCHY

Avignon coronations are discussed in detail by Bernhard Schimmelpfennig, "Eleven Papal Coronations in Avignon," in *Coronations: Medieval and Early Modern Monarchic Ritual*, ed. János M. Bak (Berkeley: University of California Press, 1990), 179–193. On the relationship between Petrarch and Cola di Rienzo, see Francesco Petrarca, Mario Emilio Cosenza, and Ronald G. Musto, *The Revolution of Cola Di Rienzo* (New York: Italica, 1996). A contemporary chronicler composed the *Vita di Cola di Rienzo* around 1358, later translated by John Wright as *The Life of Cola di Rienzo* (Toronto: Pontifical Institute of Mediaeval Studies, 1975). Regarding Cola, see Amanda Collins, *Greater Than Emperor: Cola Di Rienzo (Ca. 1313–54) and the World of Fourteenth-Century Rome* (Ann Arbor: University of Michigan Press, 2002); Ronald G. Musto, *Apocalypse in Rome: Cola Di*

Rienzo and the Politics of the New Age (Berkeley: University of California Press, 2003); Andreas Rehberg and Anna Modigliani, *Cola di Rienzo e il commune di Roma* (Rome: RR Inedita, 2004), 2 vols.; on his death, see Joëlle Rollo-Koster and Alizah Holstein, "Anger and Spectacle in Late Medieval Rome: Gauging Emotion in Urban Topography?" in *Cities, Texts and Social Networks, 400–1500: Experiences and Perceptions of Medieval Urban Space*, ed. Anne Lester, Caroline Goodson, and Carol Symes (Farnham, UK: Ashgate, 2010), 149–174. Nancy Goldstone, *Joanna: The Notorious Queen of Naples, Jerusalem and Sicily* (London: Weidenfeld & Nicolson, 2010), offers a compelling read of the queen's dramatic life. Elizabeth Casteen, "Sex and Politics in Naples: The Regnant Queenship of Johanna I," *Journal of the Historical Society* 11.2 (2011): 183–210, frames her analysis of Joanna's rule within the medieval construction of queenship, insisting on contemporary propaganda that either supported or reviled the queen. On the Hundred Years' War, see C. T. Allmand, *The Hundred Years War: England and France at War, c. 1300–c. 1450* (Cambridge: Cambridge University Press, 1988); Jonathan Sumption, *The Hundred Years War: Trial by Battle* (Philadelphia: University of Pennsylvania Press, 1991); Anne Curry, *The Hundred Years' War, 1337–1453* (New York: St. Martin's, 1993); L. J. Andrew Villalon and Donald J. Kagay, *The Hundred Years War: A Wider Focus* (Leiden: Brill, 2005); and L. J. Andrew Villalon and Donald J. Kagay, *The Hundred Years War (Part II): Different Vistas* (Leiden: Brill, 2008). On the Battle of Crécy, see Andrew Ayton, Philip Preston, Françoise Autrand, Michael Prestwich, and Bertrand Schnerb, *The Battle of Crécy, 1346* (Woodbridge: Boydell, 2005). On the Statutes of Provisors, see Cecily Davies, "The Statute of Provisors of 1351," *History* 38.133 (1953): 116–133; and Fredric Cheyette, "Kings, Courts, Cures, and Sinecures: The Statute of Provisors and the Common Law," *Traditio* 19 (1963): 295–349. Étienne Anheim has recently reconstituted Clement VI's library; see his "La bibliothèque personnelle de Pierre Roger/Clement VI," in *La vie culturelle, intellectuelle et scientifique à la cour des papes d'Avignon*, ed. Jacqueline Hamesse (Turhnout: Brepols, 2006), 1–48. On Clement VI's tomb, see Anne McGee Morganstern, "Art and Ceremony in Papal Avignon: A Prescription for the Tomb of Clement VI," *Gesta* 40.1 (2001): 61–77. On Talleyrand of Périgord, see Norman P. Zacour, "The Cardinal of Périgord (1301–1364)," *Transactions of the American Philosophical Society* 50.7 (1960): 1–83. Pierre Jugie, "Innocent VI," in *The Papacy: An Encyclopedia*, ed. Philippe Levillain (New York: Routledge, 2002), vol. 2, 794–797, offers general information on Pope Innocent VI. Regarding Albornoz's Italian campaigns, see Peter Partner, *The Lands of Saint Peter*, 262, 339–360, 378, and 446. The most complete survey of Albornoz is found in the recent edition of Juan Ginés de Sepúlveda, Jenaro Costas Rodríguez, and Maria Teresa Ferrer i Mallol, *Historia de los hechos del Cardenal Gil de Albornoz* (Pozoblanco, Spain: Ayuntamiento de Pozoblanco, 2002); and Paolo Colliva, *Il cardinale Alborno. Lo Stato della Chiesa, le "Constitutiones Aegidianae" (1353–1357)* (Bolonia: Real Colegio de España, 1977). To establish a lasting presence in Bologna, in his will of 1364 Albornoz created a college "for the benefit of poor scholars . . . of Spanish origin," to enable them "the more freely and readily to be intent upon the acquisition of knowledge." The college was named "Real Colegio Mayor Albornociano de San Clemente de los Españioles en Bolonia"; see Berthe M. Marti, ed., *The Spanish College at Bologna in the Fourteenth Century* (Philadelphia: University of Pennsylvania Press, 1966). On Pedro the Cruel of Castile, see Clara Estow, *Pedro the Cruel of Castile, 1350–1369* (Leiden: Brill, 1995). On the use of mercenaries by the papacy, see William L. Urban, *Medieval Mercenaries: The Business of War* (London: Greenhill Books, 2006); Philippe Contamine, *War in the Middle Ages* (New York: Basil Blackwell, 1984); Maurice Hugh Keen, *Medieval Warfare: A History* (Oxford: Oxford University Press, 1999); William Caferro, *John Hawkwood: An English Mercenary in Fourteenth-Century Italy* (Baltimore: Johns Hopkins University Press, 2006); and Norman Housley, "The Mercenary Companies, the Papacy, and the Crusades, 1356–1378," *Traditio* 38 (1982): 253–280. Regarding the Battle of Poitiers and the Black Prince, see Richard Barber, *Edward, Prince of Wales and Aquitaine: A Biography of the Black Prince* (London: Allen Lane, 1978); and Richard Barber, ed., *The Life and Campaigns of the Black Prince: From Contemporary Letters, Diaries and Chronicles, Including Chandos Herald's Life of the Black Prince* (Woodbridge: Boydell, 1986); Jonathan Sumption, *The Hundred Years War: Trial by Fire* (Philadelphia: University of Pennsylvania Press, 1999); David Green, *Edward, the Black Prince: Power in Medieval Europe* (Harlow: Longman, 2007); and Peter Hoskins, *In the Steps of the Black Prince: The Road to Poitiers, 1355–1356* (Woodbridge: Boydell, 2011). Françoise Autrand, *Charles V: Le sage* (Paris: Fayard, 1994) offers a biography of the French king Charles V. On Jean de Roquetaillade, see Leah DeVun, *Prophecy, Alchemy, and the End of Time: John of Rupescissa in the Late Middle Ages* (New York: Columbia University Press, 2009). On the archbishop of Armagh, Richard FitzRalph, and his vituperations against the mendicants, see Katherine Walsh, "Archbishop Fitz-Ralph and the Friars at the Papal Court in Avignon, 1357–60," *Traditio* 31 (1975): 223–245.

3: RETURNING TO ROME

Regarding Urban, see Anne-Marie Hayez, "Urban V," in *The Papacy: An Encyclopedia*, ed. Philippe Levillain (New York: Routledge, 2002), 1556–1557; Yves Chiron, *Urbain V: Le bienheureux* (Versailles: Via Romana 2010); Paul Amargier, *Urbain V: Un homme, une vie (1310–1370)* (Marseille: Société des médiévistes provençaux, 1987); and Anne-Marie Hayez, "L'entourage d'Urbain V: Parents, amis et familiers," *Annuaire de la société des amis du Palais des papes* (1988–1989): 31–45. For Urban's love of gardens, see Élydia Barret, "Les 'vergers' de la papauté d'Avignon: Avignon, Pont-de-Sorgues et Villeneuve (1316–1378)" (PhD diss., École des chartes, 2004). Regarding Urban's *camerarius*, Arnaud Aubert, and the return of the papacy to Rome, see Daniel Williman, *Calendar of the Letters of Arnaud Aubert, Camerarius Apostolicus 1361–1371* (Toronto: Pontifical Institute of Mediaeval Studies, 1992). For general politics, see Maurice Prou, *Études sur les relations politiques du pape Urbain V avec les rois de France Jean II et Charles V (1362–1370)* (Paris: F. Vieweg, 1888). The dates and details of the returns to Rome of Urban V and Gregory XI are found in Mollat, *The Popes at Avignon*, 111–128; Favier, *Les papes d'Avignon*, 530–538; and Michel Hayez, "Avignon sans les Papes (1367–1370, 1376–1379)," in *Genèse et début du Grand Schisme d'Occident*, ed. Jean Favier (Paris: De Boccard, 1980), 143–157. See also Johann Peter Kirsch, *Die Ruckkehr der Päpste Urban V. und Gregor XI. von Avignon nach Rom: Auszuge aus den Kameralregistern des vatikanischen Archivs* (Paderborn: F. Schoningh, 1898). On Urban's reforms, see Ludwig Vones, "La réforme de l'église au XIV siècle: Tentatives pontificales dans l'esprit bénédictin et courants spirituels dans l'entourage d'Urbain V," in *Crises et réformes dans l'Église, de la réforme grégorienne à la pré-réforme, 115e congrès national des sociétés historiques et scientifiques Avignon, 1990* (Paris: Comité des travaux historiques et scientifiques, 1991), 189–206. Regarding the Sabran and their spiritual marriage, see Dyan Elliott, *Spiritual Marriage: Sexual Abstinence in Medieval Wedlock* (Princeton, NJ: Princeton University Press, 1993); and P. H. Cullum and Katherine J. Lewis, *Religious Men and Masculine Identity in the Middle Ages* (Woodbridge: Boydell & Brewer, 2013). The *terrier* of Anglic

Grimoard, describing Avignon episcopal parcels and rents, has been edited by Anne-Marie Hayez, *Le terrier Avignonnais de l'évêque Anglic Grimoard: 1366–1368* (Paris: CTHS, 1993). On Peter of Lusignan's crusades, see Peter W. Edbury, *The Kingdom of Cyprus and the Crusades, 1191–1374* (Cambridge: Cambridge University Press, 1991). Regarding the Avignon papacy and crusades, see Norman Housley, *The Avignon Papacy and the Crusades, 1305–1378* (Oxford: Clarendon, 1986). On the Hundred Years' War, see Jonathan Sumption, *The Hundred Years War: Volume II, Trial by Fire* (Philadelphia: University of Pennsylvania Press, 1999). On the Viterbo rebellion, see Joëlle Rollo-Koster, *Raiding Saint Peter: Empty Sees, Violence, and the Initiation of the Great Western Schism (1378)* (Leiden and Boston: Brill, 2008), 148–157. Regarding the cult of Urban V, see Claudia Bolgia, "Cassiano's Popes Rediscovered: Urban V in Rome," *Zeitschrift für Kunstgeschichte* 65.4 (2002): 562–574; John Osborne, "Lost Roman Images of Pope Urban V (1362–1370) for Julian Gardner," *Zeitschrift für Kunstgeschichte* 54.1 (1991): 20–32; Gérard Veyssiere, "Le rayonnement géographique du culte d' Urbain V," *Mémoires de l'académie de Vaucluse*, 7th series, 6 (1985): 137–152; Joseph-Hyacinthe Albanès and Ulysse Chevalier, *Actes anciens et documents concernant le bienheureux Urbain V Pape: Sa famille, sa personne, son pontificat, ses miracles et son culte* (Paris: Picard, 1897); and Gérard Veyssière, "Miracles du bienheureux pape Urbain V," in *Avignon au Moyen Âge: Textes et documents*, ed. IREBMA (Avignon, 1988), 161–166. Regarding Gregory XI, see additionally Guillaume Mollat, "Grégoire XI et sa légende," *Revue d' histoire ecclésiastique* 44 (1954): 873–877. On the pope's return to Rome, see Michel Hayez, "Avignon sans les papes (1367–1370, 1376–1379)," in *Genèse et début du grand schisme d'occident*, ed. Jean Favier (Paris: Éditions du Centre national de la recherche scientifique, 1980), 143–57; and Richard C. Trexler, "Rome on the Eve of the Great Schism," *Speculum* 42 (1967): 489–509. On the pope's relation with the East, see James Muldoon, "The Avignon Papacy and the Frontiers of Christendom: The Evidence of Vatican Register 62," *Archivum historiae pontificiae* 17 (1979): 125–195; and *Popes, Lawyers, and Infidels: The Church and the Non-Christian World, 1250–1550* (Philadelphia: University of Pennsylvania Press, 1979). On the Treaty of Bruges, see Maurice Keen, *England in the Later Middle Ages: A Political History* (London: Routledge, 2003). On relations with Savoy, see Eugene L. Cox, *The Green Count of Savoy, Amadeus VI and Transalpine Savoy in the Fourteenth Century* (Princeton, NJ: Princeton University Press, 1967); and the more recent

Bruno Galland, *Les papes d'Avignon et la Maison de Savoie, 1309–1409* (Rome: École française de Rome, 1998). Regarding the war with Florence, see Samuel Kline Cohn, *Lust for Liberty: The Politics of Social Revolt in Medieval Europe, 1200–1425: Italy, France, and Flanders* (Cambridge, MA: Harvard University Press, 2006); *Popular Protest in Late-Medieval Europe: Italy, France and Flanders* (Manchester: Manchester University Press, 2004); and John M. Najemy, *A History of Florence 1200–1575* (Malden, MA: Blackwell, 2006). On Baldo degli Ubaldi, see "Civil Violence and the Initiation of the Schism," in *A Companion to the Great Western Schism (1378–1417),* ed. Joëlle Rollo-Koster and Thomas Izbicki (Leiden: Brill, 2009), 9–66. On Pierre of Cros, the pope's camerlengo, see Daniel Williman, *The Letters of Pierre De Cros, Chamberlain to Pope Gregory XI, 1371–1378* (Tempe: Arizona Center for Medieval and Renaissance Studies, 2009).

4: CONSTRUCTING THE ADMINISTRATION

The École française de Rome, *Le Fonctionnement administratif de la papauté d'Avignon: Aux origines de l'état moderne* (Rome: École française de Rome, 1990) and Armand Jamme and Olivier Poncet, *Offices et papauté, XIVe–XVIIe siècle: Charges, hommes, destins* (Rome: École française de Rome, 2005) are the most recent surveys of the papal administration. Bernard Guillemain, *La cour pontificale d'Avignon: Étude d'une société* (Paris: De Boccard, 1966) remains an invaluable source on the topic. On the papal mint, see Marc Bompaire, "La monnaie de Pont-de-Sorgues dans la première moitié du XIVe siècle," *Revue numismatique* 25 (1983): 139–176. The system of communication of the popes has been well studied. See Anne-Marie Hayez, "Les couriers des papes d'Avignon sous Innocent VI et Urbain V (1352–1370)," in *La Circulation des nouvelles au Moyen Âge: XXIVe Congrès de la S.H.M.E.S. Avignon, juin 1993* (Rome: École française de Rome, 1994), 49–62; and Yves Renouard, "Comment les papes d'Avignon expédiaient leur courier," *Revue historique* 180 (1937): 1–29. Regarding the political transitions, see Ralph A. Giesey, *The Royal Funeral Ceremony in Renaissance France* (Geneva: Droz, 1960); Alain Boureau, *The Myth of Pope Joan,* trans. L. G. Cochrane (Chicago: University of Chicago Press, 2001); Sergio Bertelli, *The King's Body: Sacred Rituals of Power in Medieval and Early Modern Europe,* trans. R. Burr Litchfield (University Park: Pennsylvania State University Press, 2001); and my *Raiding Saint Peter: Empty*

Sees, Violence, and the Initiation of the Great Western Schism (1378) (Leiden and Boston: Brill, 2008). Guy de Chauliac was without a doubt the most famous surgeon of his time. His *Chirurgia* remained the standard of surgery until the seventeenth century. See Guigonis De Caulhiaco (Guy de Chauliac), *Inventarium Sive Chirurgia Magna*, ed. Michael R. McVaugh and Margrete S. Ogden (Leiden: Brill, 1997), 2 vols. On confessors, see Xavier de La Selle, *Le service des âmes à la cour: Confesseurs et aumôniers des rois de France du XIIIe au XVe siècle* (Geneva: Droz, 1995); and regarding music at the papal court, see Andrew Tomasello, *Music and Ritual at Papal Avignon, 1309–1403* (Ann Arbor, MI: UMI Research Press, 1983). The Pignotte, the papal almshouse, has recently been studied by Daniel Le Blevec in his monumental *La Part du pauvre: L'assistance dans les pays du Bas-Rhône du xiie siècle au milieu du xve siècle* (Rome: École française de Rome, 2000), 2 vols. Marc Dykmans has edited and published most medieval ceremonial books, also called *ordines*; see *Le cérémonial papal de la fin du Moyen Âge à la Renaissance* (Brussels: Institut historique belge de Rome, 1977), 4 vols.; *L'oeuvre de Patrizi Piccolomini, ou le cérémonial papal de la première Renaissance* (Città del Vaticano: Biblioteca Apostolica Vaticana, 1980), 2 vols.; and *Le pontifical romain révisé au XVe siècle* (Città del Vaticano: Biblioteca Apostolica Vaticana, 1985). Regarding double burials and the Avignon cardinals' endowments to the city, see Julian Gardner, *The Tomb and the Tiara: Curial Tomb Sculpture in Rome and Avignon in the Later Middle Ages* (Oxford: Oxford University Press, 1992), especially 133–171; and Cathleen A. Fleck, "Seeking Legitimacy: Art and Manuscripts for the Popes in Avignon from 1378–1417," in *A Companion to the Great Western Schism*, ed. Joëlle Rollo-Koster and Thomas Izbicki (Leiden: Brill, 2009), 239–302. For a case study of cardinals, see Blake R. Beattie, *Angelus Pacis: The Legation of Cardinal Giovanni Gaetano Orsini, 1326–1334* (Leiden: Brill, 2007); Margaret Harvey, "The Household of Cardinal Langham," *Journal of Ecclesiastical History* 47.1 (1996): 18–44; and Norman P. Zacour, *Talleyrand, the Cardinal of Périgord, 1301–1364* (Philadelphia: American Philosophical Society, 1960). See Pierre Jugie, "Les *familiae* cardinalices et leur organisation interne au temps de la papauté d'Avignon: Esquisse d'un bilan," in *Aux origines de l'état moderne: Le fonctionnement administratif de la papauté d'Avignon* (Rome: École française de Rome, 1990), 41–59, for the most recent survey of cardinals' households. Norman P. Zacour, "Papal Regulation of Cardinals' Households in the Fourteenth Century," *Speculum* 50.3 (1975): 434–455 studies papal attempts at reining in their expenses.

On the diplomacy of Avignon's popes, see Karsten Plöger, *England and the Avignon Popes: The Practice of Diplomacy in Late Medieval Europe* (London: Legenda, 2005). On universities in western Europe and Avignon in particular, see Walter Rüegg and Hilde De Ridder-Symoens, *A History of the University in Europe: Universities in the Middle Ages* (Cambridge: Cambridge University Press, 1992).

5: AVIGNON: THE CAPITAL AND ITS POPULATION

See Iris Origo, *The Merchant of Prato: Francesco di Marco Datini* (New York: Knopf, 1957) for Datini's biography. Regarding Avignon's seven parishes, see Anne-Marie Hayez, "La paroisse Saint-Agricol au temps des papes à Avignon," *Annuaire de la société des amis du Palais des papes et des monuments d'Avignon* 71–72 (1994–1995): 67–97; "La paroisse Saint-Geniès d'Avignon à l'époque pontificale," *Annuaire de la société des amis du Palais des papes et des monuments d'Avignon* 73 (1996): 83–98; "La paroisse Saint-Symphorien au temps des papes d'Avignon," *Annuaire de la société des amis du Palais des papes et des monuments d'Avignon* 74 (1997): 25–50; "La paroisse Saint-Étienne au temps des papes d' Avignon," *Annuaire de la société des amis du Palais des papes et des monuments d'Avignon* 75 (1998): 83–98; "La paroisse Saint-Pierre au temps des papes d'Avignon," *Annuaire de la société des amis du Palais des papes et des monuments d'Avignon* 76 (1999): 11–38; "La paroisse Saint-Didier au temps des papes d'Avignon," *Annuaire de la société des amis du Palais des papes et des monuments d' Avignon* 78–79 (2001–2002): 19–40; "La paroisse Notre-Dame-La-Principale au temps des papes d'Avignon," *Annuaire de la société des amis du Palais des papes et des monuments d'Avignon* 80 (2003): 85–108. Regarding the condition of Avignon's Jewish population, see Léon Bardinet, "Condition civile des juifs du Comtat Venaissin pendant le séjour des papes à Avignon, 1309–1376," *Revue historique* 12 (1880): 1–47; and "Les juifs du Comtat Venaissin au moyen âge: Leur rôle économique et intellectuel," *Revue historique* 14 (1880): 29–35; Elizabeth A. R. Brown, "Philip V, Charles IV and the Jews of France: The Alleged Expulsion of 1322," *Speculum* 66 (1991): 294–322; William C. Jordan, "The Jews and the Transition to Papal Rule in the Comtat Venaissin," *Michael* 12 (1991): 213–232; and Valérie Theis, "John XXII et l'expulsion des juifs du Comtat Venaissin," *Annales, histoire, sciences sociales* 67 (2012): 41–77. On the convent for repentant prostitutes, see Joëlle Rollo-Koster, "From Prostitutes to Virgin Brides of

Christ: The Avignonese *Repenties* in the Late Middle Ages," *Journal of Medieval and Early Modern Studies* 32 (2002): 109–144. For details on Avignon's population and the *Liber Divisionis*, see Joëlle Rollo-Koster, "Mercator Florentinensis and Others: Immigration in Papal Avignon," in *Urban and Rural Communities in Medieval France*, ed. Kathryn L. Reyerson and John Drendel (Leiden: Brill, 1998), 73–100; and *The People of Curial Avignon: A Critical Edition of the Liber Divisionis and the Matriculae of Notre-Dame la Majour* (Lampeter, GB, and Lewiston, NY: Edwin Mellen, 2009). On the Italian membership of Avignon's confraternities, see Joëlle Rollo-Koster, "Forever After: The Dead in the Avignonese Confraternity of Notre-Dame la Majour (1329–1381)," *Journal of Medieval History* 25 (1999): 115–140; and "Amongst Brothers: Italians' Networks in Papal Avignon (1360s–1380s)," *Medieval Prosopography* 21 (2000): 153–189. Regarding Avignon's women, see Joëlle Rollo-Koster, "The Women of Papal Avignon, A New Source: The *Liber Divisionis* of 1371," *Journal of Women's History* 8 (Spring 1996): 36–59. Regarding prostitution and the reintegration of prostitutes in medieval Avignon, see Joëlle Rollo-Koster, "Prostitutes," in *Women and Gender in Medieval Europe: An Encyclopedia*, ed. Margaret Schaus (New York and London: Routledge, 2006), 675–678. For plundering papal goods at a pope's death and election, see Joëlle Rollo-Koster, *Raiding Saint Peter: Empty Sees, Violence, and the Initiation of the Great Western Schism (1378)* (Leiden and Boston: Brill, 2008).

6: THE GREAT WESTERN SCHISM AND AVIGNON

On Gregory's return to Rome, see Joëlle Rollo-Koster and Alizah Holstein, "Anger and Spectacle in Late Medieval Rome: Gauging Emotion in Urban Topography?" in *Cities, Texts and Social Networks, 400–1500: Experiences and Perceptions of Medieval Urban Space*, ed. Anne Lester, Caroline Goodson, and Carol Symes (Farnham, UK: Ashgate, 2010), 149–174. On the Great Western Schism, see the collection of essays edited by Joëlle Rollo-Koster and Thomas Izbicki, *A Companion to the Great Western Schism (1378–1417)* (Leiden: Brill, 2009); E. Delaruelle, E. R. Labande, and Paul Ourliac, *L'église au temps du Grand Schisme et de la crise conciliaire (1378–1449)* (Paris: Bloud & Gay, 1962); Paul Ourliac, "Le schisme et les conciles (1378–1449)," in *Histoire du christianisme des origines à nos jours*, ed. Jean Marie Mayeur (Paris: Desclée, 1990), 89–139; and Howard Kaminsky, "The Great Schism," in *The New Cambridge Medieval History*, ed.

Michael Jones (Cambridge: Cambridge University Press, 2000), vol. 6, 685–696, offers an excellent introduction to the topic. I have written at length on sacking and pillaging at the deaths of popes; see Joëlle Rollo-Koster, *Raiding Saint Peter: Empty Sees, Violence, and the Initiation of the Great Western Schism (1378)* (Leiden: Brill, 2008). On the responsibility of cardinals, see Stefan Weiss, "Luxury and Extravagance at the Papal Court in Avignon and the Outbreak of Great Western Schism," in *A Companion to the Great Western Schism,* ed. Joëlle Rollo-Koster and Thomas Izbicki (Leiden: Brill, 2009), 67–97. On Raymond de Turenne, see Noël Valois, *Raymond Roger, vicomte de Turenne, et les papes d'Avignon (1386–1408) d'après un document découvert par M. Camille Rivain* (Paris: Picard, 1890). I have discussed Avignonese confraternities in Joëlle Rollo-Koster, *The People of Curial Avignon: A Critical Edition of the Liber Divisionis and the Matriculae of Notre Dame la Majour* (Lampeter, UK, and Lewiston, NY: Edwin Mellen, 2009), especially 77–160; "Forever After: The Dead in the Avignonese Confraternity of Notre Dame la Majour (1329–1381)," *Journal of Medieval History* 25 (1999): 115–140; and "Amongst Brothers: Italians' Networks in Papal Avignon (1360s–1380s)," *Medieval Prosopography* 21 (2000): 153–189. I discussed the subtraction of obedience in detail in Joëlle Rollo-Koster, "The Politics of Body Parts: Contested Topographies in Late Medieval Avignon," *Speculum: A Journal of Medieval Studies* 78 (2003): 66–98. On the repairs done to the palace after the Catalan War, see Claude Faure, "Les réparations du palais pontifical d'Avignon au temps de Jean XXIII (1413–1415)," *Mélanges d'archéologie et d'histoire* 28 (1908): 185–206; and Germain Butaud, "Les deux sièges du palais apostolique d'Avignon (1398–1411)," in *Villes en Guerre: XIVe–XVe siècles,* ed. Christiane Raynaud (Aix-en-Provence: Publications de l'université de Provence, 2008), 103–126. Regarding saints of the Schism, see Renate Blumenfeld-Kosinski, *Poets, Saints, and Visionaries of the Great Schism, 1378–1417* (University Park: Pennsylvania State University Press, 2006); and Laura Ackerman Smoller, *The Saint and the Chopped-Up Baby: The Cult of Vincent Ferrer in Medieval and Early Modern Europe* (Ithaca, NY: Cornell University Press, 2014). On John Chrysostom, see J. N. D. Kelly, *Golden Mouth: The Story of John Chrysostom, Ascetic, Preacher, Bishop* (Ithaca, NY: Cornell University Press, 1995); and Jaclyn L. Maxwell, *Christianization and Communication in Late Antiquity* (Cambridge: Cambridge University Press, 2006).

Index

abbreviators, 165, 167

absolution in *mortis articulo*, 113, 115

Acre, 36, 37

Aigrefeuille, Guillaume de, cardinal, 86, 111, 119, 256

Ailly, Pierre de, 261, 265, 268

Aix, Union of, 253–254, 258

Albornoz, Gil Álvarez Carillo, cardinal and Papal Legate, 75, 89–93, 109, 112, 121–122, 124, 127, 133, 134, 136, 145, 202

Alexander V, pope, 244, 270

Alfonso XI, king of Castile, 89, 100

alms, 5, 172–173, 215, 223, 228, 276, 277, 279

Alpartil, Martin de, 232, 262

Amadeus VI of Savoy, 134

Anagni, 25, 27, 27–28, 30–31, 33–34, 38, 40, 143, 195, 241

Ancona, 41, 91

Anjou, John of, 42

Anjou, Louis II of, 251, 252, 253, 254, 267

Anjou, Louis of, 125, 130, 140, 141, 228, 230, 243, 251–252, 253, 253–254, 265

Anjou, Robert of, king of Naples, 42, 52, 76, 77

annates, 160, 248, 250

Annibaldi, Roman family, 29–30

Apostolic Chamber, 4, 10, 14, 91, 97, 99, 124, 128, 135, 150, 155–164, 171, 172, 175, 180, 183, 197, 258, 279

apostolic poverty, 48–53

Aquitaine, 61, 94, 95, 97, 126

Aragon, 23, 36, 41, 76, 89, 100, 101, 119, 158, 243, 261, 265, 269

Arezzo, 41, 134

assignation, 10, 161, 173, 181, 206, 243

assignation officers (*assignatores*), 181

Aubert, Étienne. *See* Innocent VI, pope

Austria, Frederick of, 43, 52

Avignon, Parish of: Notre-Dame la Principale, 180, 199, 215–216, 217, 220, 221, 255; Saint-Agricol, 179–180, 199, 218–220, 221; Saint-Didier, 180, 199, 216, 217–218, 220, 221, 231, 263; Saint-Étienne, 176, 179, 200, 207, 208; Saint-Geniès, 180, 199, 214–215, 217; Saint-Pierre, 180, 199, 210–213, 219, 220, 221; Saint-Symphorien, 180, 199, 208–210

Babylon, 2

Babylonian Captivity, 23, 70

Baluze, Étienne, 3–4, 8, 33, 69, 72, 124, 128, 142

banderesi, 143

bankruptcies, 132

Battle of: Cocherel, 117; Crécy, 80–81; Poitiers, 93–96, 98

Bavaria, Louis of, Holy Roman emperor, 43, 49, 51, 59, 61, 70, 78, 80, 89

beatific vision controversy, 54–56

Benedict XI, pope, 31, 195

Benedict XII, pope, 6, 54, 56–62, 69, 72, 84, 110, 132, 155, 171, 176–177, 182, 207, 219, 288

Benedict XIII, pope, 232, 244, 254, 261–272

Benedictines, 57, 70, 110, 111, 113, 199–200, 217, 220

benefices, 25, 45, 57, 62, 71, 73, 81, 102, 111, 113–114, 128, 150–151, 155, 156–158, 159, 160–161, 163, 164, 164–165, 183, 184, 185, 205, 209, 249, 250, 258, 262, 265, 270, 276, 288

Bernier, Jean, collector, 160

Berry, duke of, 141, 228, 251, 258, 261, 262, 264, 268, 279

Index